*The Lost Lectures
of C. Vann Woodward*

The Lost Lectures of C. Vann Woodward

Edited by

NATALIE J. RING AND
SARAH E. GARDNER

Foreword by Edward L. Ayers

OXFORD
UNIVERSITY PRESS

OXFORD
UNIVERSITY PRESS

Oxford University Press is a department of the University of Oxford. It furthers
the University's objective of excellence in research, scholarship, and education
by publishing worldwide. Oxford is a registered trade mark of Oxford University
Press in the UK and certain other countries.

Published in the United States of America by Oxford University Press
198 Madison Avenue, New York, NY 10016, United States of America.

© Oxford University Press 2020

All rights reserved. No part of this publication may be reproduced, stored in
a retrieval system, or transmitted, in any form or by any means, without the
prior permission in writing of Oxford University Press, or as expressly permitted
by law, by license, or under terms agreed with the appropriate reproduction
rights organization. Inquiries concerning reproduction outside the scope of the
above should be sent to the Rights Department, Oxford University Press, at the
address above.

You must not circulate this work in any other form
and you must impose this same condition on any acquirer.

Library of Congress Cataloging-in-Publication Data
Names: Woodward, C. Vann (Comer Vann), 1908–1999, author.
| Ring, Natalie J., editor. | Gardner, Sarah E., editor.
Title: The lost lectures of C. Vann Woodward / edited by Natalie J. Ring
and Sarah E. Gardner ; foreword by Edward L. Ayers.
Identifiers: LCCN 2020013093 (print) | LCCN 2020013094 (ebook) |
ISBN 9780190863951 (hardback) | ISBN 9780190863975 (epub) |
ISBN 9780190863968 (ebook)
Subjects: LCSH: Dissenters—Southern States—History. |
Reconstruction (U.S. history, 1865–1877) | Southern States—History. |
LCGFT: Lectures.
Classification: LCC F209 .W625 2020 (print) |
LCC F209 (ebook) | DDC 973.8—dc23
LC record available at https://lccn.loc.gov/2020013093
LC ebook record available at https://lccn.loc.gov/2020013094

Contents

Foreword by Edward L. Ayers   vii

Introduction   1
Editorial Note   52

The Fleming Lectures: Southern Dissenters in Exile

Lecture I: The Men of the Thirties   57
Lecture II: The Men of the Fifties   75
Lecture III: The Way of the Exile   91
Chapter I: The Process of Alienation   108
Chapter II: The Year of Decision   128

The Messenger Lectures: The First Reconstruction in the Light of the Second

Lecture II: The Fear of Freedom   167
Lecture III: The Paradox of Loyalty   184
Lecture IV: The Conservatism of Northern Radicals   200
Lecture V: Radicalism for Southern Conservatives   214
Lecture VI: Did the North Really Mean It?   230

The Storrs Lectures: Slavery to Freedom: An American Failure

Lecture I: The Problem of Failure in American History   249

Acknowledgments   265

Index   268

Foreword

EDWARD L. AYERS

C. VANN WOODWARD emerged as a leading American intellectual in the middle decades of the twentieth century. His remarkable series of important books between 1951 and 1955 attracted interest across the United States and beyond, supporting the struggle for civil rights in the South. As this fascinating collection shows, the very passion that drove Woodward to write history, his determination to foster a more just South, proved increasingly difficult for him as history changed around him.

The early 1950s witnessed profound events in the South. African Americans drove forward in their challenges to segregation, demanding equal schools, voting registration, fair treatment on public transportation, and equitable city services. Defenders of white supremacy railed and inflicted violence against the movement. White southerners who expressed good will toward individual black people remained silent or counseled caution.

As the South stirred, Woodward and other white southern liberals searched for the appropriate voice. Woodward had long opposed segregation and had left the South and the injustices the stifling environment those injustices bred. He had abandoned his native Arkansas in the early 1930s for Atlanta, and then New York, Chapel Hill, Gainesville, Charlottesville, and California. From 1946 through the 1950s Woodward occupied an outpost on the northern edge of the South, a professorship at Johns Hopkins University in Baltimore.

Woodward's magisterial book of 1951—*The Origins of the New South*—won him a new place of respect, stature, and stability. He enjoyed a broad network of friends and allies, white and black, in academe and beyond, in the South and beyond. Lecturing and writing widely, Woodward was admired and celebrated. Without a personal stake in any particular southern community, he spoke and wrote of the South with a detached vision and an ironic tone.

Invited to give the prestigious Walter Lynwood Fleming Lectures at Louisiana State University in 1951, Woodward chose the theme of southern dissenters. Those dissenters, from the era of slavery before the Civil War, displayed bravery but became outcasts. Living as exiles, they tried to move the South at a distance, using their writing and speaking to persuade fellow white southerners to abandon slavery and the sins and suffering slavery brought. They failed, purchasing only disdain and denunciation with their bravery.

Woodward's lively portraits of southern dissenters in the lectures radiated the strengths displayed in his other writing of the period: subtlety, complexity, and elegance of composition. But the portraits did not do the work Woodward himself most wanted them to do: offer useful examples for his current generation of southern dissenters. Woodward emphasized the eccentricity of the exiles and criticized their simplistic portrayal of the South as well as their personal unhappiness and failure. Woodward promised himself and his editors that he would turn the lectures into a book, but years passed and he never did. The press eventually stopped requesting them.

Instead, Woodward gave another set of lectures, at the University of Virginia in 1954, that became the basis of his most popular and influential book, *The Strange Career of Jim Crow*. Written under the stimulus of the *Brown v. Board of Education* decision of that year, Woodward's portrayal caught the wave of history. Emphasizing the contingent and recent origins of segregation, Woodward found himself with a controversial but profoundly important work of engaged history.

Buoyed by the reception of *Strange Career*, Woodward envisioned and embarked upon a full-dress history of the Reconstruction era. In the early 1960s, he visited southern archives to explore sources and signed two contracts for the book. In the meantime, he agreed to give the Messenger Lectures at Cornell University to work out some of his major themes.

As Woodward mapped out Reconstruction, however, history complicated his task. The civil rights era gave way to the bold declarations of the black power movement. The history of Reconstruction itself shifted abruptly. The contempt directed at the Radicals and the freedmen since the 1880s suddenly reversed. White and black Republicans who had been vilified and ridiculed in popular histories, novels, and films over three generations suddenly appeared as farsighted advocates of justice and equality. Former Confederates, routinely portrayed as heroic defenders of their homes, became ruthless and violent enemies of democracy.

Some of Woodward's own students and friends participated in the revision and he supported them. But he could not bring himself to agree with them.

In Woodward's eyes, the Republicans of the North had been unsteady and insincere allies, ready to abandon their black partners at the first opportunity. Republican leaders spoke in lofty language about rights even as they pursued economic and political strategies that benefited their own region, their party, and themselves rather than the South they claimed to be liberating. They sustained segregation and disfranchisement in their northern states in fact if not in name. The Republicans demanded declarations of unbroken national loyalty they knew that almost no white southerners could honestly make.

Woodward did not celebrate the democratic potential of black southerners as the revisionists did. The freedpeople in his account seem lost, with no clear sense of purpose or identity. Woodward's emphasis on the physical suffering, hunger, and illness of the recently enslaved people fit poorly with the celebratory tone of the revisionists even though it foreshadowed recent accounts of the refugee camps in which tens of thousands of black people died. Woodward could not convert his skeptical vision into the interpretation his times seemed to demand.

In the face of these obstacles, Woodward concluded his lectures with the somber judgment that "it is my contention that the experiment was doomed at a very early stage. In fact almost from the start." Moreover, Reconstruction could not offer genuine encouragement to the activists and reformers of his own day: "To those who look to the First Reconstruction either for sources of inspiration or reasons for frustration of the Second it might be said that they will look in vain. For the First Reconstruction really never was tried. The conviction drained out of the enterprise before it was fairly under way. The North never really meant what it said, and the South sensed that from the start." Woodward saw in the white North of the 1960s the same hypocrisy its leaders had displayed in the 1860s.

Woodward lost faith in his own Reconstruction project in the late 1960s. Instead, he launched influential efforts at comparative history, hoping for new perspective and insight. The comparisons, however, only confirmed what he had come to believe: the failure of Reconstruction had been foreordained by slavery itself and the halfhearted and insincere measures to redeem it. Everywhere in the world, some form of forced labor and generations of injustice followed the destruction of slavery. The American South was no different. America was no different.

C. Vann Woodward searched for inspiration in the past but failed. Looking to the lives of southern dissenters for inspiration, he found mainly isolation and failure. Looking to Reconstruction for an example of bold reform, he found mainly bad faith and selfishness. Other historians shifted the frame of

Reconstruction, finding in black southerners, prominent and otherwise, the virtues of bravery, vision, and persistence that Woodward had sought in white Americans and found missing.

The story of C. Vann Woodward cannot, of course, be counted a story of failure. He accomplished too much, his work has endured for too long. But, in a sense Woodward himself might have acknowledged, his story was ironic: his public calling conflicted with what his craft seemed to reveal. These lost lectures and the insightful framing of Natalie Ring and Sarah Gardner help us understand that irony, to appreciate the challenges of writing history while history changes around us.

*The Lost Lectures
of C. Vann Woodward*

Introduction

C. VANN WOODWARD'S career spanned seven remarkable decades. At the time of his death in 1999 at the age of ninety-one, tributes to the historian described him as "the 20th century's greatest American historian," "a writer with unquestioned literary flair" and "the model of intellectual integrity."[1] During his professional life he produced nine books and six edited volumes. His first book, *Tom Watson: Agrarian Rebel*, published when he was not quite thirty years old, was released to great fanfare.[2] From 1951 to 1955 Woodward entered a particularly fertile stage with the publication of *Origins of the New South, 1877–1913* (1951), *Reunion and Reaction: The Compromise of 1877 and the End of Reconstruction* (1951), and *The Strange Career of Jim Crow* (1955).[3] In 1960 he released a collection of essays titled *The Burden of Southern History*, further cementing his reputation as the master of irony and the highest authority on the history of the late nineteenth- and twentieth-century South.[4] Even today southern historians must contend with Woodward's sweeping interpretations about the inherent discontinuity of southern history, the centrality of economic and political conflict in the New South, and his claim that segregation, following a period of fluid race relations, did not crystallize until the late nineteenth century.

What is less known about Woodward are the works he did not publish, those unfinished projects with which he struggled. In this material he demonstrated an interest in the history of white antebellum southern nonconformists, the immediate consequences of emancipation, and the history of Reconstruction in the years prior to the Compromise of 1877.[5] Woodward's unpublished writings and lectures display the elements we come to associate with his scholarship, including his preoccupation with irony, the tragedy of failure, the call for a usable past, the existence of forgotten alternatives, and his rejection of historical continuity. He gave three sets of lectures on these topics that yielded twelve addresses: the Walter Lynwood Fleming Lectures in Southern History at Louisiana State University titled "Southern Dissenters in Exile" (1951); the Messenger Lectures at Cornell University titled "The First Reconstruction in the Light of the Second" (1964); and the Storrs Lectures at Yale University Law School titled "Slavery to Freedom: An American Failure" (1969).[6] In addition to these lectures, Woodward spent more than a decade intermittently researching and thinking about writing a history of Reconstruction meant to be the equal of his tour de force, *Origins*.[7] This volume uncovers the intellectual process he went through as he grappled with and ultimately failed to attain his goals.

The Lost Lectures of C. Vann Woodward introduces Woodward's overlooked research on the contours and limits of nineteenth-century liberalism by releasing his unpublished lectures from the Fleming and Messenger series, one from the Storrs series, and two intended chapters for a book on the Fleming Lectures that was never published. The Fleming Lectures document the alienation of white southerners who challenged the proslavery orthodoxy of their friends and families and ultimately fled to the North seeking a more tolerable climate. The Messenger and Storrs Lectures highlight Woodward's interpretation of Reconstruction, which anticipate the work of a current generation of scholars who have tended to stress the limits and frustrations of the era or to advocate thinking about it in broad comparative ways.

These lectures and chapters have never been seen in the form in which they appear here because of Woodward's demanding academic career and his own doubts about their value. In the 1950s and 1960s Woodward expected to publish the Fleming Lectures as a full series for Louisiana State University Press and the Messenger Lectures as pieces of his larger book on Reconstruction—but he failed to do so. Included here are the Fleming Lectures Woodward gave in the spring of 1951 and the first two chapters of the projected book based on the three lectures, "Southern Dissenters in Exile." The life span of the Fleming Lectures is straightforward. The lectures were delivered, revised, and abandoned in relatively quick order. Although Woodward dipped back into the material when convenient, little of it found its way in other venues.

The story of the Messenger Lectures follows a more circuitous path. Woodward drafted the lecture series, "The First Reconstruction in the Light of the Second," beginning in the summer of 1963 and delivered them in 1964. This collection, however, includes only five of the six, as the first lecture is missing from his papers.[8] In 1965 Woodward combined parts of Lectures IV and VI for a reprocessed piece that he used twice as a presentation and three times in print between 1965 and 1971.⁹ Although the hybrid piece containing segments of the two Messenger Lectures has been published or presented in various guises, it seems right to publish the extant five lectures together as a set in this collection.¹⁰ Not only is there enough new, as well as reconstituted, material to deem them "lost," but collectively they offer insight into Woodward's efforts to strike the right interpretive framework for his planned book on Reconstruction.

Finally, material from the Storrs Lectures, focusing on comparative emancipations and reconstructions, was presented at various venues between 1969 and 1976 and published in several iterations as late as 1989. The first Storrs Lecture borrowed from a paper Woodward delivered at the Southern Historical Association two years earlier in 1967, but the bulk of it was never published.¹¹ Thus this volume includes Storrs Lecture I because it can rightfully be considered "lost," and is significant in light of his never-completed book on Reconstruction.

It is generally taken as established fact that Woodward did not engage in much archival research or produce significant footnoted scholarship after publication of the prize-winning *Origins*.¹² As he noted rather drolly in the bibliography of *Origins*, "The historian is driven to manuscripts by necessity rather than zeal."¹³ Nevertheless, the footnoted Fleming and Messenger Lectures do show evidence of archival research and a reliance on primary sources. And at some point in the late 1950s he began archival research for the intended book on Reconstruction. Woodward's papers in the Manuscript and Archives Library at Yale University contain folders of notes and lengthy bibliographies on the subject of Reconstruction, as well as sections of footnoted typescript and handwritten text bundled together, the endnotes inauspiciously labeled "Chapter I Notes."¹⁴ Likewise, the second Messenger Lecture's endnotes are marked "NOTES FOR CHAPTER I," suggesting that Woodward considered at least two possibilities for the opening chapter of the book on Reconstruction.¹⁵ It does not appear that he made any further progress. In 1969 colleagues, including Eugene D. Genovese and William S. McFeeley, still believed the book on Reconstruction was forthcoming, and the content of the Storrs Lectures, given that same year, indicate that Woodward had not stopped thinking about the topic.¹⁶

Both the Fleming and Messenger Lecture Series and Storrs Lecture I evince Woodward's iconoclasm. In the 1950s, at the height of post–World War II liberalism and consensus historiography, Woodward chose to write about southern dissenters, those who felt stifled by the prevailing order that governed their society. A decade later Woodward, like W. E. B. Du Bois twenty-five years earlier, rejected the Dunning School interpretation of Reconstruction, which characterized the post–Civil War political landscape as riddled with corruption, subject to "Negro rule," and unduly punitive toward southern whites. In the 1960s revisionist historians of Reconstruction turned the story upside down, deeming the formerly enslaved as heroic protagonists who participated in the political process with great success. Woodward, though, questioned many of the revisionists' articles of faith, especially their easy assumption that a Republican Congress would have done right by the newly emancipated had it not been stymied by Andrew Johnson and his allies. In all of these lectures, then, Woodward used the past to comment on the times in which he was writing. In triumphant postwar America he cautioned against the dangers posed by conformity and consensus. And as the civil rights movement advanced he often questioned the degree to which the federal government alone could affect meaningful and lasting change.

Between the time Woodward gave the Fleming and the Messenger Lectures he delivered the James W. Richards Lectures, which were later published as *Strange Career*. The ideas emerged from his work on an amicus curiae brief for the Warren Court in the *Brown v. Board of Education* decision. Here Woodward's personal and professional interests converged. He saw his lectures and their subsequent publication effect real-world change, something he did not necessarily imagine would happen with his work on dissenters or Reconstruction. Woodward first introduced the concept of the "First Reconstruction" and the "New Reconstruction" (which he eventually called the "Second Reconstruction") in the publication of *Strange Career*. The analogy, according to Howard N. Rabinowitz, allowed Woodward to stress that "the new effort had a better chance for success than the first."[17] Over the course of the next fifteen years Woodward revised *Strange Career* three times, in part to parry the blows his critics leveled but also to account for the modern civil rights movement as it evolved over the 1950s and 1960s. As a historian committed to advocating for a usable past, it comes as no surprise that he took this route. But the subjects of the Fleming and the Messenger Lectures are frozen in time, a product of their moment—never viewed by the public or revised and resubmitted for publication by the author. The Messenger Lectures, in particular, allowed Woodward to address the failure of the First Reconstruction more thoroughly than he had time for in the Richards Lectures. Yet despite the title of the series, "The First Reconstruction in the Light of the Second," he left the analogy relatively untouched in the text. The backlash against *Strange Career* in some quarters reminded him why he had remained reluctant to consistently embrace his role as a presentist historian.

It should be noted that Woodward recycled old material when it suited his needs. He often cribbed from himself when arranging presentations or putting together edited collections. For example, volumes such as *The Burden of Southern History, American Counterpoint: Slavery and Racism in the North-South Dialogue*, and *The Future of the Past* primarily contain previously published essays, offering only two to three new essays each.[18] Indeed, Woodward revised and expanded *Burden* twice. Even when his edited collections document the origins of the reprinted material, his attributions are not always comprehensive. Sometimes Woodward republished or presented the same essay, or pieces of an essay, multiples times. An essay using repurposed material might appear in one of his edited collections, another scholar's edited collection, and a scholarly journal or popular magazine. In some instances, he gave lectures that lifted material from previously published work. Sometimes he acknowledged that he had done so. Other times he did not.[19] For these reasons, it has been difficult at times, although not impossible, to ascertain how much of Woodward's writing and lectures are new, how much is derivative, and how many times a single essay or lecture has appeared, either in whole or in part.[20] It could be that Woodward lost track himself or failed to note these distinctions in his own filing system. Not without reason, Woodward had worried about the peril of publishing too many edited collections that contained reprints. One year after the Messenger Lectures he wrote his close friend William G. Carleton, a political scientist at the University of Florida, "The professional threshold for tolerance for such self-indulgence is fairly high. I mean one is not permitted many without impunity. You risk the charge of perpetrating another non-book on the trade. Of cashing in." Woodward determined that the best time to issue a collection was "after the publication of a major book," but he confided to Carleton that the Reconstruction book was not yet ready. "I have troubles yet to be resolved there," he acknowledged.[21] Perhaps this is why he continued to repurpose segments of the Reconstruction material over the next twenty-four years.

In 1949, two years before *Origins of the New South* was released, Woodward received an invitation to give the Walter Lynwood Fleming Lectures at Louisiana State University with the expectation that Louisiana State University Press would publish them. In the summer of 1949, Woodward wrote to the director, Marcus M. Wilkerson, requesting the date of his lectures be postponed and also asking for permission to expand on chapter II of *Origins*, "The Forked Road to Reunion," as the subject of his lectures. Wilkerson agreed to schedule the lectures for the spring of 1951.[22] The second request was thornier. Wilkerson and Wendell Stephenson, the series editor for the History of the South series of which *Origins* was a part, eventually concluded that Woodward's proposal might work in terms of content, but explained the timing was problematic. Stephenson expected to release *Origins* in 1950 and feared that LSU Press might not want an inflated version of a chapter published shortly after the monograph. Stephenson also wrote that he hoped the "cream" of Woodward's research would appear in *Origins*, although he cautioned that adding more chapters might delay the book's publication.[23] Ultimately, as Woodward recounted years later, he made the choice to use his accumulated "sack full of jigsaw puzzle pieces, parts of several puzzles, with many pieces missing, all jumbled together, yet somehow related" to generate *Reunion and Reaction: The Compromise of 1877* as a freestanding book.[24] For a brief moment *Reunion and Reaction* might have become the fourteenth set of the Fleming Lectures.

Woodward, not surprisingly, chose a new topic for the Fleming Lectures that reflected his longstanding affinity for southern dissenters. One historian later observed that Woodward's participation in the series "marked a sharp break" with the speakers who had come before him.[25] His predecessors had included Charles W. Ramsdell, Avery O. Craven, Bell Irvin Wiley, and Frank L. Owsley, the rear guard of a historiographical tradition that had upheld a version of the southern past that romanticized the slaveholding South, celebrated the Confederate cause, and decried the evils of Reconstruction. Around the time the lecture series was inaugurated "a new generation of southern historians was emerging with different experiences and different examples."[26] Woodward became the exemplar of this new breed. As a graduate student he had found it difficult to swallow "the predominant literature, the scholarship, and the prevailing interpretations" in the field of southern history, he admitted decades later. "To me," he continued, "each of the masters held up as emulation seemed virtually of one mind, united not so much in their view of the past as in their dedication to the present order, the system founded on the ruins of Reconstruction."[27] Woodward also self-identified as a nonconformist. When asked during an interview what prompted his interest in southern radicalism he retorted, "Well, I was interested in the theme of dissent. Being a dissenter myself I looked for evidence of it and found it." He conceded that others had "accused" him "of exaggerating it" and he "wasn't always picking typical Southerners," especially during the time he thought about writing "a book about Southern abolitionists," but concluded, "It was part of my rebellion against the dominant historiography I was exposed to—that is, the solidarity of the South and the continuity of culture."[28] His decision to speak on southern dissenters, then, served notice. "Southern Dissenters in Exile" would not be a staid retelling of the South's antebellum past.

Of course, LSU knew what it was getting when it invited Woodward in 1949. He had already earned his reputation as an iconoclast with his biography of Populist demagogue Tom Watson in 1938. "Southern Dissenters in Exile" examines two generations of antebellum white southerners who challenged the moral authority of proslavery ideologues and subsequently fled the South because of the region's lack of political tolerance for "Jeffersonian liberalism."[29] Woodward titled his first lecture "The Men of the Thirties." He showed how this first generation of southern white abolitionists came from the planter aristocracy and was influenced by evangelical revivals and religious radicalism at outposts like Lane Theological Seminary in Cincinnati. They included figures such as James G. Birney, Angelina and Sarah Grimké, and James A. Thome. The second lecture, "The Men of the Fifties," focused on a generation he described as more secular in orientation. Moncure Daniel Conway, Hinton Rowan Helper, John Curtis Underwood, and their cohort came of age during a time of persistent sectional tension between North and South.[30] In the final lecture, "The Way of the Exile," Woodward described the physical and psychological dislocation these white southern abolitionists suffered while living as expatriates outside of the South. Regarded as turncoats, they never lost their sense of southern identity despite a lack of connection to their families. Many were plagued by a nagging sense of loneliness and a deep grief over their inability to return home. Unable to reconcile the inner conflict between their loyalty to the South and a moral commitment to speak out against the institution of slavery, they chose virtue and suffered the consequences.

Not merely subject matter signaled a departure from previous sets of Fleming Lectures. Like those who went before him, Woodward sought a usable past. But his understanding of the South's history and his vision for its future looked quite different from those imagined by the old guard. Writing during the early years of the modern civil rights movement, Woodward believed antebellum southern dissenters could serve as lodestars for those white southerners who opposed Jim Crow. "Here, in long perspective," he wrote in the first lecture, are the "projected problems of wide human significance that have relevance to our own troubled times."[31] Woodward began his first Fleming Lecture by highlighting the relevance of the southern past to the region's current moment. He ended the last lecture with the same appeal. Like the southern moralists of the 1830s and the 1850s, contemporary "reformers, novelists, playwrights, sociologists, and historians" have similarly felt compelled to "record their testimonies, to tell their story of the South."

And they had equal cause for concern that both their compatriots and outsiders might misconstrue their motives, might question their loyalties. Citing Quentin Compson's famous remonstrance in William Faulkner's 1936 novel *Absalom, Absalom!*, Woodward ended the last lecture of "Southern Dissenters in Exile" with the protest "I don't hate" the South.[32]

Woodward sought the assistance of several colleagues while working on "Southern Dissenters in Exile." In the fall of 1950, he asked Henry Steele Commager to write on behalf of his request for travel funds to support research on William Lloyd Garrison and those affiliated with the Lane Theological Seminary. Commager happily agreed but chided Woodward for requesting such a paltry sum as well as planning such a whirlwind tour. "I do think, however, that you are trying to do it all on a shoe-string," he pronounced. "I don't see how you can clean up the Garrison papers, e.g. in a matter of three days, or the stuff at Oberlin, in a couple of days. . . . It is a great mistake to try to do these things on the cheap."[33] Instead Commager remarked that he felt more comfortable supporting an application for a lengthier trip. Whether Woodward followed the senior historian's advice remains unclear. Two months after he gave the Fleming Lectures, Woodward asked David Herbert Donald to suggest additional archives to consult over the coming summer as he prepared to turn "Southern Dissenters in Exile" into a book. Woodward stated that he planned to work in collections at the University of Michigan, Smith College, and Harvard University.[34] The first two chapters of the intended book demonstrate that he completed some of this work. Woodward also petitioned Richard Hofstadter to gain him access to the Moncure Daniel Conway Papers at Columbia University.[35] Even as late as 1956, Woodward planned to visit Oberlin College, signaling that he had not given up on his treasured southern dissenters.[36]

Nevertheless, Woodward struggled to submit the final manuscript. He revised and expanded the first two lectures into two draft chapters but could not seem to eke out the third. At some point, when he sat down to convert the lectures into chapters, he lost interest in the white southern exiles of the 1850s. Instead, he decided to expound further on the generation of the 1830s. The Grimkés' story increasingly fascinated Woodward. Although he had grouped the sisters with the male reformers in the first lecture, he devoted roughly seventy-five percent of Chapter II to the Grimkés. The two draft chapters hint at what Woodward thought most salient in "Southern Dissenters in Exile." They also demonstrate the kind of heavy lifting that Woodward still had in front of him. Some citations are incomplete; others are missing altogether. Information and anecdotes are repeated. But in the end, it did not matter how he had organized his chapters or how piecemeal the citations were. His attention had been drawn elsewhere and it never returned fully to his lectures on "Southern Dissenters in Exile."

The staff at LSU Press knew very little of this. They still assumed that Woodward would deliver his manuscript at some point. Between 1951 and 1957, various members of the press wrote letters gently nudging the author to submit his lectures for publication. By 1953 they seemed particularly anxious. "Seriously, now—about the Fleming lectures. More than ever, we need them for the fall," editor Patricia Smylie wrote in March. "If you could get the MS in shape and send it by May 1, we could do it. Maybe what you needed all along was a deadline.... All you have to do is write that rich, beautiful prose." She advised hiring a graduate student to assist with the footnotes or omitting them altogether.[37] Woodward pledged to do what he could but indicated a fall deadline was more likely.[38] At the end of May, Ruth B. Hubert, secretary of the press, pushed a bit harder: "We, of course are not trying to hurry you along, but are merely seeking to learn the status of the work so that we may know whether or not to include the title in advance announcements." In a postscript at the bottom of the letter she reminded Woodward of a "little note" she "had just run across" dated from the previous year in which he had promised to submit the manuscript in June of 1953.[39] Two days later Woodward received another letter from Smylie, which opened with a more playful tone. "Relax, lad; I do not intend to remind you that you never answered my plea for a date on which the Press can expect your Fleming MS." She reminded him that she was leaving her position as editor and Joan Doyle would soon replace her.[40] On June 11 Woodward responded to Hubert clarifying that he had been busy and thought the following winter was far more likely than the fall, "promis[ing] ... to do the best I can this year."[41] Woodward's summer included giving a six-week seminar on Reconstruction at the Stanford–Tokyo University Seminar on American Studies, ironically hinting at his future intellectual direction.[42]

During the summer and fall Doyle hounded Woodward for the manuscript. On June 17 she wrote that she and Smylie were concerned about his trip to Japan, hoping that it was "not too distant for you to send us the Fleming lecture manuscript" because when "you gave them they sounded good enough to make me think you had little more to do to them than add the accent marks to Grimké." As if to appeal to his vanity she added, "You can't imagine how surprised I was to see Carl Bridenbaugh beat you into print with his epic."[43] In August her tone was more good-humored, but still direct. She informed Woodward that now "seems as good a time as any for jacking up delinquent authors" and chastised him for not responding to an "earlier attempt to smite [his] conscience." "All of this may sound very gay and informal," she pushed, "but frankly the need of the LSU Press for your manuscript is moving into the urgent category."[44] In September Doyle adopted a softer tack. "I'm sorry if I sounded cross or impatient; I'm not," she apologized. She wrote only that she was "anxious to round up all the manuscripts still owed to us, but you are a long way from being our tardiest author and we appreciate your wanting to send us nothing but the best of Woodward." Like Smylie before her, she suggested that Woodward hire a "talented graduate student" to help with the "remaining leg-work" so that he could begin "coining the golden prose."[45] Doyle sent one more letter in November of 1953, after seeing Woodward at a conference, and apologized again for being "rather tiresome" in her requests for the manuscript but promised to leave him be in the future.[46]

Beginning in 1954, inquiries about the Fleming manuscript came solely from the director of LSU Press, Donald Ellegood.[47] After one such query Woodward responded wryly, "I am still hoping to add a book to your list before I am too aged."[48] Three years later the conversation between Woodward and Ellegood appears to have ended. Perhaps after years of delays and unfulfilled promises, neither man could continue to believe in the fiction that Woodward would produce the manuscript.[49] The LSU History Department and LSU Press bore no grudges, likely because of Woodward's elevated status in the field and the fact that *Origins of the New South*, published by LSU, had won the Bancroft Prize. Thirty-four years later, the History Department invited Woodward to deliver a second set of Fleming Lectures. As one member of the department recalled, "When C. Vann Woodward returned to Baton Rouge in 1985 for his second appearance in the Fleming series, some observers... dubbed the occasion the Second Coming."[50] This time he turned around the lectures swiftly and *Thinking Back: The Perils of Writing History* was published one year later.[51] Lectures of a different sort, they did not need to be footnoted since they involved self-reflection on the significance of his decades-long career and extensive trail of critics.

The period during which LSU Press chased Woodward for the Fleming manuscript was a busy time for the historian, and there are many reasons why the staff never received a submission. In 1952 he served as president of the Southern Historical Association. Between 1952 and 1953 he conducted research for the legal team affiliated with the National Association for the Advancement of Colored People working on the brief for *Brown v. Board of Education*, producing, along with John Hope Franklin, "basic monographs" on the history of Reconstruction and segregation for the group.[52] In 1953 he spent the summer teaching in Japan. From 1954 to 1955 Woodward was in residence at the University of Oxford as the visiting Harmsworth Professor.[53] In addition, two other significant projects loomed over his life. In the summer of 1954, two months after the US Supreme Court issued its ruling in *Brown v. Board of Education* Woodward began working on the Richards Lectures. He also found himself entangled with a group of southern liberals collaborating on a symposium and book project that he believed would wrestle with the kinds of questions he faced with the Fleming Lectures.

First, the timing of the Richards Lectures was infelicitous, not because Woodward had to divide his time, but because he learned quickly the public's response to *Strange Career*. In *Thinking Back*, Woodward described "the curious reception" of *Strange Career*. The irony—and Woodward loved irony, although perhaps not as it played out in real time—was that Woodward imagined "the smallest of audiences," those who constituted the "academic circles" that moved about the University of Virginia, where he delivered the lectures. Yet *Strange Career*, Woodward explained, "gained the greatest number of readers, an enormous number, . . . more perhaps than the total number of readers of all the other books" he had written put together. "In short," he continued, "I had badly misconceived my readership." His miscalculation, he rued, "had awkward and unforeseen consequences."[54]

Woodward thought he knew his audience. He had, after all, served a brief stint on UVA's faculty. And because publication had not been promised, Woodward made "no mental distinction between audience and potential readers." He assumed that his audience would hear him out "with the degree of tolerance then prevailing in southern universities." But he could never have anticipated how the hundreds of thousands of readers who picked up a copy of *Strange Career* would respond. "They were certainly not the readers I had in mind originally, those for whom the book was written," he lamented. What's worse, these were not the readers who "shared" Woodward's background, "who understood unspoken assumptions, and who did not require the spelling out of certain subtleties and nuances."[55] And that meant that this expanded readership did not receive *Strange Career* the way Woodward had intended.

To be sure, Woodward's frustration continued well after the Fleming Lectures had been abandoned. *Strange Career* went through four editions, after all, including a revised and expanded edition in 1974. But that early befuddlement set in as Woodward thought about revising "Southern Dissenters in Exile" for publication. What's more, the full-throated opposition to the *Brown* decision, most clearly evinced in the "Southern Manifesto" delivered on the floor of Congress in early 1956, revealed just how out of step Woodward's reading of the southern past was. No wonder, then, he was reluctant to publish a set of lectures on southern dissenters who were forced into exile.

Second, Woodward found himself tied up in a symposium and book project with a group of southern liberals that included Charles Grier Sellers, Jr., Robert A. Lively, Dewey W. Grantham, George B. Tindall, David Donald, and John Hope Franklin. Sellers and Lively had approached Woodward in early 1953 about their mission to compile a selection of essays with the working title "The Southerner as American." Sellers described the project in sweeping terms: "we have turned our backs on the sectional preoccupations of the past and are striving (if this is not being too pretentious) for a reintegration of the South in the mainstream of the American liberal tradition."[56] Woodward responded that he was skittish about the possible consequences of a hard-hitting "manifesto," though. He recalled firsthand experience with the Nashville Agrarians' conservative and myopic "doctrine," noting that southern liberals, such as himself, had pushed back by fleeing to New York, embracing Marx, or "trying to be more American than the Yanks." "Nothing really was gained by denying my southernness," he presumed, "for I never got away from it. . . . I guess I am not ready to embrace an indiscriminate nationalism, any more than I am prepared to embrace an aggressive sectionalism." He continued with a candid assessment: "I would very much like to find some definition of a Southerner with which I could identify myself. And maybe your group is working toward such a definition."[57] Sellers suggested that Woodward write on twentieth-century southern liberalism and added that his essay might also provide a "comparative backward glance" to the subjects of his 1951 Fleming Lectures.[58] Woodward held back from making a firm commitment for some time, although in 1957 he complained to sociologist David Riesman about having said yes to cooperating with a group of interlocutors "who are several years younger than myself, seem pretty generally disposed to wash up the regional heritage and bury the by-gone South."[59]

The members of the group varied over the course of the 1950s. Historian Michael O'Brien describes them as a cluster of southern liberals who came of age after the New Deal and represented, "to some extent, the Southern wing of consensus historiography."[60] The southern historians staked out their position in the introduction to *Southerner as American*, which they released in 1960. "The traditional emphasis on the South's differentness and on the conflict between Southernism and Americanism is wrong historically,"" they argued. "We all agree that the most important fact about the Southerner is that he has been throughout his history also an American."[61] The authors of the volume were anxious to demonstrate their national liberal bona fides at the height of the consensus period, a scholarly moment that had produced such works as Louis Hartz's *The Liberal Tradition in America* in 1955.[62] As O'Brien explains, "the contention of Louis Hartz that American civilization was peculiarly a liberal culture put these nationalists under an obligation to demonstrate that the South was not exclusively conservative."[63] They were ready to embrace nationalism and abandon all pretenses to southern distinctiveness. The consensus wing of southern liberals, however, never quite articulated a definition of "southernness" Woodward could relate to. He remained caught between his southern identity and the imperatives of nationalism at the height of the consensus period.

Significantly, Woodward scooped the collection's editors by publishing the ideas he had been grappling with in an essay titled "The Search for Southern Identity" in the *Virginia Quarterly Review* in 1958. That influential piece also opened *The Burden of Southern History*, published in the same year as *Southerner as American*. Woodward was hesitant to discard the idea of regional distinctiveness. In the essay he observed that many of the region's faults, something that critics had always used to demarcate southern identity, had either vanished or grown less conspicuous over the course of the twentieth century in the face of modernization and industrialization. The "old monuments of regional distinctiveness" included sharecropping, segregated transportation, lynchings, the white primary, and a single party system of politics. Yet the national myth of "economic abundance," "American opulence and American success," and "innocence" did not represent southern identity. What made the South distinctive, Woodward claimed, was its history, one that contained "large components of frustration, failure, and defeat."[64]

Woodward's connection to the group continued until 1959 when he made the decision to cut ties and pull his essay out of the forthcoming collection. He dropped out of *Southerner as American* in part because he never fit and also because he began compiling *The Burden of Southern History*. In mid-1958 David Donald wrote inquiring about "our proposed symposium" and informed Woodward, "I am much vexed with Sellers and Lively for their slowness." He noted that "if it's dead" he might pull his own piece and suggested that Woodward publish his own volume of essays.[65] In 1959 Woodward resisted entreaties by George Tindall and Dewey Grantham to submit his promised essay. He explained to Grantham that he had left the project "in good faith" when LSU Press decided not to publish *Southerner as American* and that the piece would likely be the leading essay in his own collection.[66] Tindall was more perturbed. "I feel that we still have some claim upon you," he declared, given that the group's mission was inspired by Woodward's 1952 Southern Historical Association presidential address, "The Irony of Southern History." Woodward disclosed to Tindall, however, that he still owed LSU Press a book because of the Fleming Lectures he failed to submit.[67] Likely Woodward was also inspired by David Donald's suggestion that he produce his own collection of essays.

Even as late as 1964, Woodward's interest in the antebellum southern dissenters had not completely waned. He alluded to them in a commencement address at the College of William and Mary on "The Question of Loyalty." As he faced the crowd, the middle-aged historian spoke as an "exiled" southerner living in New England with empathy for southern students who felt pulled by the "great moral crisis of our time," a crisis that had only become "more urgent, more insistent, more filled with evidence of confusion of values and deep emotional conflict and internal distress." Among the many questions Woodward posed to his audience were: "Must I move North? Can I stay in the South and speak my mind? Or will I have to hold my tongue, keep my peace, conform? Will I compromise my convictions if I do? ... Can I defend the South and at the same time be critical of it? Can I defend the people I love without betraying the principles I stand for?" These were the same questions Woodward asked of his historical subjects and of himself. He thus offered the audience examples of "forgotten southerners" who had grappled with similar concerns, including the antebellum figures from his Fleming Lectures. He also celebrated late nineteenth-century southern dissenters such as George W. Cable, Lewis Harvey Blair, and Justice John Marshall Harlan, claiming they had successfully engaged in moral crusades while maintaining allegiance to the South.[68]

After the commencement address was published in the *American Scholar*, William G. Carleton wrote to Woodward twice to offer his opinion of it. Carleton took Woodward to task for his shorthand "reliance on 'names'" as a stand-in for "a realistic treatment of Southern history." "You have a way of allowing single individuals to stand for movements, to symbolize them," he asserted. "But are these individuals really symbolic of movements, of any sizable segment of mass opinion? Are they not in most cases only brilliant and idealistic mavericks?"[69] More problematic, Carleton griped, was Woodward's hopelessly naïve belief in the existence of widespread liberal sentiment in the South. "At NO time has there been an appreciable number of ordinary Southerns [*sic*] who have taken a liberal view on the Negro," he proclaimed. He finished by adding that "while it may be good propaganda, and it may be helping in a good cause ... God damnit [*sic*] I cannot see it as authentic history."⁷⁰ Not long after, Woodward replied to his friend with a sheepish letter. "You are devastatingly right," he confessed. "I should have never allowed it to be printed. It was not written to be. It was a sermon not history." But in the next breath, Woodward put forth a defense of his beloved southern dissenters, exclaiming, "I did not mean to offer them as typical. Only that we need more mavericks, that the South still produces them, and that they must be respected, even honored."⁷¹ Still, his defense notwithstanding, Woodward did not return to the Fleming Lectures he had abandoned more than a decade earlier.

Carleton not only served as a sounding board for Woodward on the topic of southern liberals, but also for the Messenger Lectures and the planned book on Reconstruction. He checked in periodically about the Reconstruction work, asking about progress as well as providing reassurance. As early as 1961, Woodward had expressed uncertainty about his ability to finish. "Something would be wrong if you did not have these doubts," Carleton remarked, for "they are an inevitable part of the creative process."⁷² Two years later, in December 1963, Carleton queried, "How goes the Reconstruction? It must be a terribly difficult job. But you are in the fullness of your powers and it will be a great contribution, I am sure."⁷³ And in December 1964 he inquired yet again: "Tell me about the progress on your Reconstruction. My spies tell me it is to be a historical essay and not a narrative, that you are moving in the direction of the Hofstadter type of history," he wrote. "This will bring you greater fame and probably a Pulitzer Prize, but still I think it is too bad we are not going to get the narrative from you.... At least I know it will have lots of new ideas, approaches, and so forth."⁷⁴ At this point Woodward had given the Messenger Lectures and found himself at a crossroads, contemplating how to move forward toward completion of a fuller archival work. What new ideas or approaches he could generate remained to be seen.

From the beginning, however, Woodward's vision was grand. Almost two years before signing the book contract he broached the topic with David Donald, who expressed skepticism about Woodward's task. "I'm afraid I sounded negative about your big research project on Reconstruction," Donald later apologized. "You know I am constitutionally incapable of enthusiasm. But I really respect you for tackling a big job and for sticking at research, even when it would be easier to sit down and turn out 'syntheses' by the hour."⁷⁵ Woodward, though, had a hard time pinning down his approach to the subject. He kept a running list of questions that guided his thinking. Some were "questions of approach." "Can I," he wondered, "avoid the century-old debate: whether Reconstruction was benevolent or malevolent, philanthropic or vindictive?" Were there fruitful comparisons to be made, "such as reconstruction in the British West Indies in the 1830s–1840s. Cuba, Brazil, Latin America; French West Indies, Germany, Japan? The French of Louisiana after 1803"? Was there "anything instructive in comparison of black man & red man as contemporaneous 'Wards of the Nation'"? How about "Attitudes of Southern whites and Western whites?" The possibilities seemed endless. Could he avoid the "traditional trap of pathos, melodrama, [crossed out: moralistic approach]; [handwritten: academic primness, sectional recrimination]"? Other questions concerned substance and coverage. Could he pull off what he had promised his editor Arthur R. Thornhill, of Little, Brown & Co.—that is, a political history rather than "a period study" or a "regional study"? And then there was the matter of organization. Was 1877 a "logical stopping point"? he asked. Did he really need to write eleven state histories? Would "sub-regional treatments" make better sense? Was there any "compromise between topical and chronological?"[76] The more questions he listed, the more complicated his task became.

The longer the project dragged on, the more Woodward felt out of step with current trends in the academy. But that discontent lay in the future. In the late 1950s, Woodward still had every reason to believe he would finish the manuscript. He wrote confidently about his plans. To his editor at Little, Brown, one of the many publishers to whom he pitched his idea, Woodward explained that this new work would have intellectual weight, like *Origins*, "but being free of obligations to a series, I think I could make it a better book."[77] Because he no longer needed to conform to a model that stressed coverage, Woodward believed this book "should consequently "have more focus, more individuality, and I hope more importance and wider interest." In this way perhaps Carleton was right to speculate that Woodward's Reconstruction would be on par with Hofstadter's oeuvre in that it would seek to engage a larger public outside the academy and focus on ideas and values rather than traditional political moments.[78] Equally important, Woodward did not envision this work "to be so narrowly regional." He would not write a book about Reconstruction in the South; rather, he would tell a story of "the relations between the regions, the impact of the North on the South, the gradual absorption of the impact, the blunting of Northern purpose, and the eventual frustration of the revolution."[79] At least that is how he envisioned his project in the fall of 1958.

Arthur H. Thornhill was interested in signing Woodward to a contract that obligated him to write a study of the period from emancipation to desegregation. Woodward admitted that such a book would likely have greater significance and popular appeal. "I hope to get around to that one later on," he confessed. But he worried the project might overlap with other lingering obligations he had with Houghton Mifflin.[80] At this point in his career, both academic and trade publishers wanted Woodward on their lists. The more contracts he signed, the more projects he agreed to undertake, the more difficult it became for him to follow through. That said, he signed with Little, Brown in November 1958, planning to deliver a 200,000-word manuscript by the fall of 1962.[81]

In the meantime, Woodward corresponded with George P. Brockway, president of W. W. Norton & Co., who, prompted by Woodward's *New York Times* review of Hodding Carter's *The Angry Scar: The Story of Reconstruction*, wondered whether Woodward was "ready to write the definitive book on Reconstruction that so many await."[82] Woodward met with Brockway in New York, despite the fact that he had already signed a contract with Thornhill, and followed up with a letter that outlined his intentions. "I will be concerned with the primary results of the Civil War—the making of peace, the abortive efforts to impose a social and political revolution in the South, the resistance to those efforts, their frustration, and the resolution of conflict in reunion by compromise." His use of the word "impose" is telling, for in his notes he asked how much he needed to consider "sectional recrimination." Woodward seemed to be more confident in his pitch to Brockway. He justified his approach by listing a host of national policies that Reconstruction put into place, including "emancipation, military rule, sudden disfranchisement, sudden enfranchisement, an inverted social order, a status revolution, confiscation and redistribution of private property on a large scale, [and] terror." But those policies were experienced differently depending on region. Only the South lived through the effects of Reconstruction, Woodward maintained. At last he believed he had an entry point. "The emphasis in recent and forthcoming historiography of Reconstruction has been upon motive and causation," he explained. "I want to shift attention to effect and fulfillment—the concrete, flesh-and-blood experience, rather than the abstract plans, debates, and maneuvers." He did issue one final caveat. "Research and long rumination" often altered even the best-laid plans.[83] Still, Woodward felt fairly confident at this point.

As Woodward negotiated with Thornhill at Little & Brown and Brockway at Norton, he applied for fellowships. "I am convinced that a fresh and revisionary study needs to be made of the history of Reconstruction," he stressed in a letter to the Guggenheim Foundation's director. Most of the major works in the field were more than five decades old, he observed, though his concern went well beyond their expiration date: "They bear the strong imprint of their period and its presuppositions." New questions needed to be asked, he explained. And in order to answer those questions, Woodward had "to go back to the archives myself." He provided no detailed list, writing instead that he planned to visit collections in the "eleven Southern states concerned," in Washington, DC, "and elsewhere."[84] He closed his proposal by asserting that he "anticipated no difficulty in getting the resulting book published by a reputable press." [85] The Guggenheim Foundation awarded Woodward a fellowship, giving him much of 1960 and the summer of 1961 off.[86]

Woodward reiterated many of these points in his application to the Lilly Foundation. Older interpretations of Reconstruction had far-reaching consequences for the American polity, he argued, because "they support the conviction that the Negro is incapable of self-government and of full participation in democratic government and unacceptable as first-class citizens enjoying civil liberties guaranteed by the Constitution." This "unacceptable interpretation of history," he continued, proved an important impediment in the way of a "second reconstruction."[87] This is vintage Woodward, the scholar-activist who sought to put his studies of the past in service of the present. His thinking on Reconstruction would always be filtered through the modern civil rights movement.

Even as late as 1960, Woodward did not think of himself primarily in terms of his newfound status as a public intellectual.[88] He planned to write a standard monograph, not a think piece. Nor did he "conceive of this work as a mere synthesis of new monographs done by my students and others, rounding up and summarizing the findings of original investigations." Rather, he "proposed to do original research myself, as I did my work on the period immediately following Reconstruction from 1877–1913."[89] Woodward did not outline any of the possible approaches or themes that had vexed him. Instead, he emphasized his credentials and his preparedness for the work at hand. In late June he received word that his proposal had been successful. The Lilly Foundation would buy out his teaching contract at Johns Hopkins for the 1960–1961 academic year. With two sources of external funding, Woodward would be free to pursue his research.[90] The book contract was another matter. Woodward's attempt to woo both Thornhill and Brockway turned out to be a rockier situation, although he ultimately settled on the former and expected to make good use of his money and time.[91]

At first blush, the timing seems propitious. Avenues for the dissemination of Woodward's research were beginning to open up, for example. Cornell University had approached Woodward in the fall of 1959 about delivering the

Messenger Lectures on the Evolution of Civilization. The Messenger Lecture Committee desired Woodward because of the notoriety he had achieved with the Richards Lectures. Woodward was a recognizable commodity, and the committee was likely banking on the success of another *Strange Career*.[92] Established in 1923 and funded by alumnus Hiram Messenger, the Messenger Lectureship Series was designed with "the special purpose of raising the moral standard of our political, business, and social life."[93] Although Messenger had not limited the series to the subject of history, Woodward was not an unlikely selection given his status in the field. The invitation in 1959 also arrived as Americans were busy reassessing the problem of racial equality. By the time Woodward drafted the lectures four years later, President John F. Kennedy had underscored what was at stake. "We are confronted primarily with a moral issue," he announced to the American people. "It is as old as the scriptures and is as clear as the American Constitution."[94] Woodward as the scholar-activist, who used history to inform the present in moral terms, was the ideal choice of speaker.

Knight Biggerstaff, chair of Cornell's history department, emphasized Woodward would have free rein to choose the lecture's subject matter. He also made clear that most lecturers prepared manuscripts, "subsequently published by Cornell University Press."[95] Both points concerned Woodward. Cornell initially wanted Woodward to deliver the talks in the fall of 1961. The possibility that he might teach overseas allowed him to defer, but he still needed to address the larger issues at hand. While explaining "his research program" was such that he thought a later date preferable, he disclosed that he was unsure of the subject matter for his lectures. His Reconstruction manuscript was already under contract and he could not in good conscience draw on that material for his lectures. If he could come up with a different angle—one that would not find a home in his proposed book manuscript—and if Cornell could agree to publish his lectures with the understanding that the subject matter of the two works would overlap but "with no infringement on or duplication of his book," he would be delighted to accept the invitation.[96] Biggerstaff quickly agreed to Woodward's terms, delaying the date of his lectures to fall 1962, and promised that publication was not a requirement since he understood the material was contracted elsewhere.

Woodward's plans to complete the Messenger Lectures, and ultimately the book he promised to deliver to Thornhill in 1962, were stymied by his decision to leave Johns Hopkins for a position at Yale University that fall. Perhaps Woodward also underestimated the amount of research it would take to complete a sweeping history of Reconstruction in eleven states, as described to Brockway in 1959. As a result, Woodward asked Biggerstaff if Cornell could move the lectures yet again, to 1963 or 1964.[97] The University Lecture Committee easily agreed to his request.

In the years preceding the drafting of six Messenger Lectures, and as preparation for the book, Woodward undertook several visits to the archives. In 1961 and 1962 he traveled to Alabama, Mississippi, Louisiana, Texas, and Tennessee. He frequently requested assistance from colleagues stationed in various towns across the South, often asking them for their opinion on which archival collections had the most to offer.[98] As part of the process, he also borrowed archival notes on Reconstruction topics from former students and colleagues, including James McPherson and T. Harry Williams.[99] Notwithstanding the optimism and expertise highlighted in his funding applications, Woodward was frequently plagued by doubts about his professional decisions. In a letter to William Carleton he revisited concerns they had discussed during a prior visit. "But the heavier crisis is the conjunction of two major challenges (self-selected, inflicted)—the new job *and* the new book," Woodward lamented. "Hard to say which is the more severe." He thanked Carleton for his counsel, noting, "I took what comfort I could in your deprecation of my fear of the new book."[100] Woodward's feelings toward the project, though, oscillated between apprehension and exhilaration. After one research trip in the winter of 1962, he informed Carleton that he was "getting dirty in [the] archives as if I were a real historian again." He clarified the nature of his work, however, observing that "it wasn't really research but accumulation—a begging, copying, photographing, filming, looting, borrowing expedition." Regardless, he was excited. "Maybe I can eventually make something of it. The loot sitting around does send up some savory smells," he reported. "As periods go, this one seems to me to have more than its share of the standard stuff of history—rape, robbery, mass murder, torture, endless brutality, hypocrisy, heroism, saintliness. The cumulative impact of exposure to all this raw material would best be represented as a piercing scream."[101]

Woodward incorporated material from his archival trips into the Messenger Lectures to underscore his principal contention that Reconstruction did not engender any meaningful change. Although Woodward was careful not to use the phrase "destined to fail," his description all but suggested that failure was preordained. At the time he delivered the lectures, Woodward's insistence on the failure of Reconstruction and his bedeviling pessimism about the present made him an outlier during the heyday of revisionist historiography in the early to mid-1960s.[102] Revisionists celebrated Radical Republicans as principled crusaders who were driven by idealism rather than self-interest and viewed African Americans as efficacious agents of their own destiny.[103] Woodward was critical of their inability to reconcile so much achievement with the eventual downfall of Reconstruction. He was interested in the tragedy and irony of failure, as he had been in his earlier scholarship. When the post-revisionists arrived in the 1970s the historiography shifted yet again. This generation of historians viewed the era as unequivocally moderate and pointed out that little had changed. In this sense they had more in common with Woodward, although the bulk of the post-revisionists argued for the continuity of racial thought and economic conditions in the South which still left Woodward as the iconoclast.[104]

As Woodward continued to draft the lectures, he reminded himself of his goals. He handwrote in pencil a brief one-page outline titled "Messenger Lectures." It reads, "1. No substanture [sic], no narrative, no summary 2. Topical." Underneath the word *topical* are listed the following themes: "Defeat, Victory, Liberation, Loyalty, Radicalism, Reactionism."[105] The five extant lectures in this volume still function more like a political history, just as he had promised Thornhill in 1958, although the themes of liberation, defeat, loyalty, and radicalism do run through the series. Woodward stuck closely to the archival material and primary sources and footnoted his work. These notes and revisions hint at his ongoing efforts to offer a substantively new interpretation of Reconstruction. The lecture series was not intended to be a superficial narrative summary because Woodward had the broader book in mind. He began the discussion in 1865 with emancipation and its immediate consequences, and ended in 1872 with Senator Charles Sumner's failed civil rights bill and the successful passage of the Amnesty Act permitting ex-Confederates, formerly excluded under the Fourteenth Amendment, to hold office. Woodward marked the end of Reconstruction in 1872 rather than 1877 as he did in *Origins* and *Reunion and Reaction*, demonstrating that his ideas had shifted and perhaps to underscore how swiftly the end had arrived. The typescripts he produced show evidence of his own copyediting as well as meaty comments from others in pencil, including those that appear to be from one of his students, Willie Lee Rose, who jokingly wrote upon return, "Good lord—I haven't lost your last 5 footnotes, have I??"[106] Turns out she had, but Woodward remained undeterred.

Taken as a whole, the lectures elucidate why the First Reconstruction failed rather quickly. Woodward described the northern commitment to Reconstruction as tentative, limited, and decidedly not revolutionary. In Lecture IV, "The Conservatism of Northern Radicals," and Lecture VI, "Did the North Really Mean It?" he demonstrated how the Republican Party was divided in purpose. On the question of racial equality, aside from a few figures such as Senators Charles Sumner and Thaddeus Stevens, the bulk of the party held moderate to conservative views. Party leaders drew their support from a political constituency dedicated to a belief in the superiority of the white race. Before the war, northerners had established segregation in public spaces and disenfranchised black voters in their own states. After the war, northerners' interest in racial equality proved to be halfhearted and reflected existing prejudices. The Freedmen's Bureau often tolerated the use of coercion by white landowners in the labor system. Without land redistribution, full integration, or guaranteed suffrage backed by federal protection, the project was doomed.[107]

Woodward relied heavily on Leon F. Litwack's book *North of Slavery: The Negro in the Free States, 1790–1860* as he wrote these two Messenger Lectures. He borrowed Litwack's argument about widespread patterns of northern segregation and the prevalence of conservative northern views on race before the Civil War.[108] Litwack's work also informed Woodward's cynical view of the Radical Republicans' motives during the First Reconstruction. Two years later when Woodward revised *Strange Career*, he included the same passage from *North of Slavery* that had been introduced in the fourth Messenger Lecture.[109] Two things are worth noting. First, Woodward always reevaluated his work in light of new scholarship. Second, he was attuned to the reception of his own writings. Historians had criticized *Strange Career* for Woodward's tendency to exaggerate the distinctive and fluid nature of race relations, those "forgotten alternatives," in the late nineteenth-century South. Woodward's inclusion of Litwack marked an acknowledgment to his critics that he understood their doubt and pessimism about the possibility of racial equality in the nineteenth and twentieth centuries.

Then again Woodward knew there was plenty of blame to go around for Reconstruction's failure. In other lectures, he located it not just in the attitudes and actions of northern reformers, but also in those of white southerners. In Lecture III, "The Paradox of Loyalty," he stated that Presidential Reconstruction had made little headway not just because of President Andrew Johnson's intransigence and leniency toward former Confederates, but also because loyalty to church, tradition, and locality precipitated a crisis. One could not be both loyal to the nation and loyal to the region. The penalty for not affirming both "anti-Confederate" and "anti-Southern" sentiment was social ostracism by the community.[110] In Lecture V, "Radicalism for Southern Conservatives," Woodward described how southern radicals often proved to be reluctant supporters of change because of their own racism, even as they were reviled by their neighbors for having been traitors. Southern radicals did lend a hand in building the Republican Party in the South, although their strength and engagement varied depending upon the locale. He illustrated how white southern supporters of the Republican Party tended to come from poorer regions of the South, exhibiting intense class resentment against the planters. The party's promise of economic reform in the region attracted white southern radicals as well as the formerly enslaved.[111]

Lecture II and a small section of Lecture V turned to the experience of the formerly enslaved. "The Fear of Freedom," opened with a lengthy quotation from W. E. B. Du Bois's *Black Reconstruction in America* identifying the period of Reconstruction as "the Apocalypse." Woodward was touched by the "hauntingly lyrical" quality of Du Bois's writing, noting that it had "sustained the hopes and aspirations of a whole people," even a century later.[112] In the Messenger Lectures he depicted freedom as an unfolding process, one of advancement and retreat, and one that had both physical and psychological consequences. The formerly enslaved experimented with various acts of self-determination such as immediate "uninhibited motion," insubordination, and demands of payment for labor. Any "fear of freedom" was alleviated by the possibility of land redistribution and sustained by the assertive demeanor of African American troops. With the onset of Congressional Reconstruction, freedpeople adopted a radical political sensibility, participating in Union Leagues and registering to vote in high numbers. Yet, the formerly enslaved in Woodward's story faced hunger, disease, and death, all engendered by the squalid conditions of the refugee camps and the limitations of life on the move. So appalling was the "second exodus" that he deemed it reminiscent of the "horrors" of the Middle Passage.[113]

By the time Woodward delivered the Messenger Lectures, he had already published a number of essays on Reconstruction in such venues as *Commentary*, *American Scholar*, and the *Journal of Negro Education*. Many of them invoked the analogy between the First and Second Reconstructions. In 1956 Woodward appreciated the First Reconstruction, describing how "an enormous amount of idealism and noble motives went into its making." Writing in *Commentary* he intended to furnish hope to contemporary activists who feared that only two years after the *Brown* decision the movement was "doomed . . . to repeat the failure and frustration" of the first. Woodward advised that while change would come through a process of "gradualism," "the New Reconstruction seem[ed] to promise more enduring results."[114] Yet his sanguinity was short lived. In 1957 and 1958 he expressed greater ambivalence, even verging on pessimism, about the possibilities of the Second

Reconstruction. Congressional debate over the 1957 Civil Rights bill had revealed deep sectional division and white southerners' defiance of court orders to desegregate southern schools (known as massive resistance) persisted, particularly in the Lower South. "There is no apparent prospect of early compliance or of easy solution," he concluded. "The white South is resisting, and a reactionary part of it is defiant. The resistance is stubborn."[115] Woodward also cautioned against viewing "the First Reconstruction as if it was in some ways a sort of Golden Age." While he sympathized with the sentiment, he also warned that it was folly because "there is too much irony mixed with the tragedy for that."[116]

Despite the title of the Messenger Lecture Series, Woodward surprisingly spoke very little of the First Reconstruction in the context of the Second. He had grown weary of the analogy and perhaps considered it less historically useful in 1964. In the 1957 version of *Strange Career* a more detailed comparison allowed him to highlight how much better were the prospects of victory in the mid-1950s than in the 1860s and 1870s—a story of discontinuity versus continuity. Except now the possibility of success seemed even less certain. The struggle continued to face robust resistance, particularly in Mississippi, and passage of the 1964 Civil Rights Act was still several months away. Woodward referenced the analogy only twice in the Messenger Lectures. As in other places, he offered a stern admonition in Lecture IV about employing the analogy. "The temptation is strong" to view the "leaders" of Reconstruction as "prophets and ideologists" for the twentieth century and to "read into their words and deeds our own thoughts and motives." This was imprudent and reflected an unrealistic desire to make good on the unfulfilled pledges of the past. "To be conscious of the temptation is—or should be—to be on guard against it," he advised.[117] In the final lecture he explicitly cautioned against seeking insight in the 1860s and 1870s. "For the First Reconstruction was really never tried," he insisted. "The North never really meant what it said and the South sensed that from the start." If the Second Reconstruction were to succeed, Woodward concluded, it would require self-reflection on the part of the North, not just criticism of the South. Hypocrisy on either side was no solution for national progress on racial equality.[118] In 1966 when he revised *Strange Career*, he eliminated those portions of the last chapter that contained "an extended comparison of the two reconstructions."[119]

Although Woodward abandoned his plans to publish the Messenger Lectures and anticipated incorporating them into the larger monograph, some of the material, nonetheless, trickled out. He expanded on his ideas, generating new prose, except in the case of one short piece for which he copied material verbatim from Messenger Lectures IV and VI. The product, "Seeds of Failure in Radical Race Policy," underscored the lack of radicalism among the Radicals. Woodward recycled this new hybrid piece in dizzying fashion. In April of 1965 he presented "Seeds" as a speech at the American Philosophical Society, published a year later with no revision.[120] Later that month he retitled the paper as "Reformers and Reconstruction" and delivered it at a conference on Reconstruction at the University of Illinois for university and secondary schoolteachers.[121] When Woodward agreed to join the symposium, he neglected to inform the host, Harold M. Hyman, that he had already committed the paper for publication.[122] One month later, Hyman came seeking Woodward's piece with his hackles raised. Having heard that Woodward had promised it to the APS, Hyman suggested that the piece be reprinted in the forthcoming volume following release of the APS essay. After all, Woodward owed them. At this point Woodward tried to back out, informing Hyman that, while he could get permission to reprint it, his publisher was not keen on seeing "publication of material in book form" since it was already under contract for the larger Reconstruction book.[123] Hyman was livid, and after much back and forth, Woodward ultimately relented.[124] Finally, Woodward published the piece a third time in 1971 in his collection *American Counterpoint*.[125]

Woodward also borrowed ideas from the Messenger Lectures for shorter pieces written for general audiences, as was his wont. In 1965, for example, he wrote an essay printed in *Harper's Magazine* titled "From the First Reconstruction to the Second," a riff on his title for the Messenger Lectures, even though he had warned of the dangers of using the analogy. In light of passage of the Civil Rights Act of July 1964, perhaps the possibility of further accomplishments looked promising. Woodward suggested that recent events paralleled those of the 1860s and 1870s. Apparently, even discontinuity had its limits, if only up to a point: 1965, he noted, looked in many ways a lot like 1865. During Reconstruction, "the North had its way." The restoration of the states of the former Confederacy was predicated on "the Union's terms"; slavery was abolished; the newly emancipated were granted citizenship; "and the new citizens were granted the franchise and equal rights." These were the kinds of changes codified in law but not practiced on the ground. Herein lay the problem with Reconstruction. Still, Woodward believed the South had changed fundamentally between those two terminal points. "Looking back over the past one hundred years and beyond," he wrote, "one will find no period of such concentrated change in the South since Captain John Smith disturbed the tranquility of the aborigines at the dawn of the seventeenth century." What had not changed, however, was how "Southern people of both races" lived their lives. "If anything," he ruefully stressed, "old status lines were rigidified."[126]

In this piece Woodward was more sanguine about the potential for lasting change wrought by the modern civil rights movement. "This time," he wrote encouragingly, "the way people live, where they live, and how they make their living are changing massively and with unprecedented speed." And yet, the white South was recalcitrant "and more deeply alienated and defiant than it has been since 1877." The 1950s and 1960s were, Woodward believed, "a historical flashback" to the Reconstruction era. "The South has been reliving an old trauma."[127] That said, the flashback was only partial. It could have been complete, were it not for African American activists who changed the course of history. "Had it been up to the white man, North and South," Woodward surmised, "the Second Reconstruction possibly would have already gone the way of the First—the way of compromise, conciliation, and appeasement into frustration and failure. It would have been," Woodward continued, "the story of white men resolving their differences at the expense of black men." But not this time. Instead, Woodward argued, "the Negro himself was a decisive participant, not an instrument of white purpose."[128] Woodward was no naïf. He knew that to proclaim the Second Reconstruction a success in 1965 was sheer folly. The white South was "moving," but it was also "back in the old limbo, nursing new bruises to pride and licking old wounds to self-esteem." Heretofore, white southerners had looked to the past to affirm their identity. "Defeat and failure, frustration and poverty, guilt and tragedy" had defined their heritage, Woodward believed. These "Faulknerian themes" would not go away easily. Still, Woodward sensed that southerners, black and white, would look "increasingly to the future and not the past, to action and instead of memory" for self-definition.[129] Only in this way could the region move from the First Reconstruction to the Second.

As Woodward continued to ponder the relevance of the analogy, he took stock of his own work and the state of the field. He felt his optimism dwindling. As Michael O'Brien notes, the analogy "became less tenable in the late 1960s, when to [Woodward's] sharp dissatisfaction, the rise of the black power movement splintered the existing racial reform movement."[130] Woodward clung to mounting pessimism about whether the achievements of the Second Reconstruction represented any genuine accomplishment and would prove to be as fleeting as the First Reconstruction. Colleagues still expected he would produce a book on Reconstruction incorporating material from the Messenger Lectures, and they waited in anticipation for

"Reconstruction and Revision," his paper delivered at the 1967 Southern Historical Association in which he emphasized the shortcomings of a century earlier.

Woodward was even blunter about the catastrophe of Reconstruction in the SHA paper. "The ruins of two great failures dominate the landscape of American history," he began. "They are adjacent and complementary but separate and distinct." This was a story of double irony—one of southern history and its experience with defeat, and the other of national history and the federal government's failure to achieve racial equality. Woodward described these two historical moments as "exceptional" and "uncharacteristic in the American experience," noting that historians had a duty to account for these "unique failures." Revisionists, though, seemed uninterested in Woodward's engagement with irony. Their focus was squarely on success, not failure. The "new revisionists" of the 1960s were committed to rehabilitating the image of Radical Republicans as "high-minded idealists who rose above selfish political and economic interests" and African American leaders as symbols of "a gratifying amount of talent, ability, and vision." They sought not only to upend the Dunning School interpretation of the early twentieth century, but also to overturn the 1930s scholarship associated with white historians who had suggested Republicans were driven by economic self-interest rather than pure idealism. Woodward, always generous with his compliments, acknowledged the significance of the revisionists' accomplishments. "I hope the record is clear," he proclaimed, "that I have aided and abetted and egged them on, presumed to teach some of them, read many of their manuscripts and all their monographs, praised what I could and encouraged when I could."[131] As correspondence about the Messenger Lectures and the larger book indicates, the work of Woodward's students undoubtedly shaped his own understanding of Reconstruction. But, always the outlier, he still found the revisionists' scholarship wanting. If the Radicals' enthusiasm was genuine, the formerly enslaved were receptive to political change, and the southern Republican Party coalition was productive, then why didn't the goals of Radical Reconstruction prevail?

Woodward ventured that he might have an answer to the problem. "Americans have rather a thing about failure—about confronting it, confessing it, and accepting it, as well as about explaining it," he surmised. The inclination to accept the failure of the First Reconstruction without historical interrogation revealed an exaggerated, and possibly unwarranted, faith in the broad potential of the Second Reconstruction. This misplaced optimism, he noted whimsically, might even lead historians to envision a Third Reconstruction in some undetermined future. But what made reckoning with failure truly difficult for historians was their incapacity or indifference to thinking comparatively. "Comparisons are essential to all historical interpretations," he averred.[132] Certainly this was not an unfamiliar approach to Woodward. In the 1953 essay "The Irony of Southern History," he described how "the South had undergone an experience, that it could share with no other part of America—though is shared by nearly all the peoples of Europe and Asia—the experience of defeat, occupation, and resistance."[133] In the mid-1960s Woodward's intellectual trajectory shifted in a more explicitly comparative direction as his work and collaboration with other scholars demonstrates. He gathered together twenty-two American historians, including such luminaries as David Brion Davis, John Hope Franklin, Richard Hofstadter, and David M. Potter, to generate lectures on American history rooted in a comparative context and designed with foreign audiences in mind for the broadcast program Voice of America.[134] In the published volume of the lectures Woodward observed that the history of the Civil War and Reconstruction had "profited from hints, suggestions, and limited experiments of a comparative nature" but had not advanced far enough.[135]

His SHA talk extended the conversation by providing two comparative frameworks as a way of understanding the double irony of failure—comparison with foreign post emancipation societies and the US West. First, he demonstrated how emancipation in post-slave societies in the West Indies, Brazil, Mexico, Asia, and Africa consisted of some kind of forced labor. Coercion was the modus operandi, as it had been in the US South. The formerly enslaved grappled with such adversities as vagrancy and apprenticeship laws, penalties for violating labor contracts, and restrictions on land ownership. The failure of racial equality was guaranteed. Moreover, the greatest significance of such an approach, Woodward pronounced, was that "historians of Reconstruction" seeking an explanation for "the failure of that experiment" would be able to abandon the "myth of American uniqueness."[136] Woodward's early nod toward the comparative history of post-emancipations influenced decades of subsequent scholarship.[137]

Second, Woodward drew attention to similarities between the Freedmen's Bureau and the Indian Bureau. Both federal entities were born out of the same reform impulse, as military officers stationed in the South eventually made their way to the West. Ultimately, the forces of white supremacy overwhelmed any commitment to progress. Reformers pledged to give land to Native Americans and African Americans, only to rescind the offer. Promises of integration also went unfulfilled. Woodward's focus on the burdens of white supremacy not only hearkened back to the central analytic thrust of the Messenger Lectures, but also anticipated present-day trends in the historiography in his focus on the South-West Reconstruction comparison.[138]

Nestled in Woodward's comparison of the South to the West also lay a counterfactual narrative. In a note on the conference's proceedings, David Donald appreciated Woodward's willingness to entertain the idea of "revolutionary alternatives."[139] This is proverbial Woodward, invoking the same sense of tragedy and irony as he did with his "forgotten alternatives" in *Strange Career*.[140] Woodward asked, What if Thaddeus Stevens's plan for confiscation and redistribution of ex-Confederate estates had succeeded? Precedent for the idea certainly existed, he contended. The same Republican Party that had spearheaded an enormous program of government-sanctioned distribution of public lands with passage of the 1862 Homestead Act would have assumed control of Stevens's legislation. The plan entailed seizing 394 million acres and redistributing 40 million acres to the formerly enslaved. Stevens also could have advocated for the entire "liquidation of the enemy class," wiping out "white resistance down to the last unregenerate lord of the lash and the last bed-sheeted Ku-Kluxer." And why not make the Freedmen's Bureau permanent and replace General O. O. Howard with Frederick Douglass? Woodward added. In the end, Reconstruction did not turn out to be much of a revolution since "there were no mass executions, no class liquidations," and "no heads rolled."[141]

In the Messenger Lectures, Woodward had celebrated Stevens as a visionary who lost to the large group of "pusillanimous" moderates during the drafting of the Fourteenth Amendment when they deferred to states' rights and did not compel ratification of the amendment in exchange for readmission to the Union.[142] Three years later, in the counterfactual storyline presented in the SHA paper, Stevens was "not revolutionary enough" and perhaps not even much of a Radical. Neither was Charles Sumner for that matter. Stevens suffered from "bourgeois softness" and was incapable of standing up to white southerners "who scoffed at the law and ridiculed the courts." Yet even if Stevens's vision had prevailed, Woodward conceded, Republicans' experience in the West showed that Reconstruction could not have succeeded. "The will of the dominant white majority would prevail," he said, "and where whites were not in the majority it would prevail anyway."[143]

Over the course of the next few years Woodward's work on the comparative nature of emancipation and reconstruction evolved. Yale University Law School invited him to deliver the Storrs Lectures in April 1969. The series, established in 1889 in honor of alumnus William L. Storrs, showcased

American scholars who were not typically part of the university's law school but focused on "fundamental problems of law and jurisprudence."[144] In classic Woodwardian fashion, he incorporated material from the SHA paper into the first lecture, "The Problem of Failure in American History," revisiting Reconstruction historiography and stressing the double irony of failure.[145] The second and third lectures, "The Comparative Approach to Emancipation History" and "The Comparative Approach to Reconstruction History," contained largely new work, fleshing out the foreign parallels alluded to in the SHA talk. The two lectures compared various post-emancipation societies in areas that had formerly been under the control of colonial rule. As he had in his SHA talk, he referenced work by Dutch scholar Wilhelmina Kloosterboer who maintained that involuntary labor was a fundamental feature of post-emancipation societies. Still, in spite of this commonality in broader "Plantation-America," Woodward made the case for southern distinctiveness by relying on Phillip D. Curtin's recently published demographic statistics on the Atlantic slave trade showing that the South had the largest slave population at the end of the Civil War, despite having purchased the smallest number of imported slaves. Enslaved people in the United States also endured the worst coercion, he declared.[146]

Historians Genovese and McFeeley provided feedback on the Storrs Lectures, enthusiastically recommending publication, although expressing uncertainty about where they fit into the book on Reconstruction the profession had been impatiently waiting for. McFeeley divulged that he was "just a little bit hungry for some down to earth details in the manner of *Origins*" but expected those might arrive in the monograph.[147] "If you are reasonably close to the end," Genovese advised, "it would make sense to compress these into an article and put the rest right into the book. If that book is years away—I hope you have not become too discouraged about finishing it—then you ought to publish a small book right now." Genovese also specified that he missed the SHA material on the US West and the "fantasies associated with super-radical reconstruction."[148] Woodward revealed to Genovese that his plans for publishing the lectures were unresolved, and while he agreed that they should appear in print soon, he nonetheless envisioned them as "part of a larger series of reinterpretations ... some of which I have yet to write."[149] In fact, two years later Woodward included two new comparative essays in the edited collection *American Counterpoint* that advanced these "reinterpretations."[150] These essays represented his last work on comparative emancipations and reconstructions.

Yet in the 1970s and 1980s Woodward mostly found himself in an intellectual cul-de-sac. He frequently returned to half-formulated ideas and unfinished projects. Woodward reused material from the SHA paper and Storrs Lectures II and III, in particular, but seemed to have abandoned hope of completing the larger book on Reconstruction. In 1970, for example, he combined unrevised sections and presented them in Moscow at the XIII International Congress for Historical Sciences, which published the proceedings shortly thereafter.[151] In 1976 Woodward delivered the Moscow paper as part of the Chancellor's Symposium on Southern History at the University of Mississippi. It appeared in print two years later in the collection *What Is Freedom's Price?*[152] There is no evidence he was able to expand on the material. Still, Woodward could not rest. In 1989 he published the volume *Future of the Past*, noting in the "Provenance of Contents" that all but two of the essays had been previously published, including the Moscow–Mississippi essay, and one of the "new" pieces relied on "comparisons" that had "been used elsewhere."[153] The latter, titled "Reconstruction: A Counterfactual Playback," turned out to be almost a literal adaptation of a large section of the SHA paper.[154] The SHA paper had remained hidden in published form for roughly two decades, and although in print by 1989, its origins remained unnamed.

Attention to failure in the history of Reconstruction encouraged Woodward to be frank about failures of his own. In "Reconstruction: A Counterfactual Playback," as he had in prior incarnations of the SHA paper, Woodward ended the presentation with an apology. "Having invited you to consider the causes of the failure of Reconstruction," he professed, "I have produced nothing but negative results." He acknowledged having doubted the authenticity of the Radicals, questioned the usefulness of claims for American exceptionalism, and presented a "revolutionary alternative" that was not very feasible. "The problem remains unsolved," he announced. All he could offer was a buoyant recommendation for assigning the task a "high priority" in American historiography. And as if to underscore the enormity of the disappointment, he felt compelled to issue a second apology in the same paragraph: "I am obliged to confess a failure of my own, the failure to find a satisfactory explanation for the failure of Reconstruction." In this moment Woodward laid everything bare, confessing that ironically the ironist had misstepped in solving a historical misstep.[155] A handful of scholars who reviewed Woodward's last collection, *Future of the Past*, addressed the seemingly stale nature of the essay, if not the entire book, even while praising the southern historian's skills and reputation. "Woodward has, I suppose, passed beyond criticism into the canonical," Michael O'Brien decided. "Even his failings have interest."[156] John Herbert Roper concluded the book was "quite dated, even musty in today's context," and in light of the recent release of Eric Foner's magnum opus *Reconstruction: America's Unfinished Revolution, 1863–1877*, Woodward had little to add that was "useful." Roper did not recognize that "Reconstruction: A Counterfactual Playback" was two decades old. But the obsolete or familiar quality of the work mattered little in the end, "for the plain fact is that Woodward—warmed over, half-speed, rerun, or whatever words one seizes to describe him when he is at less than his best—is still classier than the rest of us at our very best."[157]

Woodward's volume of essays and Foner's book appeared within a year of each other. Indeed, Woodward reviewed Foner in the *New York Review of Books* shortly before the release of *Future of the Past*. Generally impressed with Foner's narrative, Woodward noted that the Columbia historian had successfully balanced political, economic, and social history, furnished a cohesive account of Reconstruction in eleven southern states, and "cut a maze of tunnels through the vast archives of the period." In short, it appears Foner accomplished what Woodward could not. Woodward illuminated how the histories of Reconstruction appeared in "thirty-year cycles"—1900s, 1930s, and 1960s—remarking that Foner's work represented "the distinguished fruition" of the latest "cycle of Reconstruction historiography." Given that Foner highlighted the "centrality of the black experience" and viewed Reconstruction as the first great "experiment in interracial democracy," no doubt Woodward viewed him as the apotheosis of revisionism. What of the next cycle, "that of the *fin de siècle*," though? Woodward considered it premature to identify "a cycle of the 1990s." Rather than speculate about the next cycle, he ended with a recognizable Woodwardian spin. He asserted that Foner, like those before him, had no answer to the question "What went so terribly wrong?"[158]

Once more the native southern historian offered a possible way out of this problem. Woodward challenged the notion of American exceptionalism and advocated exploring "the neglected field of comparative emancipations." As he had in many previous iterations of his SHA talk, he cited two scholars as muses: Dutch historian Kloosterboer and William R. Brock, a British historian who located the constitutional reasons for the failure of Reconstruction in a transatlantic context. Woodward flirted with the possibility of a turbocharged Thaddeus Stevens guided by revolutionary aims, only to conclude that "no heads rolled," leading the "defiant rebels" to prevail. Finally, he drew attention to Radical cross-fertilization in the South and West, invoking the analogy between African Americans and Native Americans.[159] When all was said and done, however, he aimed for a soft landing. Woodward did not mean "to suggest that Reconstruction was inevitably doomed to failure" or to "imply that historians have failed in their duty." He merely hoped to draw attention to "unanswered questions."[160] Woodward, it appears, still had not managed to find a way out of his intellectual roundabout.

It is possible that Woodward felt regret over not finishing the larger book on Reconstruction the profession had come to expect. No one seemed to hold it against him when the book failed to appear, and colleagues continued to recognize him as an expert on the subject. There are as many reasons for failure as success, and Woodward had ample amounts of both. But the book on Reconstruction proved to be too much for him to conquer. In 1962 he made a shift from Johns Hopkins to Yale University at the same moment he initiated short visits to the archives, all prompted by a sabbatical and research support from Guggenheim and Lilly. The transition proved to be difficult, and archival research was never Woodward's forte. After delivering the Messenger Lectures in 1964, Woodward's interests shifted in a comparative direction. Although the theme of failure ran through all of his work on Reconstruction, he was never able to draw a meaningful connection between the earlier and later output. The shocking and early death of his twenty-six-year-old son Peter and deaths of close friends Richard Hofstadter, David Potter, and Alexander Bickel from cancer in the late 1960s and early 1970s came at a decisive professional moment and brought untold sadness. Michael O'Brien attributes Woodward's failure to finish the book on Reconstruction to his unique role as a "literary midwife" for some "very gifted historians who would rise to prominence," as well as many others.[161] A fair number of these scholars worked on the Civil War and Reconstruction, many of them students of Woodward, and they undoubtedly shaped his thinking on the subject, particularly while he was drafting the Messenger Lectures and comparative/counterfactual essays. Certainly the time spent in this mentorship role was considerable.

One other clue can be found in the SHA paper. Woodward outlined the sequential waves of Reconstruction historiography, noting that scholarship in the 1960s appeared to have "somewhat better prospects of durability, in[sofar] as durability goes in historiography." What's more, he felt compelled to "put in a word for the synthesizers" to whom the profession owed tremendous "gratitude." "My personal debt is particularly large," he avowed, for they had essentially let him "off the hook." "For whatever contribution I may have made in this field—and it may be quite small—it will certainly not be another synthesis," he decreed. "That need seems amply fulfilled" he concluded.[162] Woodward likely forgot that he had informed Arthur R. Thornhill years earlier that he wouldn't be writing a synthesis. Regardless, three years after delivering the Messenger Lectures, Woodward, with his inadequacies on display, had seemingly abandoned the book meant to rival *Origins* in its reach. Perhaps this explains his interest in comparative emancipations and reconstructions beginning in the mid-1960s, an underdeveloped topic with endless promise. Although he had given up on writing a history of Reconstruction, even twenty years later, Woodward could still recognize Foner as an expert.

In 2014 Foner reissued his book with a new introduction to mark the 150th anniversary of Reconstruction, and similar to Woodward's previous assessments, his work recounts the current state of historiography in light of what has come before. Foner identifies two weaknesses in the current state of the field, though. First, he notes that no one has yet managed to integrate all of the new perspectives into a "comprehensive account." With no synthesis of Reconstruction available in the twenty-first century, scholars seeking a history of the era, he concludes, have nowhere left to turn but his own book. Second, Foner is circumspect about the pessimism in contemporary scholarship. He writes that "today's historians of Reconstruction tend to give as much emphasis to the disappointments of freedom as the accomplishments of emancipation. Or, they emphasis [sic] goals other than freedom—equality, justice, and fraternity—and emphasize how far Reconstruction remained from accomplishing them." Finally, he notes, they illustrate the persistence of "racism and black subordination."[163]

It appears C. Vann Woodward might have found much in contemporary scholarship he could agree with. In Messenger Lecture IV he offered a stinging indictment of the Republican Party. "On the issue of Negro equality," he averred, "the party remained divided, hesitant, and unsure of its purpose.... The historic commitment to equality it eventually made was lacking in clarity, ambivalent in purpose, and capable of numerous interpretations."[164] In Messenger Lecture VI, he was more scathing in his assessment regarding the party's accomplishments, stating that the "Fifteenth Amendment reveals more deviousness than clarity of purpose, more partisan needs than idealist aims, more timidity than boldness."[165] His assessment of Reconstruction in the SHA paper and the Storrs Lectures underscored the theme of failure as well. Woodward affirmed that Reconstruction collapsed in large part because of the party's allegiance to white supremacy. Finally, in Lecture II he described the formerly enslaved's encounter with disease and death upon emancipation as a second Middle Passage, remarking that the escalating violence they faced in light of the Republican Party's failure to offer adequate protection made a mockery of success. Ironically Woodward was ahead of his time, unaware that his work in the 1960s would resonate with some of the fourth cycle of Reconstruction historiography beginning in the 1990s.[166]

Although Woodward showed himself to be an outlier in the midst of the revisionist movement's optimism, he and Foner do share one thing in common—a heightened sense of the importance of the present to the historical past. Foner ends his anniversary introduction by noting, "Reconstruction historiography has always spoken directly to current concerns....Citizenship, rights, freedom, democracy, [and] as long as these questions remain central to our society, so too will the necessity of an accurate understanding of Reconstruction." Foner reminds Americans that the study of Reconstruction is more than just about "historical and political questions." "Reconstruction history has always been morally inflected," he concludes, "because writing about the period forces the historian to think about where he or she stands in relation to key problems in our own time."[167]

Woodward wrote about Reconstruction during the height of the modern civil rights movement, or what he referred to as the Second Reconstruction. As both a scholar and an activist, his heightened sense of the present when writing about the past allowed for moments of both pessimism and optimism. "With all due resistance to superficial parallels," he wrote in *Harper's Magazine* in 1967, "we have been unable to avoid comparisons between past history and lived experiences. For we have witnessed in our time a rising tide of indignation against an ancient wrong, the slow crumbling of stubborn resistance, the sudden rush and elation of victory—and then felt the onset of reaction and the fading of high hopes." Although Woodward noted the Second Reconstruction ended in 1966, he celebrated what made it distinctive from the First Reconstruction—that African Americans and the young had seized the initiative. The possibility of a Third Reconstruction loomed on the horizon, "struggling to be born." Where might it be headed next? The answer was clear. A third would need to be national, not regional, in scope, Woodward stressed, and focus on eradicating economic inequality rather than solely tackling legal inequities.[168]

In Storrs Lecture I, a year and a half after the *Harper's* essay, Woodward invoked the Third Reconstruction yet again. The inclination to rationalize the failure of the first as a rehearsal for the success of the second, and possibly a third, he stated, amounted to a "deferred-success approach." He saw this predisposition as "another strategy of evasion," one that "involved a familiar middle-age solution to personal problems" and presumed a younger generation would take up the mantle.[169] Woodward was still unclear about the fate of a Third Reconstruction, but articulated a role for the historian going forward. By the late 1960s, he had moved away from writing solely for traditional scholars and more toward providing guidance to the general public on one of the greatest moral issues of the moment—the question of racial equality. "I think the country suffers from a pathological complex on Reconstruction and has lived with it for a long time . . . both arising out of the same traumatic event, but experienced in different ways," he declared in Storrs Lecture I. "In the North it resulted in a guilt-shame complex" and "in the South a dirty-deal complex." After emerging victorious from the war, the North failed to live up to its ideals, leaving it wracked with guilt, self-criticism, and remorse. The South (and Woodward did not specify he meant the white South) showed a predilection for extortion, indignation, and extreme bellicosity, consistently blaming its own weaknesses on Reconstruction. The solution to what "psychologists call 'projection'" on both sides, Woodward indicated, would involve frank and honest historical mediation: "The historian would better take his cue from the therapist, who does not encourage the patient to bury the traumatic experience in forgetfulness or to transform it into a fond memory, but who insists on restoring it to full consciousness and facing all the implications and insights it provides."[170] In short, the success of a Third Reconstruction depended on the willingness of historians to serve as therapists for the national public, drawing attention to the psychological traumas triggered by the past.

We are currently at the sesquicentennial of the Fifteenth Amendment and still living through the Third Reconstruction (or possibly facing a Fourth Reconstruction if one considers President Barack Obama the fruition of the Third), a moment Woodward surmised might happen. Whether the Third Reconstruction continues to carry with it the misguided optimism that he noted impelled the Second Reconstruction remains to be seen. Today, mass incarceration, increased voter suppression, the Supreme Court's gutting of the Voting Rights Act, the attack on birthright citizenship, a presidential impeachment, and the fortification of the nation's borders give little cause for hope, even in the wake of Barack Obama's eight years in the presidency. Those problems that plagued the First and Second Reconstructions inform the Third. Woodward might not be the only one in the roundabout. Past experience does not always guarantee future results. And certainly Woodward was attuned to what he identified as the "Great Reaction" (and "Second Great Reaction"), the inevitable backlash that follows any challenge to the existing order or revolution in civil rights.[171]

But still Woodward believed in possibility and historical contingency. He was a dissenter at heart. True, he may have given up on his southern dissenters because he found so very few of them. That is, of course, the nature of dissent. But Woodward was drawn to dissenters because they point to directions not yet taken. He also believed the historian had a therapeutic role to play in connecting the present with the past. In a 1988 retrospective piece on the significance of *Strange Career* he addressed the criticism of his Reconstruction analogy in drawing such comparisons. "It is no argument against the use of analogy to say that it is dangerous. So is the historian's use of evidence, comparison, imagination, or, for that matter, metaphor," he argued. "History is a perilous craft. History without analogies, however, would be a meaner thing, no more than a social science. . . . Of course analogies never prove anything. They only provoke things. They can even provoke thought." In retrospect, Woodward defended "the use of analogy in history" even though his fondness for the conceit vacillated throughout his career.[172] His work on southern dissenters and the First and Second Reconstructions remind us of the importance of this practice, one that proves to be even more imperative during centennial, sesquicentennial, and bicentennial moments.[173]

Notes

1. Drew Gilpin Faust, "C. Vann Woodward: Helping to Make History," *Chronicle of Higher Education* 46 (January 14, 2000): B7; Richard Pearson, "Historian C. Vann Woodward Dies at 91," *Washington Post*, December 19, 1999; Richard Severo, "C. Vann Woodward, Historian Who Wrote Extensively About the South, Dies at 91," *New York Times*, December 19, 1999, Section 1, 66.
2. C. Vann Woodward, *Tom Watson: Agrarian Rebel* (New York: MacMillan, 1938). For an example, see Allan Nevins, "Tom Watson and the New South: Crucial Economic, Social, and Political History as Reflected in His Career," *New York Times Book Review*, April 3, 1938, 1, 16.
3. C. Vann Woodward, *Origins of the New South, 1877–1913* (Baton Rouge: Louisiana State University Press, 1951); C. Vann Woodward, *Reunion and Reaction: The Compromise of 1877 and the End of Reconstruction* (Boston: Little Brown, 1951); C. Vann Woodward, *The Strange Career of Jim Crow* (New York: Oxford University Press, 1955, rev. ed., 1957, 2nd rev. ed., 1966, 3rd rev. ed., 1974).
4. C. Vann Woodward, *The Burden of Southern History* (Baton Rouge: Louisiana State University Press, 1960, rev. ed., 1968, 2nd rev. ed., 1993).
5. One exception to this is the work Woodward did editing and publishing the diaries of Mary Boykin Chestnut. See C. Vann Woodward, ed., *Mary Chestnut's Civil War* (New Haven, CT: Yale University Press, 1981).
6. See C. Vann Woodward, Fleming Lectures, Box 66, Folder 59; Messenger Lectures, Box 64, Folder 23; and Storrs Lectures, Box 66, Folder 66, C. Vann Woodward

Papers (MS 1436), Manuscripts and Archives, Yale University Library (hereafter this collection is referred to as CVW Papers). During this period, Woodward also gave the Commonwealth Fund Lectures in 1954 at the University of London titled "Southern History and American Legend." Unlike the Fleming, Messenger, and Storrs Lectures, this set of eight lectures did not involve new archival work or the advancement of new ideas. Largely narrative in scope, they were intended for a general audience unfamiliar with Woodward's previous scholarship. The Commonwealth Lectures both borrow from Woodward's previously published work (often verbatim) and anticipate public material he wrote in the late 1950s. For example, they contain material from Woodward, *Origins of the New South*; "John Brown's Private War," a lecture delivered at Bennington College in 1952 and published in Daniel Aaron, ed., *America in Crisis: Fourteen Crucial Episodes in American History* (New York: Alfred A. Knopf, 1952), 109–30; "The Irony of Southern History," a presidential address at the annual meeting of the 1952 Southern Historical Association and published in *Journal of Southern History* 19 (February 1953): 3–19; and C. Vann Woodward "The Search for Southern Identity," *Virginia Quarterly Review* 34 (Summer 1958): 321–38. The lecture series can be found in two places: Box 64, Folder 34 and Box 55, Folder 661, CVW Papers.

7. C. Vann Woodward to Arthur H. Thornhill, Jr., September 27, 1958, Box 71, Folder 108, CVW Papers.

8. Woodward often shared drafts of unpublished work with friends in the profession, so it is possible that a colleague failed to return it. The staff at the Manuscript and Archives Library at Yale University initiated a thorough search of the CVW Papers, which were compiled in 2004, but could not locate the missing lecture. Cornell University does not appear to have kept copies or recordings of their guests' lectures in this time period.

9. The hybrid version includes the second half of Lecture IV and the first half of Lecture VI (with a few paragraphs missing), given as a speech at the American Philosophical Society in 1965. See C. Vann Woodward, "Seeds of Failure in Radical Race Policy," *Proceedings of the American Philosophical Society* 110 (February 18, 1966): 1–9. Woodward delivered the same paper at a conference on Reconstruction at the University of Illinois, also in 1965. Later it was published in Harold M. Hyman, ed., *New Frontiers of the American Reconstruction* (Urbana: University of Illinois Press, 1966). It appeared for a third time in C. Vann Woodward, *American Counterpoint: Slavery and Racism in the North–South Dialogue* (New York: Little, Brown, 1971), 163–184.

10. It should also be noted that Woodward lifted a few sentences from his article "The Political Legacy of Reconstruction," *Journal of Negro Education* 26 (Summer 1957): 231–40, and incorporated them into Messenger Lecture V. See pages 236–37 and 239 of the article.

11. For the full version of the SHA paper see "Reconstruction and Revision," Box 63, Folder 21, CVW Papers. Woodward presented the combined Storrs Lectures at the

XIII International Congress of Historical Sciences in Moscow in August 1969 and at the Chancellor's Symposium on Southern History at the University of Mississippi in 1976. See C. Vann Woodward, "Emancipations and Reconstructions: A Comparative Study," in *XIII International Congress of Historical Studies, Moscow* (Moscow: Navka, 1970); C. Vann Woodward, "The Price of Freedom," in David G. Sansing, ed., *What Was Freedom's Price?* (Jackson: University of Mississippi Press, 1978), 83–113. Twenty years later Woodward resuscitated these lectures, publishing them as C. Vann Woodward, "Reconstruction: A Counterfactual Playback" and "Emancipations and Reconstructions: A Comparative Study," in *Future of the Past* (New York: Oxford University Press, 1989), 145–66, 183–202. As early as 1965, some material appearing in Storrs Lecture I seems to have been used in a lecture Woodward delivered at Stanford titled "The Disturbed Mind of the South," although it is not clear how much. See Mary Kay Becker, "Woodward: Second Era for South," *Stanford Daily* Archives, January 31, 1965, https://archives.stanforddaily.com/1965/01/21?page=1#issue, accessed February 10, 2019.

12. James C. Cobb, "Therapist of the Public Mind: Woodward and the Most Burdensome Burden," in Angie Maxwell, Todd Shields, and Jeannie Whayne, eds., *The Ongoing Burden of Southern History* (Baton Rouge: Louisiana State University Press, 2012), 8; Michael O'Brien, ed., *The Letters of C. Vann Woodward* (New Haven, CT: Yale University Press, 2013), xxviii–xxx.
13. Woodward, *Origins*, 482.
14. C. Vann Woodward, Untitled, Box 71, Folder 108, CVW Papers. This version of chapter one of the proposed Reconstruction book looks at southern defeat. In the opening Woodward notes, "The South's adjustment, or lack of adjustment, to defeat is at the root of Reconstruction history" and this "collective experience" embodies "long-term patterns of behavior" linked to regional distinctiveness. See pp. 1–2 and 7. This argument echoes his often cited statement in "The Search for Southern Identity" that what made the South distinctive was its experience with "large components of frustration, failure, and defeat." See p. 333.
15. C. Vann Woodward, "II: The Fear of Freedom," Box 64, Folder 23, CVW Papers.
16. Eugene Genovese to C. Vann Woodward, May 12, 1969; William McFeeley to C. Vann Woodward, July 14, 1969, Box 66, Folder 66, CVW Papers.
17. Howard N. Rabinowitz, "More than the Woodward Thesis: Assessing the Strange Career of Jim Crow," *Journal of American History* 75 (December 1988): 852. A group of social scientists note more explicitly that Woodward used the term "New Reconstruction" in *Strange Career* but did not introduce the term until his 1957 essay "The Political Legacy of Reconstruction." See Hanes Walton, Jr., Josephine A. V. Allen, Sherman C. Puckett, and Donald R. Deskins, Jr., "Beyond the Second Reconstruction: C. Vann Woodward's Concept of the Third Reconstruction in the South," *American Review of Politics* 32 (Summer 2011): 124, 125–26.
18. The first edition of *Burden of Southern History* includes only one unpublished essay. The second edition offers one unpublished essay and one previously published essay.

The third edition contains three previously published essays. C. Vann Woodward, *American Counterpoint* offers three unpublished essays; and Woodward, *Future of the Past*, presents two unpublished essays, although Woodward notes that one of them was previously presented in Moscow and at the University of Mississippi. See *Future of the Past*, 360.

19. For example see *Future of the Past*, 359–61.
20. The Yale University Archives finding guide has sought to make a distinction between his published and unpublished work, but even that is occasionally inaccurate. "Guide to the C. Vann Woodward Papers," compiled by Tammy Ingram and Christine Weideman, January 2004, CVW Papers.
21. C. Vann Woodward to William G. Carleton, February 27, 1965, Series 7a: Correspondence Files, Box 7, William Graves Carleton Papers, George A. Smathers Library, University of Florida (hereafter this collection is referred to as the Carleton Papers).
22. Wendell H. Stephenson to C. Vann Woodward, August 3, 1949, Box 71, Folder 109. William C. Binkley of Vanderbilt University had been booked for 1950 and later published his lectures as William C. Binkley, *The Texas Revolution* (Baton Rouge: Louisiana State University Press, 1952).
23. Stephenson to Woodward, August 3, 1949, Box 71, Folder 109; Marcus M. Wilkerson to C. Vann Woodward, August 6, 1949, Box 70, Folder 103, CVW Papers.
24. C. Vann Woodward, *Thinking Back: The Perils of Writing History* (Baton Rouge: Louisiana State University Press, 1986), 49. Woodward notes that his options for using this material included expanding *Origins*, writing "a long article for a learned journal," crafting "two articles or more," or producing a book. Oddly, he does not mention that he made a plea to use this material for the Fleming Lectures as an additional option. In fact, his short memoir fails to reference the 1951 Fleming Lectures. See p. 51.
25. Burl Noggle, *The Fleming Lectures, 1937–1990: A Historiographical Essay* (Baton Rouge: Louisiana State University Press, 1992), 17.
26. Peter Novick quoted in Noggle, *Fleming Lectures*, 17. See *That Noble Dream: The "Objectivity Question" and the American Historical Profession* (New York: Cambridge University Press, 1988), 288.
27. Woodward, *Thinking Back*, 22.
28. C. Vann Woodward, interview by Jim Green, September 1, 1983, 7–8, in the John Herbert Roper Papers #4235, Southern Historical Collection, Wilson Library, University of North Carolina at Chapel Hill. Also see John Herbert Roper, "C. Vann Woodward's Early Career: The Historian as Dissident Youth," *Georgia Historical Quarterly* 64 (Spring 1980): 7–21.
29. C. Vann Woodward, "I: The Men of the Thirties," 1, Box 66, Folder 59, CVW Papers.
30. C. Vann Woodward, "II: The Men of the Fifties," Box 66, Folder 59, CVW Papers.
31. Woodward, "Men of the Thirties," 4, Box 66, Folder, 59, CVW Papers.

32. C. Vann Woodward, "III: The Way of the Exile," 24, Box 66, Folder 59, CVW Papers.
33. Henry Steele Commager to C. Vann Woodward, November 20, 1950, Box 12, Folder 136, CVW Papers.
34. C. Vann Woodward to David Donald, June 22, 1951, Box 16, Folder 175, CVW Papers.
35. C. Vann Woodward to Richard Hofstadter, July 2, 1951, Box 26, Folder 302, CVW Papers.
36. Leslie H. Fishel, Jr., to C. Vann Woodward, March 29, 1956, Box 18, Folder 213, CVW Papers. The same year historian Fishel mailed Woodward copies of several letters from the James A. Thome Collection at Oberlin. Fishel was the executive director of the alumni association at the college.
37. Pat Smylie to C. Vann Woodward, March 17, 1943, Box 33, Folder 392, CVW Papers.
38. C. Vann Woodward to Pat Smylie, March 25, 1953, Box 33, Folder 392, CVW Papers.
39. Ruth B. Hubert to C. Vann Woodward, May 27, 1953, Box 33, Folder 392, CVW Papers.
40. Pat Smylie to C. Vann Woodward, May 29, 1953, Box 33, Folder 392, CVW Papers.
41. C. Vann Woodward to Ruth B. Hubert, June 11, 1953, Box 33, Folder 392, CVW Papers.
42. See Woodward, *Thinking Back*, 104; Nicolas Barreyre, Michael Heale, Stephen Tuck, Cecile Vidal, eds., *Historians Across Borders: Writing American History in the Global Age* (Berkeley: University of California Press, 2014), 192, 286. Daniel Boorstin asked Woodward several times to submit a draft of the Reconstruction lectures he had offered in the Japanese seminar to appear as a short manuscript of around 100 pages in Boorstin's forthcoming series "The Chicago History of American Civilization" with the University of Chicago Press. See Daniel Boorstin to C. Vann Woodward, June 11, 1953, and May 8, 1954, Box 8, Folder 86, CVW Papers. In both instances Woodward declined because he said they were not in suitable shape for publication. See C. Vann Woodward to Daniel Boorstin, June 16, 1953, and May 19, 1954, Box 8, Folder 86, CVW Papers. Later, John Hope Franklin would publish the volume on Reconstruction in Boorstin's series. See *Reconstruction After the Civil War* (Chicago: University of Chicago Press, 1961).
43. Joan Doyle to C. Vann Woodward, June 17, 1953, Box 33, Folder 392, CVW Papers. Carl Bridenbaugh was a historian of colonial America who taught at MIT, Harvard University, and Brown University and gave the Fleming Lectures shortly after Woodward. Doyle was likely referring to *Myths and Realities: Societies of the Colonial South* (Baton Rouge: Louisiana State University Press, 1952).
44. Joan Doyle to C. Vann Woodward, August 22, 1953, Box 33, Folder 392, CVW Papers.

45. Joan Doyle to C. Vann Woodward, September 17, 1953, Box 33, Folder 392, CVW Papers.
46. Joan Doyle to C. Vann Woodward, November 16, 1953, Box 33 Folder 392, CVW Papers.
47. Donald R. Ellegood to C. Vann Woodward, September 9, 1954, September 20, 1954, August 12, 1955, September 20, 1955, and December 5, 1957, Box 33, Folder 392, CVW Papers.
48. C. Vann Woodward to Donald R. Ellegood, September 6, 1955, Box 33, Folder 392, CVW Papers.
49. In a 1956 letter to James M. Reid of Harcourt and Brace, regarding a squabble over royalties involving a textbook and the publisher's suggestion that Woodward possibly owed them a book, Woodward noted that he already owed one to LSU Press based on the Fleming Lectures. See C. Vann Woodward to James M. Reid, March 14, 1956, Box 23, Folder 277, CVW Papers.
50. Noggle, *Fleming Lectures*, 50.
51. Noggle, *Fleming Lectures*, 18.
52. "Brief for Appellants in Nos. 1, 2 and 4 and For Respondents in No. 10 on Reargument," *In the Supreme Court of the United States, October Term, 1953*, n.p., https://babel.hathitrust.org/cgi/pt?id=mdp.39015010310475&view=1up&seq=6, accessed February 17, 2020. Although the court case describes C. Vann Woodward's and John Hope Franklin's work as "monographs," it is unclear what form the work took.
53. Woodward was responsible for giving one lecture, "American Attitudes Toward History," while in residence. See C. Vann Woodward, "An Inaugural Lecture Delivered Before the University of Oxford on 22 February 1955," Box 73, Folder 127, CVW Papers.
54. Woodward, *Thinking Back*, 81–82.
55. Woodward, *Thinking Back*, 83, 93.
56. Charles Grier Sellers to Robert A. Lively, April 6, 1953, Box 71, Folder 111, CVW Papers.
57. C. Vann Woodward to Charles Grier Sellers, May 22, 1953, Box 71, Folder 111, CVW Papers.
58. Charles Grier Sellers to C. Vann Woodward, June 13, 1953, Box 71, Folder 111, CVW Papers.
59. C. Vann Woodward to David Riesman, January 31, 1957, Box 45, Folder 550, CVW Papers.
60. Michael O'Brien, *The Idea of the American South, 1920–1941* (Baltimore: Johns Hopkins, 1979), xx.
61. Charles Grier Sellers, Jr., ed., *The Southerner as American* (Chapel Hill: University of North Carolina Press, 1960), vi–vii.
62. Louis Hartz, *The Liberal Tradition in America* (New York: Harcourt, Brace, and World, 1955).

63. O'Brien, *Idea of the American South*, xx.
64. Woodward, "Search for Southern Identity," 322–23, 331–34.
65. David Donald to C. Vann Woodward, July 10, 1958, Box 16, Folder 175, CVW Papers.
66. C. Vann Woodward to Dewey Grantham, March 15, 1959, Box 51, Folder 606, CVW Papers.
67. George Tindall to C. Vann Woodward, February 26, 1959, Box 53, Folder 632, CVW Papers.
68. C. Vann Woodward, "The Question of Loyalty," *American Scholar* 33 (Autumn 1964): 561–62, 563–65. Woodward also briefly alluded to the "Men of the Eighties," which included George Washington Cable, in Fleming Lecture I. See Woodward, "Men of the Thirties," 3.
69. William G. Carleton to C. Vann Woodward, December 5, 1964, Box 11, Folder 115, CVW Papers.
70. William G. Carleton to C. Vann Woodward, December 18, 1964, Box 11, Folder 115, CVW Papers.
71. C. Vann Woodward to William G. Carleton, December 25, 1964, Series 7a: Correspondence Files, Box 7, Carleton Papers.
72. William G. Carleton to C. Vann Woodward, n.d., December 1961, Box 11, Folder 114, CVW Papers.
73. William G. Carleton to C. Vann Woodward, December 15, 1963, Box 11, Folder 115, CVW Papers.
74. Carleton to Woodward, December 5, 1964.
75. David Donald to C. Vann Woodward, January 7, 1957, Box 16, Folder 175, CVW Papers.
76. Undated TS Notes, Proposed Book on Reconstruction, Box 71, Folder 108, CVW Papers.
77. Woodward to Thornhill, Jr., September 27, 1958.
78. David S. Brown, *Richard Hofstadter: An Intellectual Biography* (Chicago: University of Chicago Press, 2006), 120.
79. Woodward to Thornhill, Jr., September 27, 1958.
80. Woodward to Thornhill, Jr., September 27, 1958.
81. Arthur H. Thornhill, Jr., to C. Vann Woodward, December 1, 1958, Box 71, Folder 108; Arthur H. Thornhill, Jr., to C. Vann Woodward, October 26, 1962, Box 32, Folder 386, CVW Papers.
82. Telegram, George P. Brockway to C. Vann Woodward, January 30, 1959, Box 39, Folder 470, CVW Papers.
83. C. Vann Woodward to George P. Brockway, February 21, 1959, Box 39, Folder 470, CVW Papers.
84. C. Vann Woodward to Henry Allen Moe, February 5, 1959, Box 22, Folder 263, CVW Papers.
85. Woodward to Moe, February 5, 1959.

86. Henry Allen Moe to C. Vann Woodward, April 9, 1959, Box 22, Folder 263, CVW Papers.
87. C. Vann Woodward, Undated, Application to Lilly Fund, Box 80, Folder 3, CVW Papers.
88. Woodward, Undated, Application to Lilly Fund.
89. Woodward to Thornhill, Jr., September 27, 1958.
90. Manning M. Pattillo to C. Vann Woodward, June 27, 1960, Box 80, Folder 3, CVW Papers.
91. Woodward pitted rival publishing firms against each other as he sought to secure a contract for his book on Reconstruction. He and the competing editors found the entire process unpleasant. He first signed a contract with Thornhill in November 1958. In January 1959 Brockway asked Woodward if he were interested in writing a book on Reconstruction, seemingly unaware that Woodward had already landed a contract, and offered him $10,000 to sign. Woodward jumped at the chance to switch presses and in March informed Brockway that he would seek a release from his previous contract. Thornhill was stunned and offended when he received Woodward's letter. He deemed Brockway's actions "barbaric" and accused him of behaving in a "questionable manner." Thornhill demanded that Woodward honor his contract and the historian ultimately relented before asking and receiving an additional advance. See Telegram, C. Vann Woodward to George P. Brockway, March 5, 1959, Box 39, Folder 470; Arthur Thornhill, Jr., to C. Vann Woodward, March 23, 1959, Box 71, Folder 108; C. Vann Woodward to Arthur Thornhill, Jr., March 31, 1959, Box 71, Folder 108; Arthur Thornhill, Jr., to C. Vann Woodward, April 7, 1959, Box 71, Folder 108; and C. Vann Woodward to George Brockway, April 15, 1959, Box 39, Folder 470, CVW Papers.
92. Knight Biggerstaff to C. Vann Woodward, May 11, 1959, Box 64, Folder 23, CVW Papers.
93. https://theuniversityfaculty.cornell.edu/dean/messengeruniversity-lectures/, accessed January 30, 2020.
94. John F. Kennedy, "Address on Civil Rights, June 11, 1963," *Public Papers of the Presidents of the United States, John F. Kennedy, 1963* (Washington, DC: US Government Printing Office, 1964), 237.
95. Biggerstaff to Woodward, May 11, 1959.
96. C. Vann Woodward to Knight Biggerstaff, May 18, 1959, Box 64, Folder 23, CVW Papers.
97. C. Vann Woodward to Knight Biggerstaff, May 15, 1961, Box 64, Folder 23, CVW Papers.
98. For examples, see C. Vann Woodward to Otto Olsen, March 5, 1960, Box 38, Folder 477; C. Vann Woodward to Dewey Grantham, September 22, 1961, Box 22, Folder 257; C. Vann Woodward to Thomas B. Alexander, September 9, 1961, Box 1, Folder 8, CVW Papers.

99. James McPherson to C. Vann Woodward, June 30, 1963, Box 36, Folder 421; T. Harry Williams to C. Vann Woodward, February 16, 1963, Box 60, Folder 724, CVW Papers.
100. C. Vann Woodward to William G. Carleton, December 24, 1961, Series 7a: Correspondence Files, Box 7, Carleton Papers.
101. C. Vann Woodward to William G. Carleton, April 5, 1962, Box 11, Folder 114, CVW Papers.
102. August Meir was another outlier in the 1960s. He found Reconstruction "superficial," but his work appeared a few years after Woodward delivered the Messenger Lectures and published "Seeds of Failure." See Eric Foner, "Reconstruction Revisited," *American Reviews in History* 10 (December 1982): 83n6.
103. For some examples, see LaWanda Cox and John H. Cox, *Politics, Principle, and Prejudice 1865–1866* (Glencoe, IL: Free Press, 1963); W. R. Brock, *An American Crisis* (London: St. Martin's, 1963); and Kenneth M. Stampp, *The Era of Reconstruction, 1865–1877* (New York: Knopf, 1965). For students of Woodward who are considered revisionists, see Eric McKitrick, *Andrew Johnson and Reconstruction* (Chicago: University of Chicago Press, 1960); Willie Lee Rose, *Rehearsal for Reconstruction: The Port Royal Experiment* (Indianapolis, IN: Bobbs-Merrill, 1964); James M. McPherson, *The Struggle for Equality: Abolitionists and the Negro in the Civil War and Reconstruction* (Princeton, NJ: Princeton University Press, 1964); Otto H. Olsen, *Carpetbagger's Crusade: The Life of Albion Winegar Tourgée* (Baltimore: Johns Hopkins University Press, 1965).
104. See Foner, "Reconstruction Revisited," 83–85.
105. Messenger Lectures note, Box 64, Folder 23, CVW Papers.
106. Rose to Woodward, May 10, 1964. Quotation in Woodward, "IV: The Conservatism of Northern Radicals," 20, Box 64, Folder 23, CVW Papers.
107. Woodward, "Conservatism of Northern Radicals," and C. Vann Woodward, "VI: Did the North Really Mean It?" Box 64, Folder 23, CVW Papers.
108. Leon F. Litwack, *North of Slavery: The Negro in the Free States, 1790–1860* (Chicago: University of Chicago Press, 1961).
109. See Litwack, *North of Slavery*, 97; Woodward, "Did the North Really Mean It?" 10; and Woodward, *Strange Career*, 19.
110. C. Vann Woodward, "III: The Paradox of Loyalty," 8–9, 17, Box 64, Folder 23, CVW Papers.
111. C. Vann Woodward, "V: Radicalism for Southern Conservatives," 6, 15–19, Box 64, Folder 23, CVW Papers.
112. Woodward, "Fear of Freedom," 1. Woodward first read W. E. B. Du Bois's *Black Reconstruction in America: A History of the Part Which Black Folk Played in the Attempt to Reconstruct Democracy in America 1860–1880* (New York: Harcourt, Brace, 1935) in graduate school and wrote an assigned review of it. Like any good graduate student, he addressed both the weaknesses and strengths of the book, concluding that the former outweighed the latter. He also added, perhaps

foreshadowing his own work, "But the history of Reconstruction is strewn with curiously perverse paradoxes and some of its best morals are spoiled by a twist of irony." See C. Vann Woodward's review of *Black Reconstruction*, Box 71, Folder 115, CVW Papers.
113. Woodward, "Fear of Freedom," 2–4, 8, 10.
114. C. Vann Woodward, "The 'New Reconstruction' in the South: Desegregation in Historical Perspective," *Commentary* 21 (June 1956): 502, 508.
115. C. Vann Woodward, "The Great Civil Rights Debate: The Ghost of Thaddeus Stevens in the Senate Chamber," *Commentary* 24 (October 1957): 283–91; C. Vann Woodward, "The South and the Law of the Land: The Present Resistance and Its Prospects," *Commentary* 26 (November 1958): 373–74. Quotation in C. Vann Woodward, "Equality: America's Deferred Commitment," *American Scholar* 27 (Autumn 1958): 471.
116. Woodward, "Political Legacy of Reconstruction," 240.
117. Woodward, "Conservatism of Northern Radicals," 9.
118. Woodward, "Did the North Really Mean It?" 20–21.
119. Rabinowitz, "More than the Woodward Thesis," 843.
120. Woodward, "Seeds of Failure." See enclosure in Harold M. Hyman to C. Vann Woodward, February 26, 1965, Box 27, Folder 311, CVW Papers.
121. Enclosure, Hyman to Woodward.
122. C. Vann Woodward to Harold M. Hyman, July 13, 1964, Box 27, Folder 311, CVW Papers.
123. Harold M. Hyman to C. Vann Woodward, June 8, 1965, Box 27, Folder 311, CVW Papers.
124. Woodward, "Seeds of Failure," in Hyman, ed., *New Frontiers*. This essay is identical to the APS version, but it is accompanied with a formal comment by historian Russell B. Nye. See p. 148–56.
125. Woodward, "Seeds of Failure," in Woodward, *American Counterpoint*, 163–184. Woodward's biographer John Herbert Roper states the *American Counterpoint* version was "reprinted with substantial revisions," but this does not appear to be the case. See John Herbert Roper, *C. Vann Woodward, Southerner* (Athens: University of Georgia Press, 1987), 350.
126. C. Vann Woodward, "From the First Reconstruction to the Second," *Harper's Magazine* 230 (April 1965), 127–28.
127. Woodward, "From the First," 128.
128. Woodward, "From the First," 132.
129. Woodward, "From the First," 133.
130. O'Brien, *Letters*, xxx.
131. Woodward, "Reconstruction and Revision," 1, 3–4, 7. Although Woodward had opened the second Messenger Lecture with Du Bois, in the SHA paper Du Bois dropped out of the discussion altogether.
132. Woodward, "Reconstruction and Revision," 8–9.

133. Woodward, "Irony of Southern History," 5.
134. See Carl J. Guarneri, "Reconsidering C. Vann Woodward's *The Comparative Approach to American History*," *Reviews in American History* 23 (September 1995), 552–61.
135. C. Vann Woodward, "The Comparability of American History," in C. Vann Woodward, *The Comparative Approach to American History* (New York: Oxford University Press, 1997), 15
136. Woodward, "Reconstruction and Revision," 9–10, 11.
137. In 1982 Woodward's students honored him for opening up this "intellectual pathway," which at the time was still in its infancy. See J. Morgan Kousser and James M. McPherson, "Introduction: C. Vann Woodward: An Assessment of His Work and Influence," in J. Morgan Kousser and James M. McPherson, *Region, Race, and Reconstruction: Essays in Honor of C. Vann Woodward* (New York: Oxford University Press, 1982), xxxiii. See also Steven Hahn, "Class and State in Postemancipation Societies: Southern Planters in Comparative Perspectives," *American Historical Review* 95 (February 1990): 75–98. For more recent scholarship on comparative reconstructions and post-emancipation societies, see "Introduction," in Frederick Cooper, Thomas C. Holt, and Rebecca J. Scott, *Beyond Slavery: Explorations of Race, Labor, and Citizenship in Postemancipation Societies* (Chapel Hill: University of North Carolina Press, 2000); Peter Kolchin, *A Sphinx on the American Land: The Nineteenth-Century South in Comparative Perspective* (Baton Rouge: Louisiana State University Press, 2003); Rebecca J. Scott, *Degrees of Freedom: Louisiana and Cuba After Slavery* (Cambridge, MA: Harvard University Press, 2008).
138. Woodward, "Reconstruction and Revision," 15–17, 20–22. At one point, Woodward labeled the approach he took in the SHA paper "Reconstruction, Rouge et Noir" and considered teaching a seminar on it. See C. Vann Woodward to James McPherson, January 9, 1968, and James McPherson to C. Vann Woodward, January 12, 1968, Box 36, Folder 421, CVW Papers. In a 1994 essay, William Deverell argued that historians of the West would do well to borrow the strategies of historians of the South in focusing on the categories of "race, difference, and dependence." For inspiration he cited Woodward's "Reconstruction and Revision" SHA paper. See William Deverell, "Fighting Words: The Significance of the American West in the History of the United States," *Western Historical Quarterly* 25 (Summer 1994): 203. Since then, historians have sought to broaden the scope of Reconstruction history by including the West, either in comparison or in isolation. See Elliott West, "Reconstructing Race," *Western Historical Quarterly* 34 (Spring 2003): 6–26; Elliott West, *The Last Indian War: The Nez Perce Story* (New York: Oxford University Press, 2007); Heather Cox Richardson, *West from Appomattox: The Reconstruction of America After the Civil War* (New Haven, CT: Yale University Press, 2007); Stacey L. Smith, *Freedom's Frontier: California and the Struggle Over Unfree Labor, Emancipation,*

and Reconstruction (Chapel Hill: University of North Carolina, 2013); Steven Hahn, "The Widest Implications of Disorienting the Civil War Era," in Adam Arenson and Andrew R. Graybill, eds., *Civil War Wests: Testing the Limits of the United States* (Berkeley: University of California Press, 2015), 265–74; Stacey L. Smith, "Beyond North and South: Putting the West in the Civil War and Reconstruction," *Journal of the Civil War Era* 6 (December 2016): 556–91; Elliott West, "Reconstruction in the West," in "Forum: The Future of Reconstruction Studies," *Journal of the Civil War Era* 7 (March 2017): 14. See https://www.journalofthecivilwarera.org/forum-the-future-of-reconstruction-studies/reconstruction-in-the-west/, accessed February 15, 2020.

139. David Donald, "The Thirty-Third Annual Meeting," *Journal of Southern History* 34 (February 1968): 77.
140. Woodward, *Strange Career*, 31–65.
141. Woodward, "Reconstruction and Revision," 13–20.
142. Woodward, "Conservatism of Northern Radicals," 18–19.
143. Woodward, "Reconstruction and Revision," 18–19, 24.
144. https://yalebooks.yale.edu/series/the-storrs-lectures-series, accessed February 22, 2020.
145. C. Vann Woodward, "I: The Problem of Failure in American History," Box 66, Folder 66, CVW Papers.
146. C. Vann Woodward, "II: The Comparative Approach to Emancipation History" and "III: The Comparative Approach to Reconstruction History," Box 66, Folder 66, CVW Papers. See Wilhelmina Kloosterboer, *Involuntary Labour Since the Abolition of Slavery: A Survey of Compulsory Labour Throughout the World* (Leiden, Netherlands: E. J. Brill, 1960); Philip D. Curtin, *The Atlantic Slave Trade: A Census* (Madison: University of Wisconsin Press, 1969).
147. McFeeley to Woodward, July 14, 1969.
148. Genovese to Woodward, May 12, 1969.
149. C. Vann Woodward to Eugene Genovese, May 13, 1969, Box 66, Folder 66, CVW Papers.
150. C. Vann Woodward, "Protestant Slavery in a Catholic World" and "Southern Slaves in the World of Thomas Malthus," in Woodward, *American Counterpoint*, 47–77, 78–106. Although the essays were new, they touched on topics introduced in the Storrs Lectures, such as the Curtin statistics and his comparison between Brazil, Jamaica, and the US South.
151. See Woodward, "Emancipations and Reconstructions," *XIII International Congress of Historical Studies, Moscow.*
152. Woodward, "Price of Freedom." The other participants included Willie Lee Rose, Richard Sutch and Roger Ransom, Joel Williamson, and George M. Fredrickson.
153. Woodward, *Future of the Past*, 360. This collection mostly contains reprinted essays from the 1970s and 1980s.

154. See Woodward, "Reconstruction: A Counterfactual Playback." In the collection, Woodward also included the previously published essay "What Is Freedom?" in *What Was Freedom's Price?* this time using the Moscow version's title. See Woodward, "Emancipations and Reconstructions: A Comparative Study," in ibid., 145–82.
155. Woodward, "Reconstruction: A Counterfactual Playback," 198–99. In 1980 Thomas B. Alexander delivered the Southern Historical Association presidential address and cited Woodward's SHA paper for inspiration in his own counterfactual analysis of secession on the eve of the Civil War. Woodward wrote to Alexander that he had once envisioned a book of counterfactual essays on comparative history. "You tempt me to dig that old paper of mine on Reconstruction out of the file," he announced. It is possible Alexander's address inspired Woodward to eventually publish "Reconstruction: A Counterfactual Playback." C. Vann Woodward to Thomas B. Alexander, March 3, 1981, Box 1, Folder 8, CVW Papers.
156. Michael O'Brien, review of *The Future of the Past* by C. Vann Woodward, *Journal of American History* 77 (September 1990): 628.
157. John Herbert Roper, review of *The Future of the Past* by C. Vann Woodward, *Journal of Southern History* 57 (May 1991): 370.
158. C. Vann Woodward, "Unfinished Business," *New York Review of Books*, May 12, 1988, https://www.nybooks.com/articles/1988/05/12/unfinished-business/, accessed November 13, 2019.
159. Woodward, "Unfinished Business." See Kloosterboer, *Involuntary Labour*; William R. Brock, *An American Crisis: Congress and Reconstruction, 1865–1867* (New York: St. Martin's Press, 1963). Woodward first referenced Brock in Messenger Lecture IV, quoting his assertion that "the crisis of Reconstruction was a part of the worldwide crisis of nineteenth-century liberal tradition." See Woodward, "Conservatism of Northern Radicals," 5–6.
160. Woodward, "Unfinished Business."
161. O'Brien, *Letters*, xxxi.
162. Woodward, "Reconstruction and Revision," 8. That list included David Donald, John Hope Franklin, Kenneth M. Stampp, and William R. Brock.
163. Eric Foner, *Reconstruction: America's Unfinished Revolution* (New York: HarperCollins, 1988, 2014), xl–xli.
164. Woodward, "Did the North Really Mean It?" 14.
165. Woodward, "Conservatism of Northern Radicals," 9.
166. For historiographical discussions of Reconstruction, see, for example, Gregory P. Downs and Kate Masur, *The World the Civil War Made* (Chapel Hill: University of North Carolina Press, 2015); "The Future of Reconstruction Studies: A Special Issue," *Journal of the Civil War Era* 7 (March 2017): 1–122; Bruce E. Baker and Elaine S. Frantz, "Against Synthesis: Diverse Approaches to the History of Reconstruction," in Craig Thompson Friend and Lori Glovers, eds., *Reinterpreting*

Southern History: Essays in Historiography (Baton Rouge: Louisiana State University Press, 2020), 218–44.

167. Foner, *Reconstruction*, xli-xlii.
168. C. Vann Woodward, "What Happened to the Civil Rights Movement?" *Harper's Magazine* 234 (January 1967), 29–30, 34. This piece was reprinted in the second edition of Woodward's *Burden of Southern History* in 1968. The reprint included a postscript stating that his "cautious words of optimism" in the *Harper's* essay warranted reassessment given the assassination of Martin Luther King, Jr. Woodward noted that King had moved toward a more "Northern or national orientation" and might have helped usher in the Third Reconstruction. See C. Vann Woodward, "What Happened to the Civil Rights Movement?" in Woodward, *Burden of Southern History* (2nd ed.), 186. For additional references to the "Third Reconstruction," and the *Harper's Magazine* piece, see Cobb, "Therapist of the Public Mind," 21; Leigh Ann Duck, "Woodward's Southerner: History, Literature, and the Question of Identity," in Maxwell, Shields, and Whayne, *Ongoing Burden*, 48, 51, 55. For a discussion of how the election of Barack Obama might in some ways be seen as evidence of the "Third Reconstruction," see Wayne Parent, "A Lighter Burden? Southern Political Identity in the Shrinking South," in Maxwell, Shields, and Whayne, *Ongoing Burden*, 62–79.
169. Woodward, "Problem of Failure," 28.
170. Woodward, "Problem of Failure," 15–19.
171. Woodward, "Question of Loyalty," 562, 565. Also see Woodward, "What Happened to the Civil Rights Movement?" for his discussion of the revolutionary cycle of "rise, climax, decline, reaction," 32–33. Woodward possibly adopted the phrase the "Great Reaction" from Rollin G. Osterweis, a historian who wrote about Romanticism in antebellum southern nationalism. For a discussion of Osterweis's concept of proslavery conservatism as the "Great Reaction," see Michael O'Brien, "The Lineaments of Antebellum Southern Romanticism," *Journal of American Studies* 20 (August 1986): 166. Charles G. Sellers also used the term the "Great Reaction" in his piece "The Travail of Slavery" in Sellers, ed., *Southerner as American*, 51–52, a project to which Woodward had considered contributing. Woodward appears to have coined the term "The Second Great Reaction."
172. C. Vann Woodward, "Strange Career Critics: Long May They Persevere," *Journal of American History* 75 (December 1988): 862.
173. There is evidence that historians are currently moving in this direction. Beginning in April 2011, "Disunion," a series on the Civil War in the *New York Times*, addressed the 150th anniversary of the four-year conflict. Since 2017 a substantial number of "professional historians" have contributed to the series "Made by History" for the *Washington Post*, which cites Martin Luther King, Jr.'s, understanding of "making history and being made by history" as inspiration. The goal is to "situate the events making headlines into their larger historical context" and provide a forum for

"grappling with parallels between the past and present." See Brian Rosenwald and Nicole Hemmer, "Welcome to Made by History," *Washington Post*, June 26, 2017. The University of Georgia Press recently established the series "History in the Headlines," edited by Catherine Clinton and Jim Downs, which is "committed to reaffirming the indispensable role of the intellectual in the public sphere." See https://ugapress.org/series/history-in-the-headlines/, accessed January 12, 2020. The first book in the series focuses on the history of Confederate memory and memorials in the context of the Charleston church shooting in 2015 and the white nationalist rally in Charlottesville, Virginia, in 2017. See Catherine Clinton, W. Fitzhugh Brundage, Karen L. Cox, Gary W. Gallagher, and Nell Irvin Painter, *Confederate Statues and Memorialization* (Athens: University of Georgia Press, 2019).

Editorial Note

THIS COLLECTION ABIDES by simple editorial practices. We have taken care to leave the words of C. Vann Woodward as close to the original as possible. We have corrected minor spelling errors when it is clear what he intended to say and are likely the result of poor typing. Woodward's punctuation is often idiosyncratic and we have left the errors in place. We have chosen not to correct matters of style such as his choice to capitalize Northern and Southern or use foreign spelling. Underlined words have been converted to italics. We have left off the accent mark of the surname Grimké given that Woodward's editor at Louisiana State University Press chided him for this lapse and he was aware of it. Woodward relied heavily on quoted material. Occasionally he made noticeable spelling and punctuation errors, as well as errors in transcription, in his use of quotations from primary and secondary sources. We have corrected these mistakes when we were able to ascertain their accuracy. We cannot guarantee the accuracy of every quotation, however.

Woodward's lectures and chapters are typescript and include his own penciled copyediting. Sometimes he added or crossed out words, sentences, and paragraphs and noted that material should be moved within a lecture or chapter. We have incorporated his copyedited corrections in this collection because we believe they reflect what he intended to deliver to his audiences or the publisher. In rare cases, for the sake of clarity, we did consult a first iteration and incorporate a hand-written word or phrase that did not make it into the clean copy. Some lectures and chapters, though, are more polished than others. In a few instances, Woodward appears to have left out a word or a portion of a sentence. One chapter appears to be missing the final paragraph. In those instances we have noted in brackets the missing word or have included a footnote acknowledging these errors. In a few cases we have redacted extraneous words that clearly did not belong in a sentence.

Woodward's endnotes and parenthetical citations are messy. They are frequently incomplete and inconsistently formatted. Some citations are missing altogether. Some quotations are not cited. In some cases Woodward assigned the same endnote number more than once. In other cases he wrote out the note but failed to indicate where it belonged in the text. We silently corrected these errors when possible. We kept his abbreviated citations but made the choice to fix basic issues of format involving punctuation and italicization given that he formatted some of them correctly. As a result, the lectures in this volume appear more polished than the drafts suggest. We sacrificed messiness in favor of readability. In the three Fleming Lectures we chose to convert the parenthetical citations to endnotes, as both the first two chapters of the intended book "Southern Dissenters in Exile" and the Messenger Lectures, "The First Reconstruction in Light of the Second," use endnotes. This appears to be Woodward's preferred choice. The Storrs Lectures do not contain citations because at the time Woodward delivered them he was not certain whether they would be published. Because Woodward did not include bibliographies for these lectures and chapters we decided not to include any in this volume. Intrepid readers should be able to track down most of the citations if they are interested.

April seemed to be the month of crisis in Angelina's complicated religious life, as she herself remarked. It was in "the fourth month" of 1826 that she had broken with the Episcopalian Church to join the Presbyterians, and in April 1828 that she broke with the Presbyterians to begin the quest that ended in April three two years later when she was received into membership by the Philadelphia Friends.[91] Each of these crises brought the promise of long-sought peace and fulfillment, but each in its turn proved a bitter disappointment. Neither of the sisters actually proved a "true yoked fellow" of the new faith, though Sarah the long-suffering chafed more silently under the yoke than did the spirited and restless Angelina. In small things first the two incorrigible nonconformists from Charleston irritated the Friends. Neither of them would adopt the Quaker usage of the ungrammatical challenged further disapproval by altering thee for thou, and they altered the conventional shape and material of the long-eared bonnet to protect their heads from the northern chill. But it was the chill of in the faith reproof and reserve from their brothers and sisters that they felt most keenly, and from which they could contrive no satisfactory protection.[92]

And Angelina had difficulty remembering not to call the 5th day & 6th days by the names the world has given them."

Sarah's morbidly sensitive nature was especially vulnerable to criticism. Her preparation for the ministry was handicapped by a halting and self-conscious manner of speaking that made every attendance at meeting a harrowing ordeal. "Feel I must attend the evg. mtg. at Pine St.," she recorded, and confessed, "it is hard work to go where I feel despised." She dreaded the yearly meetings like a criminal under sentence facing "the day of execution." She felt "condemned already" whenever she rose to speak. The "cutting charge" of preparing her remarks beforehand and of "going there to preach, instead of to worship" cost her "hours of anguish." This reproof was severely administered "by an Elder to whom I did a little look for kindness." Sarah's journals are filled with the conviction that she was the *vilest of sinners. "I have suffered the very torments of the fallen had become my conscience was sore to the touch all over," she wrote. Her reiterated and obsessive preoccupation with guilt bordered on the pathological.*

Photographic facsimile of page 35 of "Chapter 2, The Year of Decision," from "Southern Exiles," Fleming Lectures (MS 1436, box 66, folder 59), C. Vann Woodward Papers (MS 1436), Manuscripts and Archives, Yale University Library.

The Fleming Lectures

Southern Dissenters in Exile

In the spring of 1951, C. Vann Woodward delivered the fourteenth annual Walter Lynwood Fleming Lectures in Southern History, hosted by Louisiana State University. He took for his subject "Southern Dissenters in Exile," a topic that had long fascinated him. The series explores the experiences of two generations of white southern abolitionists who fled the South for the North seeking a more hospitable intellectual climate. Each of the lectures highlights the ways in which these dissenters sought to effect political change, whether through moral suasion or their exemplary actions. Woodward opened the lecture series by acknowledging that the South tolerated dissent in the age of Jefferson, a point made two decades earlier by journalist Virginius Dabney in *Liberalism in the South*, a book Woodward cited in *Origins of the New South*.* Dabney wished to stress the persistence of liberal modes of thinking in the region through the early decades of twentieth century. Woodward was hardly as sanguine, as his final lecture demonstrates. Although Woodward returned occasionally to these liberal dissenters, they never again occupied his scholarly attention as they had for a brief moment in the early 1950s.

---

* Virginius Dabney, *Liberalism in the South* (Chapel Hill: University of North Carolina Press, 1932); see C. Vann Woodward, *Origins of the New South, 1877–1913* (Baton Rouge: Louisiana State University Press, 1951), 443, 514, 555.

FLEMING LECTURE I
The Men of the Thirties

SO LONG AS the tradition of Jeffersonian liberalism held sway in the South there was no real necessity for social dissenters to become exiles. With the exception of a few whose voluntary exile should be considered separately, the dissenter was able to hold his own against prevailing opinion on native soil. The tradition that protected him was the broad tolerance and skepticism of the eighteenth century enlightenment. No quarter of the New World was suffused more fully with the noontide glow of the enlightenment than was the South. Participation in the Revolution shook the planter aristocracy out of its colonial provincialism and thrust it into the broad current of Western thought. Virginia and Carolina gentlemen were inspired by all the noble visions of the dignity of man that flourished in that hopeful age.

The South was then not only cordially receptive to outside influence but outgoing and positive in its participation in the world of ideas. Not only did the region supply the nation with leadership in the Virginia dynasty, but Southern leaders established relationships with European intellectuals. The impact of Southern state papers, pamphlets, and ideas was felt and acknowledged abroad as well as at home.

Even before the death of Jefferson this golden age of tolerance had begun to wane. The beginning of the new era, however, is generally dated from the turning point in the Southern attitude toward slavery. Whether that turning point is attributed to the Nat Turner rebellion and the fear of servile revolt, or the launching of Garrison's *Liberator* and the rise of aggressive Northern abolitionism, or the debate on emancipation in the Virginia legislature and the launching of the proslavery argument, it is agreed that the South had changed from an open-minded to a close-minded attitude toward the world by the early years of the 1830's. The old spirit of genial tolerance was replaced by a suspicious dread of criticism. Spacious ideas and broad sympathies gave way to narrow preoccupations and defensive attitudes. The South began a retreat from a world with which it was out of tune, a world that was felt to be vaguely hostile if not downright subversive of its vital interests. Against that world the South began to set up intellectual barricades and to withdraw into spiritual isolation. Within its borders quick evidence of conformity was demanded of newcomers, and dissenters of native birth, however well connected, fell under suspicion and suffered severe curtailment of their freedom. The more determined spirits among the native dissenters eventually found themselves expelled and proscribed from their native soil.

This was the South that produced the exiles. It persisted as a state of mind for more than half a century and it inculcated traits that have lingered into our own day. In the sixties and seventies the South's armed isolation was forcibly violated by invaders who sought for a time to impose upon the region new ideas and institutions. In this effort the invaders were only partially successful, and upon the withdrawal of their armed forces the South reverted in some measure to the ante-bellum complex of illiberal suspicion of criticism and a defensive psychology. Once again the dissenter began to find his way into exile.

There were, of course, Southerners who lived in exile throughout this entire period. A few who became outcasts in the early thirties lived on into the post-bellum period and never again returned to their native soil. It is possible, however, to classify the exiles by the decade in which they arrived at national prominence and to describe them as the Men of the Thirties and the Men of the Fifties. There were also the Men of the Eighties and later decades, but we shall be concerned only with the ante-bellum exiles.

The generation of Southerners preceding the Men of the Thirties, it is true, produced an impressive number of dissenters who moved to the North largely for reasons of conscience, but they cannot be properly considered exiles. In 1816 Charles Osborn of North Carolina moved to Mt. Pleasant, Ohio, and founded the *Philanthropist*, which holds the disputed title of being the first paper in the country to advocate immediate and unconditional emancipation.[1] The following year two South Carolina ministers, William Dickey and his brother James H. Dickey joined a growing settlement of Southern abolitionists in Ohio. John Rankin, a native of Tennessee and later a minister in Kentucky, moved to Ripley, Ohio, in 1821. A tower of strength to the cause in the West for the next four decades, Rankin was often called "the Martin Luther of abolitionism." Other Southerners who attained prominence in the Ohio antislavery movement were Alexander Campbell of Virginia, Jesse Lockhart of Tennessee, James Gilliland and William Williamson of South Carolina, and Samuel Crothers and Dyer Burgess, Presbyterian ministers from Kentucky.[2] The most prominent antislavery leader of Illinois in the 1820's was Edward Coles, a Virginian who was heir to several hundred slaves. Private secretary to President Madison from 1809 to 1815 and friend of Jefferson, Coles discussed his growing revulsion for slavery at length with the Sage of Monticello. In 1819 he departed for Illinois with all his slaves and liberated them in a dramatic scene upon a flatboat on the Ohio River. Three years later he was elected governor of Illinois by an antislavery faction and gave his administration a strong abolitionist imprint.[3]

All of the men mentioned so far left the South before the great reaction against the liberal tradition and before the turning point was reached in the Southern attitude toward slavery. They were part of the great tide of Southerners who swept into the northwestern territories and like thousands of others they cast their lot with their new states. While reasons of conscience and distaste for slavery figured largely in their decisions, they left voluntarily and remained away voluntarily. They were not outcasts but emigrants, and they may more accurately be called settlers than exiles. With the Men of the Thirties the situation was not the same.

Here in long perspective are projected problems of wide human significance that have relevance to our own troubled times. Among these are the struggles between social convictions and human loyalties, between the love of justice and the love of native soil, between conscience and family ties, between humanitarian passions and patriotism. The Southerners in exile were torn by all these conflicts and by many more. George W. Cable of Louisiana spoke for many of his forerunners when he characterized his own inner conflict. Watching the "great Reconstruction agony from the first day to the last" in his native New Orleans, Cable found his emotions painfully torn—"with his sympathies ranged upon the pro-Southern side of the issue, and his convictions drifting irresistibly to the other."

When sympathies and convictions are at war with one another in the same mind, the results are seldom happy, and the spiritual schism can be the cause of mental anguish. The history of the exiles is not a very happy one. It had high moments of courage, rare triumphs of personal fortitude, and some of the transports of martyrdom. But it is a history darkened by divided families, father alienated from son, mother from daughter, by long years of loneliness and doubting, and by bitter nostalgia in the case of some of the exiles. They were the uprooted, the homeless. In their exile they were naturally drawn into intimate association with Northerners who shared the passionate convictions that had made outcasts of the Southerners. But the Southerners sometimes discovered belatedly that their new friends could combine a laudable passion to reform the South with other objectives that were not necessarily friendly to the region and its people. In fact these latter objectives might be masked by the generous reform passions. The Southerner might also be confronted with the painful realization that the cherished reforms for which he had given up home, inheritance, and loved ones could only be achieved by subversive methods, insurrection, or outright war against his own people.

The exiles of the thirties did not spring out of the discontented, non-slaveowning classes of the Southern uplands, as had many of the earlier dissenters. They [came] typically from the most privileged class, from wealthy, slave-owning, cultured families of position and distinction. Although the father of James Gillespie Birney was a Scotch-Irish immigrant who landed in Philadelphia at the age of 16, he prospered amazingly with business ventures in the Kentucky blue-grass country, maintained a luxurious country estate with slaves, a mansion for winter residence in Danville, and was reputed to be "the richest man in Kentucky."[4,*] An Episcopalian, a staunch Federalist, and a friend of Henry Clay, the elder Birney despised the doctrines of both Calhoun and Jackson. His only son James, a slaveowner at the age of six, grew up in luxurious style, graduated from Princeton, and studied law in Philadelphia, where he lived the life of a fashionable dandy. After practicing law in Kentucky three years he married, and with the slaves he received as a wedding present moved to Alabama in 1819 and set up as a planter near Huntsville. He brought with him his blue-grass traditions of fine horses, expensive furniture, and lavish hospitality. For sixteen years he lived the life of an Alabama planter, lawyer, and politician. An elegantly dressed figure with stern, finely moulded, handsome features, a thorough conservative in politics with a reputation of massive integrity, James G. Birney appeared in 1830 to be a most unlikely candidate for the leadership of a fanatical abolitionist crusade.

Equally improbable as a nest of zealous abolitionists was the home of John Fauchereau Grimke of Charleston, justice of the Supreme Court of South Carolina, father of Sarah and Angelina (for two of the Men of the Thirties were women). The son of an old, wealthy, and distinguished Charleston family, Judge Grimke was educated at Oxford, law at the Temple in London,

---

* Woodward began with superscript notes but provided no citations. He also misnumbered the notes. Then he switched to parenthetical citations. Those begin as what is endnote 5 in this version.

and home to serve as a colonel in the Revolutionary war. The large Grimke family were straight-laced, high-church Episcopalians and leaders of the aristocratic society of Charleston. The future incendiaries, Sarah and Angelina, grew up among their kinsmen the Barnwells and Rhetts accustomed to the service of slaves and to luxury and display. An uncle was Governor of North Carolina and their first cousin, Robert Barnwell Rhett was the foremost fire-eater among Charleston nullificationists and secessionists.

Associated with Birney and the Grimke sisters as abolitionist leaders was a group of younger Southerners, all ministers or ministerial students, who went into exile in the early thirties. Among these the most prominent was James Armstrong Thome of Kentucky, whose father Arthur Thome was a prosperous slaveowner of Augusta. The father of Thome's friends William T. and James M. Allan, both abolitionist exiles, was a slaveowning Presbyterian parson of Huntsville, Alabama. A fourth of these young ministers was Henry P. Thompson of Kentucky, a slaveowner in his own right. It is obvious that the antislavery impulse among these Southern abolitionists was not economic, since it ran directly counter to their own economic interests.

The impulse common to all the exiles of the thirties was basically religious, and from Charleston to the distant Alabama frontier they all came under the powerful influence of one remarkable missionary of the Great Revival. This was Theodore Dwight Weld, foremost apostle of Charles Grandison Finney, a mighty preacher of hell-fire evangelism. Finney had swept the "burnt-over" district of upper New York with the greatest of the great revivals, and his apostles spread the flames through the West. Theodore Weld, converted by Finney in 1826, carried the brand southward through Kentucky, Tennessee, and into Alabama in 1830, spending a month in the latter state and casting his spell upon Birney and the Allan brothers. Clad in what he described as "a John the Baptist attire" consisting of "shag overcoat, linsey woolsey coat and cowhide shoes," Weld made a startling figure of a prophet. He said that he did not comb his hair once a year and that it stood "in all directions like the quills of a porcupine;" nor did he shave with any regularity, so that his beard was "generally as long as a hermits." He was unable to remember the day or the year and he would often have to go to the window to see whether it was winter or summer. He shunned publicity, dodged the society of wealthy abolitionists, and abhorred cities. The backcountry was his field. "I am a Backwoodsman," he told Lewis Tappan, "—can grub up stumps and roll logs and burn brush heaps and break green sward." He would sweep the cities by setting back fires in the country.[5] He was indifferent or oblivious to the economic aspects of slavery, "believing," as he said, "that the business of abolitionists is with the heart of the nation rather than with its purse strings."⁶ So silently did he work that it was only in recent years that historians have discovered him to be the most effective personal force in the abolitionist crusade.

All the Southern exiles of the thirties left convincing testimony of the influence Weld had upon their lives. Angelina Grimke adored and married him; and Sarah made her home with the couple. Birney esteemed him above any of the leading abolitionists and he knew them all. James Thome confessed to Weld that often "the gushings of my soul have prompted me to throw my arms around your neck and kiss you."⁷ Weld himself complained that all his fellow students of Lane Seminary had "strangely and stupidly idolized" him.⁸ The part he played in their actual conversion to the cause varied considerably, but it was greatest among those Southerners who came under his influence at Lane Seminary.

The seminary at Cincinnati was established as an outpost of Yankee religious radicalism, at the very border of slave territory. It was inspired by Finney revivalism and staffed by Finney apostles. When Finney himself declined the presidency the office was accepted by Lyman Beecher. The student body was even more radical than the staff. Characteristically, Weld turned down a professorship in order to enroll as a student. Beecher complained that Weld usurped the presidency. "He took the lead of the whole institution.... They thought he was a god," wrote Beecher.⁹ Weld had recently assisted in preparing the way for founding the American Anti-Slavery Society and he came to Lane to abolitionize the place. To him at Cincinnati flocked the young apostles he had made in his missions to the West and South. After working individually among them for several months he staged with the reluctant permission of the president the famous Lane "debates" on the question of immediate emancipation. Weld led off with four lectures or sermons in his fervent evangelical style. What followed was more in the nature of a protracted abolitionist revival of eighteen nights than it was a debate.

The young Southerners took the lead in these proceedings from the start. The emotional pitch was heightened by the revelation of "experiences" picturing with lurid details the horrors of slavery. The confessions were charged with a sense of guilt and a revulsion from "sin" that suggests the "anxious bench" of the revival. Of the seventeen students who related such experiences, eight were Southerners. In addition to Thome of Kentucky, the Allan brothers of Alabama, there were three students from South Carolina, and one from Virginia. One from the Arkansas Territory was a black Southerner, an ex-slave named James Bradley who had bought his own freedom. Altogether, according to Weld, the authors of these antislavery testimonials represented twenty-nine years' residence in Virginia, twenty-three in South Carolina, twenty-four in Alabama, twenty-two in Tennessee, twenty-three in Missouri, and sixty-four in Kentucky, besides residences of from six months to five years in Louisiana, Arkansas, Maryland, North Carolina, and Mississippi.[10] Thus in all eleven slave states were represented, though only five by natives.

The Lane "debate," needless to say, terminated with a decision in favor of immediate emancipation. Starting when there was not a single immediate abolitionist among the students, where the idea was "regarded as the climax of absurdity, fanaticism and blood," Weld had swept the place into the fold, converting every one of the Southern students, many of them right out of slaveholding homes, except one who was absent during nearly all the debate. Weld stressed the assistance he received from William T. Allan of Alabama, "born, bred, and educated in the midst of slavery . . . himself heir to a slave inheritance."[11] The debates ended, the students promptly organized the Lane Seminary Anti-Slavery Society and elected Allan president, Marius R. Robinson, a New Englander educated in Tennessee, vice-president, Thome of Kentucky secretary, and C. S. Hodges of Virginia auditor; and on the board of managers they placed, along with Weld and other Northerners, James the brother of William Allan and James Bradley, the ex-slave.[12]

With terrible earnestness the students next set to work as missionaries among the Negro population of Cincinnati, subscribing hundreds of dollars to equip schools, libraries, and other services, and working tirelessly among the Negroes themselves. One convert from Kentucky liberated the slaves on whose labor he was being supported in school, then took leave from the seminary in order to earn money to pay for his liberated slaves' education. Cincinnati seethed with excitement against the students when they preached and openly practiced social equality with Negroes. The faculty remonstrated, but Allan as spokesman of the students refused to yield an inch on the doctrine of social equality.[13] Finally the trustees outlawed the abolition society and forbade all discussion of slavery. Whereupon the incorrigible students, almost to a man, walked out of Lane for good and all. The following year a large number of them, including the Allans and Thome, enrolled in the abolitionized college of Oberlin, of which Finney had just become president. When Allan took this step he wrote Weld that he had finally "passed the rubicon."[14] Across their Rubicon of the Ohio River Thome and other Southerners followed into exile. The Lane rebels were later to form the elite corps of the abolitionist shock troops, and the Southern exiles among them held high offices.

In the conversion of James G. Birney there was nothing of the sudden impulsiveness of the college student. Eleven years older than Weld, Birney was the father of nine children, one-time mayor of Huntsville and member of the legislature, a highly respected man of property in land and slaves, and the most successful lawyer in his area. In 1824 he sold his plantation and all his slaves except five household servants. His opinions of slaveholding at that time he wrote "did not materially differ from those which prevailed among the generality of planters."[15] The change began, as in the case of other Southern abolitionists, in connections with a religious conversion in 1826, when Birney joined the Presbyterian Church. Before this occurred he pictured himself as a gambler and heavy drinker "rapidly pursuing the road to Hell."[16] Conversion brought sobriety of habits, but he still regarded abolitionists as dangerous fanatics. In 1832 he became concerned over the moral effects of slavery on his six sons, and the following year moved back to Danville, Kentucky. Giving up a prosperous law practice, he also became a traveling agent of the American Colonization Society and threw all his energies into this cause. By December, 1833, however, he discovered that within one year the South had become "very manifestly, more and more indurated upon the subject of Slavery," and that among the large planters he did not "believe that anything effectual can be done amongst them on the subject of Colonization."[17] Although he had preached colonization as "the best defence against the rash attempts of *abolitionists*," Birney now came to the conclusion that colonization was an "opiate to the consciences" of the South and a means of perpetuating slavery.[18] He forthwith resigned and simultaneously struck a blow at the organization in a pamphlet published by the American Antislavery Society.[19] He then took the next step toward abolitionism, which was to come out for gradual emancipation. He occupied this ground only briefly.[20] In June, 1834, he emancipated his six remaining slaves and publicly announced he was for immediate emancipation. He had completed his gradual conversion to abolitionism though not the evolution of his thoughts on the subject. In Boston, New York, and Cincinnati there was rejoicing among abolition leaders, for as an apostate from the rival Colonization Society and a slaveholding Southerner of high standing, Birney was the most important convert yet made.

The psychological roots of the Grimke sisters' rebellion go deeper than the slavery controversy and their spiritual alienation from the South and all its ways was more thoroughgoing. Conflict began in the home which a biographer describes as "a place of constant discord, jealousy, and unhappiness."[21] It is clear that the dissident sisters themselves did little to promote domestic harmony. Angelina, twelve years younger than Sarah, was convinced that

God had endowed her with the "power of distinguishing right from wrong" and she was given to disclosing these divine promptings to all offenders in foreseeable and uncompromising language. For several years before they left home, she and Sarah insisted on paying board to their mother regularly, a practice that scarcely endeared them to their numerous unemployed brothers and sisters, nor did it quite conform to the customs of patriarchal homelife in Charleston. In the midst of the gay fashionable social life in which they were thrown, these two puritans were overwhelmed with a sense of guilt. "Few have exceeded me," wrote Sarah, "in extravagance of every kind, and in the sinful indulgence of pride and vanity." She was, she said, "weary of the ball-room and its gilded toys" and "mortified" at her own folly.[22] And Angelina, the more brilliant of the two, pictured herself as "a poor unworthy worm, feeding on luxuries my soul abhors, tended by slaves ... whose bondage I deeply deplore." She exclaimed, "Oh! Why am I kept in Carolina?" The sisters began to practice a naïve asceticism that made them the more conspicuous in their environment. They declined pastries and wines at parties, and gave up one frill or finery after another, finally abandoning all ornament. Warned that she was making herself ridiculous, Angelina prayed for strength "to dress always in the following style: A hat over the face, without any bows of ribbon or lace; no frills or trimmings on any part of my dress, and materials not the finest." Then one solemn morning the sisters destroyed a set of Sir Walter Scott's novels, which Angelina had purchased, according to Sarah, "before she was serious." They destroyed all their other novels as well.[23]

The Grimke sisters, like James Birney, registered their first formal dissent by leaving the Episcopalian Church of their family and joining the Presbyterians. Sarah subsequently had a brief Methodist phase, but their asceticism impelled them both irresistibly toward the Quakers. Already feeling themselves to be outcasts in Charleston, they yearned to escape to the North, which Angelina pictured as "a promised land, a pleasant land." Sarah left home for Philadelphia in 1821 and Angelina followed in 1829. Angelina never saw her mother again and never returned home; Sarah returned only once in 1831. Both took the drab cloth and prim bonnets of the Friends. While the sisters had professed unhappiness over the lot of the slaves, neither of them had any thought of active opposition to slavery before they left home.[24] Association with the Friends had the double effect of stimulating their interest in abolition and at the same time restraining their expression of this interest. Soon Angelina, who quickly assumed leadership in the partnership of rebellion, was "finding it very hard to stand and wait" and complaining of a "leanness and barrenness of spirit" among the Quakers. Toward the beginning of 1835 Angelina became more "deeply interested in the subject of abolition." Abolitionism was the ultimate expression of a revolt against the South, and the path of the Charleston renegades terminated only at the doors of Garrison's *Liberator*. In August 1835 Angelina impulsively wrote Garrison a letter in which she declared: "The ground upon which you stand is holy ground; never, never surrender it;" and expressed her "deep, solemn, deliberate conviction that this is a *cause worth dying for*." She knew it for she came from "the land of slavery . . . where is found the sin of Sodom." Without asking permission Garrison published the letter in the *Liberator*, thus completing the breach. Angelina wrote Sarah: "I am an exile from the home of my birth because of slavery."[25] After overcoming her first abhorrence, Sarah also took up the banner.

The exiled Southern converts were assets of tremendous value to the abolitionist crusade, and the Northern leaders recognized them as such immediately. For one thing the Southerners were living proof that abolitionist propaganda could take effect in the South itself. Secondly the exiles were irrevocably committed to the cause, for there was no turning back for them. But most important of all was their propaganda value. Was a Boston audience incredulous of the horrors of slavery? Then listen to a former planter of Alabama on the subject. Did Cleveland doubt the moral deterioration among slaveowners? Then hear the testimony of a former slaveowner from South Carolina. It made good copy, headlines. The exiles were Exhibit A in the case for abolitionism, more effective than the fugitive slave and his scars or the torture tongs. As Weld wrote the Grimke sisters: "The *great* reason why *you* should operate upon the public mind far and wide at the north . . . is that you are *southern* women, *once* in *law* slaveowners, your friends all slave holders, etc., hence your testimony, *testimony*, TESTIMONY is the great desideratum."[26] So it was that the Southerners were pushed forward into the spotlight, and most of them took to it eagerly.

When Theodore Weld undertook to abolitionize the state of Ohio in 1835 he went to Oberlin for recruits among his fellow Lane rebels. He completed the conversion of the college to the cause in three weeks and selected six apostles to help him convert the state. Leading spirits among the six were William Allan and James Thome. They reported to Weld in Cleveland for a two-weeks intensive indoctrination course conducted at evangelistic pitch that was calculated to bring them to "*welding* heat," as Elizur Wright put it. They then scattered over the state in pairs as so many firebrands of evangelical abolitionism. "I blazed and threw sky-rockets, talked of human rights, touched upon the American Revolution and brought heaven and earth together," Thome reported to Weld of one of his speeches.[27] Mobbings and violence were expected and common features of the crusade. Heckled, egged, stoned, locked up, man-handled, and threatened, the crusaders welcomed the violence as good for their cause and gloried in their fortitude in withstanding all comers. Their personal courage in these affairs is attested by voluminous evidence. At a meeting in Granville Thome encountered a mob of two hundred with a fiddler at its head that was broken up by antislavery men armed with clubs, casualties occurring on both sides.[28] Ordinarily, however, the procedure was to offer no resistance but face down the mobs until they tired of their sport or joined the audience and were converted. Twenty-six windows were smashed in one church while Thome was speaking, and the place and audience festooned with egg yolks and battered with bricks. But the speaking continued. As for the apostles, they embraced their martyrdom and flourished under such treatment. "For the past 3 years, I have walked in a new world," wrote Thome to Weld. "My path has turned with delight. Every foot-tread has touched some spring and revealed fresh treasures of happiness. Life has been *rapture*."[29] He was, he declared, "all swallowed up in the causes which never troubled my thoughts before. Bless God! Though I have lost the favor of the gay and the smile of folly, I have secured friendship with Heaven and peace of soul."[30] Weld described his disciples as "He-goat men, who think they do God a service by butting everything in the line of their march which does not fall or get out of the way."[31] For the crucial years, 1835–1836 Weld's "he-goat" men formed the shock troops and field force of the abolitionist crusade.

No one, not even Weld, would have thought of applying the term "he-goat man" to James G. Birney, nor of describing any of his activities as "butting." He was not a ranting evangelist nor a spread-eagle spell binder. He was a gentleman of substance and distinction and he looked every inch the part. Such was the respect he commanded that in spite of the numerous hostile mobs that menaced him, some of them threatening his life, no one ever laid hands upon him in violence.[32] He was the only one of the exiles of the thirties who dared continue living and working for the cause in the South after his conversion to abolitionism, and that only in Kentucky, the most liberal of the Southern states. The boldness of his single-handed fight made him the most conspicuous and admired abolitionist within the movement.

From his native Danville, Birney set about vigorously proselytizing among planters and slaveowners. He attempted to gain a professorship in Centre College and abolitionize the students as Weld had done at Lane and Oberlin, but was thwarted by suspicious trustees. He did succeed in persuading the Presbyterian Synod of Kentucky to pronounce slaveholding a sin, and in March, 1835, he was instrumental in organizing the Kentucky Anti-Slavery

Society. An affiliate of the national society, the Kentucky branch began with forty members, mainly ex-slave-owners. As a secret agent in the pay of the American Anti-Slavery Society, Birney laid plans for the printing of an abolitionist paper in Kentucky. Excited mass meetings resolved to block this venture at all costs, even to the taking of life. Threatened with violence, deserted by some of his kinsmen, unable to secure a printer or even to hire a hall in which to defend his views, Birney finally gave up the effort and moved with his family to Cincinnati. He had started his long years of exile.

In Cincinnati Birney met with more overt violence than he had in the South. A small mob destroyed some printer's equipment in the shop where his *Philanthropist* was printed, and later in July, 1836, after a mass meeting of business and professional men had warned Birney to abandon his paper, an angry mob destroyed the press and scattered the type. The burning of his home was narrowly prevented, and Birney went into temporary hiding. It was the first major attack on the abolitionist press of the North and it made Birney a national figure. His indictment soon afterward for harboring a fugitive slave focused additional attention on him. When the American Anti-Slavery Society was reorganized in 1837, Birney was a logical—and Weld thought the ideal—choice for executive secretary of the national headquarters of the organization. In September he moved to New York to take charge.

Birney ran head on into a doctrinal schism among abolitionists over the heresies of William Lloyd Garrison. With fanatical dogmatism the editor of the *Liberator* insisted on burdening the cause of the slave by associating it with a dozen other causes of equal or greater unpopularity. These included his war against all churches, clergy, organized religion, and sabbath observance, as well as a repudiation of all forms of government in any department. Along with anarchism he championed woman's rights, pacifism, perfectionism, and spiritualism. Weld pronounced it "downright fanaticism" to attempt to promote abolition "with forty incongruous things tacked on to it."[33] Birney published a pamphlet denouncing Garrisonism in similar terms, and the exiles among the Lane rebels took the same position.[34]

The exiles were divided, however, over the issue of Garrisonism. For a time the Grimke sisters were completely under the influence of Garrison. Angelina compared the Boston editor favorably with Christ. She was convinced that "a deadly war" was raging "between Righteousness and Sin" and that "Brother Garrison is sustained by the Lord." She and Sarah hoped that he would be untrammeled in the advancement of "the Great subjects of Peace, Perfection, [No-] Government, the Clergy, Woman, etc.," as well as his own brand of abolitionism.[35] While they expressed devotion to all these causes, the sisters were peculiarly dedicated to one—woman's rights. And in that it was they who infected Garrison, rather than vice versa.

The taboos of propriety against women speaking in public were still intact. Not even the advanced and emancipated women of Boston dared defy the man-made taboo. It remained for the two frail exiles from conservative Charleston to override the barriers. They began by demanding the right to speak for the enslaved Negro, but the outcry their impropriety provoked turned their attention to enslaved women. Sarah's private revolt against Charleston started with her indignation over being denied the education a man would have enjoyed. Comparing the wrongs of the slave with those of women, the sisters concluded the grievances of their own sex were as great as those of the Negro. They appealed to "the white slaves of the North" to arise and they urged that the *Liberator* abandon abolition "as a *primary* object" and turn instead to woman's rights.[36] The romantic appeal of the Charleston abolitionists plus the notoriety of their public speaking brought a deluge of invitations to speak. They barnstormed New York and New Jersey and carried the war into New England and on to Boston, where they addressed a committee of the Massachusetts Legislature three times. New England was agog with their boldness. They were the sensation of the day, and it is pretty clear that Angelina enjoyed it. "I cannot help smiling in the midst of 'rhetorical flourishes,'" she wrote Weld, "to witness their perfect amazement at hearing a woman speak in the churches."[37] "What dost thou think," she asked another, "of some of them walking two, four, six, and eight miles to attend our meetings?"[38]

The press was outraged, and a conclave of Massachusetts ministers resolved against this female invasion of what they regarded as a masculine monopoly. The sisters were amused at Massachusetts men defending slavery against the attacks of two South Carolina women. But when Catherine Beecher, the sister of Harriet Beecher Stowe, published a book defending "All the generous promptings of chivalry, all the poetry of romantic gallantry" against the Charleston feminists and pleading for "Woman's retaining her place as *dependent*," the Grimke blood boiled. A Beecher defending chivalry, and a woman Beecher at that! Let Charleston have the floor. Angelina published an impassioned reply. No self-respecting woman, she declared "cares aught for any attention or any protection, vouchsafed by 'the promptings of chivalry.'" Instead she scorns "romantic gallantry" and "loathes such littleness, and turns away with disgust from all such silly insipidities . . . such paltry, sickening adulation."[39] Never did a Southern tradition receive such punishment as Angelina gave chivalry.

Birney was disturbed by the deviations of the Grimkes. His war against the South was largely limited to slavery and race questions. On other matters his code remained that of the tradition to which he was born. Somewhat quaintly he publicly rebuked a New England clergyman for his unchivalrous words against Miss Grimke's attack on chivalry.[40] Sarah and Angelina were amused at their fellow exile's backwardness.[41] But their Northern abolitionist friends were deeply upset. John Greenleaf Whittier implored the sisters not to put "a selfish crusade against some paltry grievance" above "the cause of the poor and miserable slave, sighing from the cotton plantation of the Mississippi."[42] And Theodore Weld, greatly exercised, undertook to set them right. "Why my dear child!" he wrote Angelina, "What is the matter with you? Patience! Rally yourself. Recollect your womanhood my sister."[43] Angelina replied in kind: "Well—*such* a lecture, I never before received. What is the matter with thee?" Such was her "bump of obstinacy," she declared, that "not even thy sledge hammer can beat it down."[44] But Theodore put aside his sledge hammer for words of courtship, confessed his love, and begged Angelina to marry him. She had previously told her suitor in the heat of argument that there was "not one man in 500 who really understands what kind of attention is alone acceptable to a woman of pure and exalted moral and intellectual worth."[45] Apparently Theodore was one in 500, however, for he was joyfully accepted. Their wedding, held on the opening day of the annual convention of the Antislavery Women and at the height of the sisters' notoriety, was the most celebrated event in the abolitionist brotherhood. The elite of the movement, including Garrison, Gerrit Smith, Lewis Tappan, and Whittier, as well as James G. Birney, were wedding guests. Everyone sought to make two liberated Grimke slaves feel at home. The ceremony was strictly of the bride and groom's devising and consisted of addresses by each. Afterward William Lloyd Garrison read the marriage certificate and the guests signed as witnesses. Thenceforth doctrinal disputes were resolved in the bosom of the family and both sisters renounced Garrisonism.[46]

Marriage made Angelina less conspicuous in the abolition crusade but did not dampen her ardor nor stop her efforts. She and Sarah were soon hard at work under Theodore's direction preparing what became the most influential of all the many antislavery tracts and the most terrible indictment of the South published, *American Slavery As It Is*. For six months they averaged six hours daily combing old Southern newspaper files, 20,000 copies they estimated, to amass the bulk of material that made up the book. The method was to indict the South by the words of the Southerners, either the unconscious testimony of the fugitive slave advertisement, or the testimony of the exiles and Southern abolitionists. Weld set out to prove, he wrote, that the slaves were "overworked, underfed, have insufficient sleep, live in miserable huts," and that "barbarous cruelties are inflicted upon them."[47] The selection of evidence is suggested by two editorial advisors who proposed that facts "which are merely *horrid* must give place to those which are absolutely diabolical."[48] The picture that Weld painted of the slave's plight strongly suggests the evangelist's picture of hell itself. Slaves, he wrote, were "made to wear round their necks iron collars armed with prongs, to drag heavy chains and weights at their feet while working in the field, and to wear yokes, and bells, and iron horns . . . to wear gags in their mouths . . . have some of their front teeth torn out or broken off . . . frequently flogged with terrible severity, have red pepper rubbed into their lacerated flesh, and hot brine, spirits of turpentine, &c., poured over the gashes to increase the torture . . . terribly torn by the claws of cats, drawn over them by their tormenters . . . their ears are often cut off, their eyes knocked out, their bones broken, their flesh branded with red hot irons; that they are maimed, mutilated and burned to death over slow fires. All these things, and more, and worse, we shall *prove*."[49] As Weld wrote Gerrit Smith, "Facts and testimonies are troops, weapons and victory, all in one."[50] And after all, this was a holy war. If there happened to be any decent slaveowners or well-fed slaves the champions of the institution would make them sufficiently well known.

All the Southern exiles were solicited for contributions by Weld or the Grimke sisters. James A. Thome was eager to be helpful, but replied: "I have really witnessed so few cases of cruel treatment in Ky., that any account I could give from personal observation would, I fear, have the impression that *cruelties were rare*. I might have stated numerous facts which have occurred in *other places*, and of which I have *heard*; but this would not have been in pursuance of the terms of your request."[51] Weld's solution was to quote an earlier speech that Thome made before the first meeting of the American Anti-Slavery Society in which he described: "Sufferings inconceivable and innumerable—unmingled wretchedness from the ties of nature rudely broken and destroyed, the acutest bodily tortures, groans, tears and blood—lying for ever in weariness and painfulness, in watchings, in hunger and in thirst, in cold and nakedness."[52] He was the sensation of the meeting, and he told the members that all his testimony was "the result either of experience or of personal observation."[53]

The exiles no doubt realized that testimony regarding their own homes made the greatest impression on Northern audiences. The Grimke sisters had never visited the fields of their father's plantation where the slaves were at work, and Angelina admitted that she "knew almost nothing of their condition," though they had, of course, known slavery in Charleston.[54] Sarah declared, however, that she had "deserted the home of my fathers to escape the sound of the lash and the shrieks of tortured victims."[55] William T. Allan of Alabama testified that "At our house it is so common to hear their screams, that we think nothing of it . . . *cruelty* is the *rule*, and *kindness* the *exception*."[56] Thome painted an even less attractive picture of Southern home life. "Let it be felt in the North," he urged, "and rolled back upon the South, that the slave States are Sodoms, and almost every village family is a brothel"—at least in the kitchen departments. "Pollution! Pollution . . . Overwhelming pollution!" he exclaimed.[57]

Birney was more restrained in his testimony, though urged on by the same compulsive sense of guilt that plagued other exiles. The first number of his *Philanthropist*, January 1, 1836, presented a strong contrast in its mildness with the strident words of the first *Liberator*, six years earlier. He set aside a "Slave-Holder's Department" in which appeared the arguments of his opponents, and he promised to treat the unrepentant sinners with justice and compassion. He printed a regular column of horrors and cruelties, but there *were* limits beyond which Birney would not go. One contribution, for example, was the story of a master who left the dinner table with a butcher knife, whacked off the head of a slave woman who had spilled gravy on the dress of his colored concubine, and returned calmly to finish his meal. This one Birney suggested was "improbable."[58] His regular column entitled "Scenes at the South," however, contained samples of all the standard atrocities known to abolitionist literature: the woman kicked to death, the stillborn babe, brutal tortures, slow death by fire.[59]

The testimony of the native Southerners, primarily that of the exiles, was esteemed among abolitionists as the most incontrovertible and effective of all. The books and pamphlets of Birney, Thome, Angelina Weld, and Sarah Grimke, and the speeches of the Lane rebels were circulated widely and systematically. Weld's *American Slavery As It Is*, the greatest of all the tracts until *Uncle Tom's Cabin*, was in large part a compendium of the Southern exiles' testimony against the South. The first year its sales exceeded a hundred thousand copies, and for a while it was the best selling book in the country.[60] It has been called "the handbook of the movement for more than a decade."[61]

One fascinated listener to the impassioned confessions of the Southern students at the Lane Debates was the president's daughter, Harriet Beecher, who later married one of the professors named Stowe. Twenty years later when she was writing *Uncle Tom* she drew upon those debates and upon the evidence of the exiles printed in Weld's tract to support her arraignment of slavery. The abolitionist indictment of the South was documented with Southern sources.

Notes

1. [note missing]
2. [note missing]
3. [note missing]
4. [note missing]
5. W-G Letters, 593–99.
6. Barnes, 79.
7. WG Letters, 642.
8. Ibid., 593.
9. *Auto of L. B.*, II, 314.
10. WG Letters, 138–39.
11. Ibid., 132.
12. Thomas, *Weld*, 72.
13. Barnes, 68, 71.
14. WG Letters, 189–90.
15. W. B., *Birney*, 424.
16. B. Letters, 242; also p. 9.
17. B. Letters, 97.
18. Ibid., 47.
19. B., Letter on Colonization, 7.
20. Corres. between B and Society of Friends, Haverhill, 1935.
21. Birney, *G. Sisters*, 68.
22. Ibid., 18–19.
23. Ibid., 51, 53, 58.
24. Ibid., 41, 92.
25. Ibid., 124–27.
26. WG Letters, 389.
27. WG Letters, 257–58.
28. Thomas, 107.
29. WG Letters, 339, 341.
30. WG Letters, 190–91.
31. Barnes, 72.
32. W. G., *Birney*.
33. Thomas, 147.
34. James G. Birney, *A Letter on the Political Obligations of Abolitionists*, with a Reply by William Lloyd Garrison (Boston, 1839).

35. WG Letters, 476–77.
36. WG Letters, 440.
37. WG Letters, 414–15.
38. Birney, *Sisters*, 195.
39. A. Grimke, *Letters to C. Beecher*, 107.
40. B. Letters, 478–81.
41. WG Letters, 552.
42. Ibid., 424.
43. Ibid., 457.
44. Ibid., 450–51.
45. Ibid., 414–15.
46. Birney, *Sisters*, 232–33; Barnes, 158.
47. WG Letters, 717.
48. Ibid., 733.
49. *Slavery As It Is*, 9.
50. WG Letters, 809.
51. Ibid., 752–53.
52. *Slavery As It Is*, 61.
53. *First Annual Report of the American Anti-Slavery Society* (New York, 1834), p. 7.
54. *Slavery As It Is*, 53.
55. Ibid., 22.
56. Ibid., 61.
57. *First Annual Report American Anti-Slavery Society*, 9.
58. Cincinnati *Philanthropist*, March 3, 1837.
59. Ibid., Nov. 18, Dec. 2, Dec. 23, 1836; Jan. 6, 1837.
60. Thomas, *Weld*, 172.
61. WG Letters, xii–xiii.

FLEMING LECTURE II
The Men of the Fifties

THE MEN OF THE thirties, who were the subject of discussion last evening, did not suddenly disappear from the scene at the end of the decade, though it is true that by far the greater part of their more significant achievements fell before that time. This was even true of James G. Birney, in spite of the fact that he ran for President as the nominee of the Liberty Party in 1840 and again in 1844. The insignificant vote that he polled was a disappointment for the abolitionists who supported him. The only practical consequence of these campaigns was that in 1844 the votes cast for Birney in New York State defeated Clay for the Presidency. But that was only one of the fortunes of politics, not the achievement of Birney, and certainly not the result of intrigue as was charged.

The nervous strain and the pull of conflicting emotions under which the Southern exiles of the 1830's lived told heavily upon their health and peace of mind. "I find my nervous system greatly shattered," wrote Birney in 1839, and complained of what he called "a distressing brainular prostration."[1] In 1845 he had a stroke of "nervous paralysis" that deprived him of the power of speech temporarily and left him an invalid the rest of his life. James Thome and Theodore Weld were also stricken with a mysterious nervous affliction of the throat that made it impossible for them to speak in public. Weld did not attempt a public address for eighteen years. Thome gave up his speaking crusade and went to the West Indies where he wrote a book on the results of abolition in the islands. Soon after her marriage in 1838 Angelina Weld suffered an injury which, according to her biographer, was "of such a nature that her nervous system was permanently impaired, and she was ever after obliged to avoid all excitement or over-exertion."[2]

The Southern exiles of the thirties lived on, with diminishing activity and effectiveness, into the fifties. Their influence and notoriety was already faded before the appearance of a new generation of exiles fresh from the South. The Men of the Fifties played their roles on a national stage peopled by a new cast of actors and animated by a spirit that differed in several respects from that of the thirties.

The exiles of the fifties shared the stage with Lincoln and Douglas, Stephens and Davis, Seward and Sumner, while their forerunners had been contemporaries of Clay, Webster, Jackson, Polk, and Cass. Like the dominant politicians of the day, the new generation of exiles were born in the nineteenth century. Few of them attained their majority before 1840 and could therefore not remember a time when there was not a more or less acute sectional controversy over slavery. They had been born into it, and from their childhood the abolitionist had been the popular bogey of the South. In the meantime sectional lines had hardened and issues were more sharply drawn. The South had become more militant and assertive in its defense and the North more aggressive in its charges.

The antislavery movement itself had changed subtly in many ways. By the end of the thirties the Great Revival had burnt itself out, and thereafter the evangelical impulse of abolitionism was supplanted by motivation of a somewhat different character. No longer was it primarily a missionary movement to save the souls of slaveowners from sin by bringing salvation through repentance. Hatred of the sin of slaveholding was transferred to hatred of the slaveholder himself, and from him to his associates, his region, to the South as a whole. The old antislavery societies declined in strength at the same time that agitation intensified in other quarters. Leadership shifted from ecclesiastical to a secular predominance. Politicians discovered that they could profitably exploit antislavery sentiment. A moral crusade was becoming a political crusade as abolitionism was incorporated into the sectional war.

It is significant that none of the Southern exiles of the fifties came from the Lower South, as had several of the Men of the Thirties. Western North Carolina, a region of small farmers with an indigenous antislavery tradition, produced three of the new exiles. These were Hinton Rowan Helper, Daniel Reaves Goodloe, and Benjamin Sherwood Hedrick. Moncure Daniel Conway was a native of Virginia, and John Curtiss Underwood was a Virginian by adoption. John Gregg Fee was one of several Kentuckians forced into exile in the fifties for their abolitionist views, and Mattie Griffith another.

While the Men of the Thirties sprang from families of wealth and distinction, the Men of the Fifties came typically from humbler stock of yeomanry or middle class. The single outstanding exception to this rule was Moncure Daniel Conway, each of whose three names belonged to one of Virginia's old families. Conway grew up among his numerous kinsfolk, associated particularly with the influential Daniel family. His father owned an estate valued at about $100,000 in addition to landed property and numerous slaves.[3] More typical was the obscure background of Hinton Rowan Helper, whose father was the son of a German immigrant. Both father and grandfather were small landholders of Western North Carolina. Hinton was the seventh of a poor family of seven children. His own statement that his father, who died when the boy was nine months old, was the owner of four slaves has been questioned on the ground that he was too poor to buy that much slave property.[4] Neither Hedrick, who was also of German stock, nor Goodloe, the third of the tarheel exiles, came of slaveholding families. The father of John G. Fee was a Kentucky farmer who, according to his son, at one time owned some thirteen slaves and was sufficiently prosperous to offer to send his son to Princeton.[5] The Fees, however, were neither prominent nor affluent. Underwood moved to Virginia from New York as a youth, married into Stonewall Jackson's family, and acquired about 800 acres of land, but no slaves.

While there was considerable antislavery sentiment latent in the South, particularly in the communities in which the North Carolina exiles grew up, the views of the men themselves do not appear to have been determined thereby. At least they thought of themselves as converts from the prevailing Southern view. Even Helper, often mentioned as an expression of indigenous antislavery thought, wrote: "As I grew from infancy to childhood, and from childhood to manhood, I learned, as ... almost every Southerner learned, to look upon negroes and negro slavery as absolutely essential constituents of the general plan, harmony and perfection of nature,—quite as essential as fire, air, earth, and water."[6] Young Conway, who was reared under very different circumstances, could write: "Slavery seemed to be as permanent a fact as the Rappahannock River."[7] Before the year 1850, when he was nineteen years of age, he said that he had never "heard any person say a word against the rectitude of slavery."[8] He had been disturbed by some half-formulated misgivings of his own. But, he wrote, "So accustomed had I been to regard Slavery as the very corner-stone of society; so bound hand and foot by my relations to it," that these misgivings "seemed to me to be a terrible secret, to be hushed and held down in my own breast."[9] Publicly, he declared that "the negro was not a man within the meaning of the Declaration of Independence."[10] He wrote for the Richmond *Examiner*, edited by his uncle John Daniel, articles full of what he described as "inflated Southernism,"[11] and he was pleased at his election as secretary of the first Southern Rights Association formed in Northern Virginia.[12]

Whether the experience was the determining event or not, each of the Men of the Fifties had residence in the free states of some extent before breaking with his native tradition and professing his conversion. In the case of John Fee this was two years of theological study at Lane Seminary in Cincinnati beginning in 1842. Weld and his converts had departed eight years earlier, and Lane was no longer the hotbed of evangelical abolitionism it had been. Nevertheless by 1844 Fee's conversion was complete. "For a time," he said, "I struggled between odium on the one hand, and manifest duty on the other." Then he surrendered. "In my bedroom on bended knee," he wrote, "and looking through my window across the Ohio river, over into my native State, I entered into a solemn covenant with God to return and there preach this gospel of love"—which was abolitionism.[13] Young Benjamin Hedrick graduated from the University of North Carolina in 1851 with first honors and accepted a clerkship in the Navy Department. He was stationed at Cambridge, Massachusetts, and while there took advanced work in mathematics and chemistry with Peirce and Agassiz at Harvard. When he returned to the Chapel Hill as professor of chemistry in 1854 he had not yet taken any public part in the slavery controversy.[14] Young Helper, a contemporary and friend of Hedrick, set forth from Carolina on his *Wanderjahre* about the same time, in the spring of 1850. He spent almost a year in New York and then sailed around the Horn to California for an unhappy sojourn of three years. After publishing *The Land of Gold*, a book ridiculing the California myth, he returned briefly to North Carolina, already a convinced abolitionist. His sojourn in the North, he wrote, had provided him "universal, irresistible and overwhelming" proof of the superiority of free labor.[15] The only one of the Tar Heel exiles who disclaimed any Northern influence in forming his abolitionist doctrine was Daniel Goodloe. "I am a home-bred anti-slavery man—not Northern," he declared in his autobiography. He dated the crystallization of his views as early as 1841, three years before he became associated with anti-slavery agitators in Washington. Before leaving his native state he had served an apprenticeship as a printer, failed as a newspaper editor, unsuccessfully attempted to practice law, and done a tour of military duty. Political advancement in the Whig party appeared to him impossible because of his privately-held views on slavery, and in 1844 he began a long career as newspaper man and freelance writer in Washington. It was not until after he entered the circle of Northern agitators there, however, that he gave public expression to his abolitionism.[16]

Southern fathers watched their sons depart for Northern colleges and seats of heresy with misgivings and anxiety. John Fee's father refused to support him at Lane when the young student showed evidence of heretical views,[17] and Moncure Conway's father took the same stand when his son set out for Harvard in February, 1853.[18] In his semi-autobiographical novel, *Pine and Palm*, Conway pictures one father reassuring himself when asked if he did not fear his son would become an abolitionist at Harvard. "I know my boy, sir," said the father. "He may have faults, but disloyalty is not among them." He would never be seduced by "crack-brained fanatics."[19] If Conway's own father ever entertained such confidence he was to be disappointed.

Conway's path led from Fredericksburg, Virginia, to Concord, Massachusetts, through a succession of sectarian faiths reminiscent of the religious experiments made by the Grimke sisters. The break with the Episcopalian Church had been made in the previous generation by his father, and Conway was born into the Methodist communion. A brief career as a Methodist circuit rider out of Baltimore left him spiritually parched and dissatisfied and he withdrew from the church. On his circuit lived a settlement of Hicksite Quakers to whom the young parson was strongly attracted, especially by their antislavery doctrine. He thought seriously of joining the Friends but was discouraged from doing so by one of the members. He turned next to Unitarianism and from that eventually to thoroughgoing rationalism. He arrived in Cambridge early in 1853 at the age of twenty-one with good letters of introduction and promptly launched his remarkable career as a tuft hunter. During his lifetime he was to establish acquaintance with more celebrities at home and abroad than any other American of his time who had no more claim to personal distinction than did Conway. He spent the summer of 1853 in Concord and added the Transcendental hierarchy to his list. He walked the shores of Walden with Emerson (noting down all his quotable remarks) and botanized with Thoreau and watched him minister to a fugitive slave. Conway was a personable young man, earnest, fearfully eager, a bit awkward, and the New Englanders took him in hospitably enough. All the more so since he was something of a curiosity as a well-connected Virginian of abolitionist tendencies. The Grimke sisters had blazed the path to the New England heart a generation before.

By May, 1854, when Boston was aflame with excitement over the arrest and delivery of the fugitive slave Anthony Burns, Conway was a conspicuous figure for one of his years. It happened that the slave Burns came from Conway's home community of Falmouth and that the owner who came to Boston to get his escaped slave was well known to the young Virginian. But when the Southern members of the Harvard student body invited him to join them in offering sympathy to the owner of Burns, Conway sent word that his sympathies were with the fugitive. Instead of joining the Southern students, he accompanied Wendell Phillips to Tremont Temple, where a number of antislavery leaders met to consider the advisability of attempting a rescue of the fugitive, and listened to an address by Theodore Parker.

News of the position he had taken in Boston was, of course, immediately taken to Falmouth. When he proposed to visit his parents the following September his father wrote advising him to postpone his visit until he had changed his views on slavery. "If you are willing to expose your own person recklessly," wrote the elder Conway, "I am not willing to subject myself and family to the hazards of such a visit. Those antislavery opinions give me more uneasiness just now than your horrible views on the subject of religion, bad as these last are." The young heretic nevertheless did visit his home in January. On the day after he arrived former schoolmates surrounded him on the main street of Falmouth and in an ugly temper told him that his presence would not be tolerated. He took leave of his family the following day. "It was a heavy moment when I left them," he wrote later. "It was exile. As I was driven by our faithful coachman, James Parker, across the bridge and along the meadows, it was with a feeling that I should never see them again." On the train he happened to meet his father's eldest brother who accompanied him to his boat upbraiding him bitterly. "I sat on the deck humiliated and weeping," he records.[20]

In the meantime Professor Benjamin Hedrick, approaching his thirtieth birthday, was doing well at the University of North Carolina. As head of the chemistry department he was successful and well liked. In the fall of 1856, however, he ran into trouble. It became known in Chapel Hill that he intended to vote for John C. Fremont for President if the Republican electoral ticket were formed in the state. In September an article appeared in the Raleigh *Standard* demanding that "our schools and seminaries of learning be scrutinized; and if black Republicans be found in them let them be driven out." This was followed by one signed "Alumnus" charging that there was such a professor at Chapel Hill and suggesting that his "poisonous influence" be extirpated and he be compelled to leave.[21] Hedrick has been pictured as a mild and gentle professor, and Hinton Helper wrote that one of his virtues was "modesty, amounting almost to bashfulness."[22] These traits may not have been inconsistent with the ones attributed to him by President David L. Swain of the University, but if not they were an unusual combination. "Hedrick has the courage of a lion and the obstinacy of a mule," Swain wrote a trustee. "He can neither be frightened, coaxed nor persuaded in anything."[23] Against the President's advice the professor fired back a double-barreled rejoinder at "Alumnus." He could fill many columns with "good 'black Republican' documents," he wrote, "all written by the most eminent Southern statesmen, beginning with Washington," and with those worthies he could not "believe that slavery is preferable to freedom." He denied to the trustees that he was an abolitionist or that he had sought to disseminate his views among students, but he stoutly defended his opinions, his right to hold them, and the cause of academic freedom. A trustee pronounced his opinions "vile pollutions," and called on his fellow trustees "to expel that traitor to all Southern interests from the seat he now so unworthily fills." Hedrick's colleagues of the faculty deserted him and charged him with "treason to his section and to the Constitution." The students' contribution was to burn Hedrick in effigy. Then the trustees, in the immemorial words reserved for such occasions, resolved that the professor had "destroyed his usefulness" at the University. Hedrick visited his home at Salisbury a few days after his dismissal, was mobbed, and literally driven from the town. He was soon on his way to join the exiles.

Hinton Helper had left Salisbury to begin his Northern exile just four months before Hedrick was mobbed in the town. It was in Salisbury that he had begun and written a large part of his famous book, *The Impending Crisis of the South: How to Meet It*. He had left the town in June, 1856, on good terms with its citizens. But upon the publication of *The Impending Crisis* in New York a year later his friends turned against him. A Salisbury paper denounced him as a "traitor to his native sod and native skies," and a "traducer of the South."[24] The Raleigh *Standard*, which had been largely responsible for firing and exile of Professor Hedrick, pronounced his fellow townsman Helper "beneath the level of contempt and infamy," because, said the editor, "There are some treasons so gross, so palpable, and so heinous that the whole world sees them, and all good men curse them, and then say no more."[25] But more was said—much more. Another Raleigh paper ironically informed Helper that he had "so many *ardent admirers* in this State," that if he would "only return to it, he may be assured that he is so well liked, that he will never be permitted to go away again. We will give him a *home in the bosom of his native soil.*"[26] Garrison's Boston *Liberator* reported that Helper believed that if he ever returned to North Carolina he would be "mobbed, perhaps killed almost immediately."[27] The hatred of Helper aroused in the South by the publication of his book was as nothing compared with the excitement two years later when the book became a national issue.

The only one of this group of exiles who found it possible to continue to live in the South and carry on his work after his conversion to abolitionism became known was John G. Fee of Kentucky. He was able to do so only under great difficulties and under continuous threats to his life. To Fee the idea of compromise was revolting. His friend and supporter Cassius M. Clay pled with him to make some concessions to expediency. "I am in heart as much a higher law man as you are," Clay confessed to Fee, "and if we were in Massachusetts we could carry it out; but here we cannot." Fee's reply was: "The utterance of moral truth should not be confined to geographical limits."[28] His was a crusade "not of expediencies, but of absolute right."[29] Between Cassius Clay and John Fee lay the issue that divided Southern antislavery men who were able to remain in the South from those who were driven into exile. Although they were personal friends, Clay denounced Fee's position publicly as "revolutionary, insurrectionary and dangerous."[30]

In defiance of hostile threats and the censure of the Presbyterian Synod of Kentucky, Fee founded three antislavery churches in the state and labored with them for years. "I was waylaid, shot at, clubbed, stoned; by force kept out of church houses," he wrote. Services were conducted at times with an armed guard posted in the surrounding woods. In 1855 he founded an antislavery school, later known as Berea College, in Madison County. For good measure he imported a teacher from Oberlin and opened Berea to Negro students. The school building was once burned to the ground, and Fee was six times taken in hand by violent mobs. He never offered physical resistance, but was pleased to note that in some mysterious way best known to a divine providence, "sudden destruction came upon the leaders" of these mobs, one by one.[31] With God clearly on his side Fee persevered. Not until the hysteria aroused by John Brown's Raid did he yield. The misinterpretation of some remarks Fee made on Brown at Henry Ward Beecher's church in New York incited a band of sixty-two citizens to descend on Berea and demand the removal of Fee and his faculty in ten days. Fee and his friends took up their exile in Cincinnati in 1859.[32]

By the mid-fifties the center of abolitionist agitation had shifted from Boston, New York, and the Western provinces to the national capital. The leading lobbyists, pamphleteers, and propagandists congregated there, especially while Congress was in session. And it was in Washington that the new generation of Southern exiles gradually formed their little coterie in the fifties, drawn together both by their common interests in a cause and by the expatriate's sense of isolation. Daniel Goodloe was the first to arrive. Having won his spurs as a Whig campaigner in 1844, he received an appointment in the Navy Department under President Taylor's administration and returned to live in the Capital in the spring of 1849. He was ousted from the position in the spring of 1853, according to his Autobiography, "for having written a letter in approval of Uncle Tom's Cabin, which was published . . . in the author's Key to her story." He remained in the city as a newspaper man, and eventually became editor of the influential abolitionist paper, *The National Era*. Conway came to Washington in September, 1854, to fill the pulpit of the Unitarian church. Helper, after the publication of his *Impending Crisis*, had considerable business to transact in the Capital. Hedrick, after his dismissal from Chapel Hill, was in and out of the city, and a permanent resident after receiving an appointment in the Patent Office in 1861. Fee came only as an occasional visitor, and was not a part of the Washington coterie.

One center of the group's activities and social life was the *National Era*. The editor, Dr. Gamaliel Bailey, who became an abolitionist at the time of the Lane debate, was an associate editor of James G. Birney's *Philanthropist*, and then editor after Birney moved to New York. The *National Era* was founded as the voice of the Washington lobby organized by Theodore Weld, and Bailey became editor in 1847. Weld retired to the background, but his influence remained a dominant one. It was in the columns of the *National Era* that Harriet Beecher Stowe's *Uncle Tom's Cabin* first appeared. Of the scores of antislavery papers, this one, according to an authority, "more than any other publication, became the organ for the antislavery host."[33] Goodloe edited the paper while Bailey was away in the summers and after the editor died in 1859, the North Carolinian took over the position himself. At the climax of the national crisis, therefore, one of the leading antislavery journals of the country was in the hands of a Southern editor.

Mr. and Mrs. Bailey established a *salon* that was a favorite rendezvous for the Southern exiles in Washington. Hinton Helper, described as "a tall, slim, peculiar looking person, with short black hair, whiskers and mustaches, a very bronzed complexion, and a fierce military expression,"[34] found a welcome at the Bailey soirees, and so did Conway and Goodloe. Antislavery congressmen, distinguished foreign visitors, and the lobbyists for abolition gathered there regularly. Conway thought that the influence of these entertainments had never been appreciated by historians of the antislavery movement. "Nothing in Washington was more brilliant than the Bailey soiree," he wrote. "The bright and pretty 'Yankee' ladies got up theatricals, charades, tableaux, and the White House receptions were dull in comparison."[35]

Young Conway's Unitarian church was another focus of exile interest. He had answered the call to this pastorate on trial and with grave misgivings regarding proslavery sentiment in Washington. He took special pains to make his position clear to the parishioners, and in his sermon immediately preceding the election of the minister he went so far as to declare slavery "the greatest of all sins." "Within fifteen minutes from the utterance of that sentiment I was elected minister," he records, "with but two contrary votes." He was vastly pleased. He knew, he said, that his position was considered "enviable by other young ministers," the salary "ample for a young bachelor of those days," and parishioners came from the upper crust of Washington society. "My discourses were written for an educated and refined congregation," he said, "there being in it none of the so-called working class and no negroes." He was gratified to see his sermons reported in the *National Intelligencer*, which had quite a circulation across the Potomac, and he was conscious that "the fact of my being an antislavery Virginian gave weight to my words." When grave political utterances were being pondered for the Sunday sermon Conway consulted Daniel Goodloe, who was a faithful member of his flock.[36]

The sectional controversy in which the exiles of the fifties participated had much wider ramifications than the one in which the previous generation of exiles took part. The Men of the Thirties were concerned almost exclusively with moral problems, and they were still able to see that although slavery itself was confined to the South the North was deeply involved in the evil. The Men of the Fifties were caught in the ever-widening whirlpool of sectional disputes, disputes that involved not merely moral recriminations, but economic rivalries, invidious comparison of social institutions, political systems, industry, agriculture, almost every phase of life in which there were differences between the rival sections. The contributions that the exiles made to the literature of this controversy gained special attention because the authors spoke as Southerners.

The most dispassionate analysis by one of the exiles was by Goodloe in a pamphlet he called *Inquiry into the Causes Which Have Retarded the Accumulation of Wealth and Increase of Population in the Southern States*. His approach was largely economic, but his argument was founded upon moral assumptions. The argument was that capital invested in slaves was unproductive and served only to appropriate the wages of labor. What Goodloe meant was that slavery was socially unproductive, and his analysis of retarded industry and commerce was in that vein. In the columns of the *National Era* he developed the argument further with comparisons of taxation policy in Northern and Southern states, and within the South itself he contrasted taxes on slave property with those on manufacturing and commerce. His conclusion was that "Slavery sits like the Old Man of the Sea upon the necks of the people, paralyzing every effort at improvement."[37]

In another publication, *The Southern Platform*, Goodloe attempted, he said, "to awaken in Southern minds those noble and generous sentiments of freedom which animated their ancestors." He compiled lengthy testimony from the works of the founding fathers of the South, mainly of the Revolutionary generation, and sought by that means to give back to Southerners their heritage of liberalism. Professor Hedrick appealed to the same authorities in his controversy with the trustees of the University of North Carolina. In declaring against slavery on principle, he said he "but uttered the sentiments of four-fifths of the best Southern patriots from the Revolution down to the present day; and I may add, of the majority of the people among whom I was born and educated."[38]

John Fee based his book, *An Anti-Slavery Manual*, not only upon the heritage from the fathers, but upon economic principles, and upon the Bible. "We appeal to the Bible," he wrote, "because the apologists of Slavery also appeal to it; and as we believe, by false interpretations, make it to support despotism of the grossest form." He also appealed to the scriptures because "The Bible in our country, is the standard of right. Its decisions are final." In grappling with the pro-slavery thinkers, Fee devoted most of his attention to scriptural texts and interpretations and gave only incidental treatment to the economic and social issues.

Overshadowing in influence and notoriety all other Southern anti-slavery tracts, and for a time all tracts Northern or Southern, was Hinton Helper's *Impending Crisis of the South*, published in June 1857. The book marked a new departure in the slavery controversy. As Helper pictured it, the struggle lay not between right and wrong, between North and South, nor between slave and master, but between the white non-slaveholder and the slave owners. It was not primarily a moral nor a sectional conflict, but a class conflict, and it was to be waged in the South itself. "Non-slaveholders of the South!" exclaimed the author in words that recall Marx's *Manifesto* of the previous decade, "recollect that slavery is the only impediment to your progress and prosperity, that is stands diametrically opposed to all needful reforms, that it seeks to sacrifice you entirely for the benefit of others.... Will you not abolish it?"[39] He dedicated his book to that class and appealed to it in incendiary words repeatedly throughout the work. At times he suggests that the class to which he appeals can attain justice only through violence and vengeance. At other times he appears to assume that peaceable methods will suffice, but whether his proposals were peaceable or not they were always couched in the rhetoric of violence.

"I have considered my subject," he said in his preface, "more particularly with reference to its economic aspects as regards the whites—not with reference, except in a very slight degree, to its humanitarian or religious aspects."[40] Like Goodloe and Fee, however, he quoted at length from the great Southern humanitarians of the Revolutionary generation to support his argument. His most important theme was an invidious comparison of North and South. By the use of the United States census of 1850 and methods of which few trained statisticians would have approved he attempted to demonstrate the overwhelming superiority of the free states in agriculture, manufacturing, trade, and wealth, in libraries, schools, churches, and literature. Professing to be "a true hearted southerner . . . who would rather have his native clime excel than be excelled" he claimed to be "deeply abashed and chagrined at the disclosures of the comparison thus instituted."[41]

In the grand manner of the inspired reformer and revolutionist, Helper simplified all the causes of Southern ills to one great cause, all the South's ills to one great ill, and all the possible remedies to one great remedy. "The causes which have impeded the progress and prosperity of the South," he wrote, "which have dwindled our commerce, and other similar pursuits, . . . sunk a large majority of our people in galling poverty and ignorance, rendered a small minority conceited and tyrannical, and driven the rest away from their homes, entailed upon us a humiliating dependence on the Free States; disgraced us in the recesses of our own souls, and brought us under reproach in the eyes of all civilized and enlightened nations—may be traced to one common source . . . *Slavery!*"[42] The simple remedy for the simple cause was of course abolition.

His program of action called for the organization of a party of non-slaveholding whites who would call a convention and write an abolitionist platform. They would firmly withhold cooperation from slaveholders, whether in politics, religion, or society, and boycott slaveholding physicians, lawyers, merchants, parsons, and newspapers. The antislavery party on attaining power would levy a tax of $60 on every slaveholder for every slave in his possession on July 4, 1863. This tax would be raised to $100 in 1869, and increased periodically until slavery would disappear by July 4, 1876. The proceeds of the tax would be used to colonize all the millions of liberated slaves in Africa, Central America, or in some distant corner of the United States.[43] It was as simple as that—and as impractical.

Although Helper promised in his preface to treat the slaveholders with fairness and moderation, he quickly lapsed into the vituperative epithets of the abolitionist agitators. He described them as "depraved," "detestable," and as "tyrants," and employed the old stereotype "lords of the lash."[44] Because of their "illicit intercourse with 'the mother of harlots'" the slaveholders, he declared had "become so depraved, that there is scarcely a spark of honor or magnanimity to be amongst them."[45] They were actually "more criminal than common murderers."[46] In the revolutionary violence of his rhetoric Helper could equal and at times outstrip Garrison himself. "We have no modifications to propose, no compromises to offer, nothing to retract," vowed Helper. "Frown, Sirs, fret, foam, prepare your weapons, threat, strike, shoot, stab, bring on civil war, dissolve the Union . . . do what you will, Sirs, you can neither foil nor intimidate us; our purpose is as firmly fixed as the eternal pillars of Heaven; we have determined to abolish slavery, and, so help us God, abolish it we will!"[47] He was, so he declared, "a thorough and uncompromising abolitionist,"[48] "an abolitionist, in the fullest sense of the term."[49] He hoped that his book would make of every Southerner who read it "a thorough, inflexible, practical abolitionist."[50]

Of course not very many of the Southerners to whom Helper addressed his book read it. The book achieved only a moderate success even in the North until the fall of 1859. Then a committee of Republicans reprinted an abridged edition called a *Compendium* for use in their campaign. And in December, while the hysteria over John Brown's Raid was at its height, the critical contest for the speakership of the House revolved entirely around the endorsement of Helper's *Compendium* by Republican candidates for the office. Stimulated by this agitation and the free advertising by Southern congressmen, sales of Helper's *Impending Crisis* reached 142,000 by the fall of 1860, and "literally millions" of the *Compendium* were circulated in the North.[51] This meant that the North Carolinian's book surpassed in circulation all previous abolitionist tracts. "It is Helper on the counter, Helper at the stand, Helper in the shop, Helper out of the shop, Helper here, Helper there, Helper everywhere," exclaimed Horace Greeley.[52]

The more he was celebrated in the North, the more he was defamed and proscribed and outlawed in the South. Copies of his book were publicly burned in his native state and in other parts of the region. A congressman accused him of theft and dishonesty in Washington. Laws of Southern states were construed to make it a penal offense to own, read, or circulate the *Impending Crisis*. A farmer was fined and jailed in Maryland, and three men were reported hanged in Arkansas for these offenses; faculty members of Universities in Virginia, North Carolina, and Georgia were dismissed for expressing approval of the book.[53] Daniel Worth, a North Carolina parson, was sentenced to two years' imprisonment for circulating Helper's work. He fled to New York in 1860 while under bond, thus becoming the last of the ante-bellum exiles.

John Brown's raid on Harper's Ferry in October, 1859, placed the severest of all strains upon the burdened consciences of the exiles. John Brown, the perpetrator of the brutal Potawottomie massacre, together with his pikes and pistols and rifles and his band of fanatical followers, seemed to offer flesh-and-blood evidence that the South had been right about the abolitionists all along. The Harper's Ferry raid proved, so the South believed, that the abolitionists would stop at nothing—including subversive tactics, conspiracy, murder, treason, and slave insurrection—in order to gain their end. Northerners and Southerners in the North were therefore watched closely for any reaction they might betray to news of the raid and to the execution of Brown and his men.

Only the most extreme Northern abolitionists and some of the New England intellectual aristocracy gave unqualified endorsement to John Brown and his raid, though many others expressed admiration for the man and outrage at his execution. The reactions of the exiles ranged from qualified approval to enthusiastic adulation. While Goodloe "entirely disapproved and condemned the conduct of Brown" in the *National Era*, he willingly paid tribute to Brown's "heroic behavior" during his captivity.[54] Likewise John Fee sought to make a distinction between John Brown's spirit and his methods. Speaking at Henry Ward Beecher's church in Brooklyn, New York, Fee declared: "We want more John Browns; not in manner of action, but in spirit of consecration; not to go with carnal weapons, but with spiritual."[55]

Such fine-spun distinctions between spirit and deed seemed unreal to the South. Angelina Weld and Sarah Grimke did not hesitate over fine distinction. They were reported to have "fully sympathized" with "the bitter and desperate feelings" which inspired John Brown. Angelina took to bed over the prospect of the hero's execution. "What a glorious spectacle is now before us," exclaimed her sister Sarah over that event. "Last night I went in spirit to the martyr. It was my privilege to enter into sympathy with him; to go down . . . into the depths where he has travailed, and feel his past exercises, his present sublime position."[56] The two South Carolinians further identified themselves with the martyr by burying the bodies of two of John Brown's raiders on the grounds of their school at Eagleswood.[57]

Moncure Daniel Conway's first reaction to the Harper's Ferry raid was to condemn it. Caught up in the whirlwind of passions that John Brown aroused in the North, however, Conway changed. "By that Northern storm I was carried off my feet," he later admitted. The "calm judgment" of his first reaction, he wrote, "was swept away by the enthusiasm and tears of my antislavery comrades."[58] In a sermon delivered two days after the execution of Brown, Conway gave the old abolitionist a eulogy that equaled those delivered by Emerson and Thoreau. "Is John Brown a hero?" he asked. "It will one day be told, to prove the stupidity of this age, that such a question was asked by sane men.... Think not that these are the words of enthusiasm," he added; "they are the words of truth and soberness." He then predicted that the man his native state had hung as a criminal and traitor "will become our saint."[59] Many years later, in a mood of somewhat greater soberness than he attained in 1859, Conway wrote that John Brown had "inflicted on America sequels of slavery worse than the disease."[60]

Notes

1. B. Letters, 499–500.
2. Birney, *Sisters*, 241.
3. Conway, *Auto*, II, 300.
4. Helper, *Noonday Exigencies*, 155–56; Lefler, *Helper*, 31; Henderson, *North Carolina*, II, 203.
5. Fee, *Auto*, 9, 20.
6. *Noonday Exigencies*, 155.
7. Conway, *Auto*, I, 72.
8. Ibid., 89.
9. Ibid., 39.
10. Ibid., 89.
11. Ibid., 65.
12. Ibid., 72, 82.
13. Fee, *Auto*, 14, 17.
14. Hamilton, Hedrick, 9.
15. Helper, *Noonday Exigencies*, 158–59.
16. Bassett, 47–52.
17. Fee, *Auto*, 20.
18. Conway, *Auto*, I, 128.
19. Conway, P & P, 4.
20. Conway, *Auto*, I, 188–91.
21. Hamilton, Hedrick, 10.
22. Bassett, A–S Leaders, 32.
23. Hamilton, Hedrick, 26.
24. Salisbury *Carolina Watchman*, September 22, August 18, 1857, quoted in Theodore V. Theobald, "Hinton Rowan Helper and *The Impending Crisis*" (MA Thesis, Columbia, 1949), 35.

25. Raleigh *Standard*, July 8, Sept. 16, 1857, in ibid., 35.
26. Raleigh *Weekly Register*, Dec. 7, 1859, in ibid., 93.
27. *Liberator*, Dec. 25, 1857, ibid., 93.
28. Fee, *Auto*, 126.
29. Ibid., 129.
30. Ibid., 103.
31. Ibid., 124.
32. Ibid., 146–47.
33. Barnes & Dumond, WG Letters, xxv.
34. N. Y. *Herald*, Jan. 10, 1861, in Theobald, 135.
35. Conway, *Auto*, I, 211–12.
36. Conway, *Auto*, I, 189, 192, 239, 248.
37. Goodloe, *Inquiry*, 13.
38. Hamilton, 14.
39. Helper, *Crisis*, 359.
40. *Crisis*, v.
41. *Crisis*, 12.
42. *Crisis*, 25.
43. *Crisis*, 155–57.
44. *Crisis*, 53, 147.
45. *Crisis*, 153.
46. *Crisis*, 140.
47. *Crisis*, 187.
48. *Crisis*, 113.
49. *Crisis*, 25.
50. *Crisis*, 32.
51. Lefler, *Helper*, 25.
52. *Tribune* quoted in Theobald, 84.
53. Theobald, 107–8.
54. *Nat. Era*, Dec. 8, 1859.
55. Fee, *Auto*, 146–7.
56. C. Birney, *Sisters*, 282–83.
57. Mattie Griffith to Maria Chapman, James Thome quoted by [?], Helper to Lysander Spooner, Oct. 28, '59. [This citation appears at the bottom of the page in Woodward's handwriting and we assume it belongs here.]
58. Conway, *Auto*, I, 302–3.
59. Redpath, Echoes of Harper's Ferry, 353–55.
60. Conway, *Auto*, II, 4.

FLEMING LECTURE III

The Way of the Exile

THE HISTORY OF the Southern exiles is a chapter in the history of the Romantic spirit in America. It is an obscure and neglected chapter, but it is at the same time a curiously significant one. The three decades from 1830 to 1860 were the golden age of romance, and the spirit flourished as vigorously in all its contradictory varieties on this side of the Atlantic as on the other. But while in England, France, or Germany all species flowered side by side in the same garden, in America they were as highly regionalized as the economy and its great staple crops. If the purchaser sought transcendentalism, perfectionism, or any of the brave new worlds of the future, utopias that were to be realized by radical and revolutionary changes, his market was in the land of the bean and the cod or its colonies to the Westward. If, on the other hand, his fancy turned instead to antique tastes and ran to utopias with feudal trimmings or "Greek Democracies," his market lay in the land of cotton and tobacco and its western colonies.

In Europe it was different. There the romantic philosopher who was convinced that man's best hope lay in swift retreat to the ideals and manners of the past could exchange ideas daily with the romantic who was equally persuaded that salvation lay in renouncing the past completely and embracing the future wholly. In America there appeared to be no common meeting ground between the romantic extremes short of the battlefield.

One interesting aspect of the Southern exiles is that they did bring into curious relationship Charleston and Boston, the Blue Grass of Kentucky and the "Burnt Over" district of New York, the Alabama slave frontier and the free-soil Michigan frontier. They did so, of course, only at the cost of becoming converts of the North and being labeled apostates, renegades, and traitors in the South. The spiritual cost of the transition was heavy, if difficult to reckon. Our first two lectures have been concerned with what the two generations of Southern exiles did and said. The third lecture will be concerned largely with the effect of their experience upon the exiles themselves and upon their thought.

Throughout the years of their exile, which in the majority of cases ended only with death, these people continued to think and speak of themselves as Southerners. It is true that Angelina Grimke in moments of impatience or exasperation could address her compatriots as "you Southerners," but she never forgot that she was a native of Charleston and often called attention to the fact. The problems that absorbed the attention of the exiles were Southern problems; the audience for whom they intended their message was for the most part a Southern audience; the dreams and ideals by which they justified their sacrifice and tried to give their lives meaning could only be realized in the South. And yet they themselves were proscribed in the South and their books and pamphlets were outlawed and systematically suppressed there.

In 1836 Angelina Grimke published her *Appeal to Southern Women* and shipped a quantity of copies to South Carolina. Most of them were seized by postmasters and publicly burned. When the mayor of Charleston learned that Angelina intended to visit her family he informed her mother that the police had been instructed to prevent her coming ashore from the steamer or from communicating by letter or otherwise with any person in the city, and that if she did succeed in landing she would be arrested and imprisoned until her ship sailed. Feeling in the city was so intense, according to her friends, that she could not expect to escape personal violence at the hands of a mob.[1] Thereafter neither she nor Sarah ever attempted to return to Charleston.

In October, 1835, a public meeting of citizens in James G. Birney's former home in Alabama resolved to "view with feelings of abhorrence and contempt" the activities of their former fellow citizen who "went North, and associated himself with the fanatics Thompson, Garrison, etc., to preach a crusade against the people of the South, to spirit up their slaves to insurrection . . . and bring down upon our country destruction." A friend came from Huntsville to tell him that should he return there he "would be in immediate danger of death or some great personal harm."[2] His former law partner in the city, a man Birney called "a bosom-friend," declined to handle a law suit for the collection of debts owed Birney, and Birney was warned that it would not be safe to send his son to receive money collected.[3] In Kentucky "The younger members of his family," wrote Birney's son, "were exposed to rude speeches and unpleasant incidents," and Birney himself "was regarded by many as an enemy to the peace of the community."[4]

Conway found his home community in Virginia "chilled by the sneers and coldness of those who once loved me; . . . my most intimate friends of former days would not appear with me in the street."[5] And he left feeling that "thenceforth I had no home there for ever."[6] Thome and Allan and Helper and Hedrick and Goodloe all found themselves in much the same plight. The burden of their common refrain was, You can't go home again. It repeats itself over and over again in their papers and memoirs.

Physical exile was perhaps of less importance than the breaking of ties between the exiles and their families. As a group they manifest the pride of family name and the deep attachment to kin so characteristic of Southerners of that day and later. That was true even of the Grimke sisters, although their revolt from the Southern tradition seems to have had its seed in family friction in the home. The first thought of Angelina when she learned that Garrison had published her letter that identified her publicly with abolitionism was of her family. "To have my name," she wrote, "not so much *my* name as the name of Grimke, associated with that of the despised Garrison, seemed like bringing disgrace upon my *family*, not myself alone. I felt as though the name had been tarnished in the eyes of thousands who had before loved and revered it. I cannot describe the anguish of my soul."[7]

In rare instances the family tie was strong enough to survive the strain. The case of James Thome is hardly a clear one, however, for unity was preserved only by the family becoming converts to the views of the exiled son. When Arthur Thome, Kentucky slaveholder and Presbyterian elder, heard that his son was going to New York to speak before a convention of the American Anti-Slavery Society, he was convinced that James had lost his mind and hastened aboard his steamboat bound up the Ohio to detain him.[8] He could not find his son. But later James made "staunch abolitionists" of his family including his father, who emancipated all his slaves.[9] John Fee made valiant and prolonged attempts to convert his father to his way of thinking, but only succeeded in making him a more stubborn pro-slavery man. Eventually the breach between father and son was completed when the elder Fee sold into slavery three of the free-born children of a woman the younger Fee had bought from his father and liberated.[10] Conway managed to keep up a strained and tenuous relation with his father and mother, even though they would not receive him. But he found that "many of those whose blood I shared regarded me as a leper."[11] Judge Grimke died before his daughters completed the road to apostasy. Mrs. Grimke kept up a tearful correspondence with the heretics until 1839, when she died an unrepentant slaveholder. Their distinguished Charleston kinsmen, prominent nullificationists and secessionists, severely censured the sisters. And a Charleston paper described them as "two fanatical women, forgetful of the obligations of a respected name, and indifferent to the feelings of their most worthy kinsmen, the Barnwells and the Rhetts."[12] Their sister Eliza stood by them loyally through abolitionism, feminism, perfectionism, and anarchism, though detesting all these doctrines; but finally in 1847 drew the line when she learned that they had willfully abandoned Sabbath observance. At that point she wrote ending all intercourse with the renegades and informing them that "her doors would be forever closed against them."[13]

Birney's family attachments were profound, particularly those with his aged father, and his solicitude for them and the suffering his heresies caused them dogged each successive step of his progress from conservatism to radicalism. Knowing this, his sister appealed to his consciousness of "our Fathers deep solicitude and continuing attachment" and implored him not to "bring sorrow nay unmingled grief, upon a tender aged parent."[14] The elder Birney threatened and for a time did break off relations with the erring son, but Birney persisted both in his radicalism and in his affection for his father. He confessed to Lewis Tappan that he was "sometimes almost borne down to the ground" by family problems. "My nearest relatives have forsaken me—they think I am mad, and that I endanger and degrade myself and them—the proud hold me in derision,—the partner of my life is . . . under incurable affliction."[15]

As a rule the Southern abolitionists began their crusades by foreswearing bitterness of spirit and promising charity to all. John Fee "endeavored to speak in a spirit of love and kindness; for we know the difficulties of those involved in slaveholding."[16] Birney did not wish "to call the slaveholders . . . *enemies*—to treat them as such" but by "forbearance, and kindness, and sober argument" to show them the error of their ways.[17] And yet even Birney, the most consistently moderate and forbearing of the exiles, after he had cut his ties with the home soil and suffered severe persecution could describe Southern slaveholders in his paper as "the most heartless and insulting aristocracy that any institution defying God has ever raised up" and call upon the North to "AROUSE,—or the chains, prepared by the slave-holding aristocracy of the South, will be fastened, hopelessly fastened on us."[18] Bitterness of spirit seemed to grow upon him as the years of exile lengthened. In 1850 he wrote his sister, refusing an interview with her: "It has been my practice for many years to have no intercourse with oppressors of their fellow-beings, except so far as *business* might require. That you are one I entertain no doubt; and that you are becoming an old one certainly makes the case no better. A disease of whatever nature—moral or otherwise,—in my own family—among my natural friends,—is surely not less to be deprecated than when it is a long way off and confined to others."[19]

So far as the exiles were concerned, slavery was, in Birney's words, "a long way off and confined to others." The exiles became as isolated from the social evil that obsessed their thoughts as were the New England abolitionists.

Outcasts from the South, the exiles found no cordial acceptance awaiting them in the North save among the abolitionist cliques, who were often at war among themselves. And it should be remembered that the extreme abolitionists constituted an unpopular and persecuted minority in the North, with constant difficulties of their own. "Again and again have I met these exiles," wrote Moncure Conway, "—the Helpers, Underwoods, Goodloes; and sometimes tender women, as the Grimkes and Mattie Griffith . . . who had once found homes and bright hopes in the South; . . . and they were forced to wander to uncongenial climates and strange lands, to begin life anew, if heart and strength for that remained. . . . and though the anti-Slavery man was no longer cast into a dungeon as was Garrison, or murdered as was Lovejoy, there was a bleak Siberia in the heart of every community to which he was sent."[20]

It is true that the bleakness of the new Siberia was tempered by fortune for some of the exiles. "There are about ten millions of dollars in that congregation," a friend of Conway's informed the young parson of his new charge in Cincinnati in 1860.[21] The abolitionist minister from Virginia was the sensation of the pulpit, and Northern congregations hung upon his stirring words as the war crisis deepened. To a born notoriety seeker such as Hinton Helper the national furor that the political crisis over his book created in 1859–1860 was the very bread of life. The colossal sale of his book however, did not make him wealthy or even well off, for by 1860 he was in financial difficulties. There was undoubtedly tangible compensation, in degrees varying with the individual, in the flattering acclaim accorded the exiles by the abolitionist elite and the intellectual aristocracy that sympathized with them in the North. Helper indicates clearly enough that he enjoyed having his views taken seriously by Garrison and Wendell Phillips. Conway always treasured the attention he received from the philosophers and poets of Concord, and he records in detail being received by President Lincoln along with a delegation that included Wendell Phillips and two of John Brown's fellow conspirators, Dr. S. G. Howe and George L. Stearns.[22] And it is quite apparent that the young provincials, fresh from Virginia, Carolina, and Kentucky, were dazzled for a time by the brilliant soirees and receptions in Washington to which they were welcomed and where they rubbed elbows with the great and near great of the antislavery politicians. There were plenty of darker experiences and some actual suffering, but these bright moments constituted a sort of compensation. *Even so* the Southerners were never entirely at home. Conway, for example, describes a sudden loneliness that overwhelmed him in the midst of an abolitionist rally in New England, and his friend Edward Emerson, son of the Sage of Concord, writes that the Virginian always carried with him "the feelings of an exile."[23]

The way of the exiles of the previous generation had been more rugged and lacking in some of the tangible compensations that tempered for the Men of the Fifties the ardors of their Siberia. At the close of his campaign for President in 1840 and after his return from England, Birney found himself in serious financial straits. He had deliberately chosen as *his* share of his father's estate in 1829 all of the slaves and had, of course, promptly given them their freedom. He was heavily obligated by the failure of a friend whose note he had endorsed, and was unable to collect bad debts that were due. He was compelled to withdraw two of his sons from Andover and to sell landed property upon which he had relied to support him in comfort in his old age. In 1841 he married the sister-in-law of Gerrit Smith, the very wealthy abolitionist and philanthropist of Peterboro, New York, and for a time settled in the same town. His wife was a lady of means in her own name, but such was the stubborn Birney pride that he absolutely refused to permit her to ease his financial embarrassment.

Instead Birney moved his family in November, 1841, to the remote frontier wilderness of upper Michigan and settled them in Saginaw, a raw community of 130 souls, visited almost daily by Indians. It was, according to Birney, "a miserable, population" given over to "lying, drinking, gambling, backbiting," who "would be pirates if they had courage."[24] There was no school and no church, and for part of the year the place was frozen in.[25] "I am here, at one of the ends of the earth," he wrote his Eastern friends, "endeavoring by working all I am capable of, by saving all that a close economy can save, to pay off what remains of my liabilities."[26] There he remained for twelve years. "I am tied to a stake," he wrote Elizur Wright, "and I must stand it—but at times it is so grievous to me, that I think I cannot stand it long."[27] When the Liberty Party rallied to nominate him for the Presidency again he asked them: "How then would they like to have their candidate for the highest office of the Gov't a laboring man—one engaged daily in farming drudgery ... hoeing potatoes or rolling logs, or chopping his own firewood or cleaning his own shoes?"[28] He fell back upon a hard, proud stoicism to stay him after his partial paralysis in 1845. "I have tried to amuse myself by writing," he entered in his Diary in 1850. "But there is hardly interest enough felt by any one even to read the pieces that I write." He published them in small local papers or occasionally sent them to the Boston and New York journals of his old associates. "I feel now," he confessed in his Diary, "perhaps, more than I ever did before—it may be because being more helpless ... the want of some person to feel an interest in what interests me with whom I can compare ideas. I do not know such an one in this part of the country."[29]

One of Birney's most embarrassing debts in the early 1840's was one that he owed to Sarah Grimke. The Welds, with whom Sarah made her home, were themselves in serious financial difficulties at the time, and Birney knew that. Theodore Weld wrote Lewis Tappan in 1840 that unless he could collect money owed him by the Anti-Slavery Society within a few days, "I don't see but we must *stop eating*—at least we shall be pretty sure to stop SLEEPING."[30] The sisters inherited slaves on the death of their mother in 1839, but like Birney they refused to profit by the inheritance. Since the slaves stubbornly declined to leave South Carolina and the laws of the state prohibited manumission, the sisters deeded them to a brother with the understanding that they should keep their wages.[31] The Weld domestic arrangements were complicated by importing two former Grimke slaves with whom the sisters insisted upon living as equals. One of the ex-slaves managed to remain intoxicated in the teetotaling household a good part of the time.

Theodore's baffling throat ailment prevented him from speaking in public for eighteen years, and that in addition to his principles, prevented his accepting a pulpit. He dug his living out of his farm by manual labor. The morale of the establishment seems to have been sustained in large part by the indomitable spirits of Angelina. There was always some new exciting notion of emancipated dress, or correct eating, or improved thinking, or elevated living, or progressive education with which to conduct ardent experiments. She and the painfully shy Sarah were among the first to appear in "Bloomer costume," the latest insignia of emancipated woman, which they wore for several years. Dietary theories practiced on Theodore, Jr., came dangerously near ending the infant's life. Child care and the more elementary branches of cooking had not been regarded in Charleston as an essential part of the education of young ladies of the Grimke sisters' social standing. Angelina's rough-and-ready solution to the problem was to cook up an entire week's rations (strictly vegetarian) on one day and serve cold victuals the rest of the time. She also had positive views upon the subject of interior decoration. On the walls of her parlor she fixed a large picture of kneeling slave framed by some forty other anti-slavery pictures. "It is just such a speaking monument of suffering as we want in our parlor, and suits my fireboard most admirably," she wrote a friend. "We want those who come into our house to see at a glance that we are on the side of the oppressed and the poor."[32] In 1844 Angelina was in a "high tension." William Miller, prophet of the Millerite millennium had foretold the second coming of the Savior by March of that year, and Angelina was pregnant. The baby arrived according to schedule in March. The fact that it was a girl did not disqualify it as an appropriate fulfillment of the prophecy in Angelina's feminist philosophy, but the expected signs and portents failed to materialize and the tension passed off.[33]

"You and dear Sarah and I are a strange trio," Theodore wrote his wife, "different from all the world beside I do believe.... Indeed our tastes, habits, modes of life and all sorts of ways I do believe would be *annoyance* to any family I know of."[34] There was probably much to what Theodore said. Yet in 1853 his "strange trio" entered optimistically into one of the associational or communal-living colonies that were the fad of the day. This was Raritan Bay Union, established in one huge building 250 feet long, not far from the more famous North American Phalanx. The effort of communal living proved to be painful to nearly all concerned, and the Union went the way of all such experiments by 1856. But the Welds rented part of the building and remained to establish a private school they named Eagleswood, run upon the most advanced notions of the day James G. Birney and his wife, who moved from Michigan to join the Union colony in 1853, remained as tenants after the association experiment was abandoned. Birney entered one of his children in the school and took great pleasure in the company of the "strange trio." Distinguished visitors dropped in from time to time—William Cullen Bryant, Horace Greeley, and Amos Bronson Alcott among them. Henry David Thoreau, who spent several weeks at Eagleswood, thought it "a queer place" and did not care for the lingering aspect of "associationism." "Imagine them," he wrote his sister, "sitting close to the wall, all around the hall, with old Quaker-looking men and women here and there. There sat Mrs. Weld and her sister, two elderly gray-headed ladies, the former Angelina in extreme Bloomer costume, which was what you might call remarkable ... and James G. Birney ... with another particularly white head and beard."[35] The whitehaired Birney continued to live there the rest of his life.

Martyrdom in some degree was part of the experience of all the Southern exiles. By his own confession Hinton Helper had courted martyrdom in publishing his *Impending Crisis*. In the early pages of the book he said that he expected to be "subjected to insult and violence," and he rather belligerently warned that he knew "how to repel indignity, and if assaulted ... to make the blow recoil upon the aggressor's head." He would despite expected persecution carry out his design, he declared, "or die in the attempt."[36] And once later in a fit of rage he invaded the floor of the House of Representatives armed with pistol and knife and attacked a congressman who had denounced him.

While none of his fellow exiles was of so inflammable a temperament as Helper, they all carried with them a consciousness of martyrdom. And to be sure this was not entirely an imaginary experience. These men and women *did* suffer persecution. They lost their jobs, jeopardized their future, some of them forfeited their inheritance, and all of them suffered the loss of friends and home ties.

"Martyrdom," wrote Moncure Conway long years after the ardors of his early exile had cooled, "is as demoralizing to the martyr as to the persecutor." It was his own experience, he wrote, that "It distorted my vision." He tells of reading *Uncle Tom's Cabin* before his conversion to abolitionism was complete and before he had suffered for his views. "But I recognized nothing in Mrs. Stowe's romance that was true of slavery in Virginia," he confessed. Then after conversion, exile, and some taste of martyrdom, he reread the novel. "I read 'Uncle Tom's Cabin' with different eyes," he said; "and ... I concluded that Mrs. Stowe's book was a photographic representation of things going on in States farther south."[37] Forty-five years earlier, in his book *Testimonies Concerning Slavery*, he described this new insight as the dropping of scales from his eyes. "Then all society and life seemed to change about me," he wrote. "Had all the slaveholders of Maryland been suddenly seized with an epidemic that they should begin to maltreat their slaves?" he wondered. He concluded that he had been blind to the same evils before. "I searched backward into my past life, and was startled to find that there arose memories, hitherto dumb and sleeping,—memories of greater wrongs than those I now saw,—which joined with these to force upon me the clear perception that there was a great Wrong coiled about the land, and that it was SLAVERY."[38] Years later he admitted that "Slavery was not death, nor the South hell," as he had once heard Garrison say, and that he "knew good people on both sides."[39] But in 1861 it seemed to him that "every step of the South had been marked by perjury, treachery, and lawlessness."[40]

Thrown into the thick of revolutionary ferment in the North, uprooted and cut off irrevocably from their native society and associates, and watched closely for their reaction to every turn of events and shift of doctrine, the exiles absorbed and adopted as their own the stereotyped propaganda image of the South and its way of life that the North was busily creating in the years before the outbreak of war. Universal immorality, cruelty, wickedness, and virtual depravity were all parts of the conventional image.

Conway, Birney, and Helper even accepted the three-class myth of Southern society—the myth that all Southerners were divided into wealthy slaveholders, slaves, and poor white trash. With less excuse than any for overlooking the great body of yeomanry and middle class, for whom indeed he presumed to be the spokesman, Helper declared confidently that five million of the six and a half million white people of the South were "poor white trash."[41] And Conway glibly repeated the Great Conspiracy propaganda in writing that "For many years the Southerners, who held the keys of every Department at Washington, were preparing secretly for the grand coup-d'etat."[42] James Birney lent support to the growing conception of the South as a weak and decadent society. It was "almost in a state of dilapidation," he said, a façade concealing internal conflicts and inherent weaknesses. "Can it be," he asked, "that the free States will longer continue to succumb to such a rotten, decaying concern as the Slaveholding States are evidently coming to be?"[43] In his youthful enthusiasm for the new light he had received, Conway embraced a position on the subject of race amalgamation that was in advance of the great majority of Northern abolitionists. "I, for one," he declared, "am firmly persuaded that the mixture of the blacks and whites is good.... Already we know that nations are great in proportion as they are of mixed races." He believed that the "Negro shall become the chief cornerstone" of the new American race.[44]

Not only the present and the future of American society, but old conceptions of the American past were altered by the exiles to conform to their preoccupations and doctrines. "The unauthorized purchase of Louisiana," wrote Birney, "must be regarded as, in its consequences, the most disastrous event for our country, to be found in its political history."[45] His judgment of the Louisiana Purchase was entirely determined, he admitted by what he pronounced "the odium and the ills which we are now suffering, from having extended and strengthened the empire of Slavery."[46] The encroachments of slavery and what he believed to be the decline in public morals weakened, if it did not destroy, Birney's faith in democracy. "I must say—and I am sorry to believe it true—that our form of government will not do," he confessed in 1842. "My confidence in it as a political structure is greatly impaired."[47] His experience at the hands of excited mobs, what he called the "loathsome" demagoguery of the political campaign of 1840 in which he was a candidate for President, and his own political frustration made him doubt seriously the ability of the mass of people to rule themselves. "It has ever been the sway of demagogues," he believed.[48]

No one of the Southern exiles was so wrapped in doctrinaire clouds and obsessed with the cause but who was aware that both in the South and among Northern friends of the South he was widely regarded as a renegade, an apostate, or a traitor, or that his fundamental loyalty was in some way called into question. Naturally none of the exiles could admit such a charge and maintain his integrity. Each of them protested his devotion and loyalty to his native soil and swore that he cherished the best interests of his people at heart. His enmity was directed not at the people but at their institutions, and more particularly against the "peculiar" institution. He was usually careful at first to distinguish between his feelings toward slavery and his feelings toward the slaveholder, but he was inclined as time passed to forget the distinction. Few of the exiles appeared to notice that Northern abolitionists with whom they were associated so intimately sometimes failed to distinguish between slavery and the South as a whole. Nor did they seem to be aware that the slavery issue was only one of many issues, most of which had no moral content whatever, that were impelling North and South into conflict, and that among those who talked excitedly about slavery were some who had other ends entirely in mind.

In the depression that began in 1837 the Abolitionists brought forward slavery as the scapegoat for the numerous ills that beset the Northern economy. Birney's former editorial associate and Goodloe's employer, Gamaliel Bailey pointed to "the baneful influence of slavery upon the currency, upon our commercial interests, upon manufactures, . . . upon free labor and the respectability of industry."[49] And Birney declared that the North "is a conquered province"[50] of the South, ruled by "a people without commerce, without manufactures, without arts, without industry, whose whole system of management is one of expenses, waste, credit, and procrastination."[51] The Liberty Party made a strong bid for the support of the depressed wheat farmers of the Northwest by seeking the removal of the English Corn Laws that blocked the foreign market for a huge surplus of American wheat. As presidential candidate of the party, Birney campaigned in England in 1840 to end restrictions on American wheat and divert British manufacturers away from American cotton to Indian cotton.[52] The effect would be to shift the advantage of English commercial interests from the South to the North. The Grimke sisters gave their support to the movement and also promoted a boycott of Southern products.[53]

The cause of reform and emancipation might take precedence over national as well as regional interests in the minds of the exiles. In 1840 James Birney opened secret correspondence with the Mexican legation in Washington to encourage the Mexican government to promote the colonization of free Negroes in Texas in order to thwart American expansion in the west.[54] He also wondered if war with England might not be the path to emancipation, and his son thought that "the flames of insurrection, or of foreign war" were the only hope.[55]

For one who was so wholly absorbed in the moral aspects of the sectional struggle, and so other-worldly and idealistic in his outlook, Theodore Weld possessed a remarkable insight into the basic forces underlying that struggle. He thought that those forces were economic and impersonal and that the different nature of the two conflicting systems was determined by climate and geography rather than by morals. "Whoever has not seen," he wrote Birney in 1842, "ever since so long ago as Jackson's veto of the U.S. Bank, that, from every quarter, the elements of conflict, the last conflict between liberty and slavery, were rushing headlong into the central focus—has been asleep." In his view the collision was begun in the struggle over currency. "A mighty pecuniary convulsion must, if of long continuance," he thought, "hurl these two systems of labor and living into mortal conflict."[56]

It was the fear of the evangelist Finney in the early phase of the movement that the sectional bitterness aroused by abolitionist propaganda would eventually result in war. He warned Weld that unless he changed his methods the country would become "embroiled in one common infernal squabble that will roll a wave of blood over the land."[57] When this warning was referred to Weld's Southern converts then studying under Finney at Oberlin, they quickly agreed with Weld that the abolitionist crusade must go forward at all costs. "I have helped to raise the storm," wrote William T. Allan of Alabama. "Shall I now avoid its fury by going into a less dangerous field? God forbid. No, my brother, come life, come death, our stand must be maintained. Onward, then, ye friends of man."[58] And James Thome declared: "As for myself, I am firm." He was more resolute than ever.[59] Through the correspondence of the exiles runs the assumption, tacit or expressed, that the South was doomed—as Birney put it by "the awful judgments of our offended God."[60] War, bloody insurrection, or some other cataclysmic upheaval seems to have been taken for granted as inevitable. But while the gathering war clouds made Theodore Weld "rejoice and leap for joy," his Charleston fiancée had other feelings. "Oh! Brother, how different it is with me," Angelina wrote Weld. "I have long despaired of our being saved except thro' judgement and believed Slavery would thus be overthrown; but as the time approximates I remember that all *my* relatives are at the South and I exceedingly fear and quake, and feel ready to go down and die for them or with them."[61]

When war finally came all the exiles then living took the Union side. Foreseeing the conflict, James Birney expressed the wish before his death in 1857 that his descendants would fight for his views when the war came. Five of his sons who were of military age saw active duty in the Union cause, and all save one of them died as the result of wounds they received or diseases they contracted in the service.[62] Angelina and Theodore Weld were pained to see their son Charles sit out the war at Harvard as a conscientious objector. Sarah and Angelina sent provisions through the blockade to their defiant but hungry rebel sisters in Charleston, but both the abolitionist Grimkes were zealous Unionists. "You see how warlike I have become," Angelina wrote Gerrit Smith. "O, yes—war is better than Slavery."[63] The Tar Heel exiles, Hedrick, Goodloe, and Helper, all took government jobs under the Lincoln administration. Helper went into foreign service as consul in 1861. Goodloe and Hedrick were employed at Washington in various duties.

None of the exiles responded with such intoxication to the rising war spirit in the North as did Moncure Conway. "All of us in those days saw in the uprisen North the splendour of a new heaven and a new earth responding," he wrote.[64] At his sermons in the days immediately before the outbreak of war, "nearly every Sunday the congregation broke into applause" at the stirring words of the young minister.[65] And when the call to arms was sounded, "a new, wild joy," as he described it, possessed his whole being. He dashed off three books of war propaganda in quick succession, advocating emancipation as a war measure. He personally rounded up his father's fugitive slaves, smuggled them dramatically through Baltimore, and settled them in freedom. He made war speeches, consulted with Senator Sumner and Secretary Chase, advised President Lincoln on policy in long letters, and set the generals straight on matters of strategy. In September, 1862, he launched a radical paper in Boston named the *Commonwealth*, backed by George L. Stearns, the capitalist who had been the chief financial supporter of John Brown's raid on Harper's Ferry. Conway's coeditor was Frank B. Sanborn, the fanatical participant in the Brown conspiracy, and the editors often consulted Garrison and Wendell Phillips.[66] Early in the war Conway grasped the fact that the South was resisting, not promoting a revolution.[67] "WE ARE THE REVOLUTIONISTS," he proclaimed. He called the spirit that he invoked "Freedom-frenzy." "Have you any Freedom-frenzy, with its superhuman strength?" he demanded.[68] What the army needed was not McClellans but John Browns as generals, "the fireheart of Peter the Hermit, the iron nerve of Cromwell."[69] Nat Turner and John Brown, "holding commissions from Almighty God," had demonstrated the true revolutionary strategy that should be followed by the Federal army in the South. They had "proved that men unarmed with ideas are as unable to cope with the kindled ferocity of wrong, as they are without guns to cope with half their number of tigers."[70] The "Freedom-frenzy" and the "kindled ferocity of wrong" that Conway preached might, he admitted, engender a lasting hatred of the Union in the hearts of Southerners. Even so, he wrote Lincoln, "for a generation we could hold them quiet," and should the hatred be transmitted to the generation that followed, "that, too, might be held."[71] In 1863 Conway transferred to England and made it his theatre of operations for the duration of the war, doing all within his power by speeches and articles to counteract the diplomacy of Confederate agents and promote the cause of the Union.

The post-war careers of those of the exiles whose lives extended beyond Appomattox need not concern our narrative. Conway continued to live in England for more than thirty years after the war, thus becoming an exile not only from his native region but from his country. Sarah Grimke and Angelina Weld carried on their private war upon Charleston sensibilities even after the fall of the city. Their final assault was to adopt two colored nephews, sons of one of their brothers and a slave woman, take them into their family, educate them, and treat them in every way as acknowledged relatives. The shock of discovering and adopting these nephews temporarily deranged Angelina's mind, but she recovered. Both sisters died in the 1870's, honored by the old guard abolitionists. The other exiles lived out relatively inconspicuous lives and died natural deaths. All, that is, save Hinton Helper, who became as violent a Negrophobe after the war as he had been an abolitionist before. He committed suicide in a room of a dingy boarding house in Washington in 1909.

So far as the record reveals none of the exiles went so far as to recant from their ante-bellum heresies in more peaceful days. The war and its consequences had, of course, in large measure rendered old heresies respectable. But it did not resolve the deeper conflicts within the minds of the exiles—conflicts between conscience and loyalty, between love of justice and love of home, between sympathy for the oppressed and ties with the oppressor. The protests and complaints and autobiographical writings of the exiles constitute evidence that these conflicts were never wholly resolved.

One of Angelina Grimke's Charleston sisters complained to her of the "bitter cup" that Sarah and Angelina had prepared for the last days of their mother's life in the pages of *American Slavery As It Is*. Angelina replied that she felt impelled to make her revelations. "Too long, too long have we hidden these things," she wrote, "prompted by a stronger feeling of sympathy for the OPPRESSOR than for the helpless and the dumb." She protested that her love of the "oppressor" only made her task more painful. "It cost us more *agony of soul* to write those testimonies than any thing we every did," she declared.[72]

All of the exiles were impelled to write their testimonies, to tell their story of the South. With some the compulsion to testify seemed to be mingled with a feeling of guilt, as in the case of the Grimke Sisters and Mattie Griffith. With others it was not always distinguishable from a craving for notoriety. Much the same compulsion and the same confusions and mixtures of motive may be found among modern Southern moralists, reformers, novelists, playwrights, sociologists, and historians. They too have felt impelled to record their testimonies, to tell their story of the South. And they too have been concerned lest their motives be misconstrued and their loyalties questioned.

One calls to mind in this connection young Quentin Compson, the narrator in William Faulkner's novel *Absalom, Absalom!* Compson has just finished telling the dark and incredible story of "Sutpen's hundred," when his Harvard roommate asks him: "Now I want you to tell me just one thing more. Why do you hate the South?"

"'I dont hate it,' Quentin said, quickly, at once, immediately; 'I dont hate it,' he said. *I dont hate it* he thought, panting in the cold air, the iron New England dark: *I dont. I dont! I dont hate it! I dont hate it!*"

Notes

1. Birney, *Sisters*, 149–50.
2. B. Letters, 262, 237–38.
3. Ibid., 237–38, 695.
4. W. B., *Birney*, 185.
5. Conway, *Testimonies*, 44–45.
6. Ibid.
7. Birney, *Sisters*, 130.
8. A. Grimke, Letters to C. Beecher, 84.
9. Weld, Grimke Letters, 502–3.
10. Fee, *Auto*, 20, 26, 61–71.
11. Conway, *Testimonies*, 44–45.
12. Quoted in Birney, *Sisters*, 182.
13. Ibid., 270.
14. B. Letters, 347–48.

15. B. Letters, 311.
16. Fee, Manual, xi.
17. B. Letters, 71.
18. Cincinnati *Philanthropist*, July 8, 1836.
19. B. Letters, II, 1136.
20. Conway, *Testimonies*, 46.
21. Conway, *Auto*, 269.
22. Conway, *Auto*, I, 377.
23. Addresses and Reprints, ix.
24. B. Letters, 798.
25. B. Diary, Nov., Dec., 1841, LC.
26. B. Letters, 757.
27. Ibid., 798.
28. B. Letters, 757.
29. B. Diary, May 5, 1850, LC.
30. W. G. Letters, 833.
31. Thomas, 219.
32. C. Birney, *Sisters*, 247–48.
33. Thomas, *Weld*, 216–18.
34. WG Letters, 629–30.
35. Quoted in Thomas, *Weld*, 233.
36. *Crisis*, 27.
37. Conway, *Auto*, I, 192.
38. Conway, *Testimonies*, 38–39.
39. Conway, *Auto*, I, 185.
40. Conway, *Testimonies*, 96.
41. Helper, *Crisis*, 32–33.
42. Conway, *Testimonies*, 94.
43. B. Letters, 624.
44. Conway, *Testimonies*, 76–77.
45. B. Letters, 792.
46. Ibid.
47. Ibid., 658–59.
48. Ibid., 733–34.
49. *Philanthropist*, May 11, 1842, quoted in Julien P. Bretz, "The Economic Background of the Liberty Party," *Amer. Hist. Rev.* XXXIV, 263.
50. B. Letters, 567.
51. B. Letters, 572.
52. T. P. Martin, "The Upper Mississippi Valley in Anglo-American Anti-Slavery and Free Trade Relations," *MVHR*, XV, 204–220.
53. A. G., Appeal to Women of Free States, 25; WG Letters, 784.
54. Birney Diary, April 1, 1840; B. Letters, 548–49.

55. B. Letters, 551, 742.
56. B. Letters, 663.
57. WG, Letters, 318–19.
58. WG, Letters, 324.
59. Ibid., 327–28.
60. B. Letters, 203.
61. WG Letters, 522.
62. Wm. Birney, *Birney*, 379.
63. Thomas, *Weld*, 245.
64. Conway, *Auto*, I, 327.
65. Ibid.
66. Conway, *Auto*, I, 364, 369.
67. Conway, *The Rejected Stone*, 77–79, 84; Conway, *Testimonies*, 132.
68. Conway, *The Rejected Stone*, 103.
69. Ibid., 58–59.
70. Conway, *The Golden Hour*, 43–44.
71. Conway, *The Rejected Stone*, 103.
72. WG Letters, 788–89.

FLEMING CHAPTER I
The Process of Alienation

NOTHING THAT WEALTH, social distinction, and public honors can do to anchor the loyalties of men to an established order would seem to have been lacking in the family background of the exiles of the thirties. They did not spring from the discontented, non-slaveholding families of the Southern uplands, as had many of the earlier dissenters. They came rather from the most privileged classes, from the big proud houses, from wealthy, slaveholding cultured families of position and distinction—or from families closely identified with those classes in outlook and interest. They were the very people who had most to lose and most to fear from the causes their alienated sons and daughters espoused in exile.

I

James Gillespie Birney, born at Danville, Kentucky, February 4, 1792, might appear at first an exception to the rule, since both his father and his mother's father were immigrants. They were immigrants, however, of an unusual sort. James Birney arrived at Philadelphia from County Cavan, Ireland, in 1783 at the age of sixteen. Five years later he began his remarkably rapid ascent to the ranks of the frontier aristocracy of Kentucky. He prospered as a merchant, a manufacturer of bagging, the president of a bank, and large-scale contractor for army supplies in the War of 1812. His accumulations were impressive enough to earn him the reputation of being "the richest man in Kentucky," and he lived in a style suitable to the reputation. In addition to the large brick house that served as a winter residence in Danville, he owned a country estate named "Woodlawn" near the town. Set deep in an elegant park and served by twenty-odd slaves, Woodlawn had all the appointments expected of the Blue-grass gentry.

Chapter I: The Process of Alienation 109

The master of Woodlawn was a man of positive opinions, vehemently expressed. A conservative and Federalist in politics, he could abide no criticism of Washington and Marshall and find no virtue in the theories of Thomas Jefferson. His favorite book was *The Federalist* and next to that Gibbon's *Rome*. For Andrew Jackson, his party, his friends, and all his works he entertained a violent antipathy. He respected Calhoun's intellect but despised his theories. Birney was a high-tariff man, a political supporter and personal friend of Henry Clay. A frequent guest at Woodlawn, Clay looked upon the elder Birney as the mainstay of his party in local politics, a devoted supporter who never sought office. In religious matters Birney adhered to the Episcopalian faith traditional in his family, took a dominant part in building the Danville church of that persuasion, and occupied his pew every Sunday morning that rolled around.

The mother of young master Birney died when he was only three. Her father, John Read, took the boy under his wing as companion and pupil. Grandfather Read, a native of Londonderry, was a political exile from the Old Country who arrived in Kentucky as early as 1779. That year he built a fort and later a house near Danville. He was also the owner of slaves and landed property. A man of inherited wealth, education, and social position, John Read was described as a tall gentleman of handsome bearing and "courtly manners." His seven children married well and endowed young Birney with a wealth of family connections that included judges, doctors, planters, and an uncle who was United States Senator from Mississippi in the 1820's. Birney and Read kin included four uncles, eight aunts, and a large number of cousins. An adored and pampered only son, the owner of a slave at the age of six and the heir to a fortune, James Gillespie Birney very definitely "belonged." He belonged in all the ways normally thought to attach men's hearts to place and people and possessions and to the faith that sustains an established order.[1]

The Grimke sisters of Charleston also belonged. Sarah Moore Grimke, born in 1792, and Angelina Emily Grimke, born in 1805, were daughters of an old, wealthy, and distinguished family of South Carolina. Their father, John Faucheraud Grimke, was sent to England for his education and received his A.B. degree from Cambridge University, where he had been a member of Trinity College, in 1774. He studied law in the Middle Temple for a year and then returned to Charleston to accept a commission as captain in the South Carolina Continental Artillery. He eventually attained the rank of lieutenant-colonel and served as deputy adjutant-general for South Carolina and Georgia until he was made prisoner at the surrender of Charleston in 1780.[2] After the war he rose rapidly in politics and before the end of the century was senior associate justice, the equivalent of chief justice, of the Supreme Court of South Carolina. He served as speaker of the state House of Representatives one year and as a member of the convention that ratified the Federal Constitution. Judge Grimke was the author of three learned books on the law, and College of New Jersey Princeton honored him with an L.L.D. in 1789. His reputation as a stern and unbending judge in the court house probably accounted for his unpopularity and for an unsuccessful impeachment procedure against him.[3]

Mrs. Grimke at the time of her marriage bore the deceptively undistinguished name of Mary Smith. As a matter of fact, she was a descendant of Thomas Smith, First Landgrave and Governor of the colony, of Sir John Yeamans, one of the Lords Proprietors, an early governor, and founder of Charleston, and of Colonel William Rhett, once Governor General of the Bahama Islands. Her relatives of the Smith descent included John Quincy Adams of Massachusetts and Robert Barnwell Rhett of South Carolina, a nephew. Her brother Benjamin Smith was an aide to General Washington, a United States Senator from North Carolina, and later a Governor of that state.[4]

Merely to accommodate family and servants the Grimke house in Charleston had to be large. Sarah was the sixth and Angelina the last of fourteen children born to Mary Grimke. The children were accustomed to the service of slaves and the family to a style of living that was lavish and expensive. In addition to the house in Charleston there was a summer residence in the Up-Country and a plantation whose slaves were managed by overseers. The Judge and his family were High-Church Episcopalians of a devout and straight-laced kind. Regular attendance of family as well as servants at morning prayers in the home was compulsory and church attendance expected.[5] Through the portals of the aristocratic little society of old Charleston the Grimkes moved with the assurance of the elite. The future incendiaries Sarah and Angelina grew up among their cousins and kin, the Rhetts, the Smiths, the Barnwells, with friends and connections and associates that ramified throughout the charmed circle of those who ran things in ante-bellum South Carolina.

Associated from time to time with Birney and the Grimke sisters in the years of their exile and alienation from the South was a group of young Southerners, all ministers or ministerial students, who also left the South in the early thirties. None of them became so conspicuous in the reform movements as Birney and the Grimkes, but like them they came from upper-class slaveholding families. James Armstrong Thome, one of the more prominent of them, was the son of Arthur Thome, a wealthy planter and slaveholder of Augusta, Kentucky, and a staunch supporter of the institution. William T. Allan and his brother James M. Allan were sons of the Reverend William Allan, a Presbyterian parson of Huntsville, Alabama. An owner of slaves himself, the Reverend Allan found nothing in his creed that militated against divine sanction of slavery. C. S. Hodges came of a slaveholding family of Virginia, and Henry P. Thompson of Kentucky was a slave owner in his own right.

Children of the Old Regime, the future incendiaries and exiles who contributed to its overthrow were heirs to all it had to offer. To their brothers and cousins this seemed enough to command the firmest attachments and deepest loyalties. Indeed, the same families that bred the incendiaries also bred some of the most effective defenders and servants of the Old Order. In one case, that of Robert Barnwell Rhett, the champion of the South quite equaled in his defense of the cause the fanatical zeal his cousins the Grimke sisters displayed in attacking it, and exceeded them in the prominence he attained in the struggle.

To discover why one brother took the path of exile and not another may sometimes prove impossible. The seeds of alienation are secret and are often buried too deep to be unearthed. The fruit of those seed[s] took many forms, some of them less conventional and presentable than abolitionism— the one form common to all the exiles of this and the later generation.

II

In the Grimke family the process of alienation began at home. The Charleston household, according to ample testimony of its members, was a distraught and normally unhappy one. Suspicion and tension between mother and children and among the children themselves appears to have been chronic and open hostility not infrequent. Sarah, in her melancholy way, refers often to "trying circumstances,"[6] and Angelina, more bitterly, to the "ungentle," "uncongenial," and "unpleasant" atmosphere. "We must always expect to be tried with the manners of those around us when we go home," observed Angelina to Sarah.[7] When her sister Eliza remarked that "she felt distressed about the state of the family," Angelina replied that "none but the dead would live here without mourning over it." "I am fully convinced," she wrote, "that it is *not* affection but interest & a sense of duty which binds the members of most families together & when I look at home this opinion is most sadly confirmed. I can testify from painful past experience that the bonds of natural affection can be totally dissolved."[8]

The children were prone to fix much of the blame for the state of the family on their mother. Mary Grimke seems to have been a devout but irritable woman, often impatient with her children and sometimes harsh with the servants. Her burdens were many, however, and not lightly borne. Judge Grimke was much away from home, and their establishment was large and difficult to manage. This did not excuse her shortcomings in the eyes of critical daughters. Sarah felt moved "to speak a few words of reproof,"[9] and Angelina, who acted readily on such promptings, believed that "Mother found it very hard to hear *our* disapproval about anything because she had for so many years held herself so far *above* us." The daughter complained of "the painful alienation" between them and told her mother that she "mourned over her coldness." She confided tearfully to her journal that she believed her mother incapable of "that deep & tender affection for me which ought to exist in a parents bosom." Mary, when taxed with coldness, assured Angelina that she loved her "but that it was not *her way* to show her love by outward caresses."[10] This did not satisfy the unhappy daughter. There were more tearful conferences with her mother and much morbid speculation on the subject in her journal.

In the lives of the exiles there usually came a period when the role assigned them in their society seemed somehow wrong. They began to feel miscast. Their actions seemed to them mechanical and without real purpose. The motivation of friends and associates appeared shallow, their lives frivolous and vain. All the striving and the things men strived for around them turned to a mockery. As the old way of life took on the taint of evil and sinfulness, the old self associated with that way of life seemed more vain and intolerable. The craving grew for a new life, a new sense of purpose, a rebirth that would dissociate them completely from the sinful old life and the rejected self. In all cases the crisis was accompanied by religious strivings and a conversion—sometimes a succession of conversions. These experiences never entirely fulfilled the craving for a new self and a new purpose, and the quest continued. The period of crisis was of varied duration and intensity and did not always occur at the same period of life.

In the life of Sarah Moore Grimke the crisis had an early beginning and a lengthy duration. She describes her childhood perfunctorily as "passed in uninterrupted enjoyment of the good things of this life," but does not enlarge on the subject. She received "what is called a good education," and at the age of sixteen "entered the grand theatre of the fashionable world" and was "initiated into the circles of dissipation & folly." In other words she "came out" in exclusive Charleston society—a gracious and perhaps gay circle, but more accurately characterized as staid and decorous than as dissolute. Looking back from a period of contrition, however, she viewed her social life as utterly sinful. "I believe for the short time that I was exhibited on this theatre," she wrote, "few have exceeded me in folly in dissipation and in sinful indulgence of pride & vanity."[11]

In the midst of these frivolities and pleasures, however, Sarah found "a sting in them which poisoned them" and she early conceived "a thorough contempt for the trifles [she] was engaged in." The mood was first induced by the promptings of frustrated intellectual ambitions. "I was naturally independent," she confessed, "longed for an education that would elevate me above the low pursuits of sense, but I was a girl & altho well educated as such, yet the powers of my mind were not called into exercise." She envied the attainments of her brilliant brother, Thomas Smith Grimke, who was educated at Yale, and resented deeply her parents' discouragement of her yearning to study Greek and Latin. "I looked with longing eyes on my brother's superior advantages," she wrote a friend, "& wondered why the simple fact of being a girl should shut me up to the necessity of being a doll a coquette a fashionable fool, my haughty spirit spurned the idea of being dependent on my father and strange & curious & various were the fancies that crowded my juvenile years to attain education & independence."[12] Her frustrated ambitions gave her no peace. "Often during this period," she wrote, "have I returned home sick of the frivolous beings I had been with, mortified at my own folly and sick at heart of the ball room & its gilded toys.... I cannot look back to those years without a blush of shame, a feeling of anguish at the utter perversion of the ends of my being."[13]

Then a new path was revealed to Sarah, an alternative to her thwarted intellectual hopes for a new life: "My ardent nature had another channel opened for it. I was converted and turned over to doing good." At the age of eighteen she had been deeply impressed by the preaching of a visiting Presbyterian parson, but had nevertheless continued her sinful course. In the spring of 1814, when she was twenty-one, after a winter season in which she had been "led in an unusual degree into the scene of dissipation & folly" and "the cup of worldly pleasure was filled to overflowing" she went to the country with a wealthy and fashionable friend. There she again encountered the parson who had impressed her three years earlier. This time she fell more deeply under the influence of his teachings. She returned to the "splendid habitation & fashionable circle" of her friend "sorrowful & very heavy." "The glory of this world was stained in my view, I no longer dared to participate in its vain & sinful pleasures—I felt ladened with iniquity and transgression... I secluded myself from Society and put away my ornaments."[14]

After a period of penance and pious works, Sarah again fell from grace, returned to worldly amusements, and resumed the wearing of ornaments. Her downward course was arrested only, she felt, by the serious illness of her father, a stroke she deemed a "merciful interposition of Providence"—to save the daughter's soul. For a year or more Sarah found a new purpose for her life in devotedly nursing her ailing father. She was the only member of the family to accompany him to Philadelphia in search of medical attention, and was the only one with him when the long illness ended with his death at Long Branch, New Jersey, in August, 1819.[15]

Returning to Charleston the December following her father's death, Sarah once more found herself bereft of purpose, loathing her old self, and craving a new personality and sense of identity. "I yielded to a spirit of impatience & melancholy," she later recalled.[16] It seemed to her that "one powerful source of dissatisfaction was Slavery," a subject she heard discussed in Philadelphia, her first visit North, when she and her father were living with a Quaker family. She brooded over her own troubles and those of the slaves "until they became like a canker, incessantly gnawing." There was no one with whom she could talk sympathetically about her new interest in slavery, for even Angelina at that time could see nothing wrong with the institution if the slaves were well treated. Sarah admitted to herself that "many circumstances" in addition to slavery contributed to her growing unhappiness. Family relations continued to deteriorate; tension between mother and daughter continued; and Sarah fancied that her brothers and sisters treated her piety with veiled derision.

New and stranger religious experiments absorbed her from time to time. For a while she found consolation and emotional excitement in the doctrine of "universal salvation" until her mother's opposition persuaded her to abandon the heresy and her life once more turned to "wormwood and gall." Then in 1820 during a visit to the plantation of her aunt, the mother of Robert Barnwell Rhett, she was powerfully attracted by a near-by congregation of shouting Methodists. On reconsidering their doctrines she rejected them before she became an adherent. Sarah's mental health deteriorated to an acute and dangerous phase. "I craved a hiding-place in the grave," she confessed to her mother, "as a rest from the distress of my feelings, thinking that no estate could be worse than the present." Her family became alarmed as her condition grew more distressing. "I cannot without shuddering look back to that period," she wrote years later. "How dreadful did the state of my mind become! Nothing interested me; I fulfilled my duties without any feeling of satisfaction, in gloomy silence.... My soul still remembers the wormwood and gall, still remembers how awful the conviction that every door of hope was closed, and that I was given over unto death."[17]

Aboard the ship on her return passage from Philadelphia Sarah had fallen in with a group of Quakers with whom she later carried on correspondence. Repelled at first by their doctrines, she read their books and ended by becoming "convinced." The new interest seemed to quiet her distress for a time, but she soon began to see and commune with spirits—a subject which her family and friends, though alarmed, found it advisable to avoid in talking with her. Another obsession, one that was to haunt her for years, was that she had a divine call to the ministry. Wrestling desperately against this prompting, obsessed with a feeling of guilt and sin, and meeting with no understanding or sympathy at home, Sarah announced that she had decided to leave home and go to live with a Quaker family in Philadelphia. The decision met with no resistance from the Grimkes, and in the spring of 1821 she took her departure.[18]

III

Angelina was sixteen when Sarah left home. Though of very different temperament, the two sisters were close and apparently affectionate in their relationship. To console her for the departure of her brother Thomas, who left for Yale shortly before Angelina was born, Sarah was granted after prolonged begging the honor of becoming godmother of her baby sister at the unusual age of twelve. She took this, like all responsibilities, with utmost seriousness and seems to have exercised an influence and received a devotion that Angelina's own mother never enjoyed. In her relation with her sister as with her father Sarah appeared in the role of rival with her mother Mary. Angelina responded in her role eagerly, often addressed Sarah in letters as "my dear mother," and referred to herself as "your daughter." She seems to have sought and received from her sister much of the affection that she complained her mother was withholding from her.

While Sarah's influence on the younger sister was strong, the contrasts between their personalities and characters were numerous and marked. The more brilliant and personally attractive of the two, Angelina had little of the humility, self-reproach, and melancholy misgivings of Sarah in her makeup. Her characteristic approach to life was one of self-reliance and headlong determination. If she piously renounced some pleasure or foible, it seemed less a mortification of the flesh than a standing rebuke to all sinners who failed to renounce that particular pleasure or foible. As an admiring biographer has observed, Angelina "was wonderfully well satisfied with her own power of distinguishing right from wrong," a power she believed to be of divine origin and one which she was not loathe to demonstrate nor press upon all comers.[19]

Like her sister, Angelina grew tired of the fashionable society life, discovered the Episcopalian faith to be too cold and formal for her taste, fell under the influence of another Presbyterian clergyman, and joined that church after renouncing the faith of her parents. Unlike Sarah, however, she seems to have made these decisions with assurance instead of forebodings, and to have entered upon each new experiment with enthusiasm—however disenchanting and empty the preceding one proved to be.

Her progress continued comparatively serene until the fall of 1827, when in her twenty-second year she was suddenly plunged into what she described as a "long & deeply trying season of mental darkness." "At first I was totally bewildered," she wrote, "& knew not what to make of it. I had heard that sin was invariably the cause of such effects & Satan who is still 'the accuser of the brethren' tormented me day & night."[20] Angelina's "season of darkness" lasted about six months and coincided, apparently by chance, with a visit of Sarah. The Quaker sister had kept posted on the religious strivings of her spiritual daughter and arrived at Charleston in November, 1827, eager to be of aid in the crisis. Sarah found circumstances at home as "trying" as ever. "I feel renewedly how responsible and dangerous a station I stand in here," she noted in her journal; "every word and action is watched not for evil but to see how far the purifying influence of the Spirit of Truth which I profess to believe in is capable of making a frail creature what she ought to be."[21]

Prayerful counselling and conference between godmother and daughter bore fruits. The first step was symbolic and momentous enough to be recorded independently in each of their journals. Angelina had purchased a set of Sir Walter Scott's novels "before she was serious," as Sarah put it. "My mind had long been troubled about them," confessed Angelina. "I did not dare either to sell them or to lend them out, & yet I had not resolution to destroy them . . ." Sir Walter was selected for sacrificial offering, and one morning in January the sisters solemnly cut the works to bits. Further to solemnize the occasion Angelina delivered over to Sarah much of her elegant finery, silks, and laces to be cut up and used to stuff a cushion. The first offering was a Cashmere mantle that had cost her twenty dollars. She had temporized earlier by trimming off the fringe, but she was no longer in a mood for half measures. She also untrimmed her hat and removed the lace lining. "I do want if I am a Christian to look like one," she declared.[22]

The transformation in the appearance of the dashing Miss Grimke naturally attracted attention. "My friends tell me that I render myself ridiculous

Chapter I: The Process of Alienation 117

and expose the Cause of Jesus to reproach on account of my plain dressing, they tell me that it is wrong to make myself so conspicuous . . ." But criticism and ridicule, instead of crushing her spirit as it did Sarah's, merely hardened her determination. "The more I ponder on this subject," she revealed, "the more I feel that I am called with a high & holy calling & that I ought to be *peculiar* & zealous of good works." She prayed for strength "to keep the resolution of dressing always in the following style—A hat over the face without any bows of ribbon or lace—no frills or trimming on any part of my dress & materials *not* the finest."[23] It would be only a few steps now to the gray, dog-eared Quaker bonnet.

Under Sarah's guidance and example Angelina withdrew further and further from society and despite much remonstrance and debate ended her cherished connection with the Presbyterians. "My mind is composed & I cannot but feel astonished," she said, "at the total change which has passed over me during the last 6 months."[24] Of a Sunday she took to attending the local Quaker meeting, frequented solely at the time by two old men who were feuding and did not speak to each other. Fashionable friends and church associates, excited by the loss of one of the most popular members, called in numbers to urge that she change her decision, but all to no effect. Some were convinced that her mind was unhinged, and indeed her health did decline. Partly to regain her health, she went to Philadelphia to spend the summer with Sarah. There she naturally fell more deeply under the influence of the Friends.[25]

Returning to Charleston in the November that saw Andrew Jackson elected President, Angelina discovered many additional flaws in life at home and much wickedness in the old city to which she had hitherto been blind. Her ideal was to bear "silent witness" against such offenses by her own bearing and conduct, but when that failed of effect her tongue was unloosed in testimony of forceable rebuke that was anything but silent. Nor could she always tell whether such testimony was prompted by the Spirit or by her own towering and stubborn pride.

For some years, while they were at home, she and Sarah had insisted upon paying their mother board. Intended or not, this gesture had the effect not only of asserting independence from a critical parent, but also of serving as a standing rebuke to various unemployed siblings who continued to help themselves at the family table as unpaying members of the household. With her new light on the subject, Angelina forthwith carried on her campaign with more explicit measures. Announcing that the food was too rich and the style of living too luxurious, she declined cakes and wine, withdrew her presence from tea parties, and remonstrated earnestly with her mother for papering a drawing room too elegantly and expensively. She reproved one brother for living off their mother and another for giving a wine party that lasted till 12:45 in the morning. She declined to buy silk stockings for one sister and refused to help another sew on frills.[26]

For the most part the family seems to have stood in considerable awe of Angelina in her new mood, but hardly a day passed without an irritating episode. Brother Henry had a little more than he could take once and exploded with some violence. "He said I had come from the North expressly to be miserable myself," reported Angelina, "and make everyone in the house so, and that I had much better go live at the North."[27] Mary Grimke strove hard for compassion and understanding but she was also sometimes tried beyond the limits of her patience. "It was very bad she said [to Angelina] that she could not give her children what food *she* chose or paper a room without being found fault with, indeed she was weary of being continually blamed about everything she did, she wished they would let her alone for she saw no sin in these things."[28] The daughter assured her that the remonstrances were divinely inspired and not lightly intended. "I am acting in reference to that awful hour when I shall stand at thy death-bed, or thou by mine," she said.[29]

Angelina was occasionally assailed by doubts and embarrassed by lapses in the performance of her new role, which she acknowledged was not native to her. Once she caught herself up sharply for joining in a joke and reminded herself that "solemnity ought always to pervade my mind too much to allow *me* ever to joke, but my natural vivacity is hard to bridle and subdue." So was her pride. "I am all pride," she once lamented, "and I fear that I am even proud of my pride." Far from being appalled by the call to the ministry and to mighty deeds of mercy as was Sarah, Angelina was uplifted by it. "My restless, ambitious temper, so different from my sister's," she said, "craves high duties and high attainments.... These are my temptations. For a long time it seemed to me I did everything from a hope of applause. I could not even write in my diary without a feeling that I was doing it in the hope that it would one day meet the eye of the public."[30] She had now donned Quaker garb, or a modified form of it, and there is a suggestion that she even took perverse pride in the sensation she created in it. "I sometimes wonder at my quietness of feeling," she confessed, "when I walk down King Street among the gay and fashionable, I am literally 'as a wonder to many.'"[31] And the more King Street wondered, the more Angelina despised King Street and all it stood for.

After her return from Philadelphia, the faults of luxury, sloth, wickedness, and pride in her home and in her native city came more and more to seem symbolized and summed up in slavery. Prior to her visit in the North, she had not considered slavery sinful, though she had complained of cruelty to slaves. She had once taken ownership of a slave woman named Kitty whom her mother was unable to manage, then later placed the woman in a more congenial home and returned ownership to her mother. When Angelina, after receiving her new light on the subject, criticised her mother for the way Kitty was treated, Mary Grimke indignantly reminded her daughter that it was the treatment she herself had recommended and taxed her with inconsistency. Angelina admitted she had changed but heatedly asked, "Dear mother, what but the *power* of God could ever have made *me* change my sentiments?"[32] Knowing her daughter's nature as well as she did, Mary probably found that question hard to answer.

"For two or three months after my return here," wrote Angelina, "it seemed to me that all the cruelty and unkindness which I had from my infancy seen practiced towards them [the slaves] came back to my mind as though it was only yesterday."[33] She did not have to depend upon memory for evidence of oppression, suffering, mistreatment, and cruelty. She saw it now all around her—in the parlor, in the streets, in the kitchen, in the repulsive workhouse of the city where slaves were sent for punishment—and noted the evidence almost daily in her journal. The merciless flogging and cursing her brother Henry gave his slave John distressed her immensely, and the callousness and indifference with which her family and friends accepted these scenes stirred her sensibilities to the pitch of revolt. She began to yearn for the North, which seemed to her like "the land of Canaan. [...] a promised land, a pleasant land, because it is a land of freedom." In fact she already felt "like an exile, a stranger in the place of her nativity . . . and one of the very least where she was once among the greatest."[34]

"All the sacred & endearing ties of christian fellowship which once bound me to Charleston seem to be entirely dissolved," wrote Angelina in a mood of utter despair. "I go out to pay visits merely because I think it is right to do so, & I try to watch for every impression of duty . . . not that I expect to receive any satisfaction in the visits, except that, derived from a consciousness of having done my duty. Here no one delights in me & I delight in no one. I feel like an isolated being in the midst of those with whom I have often take [*sic*] sweet counsel."[35] With Angelina the process of alienation was complete before she became an abolitionist, before she even left home. In fact she was, as she said, an exile *in* her home. "Often of late whilst in social circles," she declared, "have I involuntarily exclaimed to myself this people is *not my* people, neither is their God *my* God."[36]

The only thing that kept her in Charleston, she said, was the hope that she "contributed to dear Mother's happiness." But her way of doing that was to read the poor woman anti-slavery tracts "greatly against her will."[37] Once while the family was at the dinner table lightning struck nearby and her mother's face "actually fixed with fear" and bore "the semblance of death." Angelina assured her that "the thing required of her is to give up slavery."[38] Mary remained unrepentant, however, and Angelina was convinced "lost."

Finally Angelina gained permission to leave and join Sarah to live in Philadelphia, and in October she told her mother and Charleston goodbye. She was never to see her mother again, for in the forty years of life that remained to her Angelina Grimke never again crossed Mason and Dixon's line.

IV

With all the marvelous advantages that hindsight bestows, one still finds it difficult to see in the youth and early manhood of James G. Birney the future leader of the party of abolitionism. It is much easier to see instead the fulfillment in all particulars of the youth and manhood to be expected of a bright son of the rich, slaveholding, bluegrass aristocracy. He had rather more advantages, opportunities, talents, and useful connections than usual, and he made rather wiser use of them than ordinary. But all this pointed toward a career as a statesman of compromise and conciliation, such as some of his brilliant Kentucky contemporaries achieved. If there are any hints of impending alienation from his background they are smothered by evidence of thorough identification with it, and if there are any portents of rebellion they do not appear until very late.

A handsome, active, and robust boy, fond of the out-of-doors, of sports, and of girls, James was the pride of his father and a pet among his well-to-do relatives. At eleven he was sent to Lexington, where he was taught elementary subjects at Transylvania University for three years, and then returned to Danville to prepare for college in a local "seminary." In 1808, at the age of seventeen, he left home for Princeton to enter the College of New Jersey. He was apparently able to establish a good reputation as a scholar without permitting studies to interfere with normal convivialities. Twice during his three years at Princeton the faculty suspended him and sent him home for the offense of appearing in a tavern and again in the classroom intoxicated.[39] He was nevertheless graduated in good standing in September, 1810. After a brief visit home, during which he did a bit of campaigning for the young War Hawk,

Henry Clay, Birney departed for Philadelphia to study law in the office of Alexander J. Dallas.

Between the life he led in Philadelphia and that pursued by Sarah Grimke in the same city there were some striking contrasts. James's father, "who insisted that he should live in all respects as a man of fashion," liberally supplied the means for his son to indulge expensive tastes and move in the most fashionable circles. A gay young bachelor of military age, James spent the piping war years in peaceful pursuit of learning and pleasure. From the Woodlawn pastures came a pair of blooded bays which he drove tandem about the city, wearing "high, fair-topped, tasseled boots when he drove." For three and a half years, much longer than that age thought necessary for training in the field of law, Birney prolonged his career of student and man-of-fashion in Philadelphia. He did not return to Danville to hang out his shingle until the summer of 1814.[40]

It was a splendid dawn of a day for a young man of twenty-two to start a career in Kentucky. The war was about over and in January came the news of the Battle of New Orleans that gave a fillip to the illusion of victory and to the West's already towering confidence and boundless optimism about wonderful things to come. A thriving law practice was waiting almost ready-made for young Birney at Danville. He pitched into politics at once to campaign in 1815 for his friend Clay, for whom his admiration was still growing, and to elect George Madison governor. The next year he married Agatha McDowell, a niece of Governor Madison and daughter of a Federal judge. His political connections thus strengthened, he was elected almost without opposition and as a matter of course to the lower house of the state general assembly.

For all his brilliant prospects in Kentucky, the frontier looked even brighter. A visit to the Alabama Territory in 1817 persuaded him to cast his lot with the new country opening up to the south. He bought a plantation near the Tennessee River about a two-hour horseback ride from Huntsville, where he proposed to practice law while he ran his plantation with an overseer. In February, 1818, he wound up his affairs in Kentucky and the following autumn moved his wife, small son, and property overland to his Alabama plantation.

Part of the property Birney took with him were the ten slaves he had accepted from his father as a wedding present together with slaves that were gifts from his grandfather and Mrs. Birney's father. Much has been made of the anti-slavery influences that played upon the youth of the future abolitionist leader. Such sentiment was undoubtedly to be found in his environment, but it was a sentiment native to his father's generation—not his. Even in his father's generation, even among those who were articulate in their opposition, anti-slavery sentiment rarely prevented the slaveholder from continuing in the possession of his slaves. Nothing in young Birney's convictions at the time stood in the way of accepting slaves from relatives or, for that matter, buying them from strangers. In spite of his son William's statement that his father "never bought a slave in the market,"[41] Birney's plantation records show that during his first three years in Alabama he bought nineteen slaves from four different states. These slaves added to those given him by his relatives and the eleven born of his slaves made a total of forty-three that he owned.[42]

Attainment of stature as a Southern man-of-affairs, the goal for which Birney seemed clearly destined, was a three dimensional ambition. Success as a planter, a politician, and a lawyer was required of the aspirant by immemorial precedent. Unlimited opportunity in all three departments appeared open to young Birney when at the age of twenty-six he arrived in Huntsville. Within a very short time, however, he found his way blocked and his ambition frustrated in two of the three fields.

Birney entered Alabama politics just as the territory was becoming a state. The convention that framed the first constitution met in Huntsville, and Birney was able to render conspicuous service in the work even though he was not a member of the convention. He was, however, elected a member of the first General Assembly of the new state. Shortly after that body convened at Huntsville in the fall of 1819, General Andrew Jackson arrived in town with a string of horses to attend the races and incidentally to improve his acquaintance among the members of the legislature. In the midst of the enthusiasm stirred by the hero's visit, the state assembly adopted a highly complimentary resolution, and endorsed the general. Birney not only voted against the resolution but explained in forcible terms that he did not consider the general a fit nominee for the Presidency. At the peak of Jackson's popularity, in a state that was strongly and consistently Jacksonian in allegiance, Birney had deliberately taken a step that closed his future as an Alabama politician. Although he served his community and his state in appointive offices and other ways with distinction, he never again won an elective office in Alabama though he ran for office twice. Year after year he saw men of smaller talents and lesser caliber take the honors from which he was excluded.

His career as a cotton planter likewise fell under an early blight. The year 1818 was not an auspicious one to begin. The panic of 1819 brought on hard times; his cotton crops, tended by inexperienced Kentucky hands and managed inexpertly, proved unsuccessful; heavy gambling losses piled up; friends defaulted on notes for which he was security. More than $10,000 in debt before the end of 1820, he was compelled to mortgage his land, livestock, furniture, and twenty-eight of his slaves, and still face hard sledding.[43] "My habits at this period of my life," he wrote, "tended more to the dissipation than to the accumulation of wealth." Fine horses, expensive wines and furniture, and lavish hospitality in the bluegrass tradition was hardly the road to solvency. His financial embarrassments continued through 1822. In 1823 he moved into Huntsville and the following year sold most of his slaves to a master he considered humane and gave up planting.[44]

In fortunate contrast to his failure as a politician and a planter was his brilliant success as a lawyer. It was an unusual compliment to his ability and reputation that an almost solidly Jacksonian legislature should have elected Birney, an outspoken opponent of the General, as solicitor for the Fifth Alabama Circuit. A lucrative post in its own right, the position did not preclude private practice on the side. He soon gave up the solicitorship to devote himself to private practice, which came to him in greater quantities than he could handle. According to his son, "he became the most successful practitioner in North Alabama, with the largest professional income."[45] He built a large house in Huntsville, sold it and built a larger one, and bought a stock farm in which he dabbled as an avocation.

"Till I was 34 years old [in 1826]," wrote Birney, "I was wild—much inclined to dissipation—and ambitious. I was however too much given to pleasure, to pursue with any systematic effort, the common objects of ambition . . ."[46] These are the words of a penitent, whose report of his own wickedness is doubtless subject to some discount. Nevertheless, he repeatedly described his habits in these terms, specifying gambling, drinking, and godlessness among his offenses, and declaring that he "was rapidly pursuing the road to Hell."[47]

In 1826 Birney underwent some sort of religious experience and joined the Presbyterian Church, of which his wife had been a lifelong member. It was the first departure from the ways of his father, who was "deeply wounded" at his son's defection from the traditional Episcopalian faith of the family. As was his rule in such decisions, the step was taken only after soul searching deliberation, and it was to have far reaching consequences.[48] Although he later became something of a religious skeptic, he wrote that "for several years after I made public profession of my faith, my religious emotions in contemplating the character of God . . . were often transporting."[49]

The new mood suffused his whole way of life and animated into brisk and purposeful activity submerged philanthropic impulses in several different fields. Not only did he abandon dissipations, frivolities, and gay companions, but undertook at considerable trouble a host of good works. For one thing he became counsel for the Cherokee Indians of northern Alabama and Georgia, a post he had previously avoided. As champion and defender of that oppressed and unpopular minority, he fought hard against the injustices inflicted on them, sought to mend their relations with the dominant whites, and labored to improve their hard lot.[50] He became an elder in his Church, an officer of the Sunday school, the president of a local tract society for distributing pious publications, and a guiding hand in educational institutions. It was natural for his fellow townsmen to turn to Birney to lead the struggle against crime and violence that plagued the community and to make him their mayor for two terms. When the state university needed a president and several faculty members in 1830, it was Birney whom the Governor commissioned to scout out the necessary talent. With letters of introduction from Henry Clay and other western notables, he toured the eastern states, visited Harvard, Yale, and Princeton, interviewed Daniel Webster, Edward Everett, and scores of prominent men, and returned with his mission accomplished.[51]

Nothing about all this activity suggested the meddling of a neurotic spinster. It was the bustling expression of a man in full possession of his powers, assured of the confidence of his fellows, and confident of the righteousness of his course. And apart from his concern for the Indians his activities were of the sort that met with at least the full public approbation of his peers. It was only his concern for the Negro slaves that eventually brought about his alienation, and for a long time this concern took wholly acceptable if not conventional forms. Birney did not arrive at abolitionism suddenly as the result of some Pauline experience, but only gradually after exploring, and for varying lengths of time occupying, each successive stage of gradualism from right to extreme left. Each transition from one stage to the next was made after struggle and strain.

As late as 1824, when he negotiated the sale of a large number of his slaves, Birney admits that his "opinions on the subject of slaveholding did not materially differ from those which prevailed among the generality of planters."[52] He continued to own, sell, buy or hire slaves in small numbers for ten more years, but his opinions were in the meantime changing.[53] He had fostered the adoption of liberal provisions for the administration of justice for slaves in the framing of the Alabama constitution and in 1827 promoted a bill that was adopted prohibiting the importation of slaves into the state for sale or hire. For a time Birney entertained hopes for the emancipation movements in the border states, especially Virginia and Kentucky. Returning from his eastern tour in 1830 he visited in his native state and took part in the organization of a Gradual Emancipation Society. He also called on his old friend Henry

Clay, in whom he still saw hope of national leadership for the cause of gradual emancipation. But the new society came to nothing and his talk with Clay led him to abandon the Senator as a lost leader and sever his political ties with him. Then a succession of blows fell upon his hopes for the South: the emancipation movement in Virginia collapsed; Alabama removed the recently adopted prohibition against importing slaves; and in 1831 came news of the Nat Turner rebellion at Southampton, and following that news of a wave of reaction across the South on the slave issue.[54]

So discouraging did the outlook appear to Birney that he decided to move his family out of the South. He had become "fully convinced," he wrote, "of the corrupting influence of *slavery* on the character of the *young* amongst us, especially those of our own sex—and six of my seven children are boys . . ." He had just returned from a trip to Illinois in quest of a place to live and had already advertised his property in Alabama for sale when in June, 1832, he received an offer that he considered "providential." It was a letter from Ralph R. Gurley, secretary of the American Colonization Society, inviting him to become general agent of the organization for the[*]

Notes

1. William Birney, *James G. Birney and His Times* (New York, 1890), 2–10; Calvin M. Fackler, *Early Days in Danville* (Louisville, 1941), 131 and passim.
2. "Order Book of John Faucheraud Grimke, August 1778 to May 1780," *South Carolina Historical and Genealogical Magazine*, XIII (1912), 42–43.
3. John B. O'Neall, *Biographical Sketches of the Bench and Bar of South Carolina* (Charleston, 1859), I, 39–41.
4. A. S. Salley, "The Family of the First Landgrave Thomas Smith," *South Carolina Historical and Genealogical Magazine*, IV (1903), 41–42.
5. Catherine H. Birney, *The Grimke Sisters* (Boston, 1885), 7, 11.
6. Sarah M. Grimke, Journal, April 7, December 5, 1827, Weld-Grimke Papers, Clements Library.
7. Angelina E. Grimke to Sarah M. Grimke, January 6, 1832, ibid.
8. Angelina E. Grimke, Journal, June 14, 18, 1829, ibid.
9. Sarah Grimke, Journal, April 7, 1827, ibid.
10. Angelina Grimke, Journal, April 6, 10, 12, 19, 1829, ibid.
11. Sarah Grimke, Journal, June 3, 1827, ibid.

---

[*] Chapter one ends suddenly. There is one additional end note, number 55, suggesting that Woodward was almost finished with the chapter. It reads: Ralph R. Gurley to Birney, June 12, 1832; Birney to Gurley, July 12, 1832, in Dumond, *Letters of Birney*, I, 5–12.

12. Sarah Grimke to Augusta Wattles, undated [1848?], ibid.
13. Sarah Grimke Journal, June 3, 1827, ibid.
14. Ibid.
15. Birney, *Grimke Sisters*, 20–24.
16. Sarah Grimke, Journal, June 3, 1827, Weld-Grimke Papers.
17. Birney, *Grimke Sisters*, 25–28.
18. Ibid., 29–33.
19. Ibid., 46–47.
20. Angelina Grimke, Journal, March 29, 1829; Angelina Grimke, Memorandum, November 14, 1828, Weld-Grimke Papers.
21. Sarah Grimke, Journal, December 5, 1827, ibid.
22. Angelina Grimke, Journal, January 11, 1828; Sarah Grimke, Journal, January 10, 1828, ibid.
23. Angelina Grimke, Journal, February 23, 1828, ibid.
24. Ibid., April 20, 25, 1828; William A. McDowell, Presbyterian Pastor, to Angelina Grimke, May 14, 1828; ibid.
25. Angelina Grimke to Elizabeth Bascom, April 18, 1828; Sarah Grimke, Journal, June 11, 13, 1828, ibid.
26. Birney, *Grimke Sisters*, 67–70; Angelina Grimke, Journal, July 14, 1829, ibid.
27. Birney, *Grimke Sisters*, 77.
28. Angelina Grimke, Journal, June 11, 1829.
29. Birney, *Grimke Sisters*, 71.
30. Ibid., 79, 81, 82.
31. Angelina Grimke to Sarah Grimke, March 8, 1829, Weld-Grimke Papers.
32. Birney, *Grimke Sisters*, 41, 71.
33. Ibid., 74.
34. Ibid., 79, 88–89.
35. Angelina Grimke, Journal, April 30, Weld Grimke Papers.
36. Ibid., July 13, 1829.
37. Ibid., October 11, 1829.
38. Angelina Grimke to Sarah Grimke, August 5, 1829, ibid.
39. Betty L. Fladeland, "James Gillespie Birney: Exponent of Political Action Against Slavery" (University of Michigan dissertation, 1952), 15.
40. William Birney, *J. G. Birney*, 30.
41. Ibid., 42.
42. Fladeland, "Birney," 27–28.
43. Ibid., 36.
44. J. G. Birney to Colonel William L. Stone, May 2, 1836, in William Birney, *J. G. Birney*, 423.
45. Ibid., 48–49.
46. J. G. Birney to Elizur Wright, Jr., March 4, 1844, in Dumond (ed.), *Letters of Birney*, II, 797–98.

47. J. G. Birney to Gerrit Smith, September 13, 1835, ibid., I, 242.
48. Fladeland, "Birney," 58; William Birney, *J. G. Birney*, 6.
49. James G. Birney Diary, February 4, 1840, Birney Papers (Library of Congress).
50. Fladeland, "Birney," 63, 65; William Birney, *J. G. Birney*, 55–56.
51. James G. Birney Diary, August 31–October 1, 1830, Birney Papers (Library of Congress); Henry Clay to Edward Everett, August 9, 1830, Everett Papers (Massachusetts Historical Society).
52. Birney to Colonel William L. Stone, May 2, 1836, in William Birney, *J. G. Birney*, 424.
53. Birney to Robert H. Folger, July 24, 1844, in Dumond (ed.), *Letters of Birney*, II, 424–27.
54. William Birney, *J. G. Birney*, 96–104.

FLEMING CHAPTER II
The Year of Decision

NONE OF THE Men of the Thirties became exiles in any irrevocable sense until the year 1834. For all of them that became the year of decision, and in every instance the crisis came over the issue of abolitionism. As a rule the decision was but the climax of a succession of lesser defections from the Southern way, but it sometimes came as a sudden and apocalyptic conversion. The basic impulse and inspiration common to all the exiles was religious, and from Charleston to the remote frontier they all came under the powerful influence of one extraordinary missionary of the Great Revival—Theodore Dwight Weld.

I

Since the beginning of the nineteenth century the country had been periodically swept by the fire of evangelical revivals—the South as well as the North. But while in the North these passionate upheavals often found expression in crusades for reform movements, radical ideas, and social experiments, revivalism in the South tended rather to promote conformity and social reaction. This was especially true after about 1830, when the South became increasingly absorbed with the defense of slavery and the Northern evangelical sects became more and more infiltrated with antislavery sentiment.

None of the revivalist upheavals stirred the North more deeply nor more truly typified the distinctive Northern blending of evangelism and reformism than the Great Revival of Charles Grandison Finney. A mighty preacher of hell-fire evangelism, Finney swept the "burnt-over" district of western New York and stirred Yankees as they had not been stirred before. While his numerous apostles spread the flames through the West, Finney moved on to

New York City in 1832. Theodore Weld was converted by Finney in 1825 after a sensational struggle.

A striking figure of a prophet, Weld was gaunt to the point of emaciation, "a mere skeleton," he said, weighing ten pounds less than had at sixteen when he was more than twice that age. He habitually wore what he described as "a John the Baptist attire" consisting of "shag overcoat, linsey woolsey coat and cowhide shoes."[1] "I have always been slovenly and careless in my appearance," he wrote, probably with exaggeration, "a slouching gait, a listless air, shoes slip shod, not blacked once a month, coat not brushed as *often* as that, beard generally as long as a hermit's, never yet had any fixed time for shaving.... Now as to my hair—I don't comb it once a year." He had serious difficulty remembering the names and faces of people or the day of the week or month, and he would often have to go to the window to see whether it was winter or summer. Wild impulses seized him uncontrollably. "I expect as long as I live," he wrote at the age of thirty-five, "to *cut all sorts of boyish capers* with a perfect *zest*, to get out of sight and hearing (I mean of all such as would be *appalled* and *horrified* at it) every day if possible and then jump and hop and scream like a loon and run on all fours and wrestle and throw stones and play 'tag' and 'hide and seek' and 'blind mans buff' and all those childish rompings.... They are *part* of me; take them away and you destroy my *identity. I must cut capers.*"[2]

Born in Hampton, Connecticut, in 1803, Weld was the son of a poor Congregational minister and the descendant of a line of New England clergymen that included Hutchinsons, Dwights, and Edwardses. During his childhood the family moved to western New York and settled near Utica. At seventeen the boy struck out on his own and supported himself for three years by giving public lectures on how to develop memory, lectures that succeeded despite the lecturer's own confessed embarrassments over lapses of memory. Back in Utica again Weld entered Hamilton college, but was soon distracted from this, as he was from all his successive attempts to apply himself to study. The powerful distraction in this instance was the revivalist Finney, who converted him after a sensational struggle in 1825 and became his patron as well as his spiritual guide. Weld joined Finney's "Holy Band" and followed the evangelist from town to town, interceding with sinners in the struggle for their souls. He worked especially with the young men and began to build up a strongly attached personal following among the more dedicated Finneyites. At Utica he acquired another patron in Captain Charles Stuart, a retired British army officer and bachelor who was principal of a local boys' school and another member of Finney's "Holy Band." Stuart's passionate attachment with young Weld was described by the latter's biographer as "almost rapturous," but unperverted. It was a result of Stuart's persuasion and with his financial aid that Weld enrolled at Oneida Institute at Whitesboro, New York, to prepare for the ministry.³

An academy for Christian spartans, Oneida was distinguished for its discipline of compulsory manual labor and its regimen of rigorous living and good works. Students began their labors at 4 o'clock in the morning, attended some classes before breakfast, and ate their frugal meals while listening to readings or discourses. Weld ran the milking class and had charge of some thirty cows. His studies were interrupted not only by these labors, but even more by his good works in the form of numerous lecture tours in the cause of temperance and sabbath observance. He also willingly complied with the request of the president of Oneida that he undertake travels to solicit contributions for the school. His work brought him to the notice of the Tappan brothers, Arthur and Lewis, of New York, future underwriters of the abolitionist crusade. Puritanical philanthropists at large, the Tappan brothers became interested in Oneida Institute by their friend Finney, and Lewis enrolled his two sons at the school. Greatly impressed by Weld's oratorical talents and moral zeal, the Tappans determined to bring him within their orbit of philanthropic works and invited him to New York in the summer of 1831 to discuss the launching of a national antislavery movement and to urge him to become pastor of a church they proposed to establish in the city. The abolitionist movement was postponed pending the outcome of developments in that line in Britain, and Weld declined the pastorate on the ground that he was not yet prepared for it. He was persuaded, however, to become general agent for the Society for Promoting Manual Labor in Literary Institutions, recently established by the Tappans.

In the fall of 1831 Weld quit Oneida and embarked on his mission for the Manual Labor Society with instructions to visit schools and colleges all over the country, spread the new gospel of educational salvation as well as temperance, and incidentally to find and recommend a suitable site for a new manual labor institution in the West. He flung himself into the task with characteristic, headlong zeal and totality of commitment. Reckless of health and heedless of personal comfort, he delivered 236 lectures in a little more than a year, during which he traveled 4,575 miles, much of it by horseback or afoot, all over the Middle West and deep into the Southwest. Exertions and accidents came near wrecking his health for a time. He has been aptly characterized as "a man of reckless righteousness."⁴

The countenance of the reformer alone was enough to compel attention and even provoke dismay. Gaunt and deeply seamed, it was a tortured, haunting face, slightly disfigured by a twisted nose and a deep dent over one eye. "Its SEVERITY," exclaimed an artist who was trying to paint a miniature of him, "is like a streak of lightning." Yet it was a face that could melt into a benign and winning charm. Elizabeth Whittier, sister of the poet, thought it "angelic." For social graces and small talk Weld had little but scorn. He confessed he sometimes felt an "irresistible propensity to *taciturnity*" and would go for a whole day without speaking a word. In the midst of a conversation he would, he wrote, "very often swing like a pendulum in a dreamy totally abstracted revery" and reply to all questions by "making a sort of inarticulate nasal um, um, um, um" without hearing a word that was said to him.[5] For the artificial manners and standards "among the educated and wealthy not only, but among the middling classes," Weld expressed "disgust and loathing." The great annual conventions of the abolitionist societies struck him as "ostentatious display, a mere make believe and mouthing, a sham and show off. It is an element I was never made to move in." He shunned the society of the well-to-do, abhorred publicity, and for a long time avoided cities. The backcountry was his own field. The Tappan brothers continued to urge him to come to New York and the limelight, but his answer to Lewis Tappan was: "I am a Backwoodsman—can grub up stumps and roll logs and burn brush heaps and break green sward. Let me keep about my *own* business and stay in my *own* place."[6]

So silently and anonymously did he go about his work, so self-effacing was he in his accomplishments, that it was more than a century before historians began to recognize his importance. A recent historian of the movement has gone so far as to say that "Weld was not only the greatest of the abolitionists; he was also one of the greatest figures of his time."[7] Whatever the final estimate of his significance may be, his contemporaries took his measure. William Lloyd Garrison, a rival and opponent, remarked of a gathering of the leading lights of the antislavery movement in 1836 at Boston that "Weld was the central luminary around which they all revolved."[8] And Wendell Phillips observed that "in the first years of the antislavery cause, he was our foremost advocate."[9]

A figure more incongruous with the Southern way of life than this Theodore Dwight Weld, one more uncongenial with Charleston drawing room, Alabama plantation, or Bluegrass country seat, it would be hard to imagine. And yet for the Southerner who was perplexed and sought certainty, for the disenchanted who yearned for a cause that would possess them wholly, for those who felt their lives empty and wanted them to be filled, for seekers after martyrdom and the ennobling deed, for true believers and comeouters generally, Weld was an irresistible magnet. He was a man who was absolutely sure.

All the Southern exiles of the thirties left convincing testimony of the influence Weld had upon their lives. Angelina Grimke adored him and after a passionate courtship married him. Sister Sarah, who hung upon his words, made her home with the couple the rest of her life. James G. Birney esteemed him above any of the leading abolitionists, and he knew them all. Young James Thome of Kentucky made passionate confession of his adoration. "The gushings of my soul," he wrote Weld, often "have prompted me to throw my arms around your neck and kiss you."[10] Weld himself complained that Thome, William T. Allan, and others of his converts at Lane Seminary "strangely and stupidly idolized" him. It is clear that the impact of Theodore Weld's personality upon all the Southern exiles was powerful, but the part he played in their conversion to abolitionism varied considerably. In the conversion of the Grimke sisters he had no part whatsoever, as great as his influence upon them later became, since both of them had become full-fledged abolitionists before they met Weld. Although Birney would probably have found his way into the abolitionist fold eventually without guidance, the inspiration and example of Weld was certainly an influence upon his development that cannot be overlooked. But in the conversion of Thome, the Allan brothers, and the other Southern students at Lane Seminary the Weld influence was undoubtedly decisive.

In the summer of 1832, still on his lecturing mission for the Tappans, Weld turned southward and made his way down through Kentucky, Tennessee, and into Alabama. "I also lectured from time to time on Temperance," he later wrote, "and conversed freely, wherever I had a chance, with young men on the subject of slavery." He found that at that time "there was entire freedom to converse on the subject every where, provided we kept out of the hearing of the slaves."[11] Eighteen months after the founding of Garrison's *Liberator*, Weld said that neither he nor anybody in the country he traveled had heard of it.

In June he arrived in Huntsville, Alabama, with a letter of introduction to James G. Birney. Finding the judge out of town attending court, Weld turned instead to Birney's pastor and neighbor, the Reverend William Allan, and was taken in as a guest. Two sons of the preacher, William Thomas, who had just graduated from college, and James a younger son, were living with their father. Dr. Allan was minister of the Presbyterian church and the owner of fifteen slaves. Weld's visit with the Allans stretched on for a month. He had often talked with slaveowners about slavery in the southeastern slave states and found them, he wrote, "not only tolerating my dissent, but even encouraging it by never showing irritation or impatience; and always (indeed, I can recall no exception) condemning it as a system, but generally were hopeless of deliverance." That had been ten years or more earlier. "But though I had thus much talk with slave-holders previously," he wrote, "Dr. Allen [sic] was the only one with whom I had in such length and minute detail discussed the question."[12]

After the talks had been in progress for a week, Birney returned home and was invited to dinner by Dr. Allan to meet Weld and take part in the discussions. Birney asked to be briefed on both sides of the discussion so far. Weld undertook a summary. The gaunt Yankee was twenty-nine and Birney forty when they first met. Recalling the conversation after the lapse of half a century, Weld wrote: "Indeed, during the whole afternoon, as I went on in the rehearsal from one point to another, I felt assured that he was with me, head and heart, in the positions which I had taken throughout." Although he asked many questions, Birney made no contribution to the discussion at that time, but left after inviting Weld to dine with him the following day. The two men returned to the subject then and in the days following. According to Weld's memory of the talks, Birney expressed full agreement that the legal right to hold slaves was a "monstrous moral wrong" and declared his intention to free his own slaves as soon as he could make suitable arrangements for them.[13]

This is not to say, as has been claimed, that Weld "converted" Birney to abolitionism. In the first place, as we have already seen, Birney had arrived at the decisions he confessed to Weld before the two met. And in the second place, neither of the two men had at that time yet arrived at the position of immediate abolition.[14] The encounter did occur at a crucial moment for Birney, however, and undoubtedly had an influence upon the decisions with which he was grappling at just that time. These were the problems that confronted him as a result of the "providential" invitation to become an agent of the American Colonization Society, which he had received but not accepted when Weld arrived on the scene. Weld urged him to accept and wrote back from Tennessee on his way north: "I can hardly tell you my dear brother how much I am interested in your decision upon the *great question* which you have under consideration." In September, 1832, colonization still seemed to Weld the only way of dealing with the slavery problem. "I am ripe in the conviction," he wrote Birney, "that if the Colonization Society does not dissipate the horror of darkness which overhangs the southern country, we are undone. Light breaks *in from no other quarter*.[15]

Weld's last letter was mailed from Cincinnati, to which he planned to return the following spring to enroll as a student at Lane Seminary. He sent greetings to Dr. Allan and to his son William Thomas, who together with his brother and other Southern youths Weld had enlisted were planning to join Weld at Lane in the spring.

Lane Theological Seminary at Cincinnati was a Yankee outpost of aggressive religious radicalism boldly thrust against the borders of South and West. The gateway city to those regions, Cincinnati was predominately Southern in population, as well as in culture, politics, economic life, and sentiment. Planters from across the Ohio River thronged its markets, banks, and hotels, and the slave-grown products of their plantations crowded its wharves along the waterfront. Yankee merchants and drummers cherished their Southern customers and thrived on their trade. Two steam-powered ferries kept the traffic flowing between the Ohio city and Covington on the Kentucky side of the still unbridged river. Among the city's population of thirty thousand was a settlement of some twenty-five hundred free Negroes. Slaves were sometimes hired as household servants from Kentucky masters. Slavery and freedom met and mingled in Cincinnati and prospered under a benevolent compromise. Any threat to that amiable compromise was a threat to the prosperity of the city.[16]

The new seminary under Presbyterian auspices did not seem such a threat at first. Chartered in 1829, the school remained in a state of suspended animation for three years while "Old School" Presbyterians, conservative and mainly Southern, bitterly contested control of the new seminary with "New School" Yankee radicals. The Yankees won out in the struggle, and the most radical ones at that. They assured and confirmed their control with financial aid solicited from Eastern men of wealth. Although the original donation had come from New Orleans, it had been made by Ebenezer Lane and his brother, merchants who came from Maine. Theodore Weld persuaded the Tappan brothers that Cincinnati was the ideal place for their Western manual labor institute and that the already-founded Lane Seminary was suited to the purpose. Arthur Tappan agreed to give the income from $20,000 provided Lyman Beecher of Boston were made president. An unsuccessful attempt had already been made to persuade Finney to accept the place. Other donations were pledged on condition of Beecher's acceptance, which was finally secured in June, 1832.[17]

A man of ferocious and untamed physical vigor, Beecher was the son and grandson of New England blacksmiths. Like Theodore Weld he made a cult of exercise and labor, and was given to shoveling huge piles of sand from one side of his basement to the other, twirling dumbbells, and grubbing stumps. Of an unstable emotional nature, he burst into tears o[f] hilarity on a slight provocation and delighted in horseplay and crude practical jokes. By many he was regarded as the foremost preacher of his time, a reputation he had built up in Litchfield, Connecticut, Boston, and New York by his emotional revivalism, his tirades against alcohol, and his fiery and intolerant attacks upon Catholics. He rejoiced in violent controversy, and soon after his arrival in Cincinnati he was answering formal charges of heresy, slander, and hypocrisy brought against him by conservative Presbyterians. Among his thirteen children, six of whom he brought with him to Lane, were several leaders of abolitionism in the next generation, including Henry Ward and Harriet. Twenty-one when she arrived at Lane, Harriet was later to marry one of the professors, Calvin E. Stowe.[18]

"Students are thronging in, and we have no where to stow them," wrote one of Lane students to Weld.[19] They began to pour in before the president arrived and the faculty was assembled. Twenty-four of them were former schoolmates of Weld at Oneida, and the Finney converts and disciples bulked large in the enrollment. Matriculation at Lane was a gathering of the Yankee hosts on the cultural frontier. The antecedents of thirty-seven of the first theological class of forty are known, and of them thirty-one hailed from upstate New York or New England.[20] They were for the most part mature, in their middle or upper twenties, six of them married. "It was a noble class of young men," wrote a son of President Beecher, "uncommonly strong, a little uncivilized, entirely radical, and terribly in earnest."[21] Their earnestness and their radicalism were apparent from the beginning. They seized the initiative by instituting the Oneida discipline of manual labor for the students, and a group of them, including the whole Oneida contingent, petitioned the boarding house to cease the serving of coffee.[22] Conspicuous among the newcomers for his color was James Bradley, an ex-slave who came originally from Guinea and was permitted to earn his freedom by a master in Arkansas.

Into this newly swarmed hive of Yankees, Yankee notions, and aggressive Yankee proselytism walked a handful of young Southerners, fresh from right-thinking, slave-owning homes in Alabama, Kentucky, South Carolina, and Virginia. The two sons of Dr. Allan, Birney's neighbor and Weld's host in Huntsville, William T. Allan and James Allan, came up from Alabama. James Armstrong Thome, twenty-three, the son of a slaveowning planter from Augusta, came from Kentucky. So also did Henry Thompson of Jessamine County, the owner of two slaves upon whose hire he proposed to support himself at Lane Seminary. Thomas Williamson, George G. Porter, and Josiah

Porter came all the way from South Carolina. For most of them it was the first venture abroad. But merely by crossing the Ohio River at Covington, Kentucky, and climbing the hill to the new Lane campus the Southerners put more spiritual distance between themselves and home than they would have had they been whisked off to the valleys of Vermont. For some of them it was the first step in a long and one-way journey.

Among the students, especially those from Oneida, there was great impatience and yearning for the arrival of Theodore Weld, their real leader. He did not put in his appearance until June, 1833. With three student friends he bought a boat for six dollars and floated down French Creek to the Allegheny and then to Pittsburgh. There they arranged to work their way on a passenger boat to Cincinnati. "We had great times," wrote Weld, "discussing anti-slavery, and stopping occasionally to get supplies, hold prayer-meetings, or find a place to sleep."[23] Weld came to Lane as a student, but a student of extraordinary background. In the selection of the site of the school, in the picking of its faculty, the election of the president, and the raising of funds he had played an important and sometimes decisive role.[24] With characteristic self-abasement, he had refused a professorship in the institution and entered it as a student. Yet his influence over both the students and the Tappan brothers, foremost benefactors and patrons, exceeded that of the president or any member of the faculty.[25]

It is little wonder that the new president of Lane eyed this thirty-year-old student with some misgivings. Harriet Beecher watched him during a public examination of her brother. "There is Theodore Weld," she wrote, "all awake, nodding from side to side, and scarce keeping still a minute together."[26] In later reminiscences Lyman Beecher observed ruefully, "Weld was a genius. First-rate natural capacity, but uneducated. Would have made a first-rate man in the Church of God if his education had been thorough. In the estimation of the class, he was president. He took the lead of the whole institution. The young men had, many of them, been under his care, and they thought he was a god."[27] His influence and prestige were further enhanced by the selfless and heroic devotion with which he nursed stricken students through an epidemic of cholera that threatened to wipe out the school at its very opening.[28]

Between the time of his talks with Birney in Huntsville and his arrival in Cincinnati to attend Lane, Weld had undergone an important change of mind on the slavery question. In September, 1832, he had written Birney that colonization seemed the only hope of solving the problem.[29] Charles Stuart, then in England reporting to his friend the triumphs of British abolitionism, was one of the influences that turned Weld away from the gradualism of colonization to the doctrine of immediate abolition.[30] Another was his contact with Elizur Wright and others of the Western Reserve. Instead of the only hope, colonization now seemed to him the worst enemy of abolition, a dishonest evasion of the problem, and opiate of the conscience, a thing to be discredited, exposed, and rooted out.[31] The same transition from gradualism and colonization to immediate abolition was simultaneously being made in the minds of the Tappan brothers of New York and in the minds of many of their associates in philanthropy there and in New England. The birth pangs of the national abolitionist movement coincided with those of Lane Seminary. In the spring of 1833 the *Emancipator* was started as the organ of the movement; in October the New York Anti-Slavery Society was founded in Finney's chapel; and in December it combined with Garrison's New England Anti-Slavery at a meeting in Philadelphia to found the American Antislavery Society. Arthur Tappan was elected president, and Elizur Wright, Jr., another of Weld's friends became the corresponding secretary.

Weld himself did not attend the Philadelphia meeting, but accepted from its hands a commission as one of the four agents of the new society.[32] Both he and the Tappans were greatly disappointed to find that Lyman Beecher had not kept step with the swing from colonization to immediate abolition that had occurred since he left New York. The new school they hoped to make the center and spearhead of abolitionism in the West was saddled with a president who was, from their new point of view, an obstructionist. "I am not apprised of the ground of controversy," Beecher wrote in reply to an inquiry for his views from Arthur Tappan, "between the Colonizationists and the Abolitionists. I am myself both, without perceiving in myself any inconsistency." He saw no justification for a war upon the colonizationists and "no need that the two classes of philanthropists should fall out by the way."[33] It was Weld's mission to Lane to root out the growth of colonization error completely, regardless of Beecher's views, and to abolitionize the place from top to bottom.[34] From Lane he wrote to Arthur Tappan and other officials of [the] movement: "I am deliberately, earnestly, solemnly, with my whole heart and soul and mind and strength, for the immediate, universal, and total abolition of slavery."[35]

When Weld arrived at Lane there was already a branch of the Colonization Society founded and flourishing in the seminary. He reported to Lewis Tappan that "there was not a single immediate abolitionist" at the school other than himself. In fact, he wrote, "abolitionism was regarded as the climax of absurdity, fanaticism and blood."[36] Weld set to work quietly, but with all the tremendous influence he exerted on the students, to neutralize and discredit the

Colonization Society and make converts for his cause. Working individually, he employed the techniques he used as a member of Finney's "Holy Band" to convert sinners. He selected one of the Southern students, William T. Allan of Alabama, as his first target. In addition to the advantage of gaining as a recruit a Southerner and the heir of a slaveholder, Weld considered Allan "an individual of great sway among the students." After some weeks of "struggling with his conscience, his noble soul broke loose from its shackles."[37] The experience evidently plowed deep into the emotions of the young Southerner, for "the morning after his conversion, he rose very early & went into his [Weld's] room & sat down by his bedside & poured out his feelings on this subject with an energy and delight he [Weld] could never forget."[38]

Weld's strategy of abolitionizing Lane had for a climax the staging of a public "debate," the object of which was a repudiation of colonization and an open commitment to the doctrine of immediate abolition. "A great work was to be done," he wrote, "in preparing the way for an open discussion." This was the individual work of proselytizing and conversion which he continued from June to February and to which he assigned his Southern converts as assistants. "Those of us who sympathized together in our abhorrence of slavery," he explained, "selected each his man to instruct, convince, and enlist in the cause. Thus we carried one after another, and, before ever we came to public debate, knew pretty well where we stood."[39] In other words, the outcome of the "debate" seemed pretty much assured before it was ever begun, though Weld reported to Lewis Tappan that "a majority was still opposed" at that time.[40]

When all was in readiness and President Beecher's reluctant consent was gained, the debates were begun early in February, 1834. They were to continue for eighteen nights and were attended by nearly all the students and most of the faculty. They more closely resembled a protracted religious revival than a debate. The master evangelist Weld was in charge and for the first two nights he bent all his magnificent talents to the task. The first question was put formally as, "Ought the people of the slaveholding states to abolish slavery immediately." But procedure conformed closely to the rubric of the revival meeting: the excoriation of a sin, prayerful urging of salvation, personal conviction of guilt, confession by public revelation of "experience," repentance and repudiation of error, and finally conversion. Southern students were put forward as the most conspicuous and effective speakers. Of the eighteen who spoke during the debates, according to Weld, "eight of them were born, and had always lived, in slave states," and the ten remaining speakers though not of Southern origin, "had resided more or less in slave states," from six years to six months. Making as much as possible of the Southern origin or experience of the participants, Weld wrote that, "The eighteen speakers gave, in their addresses, the results of residence and personal observation for years in each of the following states. Virginia, twenty-nine years; South Carolina, twenty-three; Alabama, twenty-four; Tennessee, twenty-two; Missouri, twenty-three; Kentucky, sixty-four. Besides these, they gave the result of observation during residences of from six months to five years in Louisiana, Arkansas Territory, Maryland, North Carolina, and Mississippi."[41] According to the account of Henry B. Stanton, all the native Southerners were sons of slaveholders; one was himself a slaveholder, and one the former slave from Arkansas.[42]

The speeches of the first nine nights consisted mainly of stories of brutalities, tortures, and atrocities inflicted on slaves. The significance of these stories did not lie in their novelty, for they contained all the properties familiar to readers of abolitionist literature—the red-hot tongs, the perforated, gore-spurting paddle, the still-born child, the tanned souvenir of the slave flayed alive. The significance lay in the Southern origin of the testimony.

The first of the Southerners to speak was William Allan of Alabama, who took up nearly three of the sessions. "At our house," he declared, referring to his father's parsonage in Huntsville, "it is so common to hear their screams from a neighboring plantation, that we think nothing of it. The overseer of this plantation told me one day, he laid a young woman over a log, and beat her so severely that she was soon after delivered of a dead child." He followed that with the story of a master who tied up a naked slave "in plain sight of the academy and the public green" of Huntsville and beat him with a perforated paddle. "He continued leisurely all day. . . . No one took any notice of it. No one thought any wrong done." Nor were these instances at all exceptional. "And lest any one should think that *in general* the slaves are well treated, and these are exceptions," said Allan, "let me be distinctly understood: —Cruelty is the *rule*, and *kindness* the *exception*." According to Augustus Wattles, one of the students reporting the speech, Allan's dictum on cruelty as the rule was "assented to and corroborated by all from the slave states."[43]

Henry P. Thompson, the Kentuckian who owned two slaves, said that "Cruelties are so common, I hardly know what to relate." But he then produced the story of a slave who was casually and sadistically beaten to death. James Thome related heart-rending stories of the internal slave trade, the separation of families, and the maltreatment of children. The Virginian C. S. Hodges told of the mistress of a home who made it a regular practice to "beat the woman who performed the kitchen work, with a stick two feet and a half long, and nearly as thick as my wrist; striking her over the head and across the small of her back, as she bent over her work." Andrew Benton of Missouri, a relative of Senator Benton but a native of Connecticut, told in circumstantial detail how a mistress slowly and meticulously tortured to death a slave woman with red-hot tongs: "first upon the bottoms of her feet; then upon her legs and body; and finally, in a rage, took hold of her throat."[44]

After the first nine nights of debate the vote was taken and all voted in favor abolition with the exception of four or five who excused themselves from voting on the ground that their opinions were still unformed. The Southerners were among the most ardent converts. In fact every one of them at Lane, except one who was absent during the debates became abolitionists. It was apparent from the phrasing of the question that abolition was to be accomplished, not by the North or the Federal Government, but by Southerners themselves. "The result has convinced me of another thing," wrote Henry B. Stanton, "which I hail as the bright bow of promise to this holy cause. That is that southern minds, trained and educated amidst all the prejudices of a slaveholding community, can, with the blessing of God, be reached and influenced by *facts and arguments, as easy as any other class of our citizens.*"[45]

The remaining nine nights were devoted to the rather moot question: "Are the doctrines, tendencies, and measures of the American Colonization Society, and the influence of its principal supporters, such as to render it worthy of the patronage of the Christian public?" After the speakers had completed their exposure of the shortcomings of colonization only one vote was cast in its support. Former members of the Colonization Society at Lane repudiated all its works, and according to Stanton they could not "find words to express their astonishment that they should have been so duped into support of this Society, as a scheme of benevolence towards the free blacks, and a remedy for slavery. They now repudiate it with all their hearts."[46]

In the case of the Southerners particularly, it was plain that these decisions and votes amounted to more than the scoring of debaters' points and the altering of opinions. They were accompanied by emotional upheaval, a profound sense of personal guilt, and deep religious stirrings. "And when thoroughly converted," observed Stanton of his fellow students from the South, "they manifest an ardor in behalf of the deeply injured black, which astonishes while it delights."[47] James Thome, former leader of the colonization movement at Lane described his conversion in mystical terms: "the great principles of duty stood forth, sin revived and I died. And, sir, though I am at this moment the heir to a slave inheritance . . . yet I am bold to denounce the whole system as an outrage, a complication of crimes and wrongs and cruelties that make angels weep. . . . Indeed, I know of no subject which takes such strong hold of the man as does abolition. It seizes the conscience with an authoritative grasp—it runs across every path of the guilty, haunts him, goads him, and rings in his ear the cry of blood. It builds up a wall to heaven before him and around him; it goes with the eye of God, and searches his heart with a scrutiny too strict to be eluded. It writes a 'thou art the man' upon the forehead of every oppressor."[48]

In the exalted mood of dedication with which they completed the eighteen nights of debate, the students proceeded at once to organize an anti-slavery society and affiliate with the national society of which Arthur Tappan was President. Again the Southerners either took, the places of prominence or were thrust forward into them. William Allan of Alabama was elected president of the new abolitionist society; James Thome of Kentucky, treasurer; C. S. Hodges of Virginia, auditor; and James Allan of Alabama, one of eight "managers." Without claim to Southern birth, but with several years of residence in slave states, Marius R. Robinson of Tennessee was made vice-president, and Andrew Benton of Missouri, recording secretary. Bradley, the former slave, was one of the managers.[49]

Faith without works was unthinkable to theologians in their frame of mind, and works followed in profusion. Henry Thompson not only returned to Kentucky and liberated the slaves upon whose hire he was educating himself, but went to work to support their education. Two sons of slaveholders vowed that they would give their parents no rest on the subject until their consciences were cleared and the slaves freed.[50]

An immediate outlet for the zeal of the new converts lay at hand in the 2,500 or more Negroes of Cincinnati. Weld and his disciples went from home to home to discover their condition and found that three-fourths of the adults had worked out their own freedom, that many were working to buy the freedom of relatives, and that an endless amount of good works were to be done for them. Without hesitation, the Lane missionaries founded two day schools, free evening schools, lectures in elementary education, three large Sunday schools, Bible classes, a library, reading room, and hall. Two students dropped out of Lane to devote full time to the work and other contributed large parts of their time—"an immense amount of labor among them, without interference with our studies," according to Weld. Arthur Tappan contributed a thousand dollars and the expenses of four young women from New York to help. The students announced as one of their fixed principles "social intercourse according to character, irrespective of color," and proceeded to put the principle into practice at once and conspicuously—to the dismay of faculty and trustees of Lane and the indignation of the citizens of Cincinnati.[51]

News of the part the Southerners played in the events at Lane Seminary was spread abroad in the antislavery press. Commenting editorially upon one report of the debates that stressed Southern testimony, the *Emancipator* remarked: "It more than vindicates the northern abolitionists in their representations of the horrors of slavery, which have been deemed so extravagant. We shall hear no more from the *intelligent* men, after this, of the 'exaggerations of northern fanatics who were never south of the Potomac, and know nothing of the matter.' Nor can it longer be urged that the instances of cruelty are only the exceptions to the general rule. Southern men have now attested the contrary." As a witness of the debates, Wattles emphasized the same point in reporting them. "I am aware that it will be said, this is not a fair picture of slavery," he wrote. "But sir, if I can judge from the conversation of gentlemen who have lived and been brought up amongst it, . . . I know the picture has never been presented to the public in all its ugliness. Such facts as *these* are common to them as household affairs; and so common are they in the community where they occur, that little notice is taken of them. They produce no effect upon the public heart. They enlist no sympathy. They call up no pity."[52]

Despite the moral obtuseness and callousness of the South repeatedly pictured by the Southern converts to abolition, it was the rather inconsistent conclusion drawn from their testimony that the way to achieve abolition was through appeals to the conscience of the slaveholder. The successful conversion of the Southerners at Lane proved it! "I fling to the winds the unworthy imputation," declared Weld, "that the people of the southern states are such compounds of prejudice, passion and cowardice, as to shun the contact of those, whose opinions upon the subject of slavery differ from their own, and who profess to sustain their opinions by arguments."[53] The Southern heart and mind was open to argument and reason, and the clear duty of the Northern abolitionist lay in carrying home to the South his appeal.

The great sensation of the first annual meeting of the American Antislavery Society, which opened in New York on May 6, 1834, was a long address by James A. Thome. He and Henry B. Stanton had been sent to the big city as delegates from the Lane Antislavery Society. They found Chatham Street Chapel crammed to capacity with the great and near-great of Eastern abolitionism and the provinces. The Tappan brothers, Arthur presiding, were in evidence, along with Elizur Wright, Jr., Samuel J. May, John Greenleaf Whittier, and William Goodell. Twenty-five years old and full of his message, Thome gained the floor the first day to speak to the resolution, "That our principles commend themselves to the consciences and interests of slave-holders; and that recent developments indicate the speedy triumph of our cause." Thome's participation in the Lane debates was known through the abolitionist press, and he was the first of the Southern converts the East had seen.

"Of the truth of the first proposition contained in this resolution," he told them, "... I have the honor to stand before you as a living witness. I am from Kentucky. There I was born and wholly educated. The associations of youth and the attachments of growing years; prejudices, opinions and habits forming and fixing during my whole life, conspire to make me a Kentuckian indeed. More than this; I breathed my first breath in the atmosphere of slavery—I was suckled at its breast and dandled on its knee. Black, black, black was before me at every step—the sure badge of infamy."

He plunged next into an account of the sufferings of the slave in Kentucky where the institution wore its "mildest features." "Such sufferings too!" he exclaimed, "Sufferings inconceivable and innumerable—anguish from mind degraded—hopelessness from violated chastity—bitterness from character, reputation, and honor annihilated—unmingled wretchedness from the ties of nature rudely broken and destroyed, the acutest bodily torture in every muscle and joint—groans, tears and blood..." But the most shocking revelations of Thome did not concern the slave, but the morals of the slaveholder. "Pollution! Pollution!" he exclaimed. "Young men of talents and responsibility, fathers, professors of religion, ministers—all classes! I have facts—but I forbear to state them—facts which have fallen under my own observation, startling enough to arouse the moral indignation of the community." Nor were these isolated and unusual instances. "I would not fail to have you understand that this is a general evil. Sir, what I now say, I say from deliberate conviction of its truth; let it be felt in the north and rolled back upon the south, that the slave states are Sodoms, and almost every village family is a brothel." He added in parentheses, "In this, I refer to the inmates of the kitchens, and not to the whites." But the parenthetical qualification was forgotten when the statement was quoted, as it often was. He concluded by an appeal to Northern abolitionists: "Come and tell us what shocking scenes are transpiring in our own families under the cover of night. Go with us into our kitchens and lift up the horrid veil—show us the contamination, as it issues thence and wraps its loathsome folds about our sons and daughters."

At a meeting of a colonization society in New York the following day the Reverend Robert J. Breckinridge, a member of the distinguished Kentucky family, who in 1831 had been defeated for reelection to the state legislature on an antislavery platform, publicly challenged Thome's description of morals in their native state and called for a retraction. Thome replied the next day on the floor of the antislavery meeting. "I have been called upon to retract," he said. "Sir, I cannot retract a word. Would to God I could do it. If truth, which I knew, would allow it, I would heartily yield to him as my elder. But I again repeat what I said. The slave states are Sodoms, and well nigh every village kitchen is a brothel."[54]

The effect of all this upon the abolitionist audience is not difficult to imagine. "The Lord be praised for giving us Lane Seminary," wrote Elizur Wright to Weld, "The visit of our dear brethren Thome and Stanton has aroused into activity thousands of stupefied consciences in this city. The speech of brother Thome electrified about as large a mass of mind as our connection with the physical world will allow to be crammed into Chatham St. Chapel. The results were the best possible under the [laws] of mind. The grand generalissimo of the powers of darkness was thrown into a rage, in which 'his zeal got the better of his judgment' as events of the week showed."[55]

The most spectacular Southern convert was yet to join the ranks of the abolitionists. This occurred in the month following Thome's speech in New York when James G. Birney publicly renounced the colonization movement, of which he was then one of the well-known national leaders, and proclaimed his adherence to the doctrine of immediate abolition. Birney's road to abolitionism was a long and slow one, full of obstacles and painful decisions.

It was some two months after his talks with Weld in the summer of 1832 that Birney decided to accept the urgently pressed agency of the American Colonization Society for the southwestern states. Once he gave up his profitable law practice, accepted the sever[e] financial sacrifices involved, and turned his back upon his plan to escape slavery by moving his family to the North, he plunged into the colonization work with great optimism. "I cannot but trust, my dear Sir," he wrote Ralph Gurley, "that the Sun of prosperity is about to break out with great warmth and brilliancy upon the cause of unhappy Africa . . ."[56] His main duties lay in traveling over the vast territory of Tennessee, Alabama, Mississippi, Arkansas, and Louisiana, giving lectures, soliciting contributions, organizing and reviv[ing] local societies, and finding suitable emigrants for the Liberian colony. After gaining the agreement of Gurley to his proposition that, "in the South, he must travel as a gentleman in good circumstances would do, not employed on an Agency,"[57] Birney set forth hopefully on his mission. He turned first to neighboring areas of the Tennessee Valley, on to Nashville and other Tennessee towns, then in December to the Lower South, to Tuscaloosa, Montgomery, Mobile, New

Orleans, and up through the Delta country to Natchez. He was working in the heart of the Cotton Kingdom of the Southwest in "flush times." He was appealing to slaveowners in an expansive and confident mood of boom times, when slavery and cotton were the road to riches and the future held unlimited possibilities.

Birney well knew that there was a basic ambiguity in the appeal the colonizationists made to the South in promising to remove the free Negroes. On the one hand they addressed the liberal conscience, offering colonization as an inducement to facilitate voluntary emancipation, a gradualist approach to the removal of slavery. On the other hand they reminded the conservatives that the presence of the free colored people in the South was a constant threat to the institution and that their removal would work for the security and stability of slavery. At one and the same time colonizationists therefore appealed to the hopes of the liberals and to the fears of the conservatives, to idealism and to selfish interests. Birney was prepared to use both of these contradictory appeals in the propagation of the doctrine, but a few months of experience convinced him that "the *selfish* principle is the only one to which an appeal can be made in the South." As he explained to Gurley, "Our cause is approved by many under the very just impression, that its success will give them a more quiet and undisturbed *possession* of their slaves."[58] It was altogether a curious and unhappy position for one whose basic motivation was a moral condemnation of slavery to find himself. Yet he persevered for nearly a year and a half with great energy and with the prayer: "May the Lord give me boldness and utterance with the people of the South, whose jealousy is so excitable on the subject of Slavery."[59]

So eager was he to temper boldness with caution and propitiate suspicion, however, that he announced that he would never "knowingly violate public sentiment."[60] It was the policy of the Colonization Society, he declared, to "approach with fastidious delicacy even the prejudices of the South," and to guard "with scrupulous care against all appearance of dictation; abjuring the spirit of dogmatism," and bearing always "the banner of peace and conciliation."[61] "There must be no bullying, no threatening, nothing like an association with . . . the *cause of abolition*," he wrote. "Indeed the opposition of the Abolitionists I consider one of the strongest grounds for recommending it to the people of the South."[62]

Birney addressed his appeal not only to the self interest of slaveholders but increasingly to their fears—fears of the free Negro's threat to slavery, fears of the slave himself, and fear of the abolitionist. He warned that "the presence of the *free colored class* must produce discontent in the minds of the slaves," that the "coming danger" was the increasing proportion Negroes over whites, and that this would cause the *"abandonment of a large portion of the South,*—the catastrophe that is now hurrying upon us with the stride and strength of a giant." He warned especially against the "ruthless spirit" and the "rash hand" of the abolitionist.[63] When Clement C. Clay was quoted as saying that abolition was "the ultimate purpose of colonization," Birney protested to the Alabama politician that "in numerous public addresses" he had recommended colonization "on the very ground that it did not interfere, in any manner, with the right of the Master to his slaves as property, and that it furnished the best defence against the rash attempts of *abolitionists.*"[64]

In a series of fifteen articles on colonization he prepared for the press in the summer of 1833, Birney devoted much of his space to attacking the arguments, tactics, and aims of the abolitionists. He emphasized particularly the antagonism between the two movements, maintaining that there was "no class of men in the United States, against whom the leading abolitionists have manifested a hostility so unappeasable as against the advocates of Colonization." And he quoted Garrison as evidence.[65] Such was the fanatical blindness of the abolitionist that he would "at once tear down the whole existing structure of society amongst us—and, in his desire for the advancement of human happiness, instigate one portion of the community to the slaughter and destruction of the other."[66] One by one he went through all the arguments of the abolitionists, replying in detail.[67] He never appears to have gone to the length of questioning their sincerity, but there was little else about abolitionism and all its works that this future leader of the national party of abolitionists did not question, denounce, and firmly reject.

In his reply to the "atrocious charges" of abolitionists against the South and the morals of slaveholders, Birney sometimes sounded very much like the whole-hearted Southern apologist. He urged the Northern agitators to visit the South and see for themselves "the care and kindness with which our menial servants are treated—the regular and abundant provision made for their wants and comfort; the meliorated condition of the field hands . . . ; witness the freedom with which the subject of slavery is discussed in ordinary conversation—the acknowledgment of the evil—the desire, everywhere expressed, to get rid of it." He denounced the wicked misrepresentations of the abolitionists, called upon them to acknowledge "the rapid march of that benevolence" in the South, and demanded that they "be ashamed and repent of the atrocious charges which you have trumpeted against us to the world for our moral condemnation."[68]

It is quite apparent that Birney felt that his office as agent of the Colonization Society obliged him to take a more optimistic view of his work in public than he expressed in private. His private reports to Secretary Gurley were filled with discouraging accounts of poorly attended lectures, meager response in contributions, and withering interest in the movement. He was "greatly disappointed at the insensibility of the *religious* community on the subject of Slavery," and "almost sickened" when such people repeatedly told him, "they cannot live in the South without slaves."[69] Everywhere he encountered apathy and indifference. At great trouble he supervised the collection of some one hundred and fifty free Negro emigrants for Liberia at New Orleans, arranged for their transportation and supplies, and went to "great exertion to attract public attention to the sailing of this Expedition." He stood on the river wharf and with "exalted and soul-stirring emotion" watched while the brig set sail, but the meeting he called on the strength of the sailing "failed utterly."[70] New Orleans was "deplorably inert" and in southern Alabama there was "a deadness to the subject."[71] He found the large planters generally "as blind to the natural rights of their Slaves, as the *whites* of the West Indies were" and that they thought that "the self evident principle *that all men are created equal*, is about as ridiculous nonsense as was ever published." The subject of slavery, as a rule, they were "determined not to have touched *in any way*." By December of 1833 he came to the conclusion that within the previous year the people of the Southwest had "become, very manifestly, more and more indurated upon the subject of Slavery" and that under these circumstances he did not "believe that anything effectual can be done amongst them on the subject of Colonization."[72]

He had already announced his decision to Secretary Gurley in September to give up his agency with the Colonization Society and leave Alabama. In part the decision was no doubt dictated by the discouragement with which his work had been met, but underlying this was the moral confusion and contradiction in which he was involved. With a mind that he confessed was "ill at ease upon the subject of retaining my fellow creatures in servitude," he could not be happy in promoting a cause that, by his own confession, justified and defended slavery.[73] For a time he returned to his earlier plan of moving to Illinois but yielded to the wishes of his wife and father, who wanted him to return to Kentucky. He moved his family to land he bought adjoining that of his father in Danville, and after selling all of his considerable property holdings in and around Huntsville, joined them in November.

Birney did not regard the move as the abandonment of a cause or as a rout, but as a strategic retreat in order to retrench and reform his lines. He realized that he had advanced to a position that was no longer tenable in the Lower South. That position was not yet abolitionism, though he was moving in that direction. Nor had he yet wholly abandoned colonization, though he admitted its weaknesses. and complained of its moral contradictions. It was admittedly a time of transition and deep self-searching for him. What the future held for him was uncertain. He only knew that he had been on the wrong track and must make a new start—even at the cost of uprooting a large family and abandoning a career at the age of forty-two.[74]

The wishes of wife and father were not the only reasons determining his settlement in Kentucky. Of "commanding importance," he said was the fact that he regarded his native state "as the *best site in our whole country for taking a stand against slavery*."[75] While he doubted that "any thing effectual can be done *South* of Tennessee," he believed that the only hope lay in the border states from the slave states.[76] Even in Nashville, Tennessee, he discovered with elation that his arguments, while "much bolder than they had ever been elsewhere," did not appear to shock his hearers.[77] And in Kentucky the outlook was even brighter. For there the old antislavery sentiment of the Revolutionary period had never really died out, and among his friends were numerous men of standing who were still outspokenly in favor of emancipation. Among them were John C. Young, president of Centre College, and Gideon Blackburn, his predecessor, Judge Joseph R. Underwood, later United States Senator, the Reverend Robert J. Breckinridge, the colonizationist who leaned to emancipation, and his cousin John Green. "There are many," he wrote Gurley, "who like myself look upon it [colonization] as impracticable to arouse the South sufficiently to make it the means of ridding us of *Slavery*."[78]

He had scarcely settled in Danville before he was invited to a meeting in Lexington called to revive a gradual emancipation movement. Since he was "for doing at least this much, if more cannot be done," Birney attended and took a leading part in the organization of "The Kentucky Society for the gradual relief of the State from slavery." The constitution made any white citizen of the state eligible for membership who would give his pledge "to emancipate any slave which may be born his or her property *thereafter*—when such slaves may have attained the age of 25 years, and if a female, her offspring with her." Birney prepared an "Address" to accompany publication of the constitution in which he made it plain that the object of the society was "*the total abolition of slavery throughout the Commonwealth*." This did not mean immediate emancipation, for which neither the slaves nor the whites were yet prepared, but "*immediate* preparation for *future* emancipation." The important thing was the decision *"that slavery shall cease to exist—absolutely, unconditionally, and irrevocably."* The institution stood condemned in the eyes of the civilized world, it was "unchristian," it would be "the ruin of us as a people," and there was no longer any excuse for procrastination.[79]

John J. Crittenden was elected president of the society, and Birney worked actively in the early months of 1834 lecturing over the state to promote its doctrines. There was actually little to distinguish the type of gradualism proclaimed by the Kentucky society from that of the American Antislavery Society save for the failure of the Kentuckians to pronounce slavery a "sin" and to denounce colonization as a method. And on these two points Birney himself was rapidly moving away from the Kentuckians and toward the Northern point of view. He followed the current progress of British abolitionism and collected and pored over a large library of English and American abolitionist literature.[80]

Birney still owned slaves, though he had come to believe slaveholding sinful, and he still condoned colonization, though he no longer believed in it. Toward the gradualism he practiced in Kentucky, he came to feel more and more as he had toward the colonization he practiced in Alabama—that it was an evasion of the real problem and an inadequate, if not inconsistent, expression of his moral convictions. But his transition from gradualism to outright immediatism was accomplished much more rapidly than his evolution from colonization to gradualism.

The accounts of the student debates at Lane Seminary, which he read in the *Emancipator* during March and April, struck home to him with particular force. They grappled with the same problems he was confronting, and they recalled his conversations with Theodore Weld in Huntsville two years before. In May Birney went to Cincinnati to renew his acquaintance with Weld and talk over his problems. He found the spell of the strange man as powerful as ever. "I have seen in no man," he remarked in his diary four months later, "such a rare combination of great intellectual powers with Christian simplicity. He must make a powerful impression on the public mind of this country, if he lives ten years."[81] Weld and some of "the enlightened students took him in and expounded unto him the way of God more perfectly."[82] Whatever they contributed to his decision, Birney told Weld that he was ready to renounce gradualism and colonization and go the whole way.

Another point of crisis had been reached, and Birney set about once more squaring his deeds with his convictions. In May he resigned his office in both the Colonization Society and the Gradual Relief society. Then on the morning of June 2 he assembled all the members of his household and with his two older sons as witnesses, solemnly emancipated all his remaining slaves. There were only six of them left—Michael, his wife and three children, and a mulatto girl of six or seven years. In the deed of manumission he read, Birney declared slavery "inconsistent with the Great Truth that all men are created equal" as well as with the admonition of the Golden Rule. To Michael, forty years of age, he paid back wages with interest for all the years of his labor as a slave. The Negroes were to remain with the family on wages.[83]

Having thus cleared his conscience, Birney undertook next to make public confession of his change of heart and face the consequences in his native state. The confession of faith, it was decided, would take the form of a long letter addressed to the Reverend Thornton Mills, secretary of the Kentucky Colonization Society, denouncing colonization and advocating immediate abolition. Birney kept in close correspondence with Theodore Weld, who together with his Lane Seminary colleagues advised him in detail on the composition and publication of the letter. Weld was determined that "it must produce an *immense effect*" and assured Birney that it would "accomplish more for the *Great Cause* than the operation of all other instrumentalities [*sic*] employed hitherto." This was due not to the argument but to the source of the letter. Weld argued that Birney could do more for abolition "than any other man in the Union." Here was no fledgling theological student, but a man of mature years, a Southerner of aristocratic connection, an ex-planter, a slaveholder of long experience, and, most important of all, a prominent colonizationist of national standing. Here was a defection that would rock the opposition on their heels. It was the first time anything of the sort had happened. It was no wonder that abolitiondom buzzed with the rumors that Weld, with Birney's advice, set afloat as "*something* REPORTED *not definitely known*.[84]

Birney's *Letter on Colonization* was a blunt and hard-hitting polemic. Many an intelligent slaveholder, he wrote, knew perfectly well that "the dark system in which he has involved himself, his posterity and their interests, will remain as unaffected by it [colonization], as mid-ocean by the discharge of a pop gun on the beach." The fact was that colonization doctrines served as "an opiate to the consciences of many, who would otherwise, in all probability, feel deeply and keenly, the injustice and the sin of slavery. They are the purchase of a little more sleep, a little more slumber." He would have it known that "The views contained in this letter are my own, and they have been the result of my own reading, observation and thought. I am a member of no antislavery society—nor have I any acquaintance, either personally or by literary correspondence, with any of the Northern abolitionists."[85]

Weld agreed that it was important to have the initial printing of the letter done in Kentucky, and with considerable difficulty a printer was finally found in Lexington. The expense was borne by a collection among the members of the Lane Anti-Slavery Society, who not only handled the circulation to lists of names supplied by Birney and others, but carried bundles of them along with them as they scattered over the country since they were just leaving Lane at the end of term. William Allan of Huntsville was assigned the important mission of carrying a supply back to Alabama for circulation among Birney's former colonizationist friends in the Lower South. and dropping off 3,000 copies with Birney in Danville. Eight thousand were thus circulated, but Weld had plans for publishing an edition of 100,000 in the East. Later the Seminarians acquired use of a press themselves, and Weld pictured them keeping it in operation all day "and the *whole of the night.*" He reported to Birney that "the document is producing a *great effect* upon those Colonizationists who have read it. Let us bless the Lord and magnify his name together . . ."[86] The Colonization Society was indeed thrown off balance by this sudden defection. Their journal, the *African Repository*, reported that it had been on the point of undertaking a defense of their former agent for being too hard on the abolitionists and too proslavery in tone in Alabama, only to learn that he had turned abolitionist himself. Gerrit Smith, the philanthropist of Peterboro, New York, who was still a colonizationist but was soon to join and surpass Birney as a fiery abolitionist, attacked him for misrepresenting slavery.[87]

The abolitionist hosts of the North were of course elated by their latest Southern recruit. Elizur Wright wrote Weld that he had been "electrified by that noble letter of Birney" and was personally writing to two hundred abolitionist societies and friends "to engage them in one thorough simultaneous effort to make the most of the *letter.*"[88] Lewis Tappan, whose house in New York had just been sacked by a mob, wrote Weld that he read the letter "with tears of joy and gratitude" and wanted Birney *"employed exclusively for this work."*[89] As a matter of fact, Birney had already proposed such employment himself to Theodore Weld. Weld assured him that the salary he required would be forthcoming and that "this can be done you know *out of sight.*" The Tappans put up the initial sum, and Birney went to work secretly as a full time abolitionist, employed by the American Anti-Slavery Society.[90]

Angelina Grimke sailed from Charleston for Philadelphia in October, 1829, with a powerful feeling of release. She was at last free from "the land of slavery." She was also escaping an uncongenial home full of unsympathetic and critical relatives, as well as the scornful eye of King Street. Northward lay "the promised land," and to her Philadelphia seemed the "Land of Canaan." At twenty-four Angelina was prepared to start life anew.[91]

In Philadelphia she made her home with Sarah, who lived with Catherine Morris and her Quaker family. Under Sarah's influence, Angelina was quickly submerged in the life of the Quaker community, which centered in the "First-day," "Quarterly" and "Yearly Meetings." Angelina was resolved to don the "longeared cap" of the Friends on her twenty-fifth birthday in February. "But when the time came," she admitted in her journal, "my soul was humbled within me." She only put on the cap after encouragement from others.[92] In April, 1831, however, Sarah rejoiced that "My beloved Sister Angelina was this day received into religious membership with the Friends," and added, "Oh that she may have been rightly prepared to become a true yoked fellow in the Gospel of our Lord."[93]

April seemed to be the month of crisis in Angelina's complicated religious life, as she herself remarked. It was in "the fourth month" of 1826 that she had broken with the Episcopalian Church to join the Presbyterians, and in April 1828 that she broke with the Presbyterians to begin the quest that ended in April two years later when she was received into membership by the Philadelphia Friends.[94] Each of these crises brought the promise of long-sought peace and fulfillment, but each in its turn proved a bitter disappointment. Neither of the sisters actually proved a "true yoked fellow" of the new faith, though Sarah the long-suffering chafed more silently under the yoke than did the spirited and restless Angelina. In small things first the two incorrigible nonconformists from Charleston irritated the Friends. Neither of them would adopt the Quaker usage of the ungrammatical *thee* for *thou*, and Angelina had difficulty remembering not to call "the 5th day & 6th days by the names the world has given them." They challenged further disapproval by altering the conventional shape and material of the long-eared bonnet to protect their heads from the northern chill. But it was the chill of reproof and reserve from their brothers and sisters in the faith that they felt most keenly, and from which they could contrive no satisfactory protection.[95]

Sarah's morbidly sensitive nature was especially vulnerable to criticism. Her preparation for the ministry was handicapped by a halting and self-conscious manner of speaking that made every attendance at meeting a harrowing ordeal. "Feel I must attend the evg. mtg. at Pine St.," she recorded, and confessed, "it is hard work to go where I feel despised." She dreaded the yearly meetings like a criminal under sentence facing "the day of execution." She felt "condemned already" whenever she rose to speak. The "cutting charge" of preparing her remarks beforehand and of "going there to preach, instead of to worship" cost her "hours of anguish." This reproof was severely administered "by an Elder to whom I did a little look for kindness." Sarah's journals are filled with self-recrimination and the conviction that she was the vilest of sinners. "I have suffered the very torments of the fabled hell because my conscience was sore to the touch all over," she wrote. Her reiterated and obsessive preoccupation with guilt bordered on the pathological. Every slight or reproof, every disappointment or failure was declared to be "a shaft from the hand of Omnipotence." It is difficult to see what comfort or satisfaction she got out of her religion, and yet with unflagging self-immolation she continued for years to submit to its discipline and the slights and reproofs of its elders.[96]

Angelina was far less submissive and resigned to her disappointments. Her youth was slipping away, and the high hopes and towering ambitions with which she had set forth from Charleston for the "promised land" remained unfulfilled. "Weeks & months have passed in mental suffering," she wrote in 1831. "'Every heart knoweth its own bitterness' & whilst my countenance has been clothed in smiles my heart has often been filled with sorrow & sighing, for daily, yea, almost hourly do I maintain a conflict for resignation to my present allotment."[97] Her restless energy and ambition were hard to harness under the repressive discipline of the Friends. "I have been led to doubt if it was right for me ever to have worn the dress of a Quaker," she confessed in a mood of rebellion, "for I despised the very form in my heart, and have felt it a disgrace to have adopted it, so empty have the people seemed to me, and sometimes it has seemed impossible that I should have ever be willing to join them. My heart has been full of rebellion, and I have even dared to think it hard that I should have to bear the burdens of a people I did not, could not, love."[98]

Most of all, Angelina was "finding it very hard to stand and *wait*," and to heed the Quakerly admonition, "be *still*." She plunged into the assigned routine of meetings and benevolent duties—the visiting of prisons, hospitals, and alms-houses—but this did not absorb her energy nor satisfy her craving for fuller expression and mightier tasks. Sarah returned to Charleston for a long visit with her mother in 1831, but Angelina did not accompany her. Turning back was not Angelina's way. Whatever it was she was seeking lay ahead. She still had visions of becoming a great preacher, but the Quaker preparation for the ministry was tedious and slow. A passion for self-improvement and a desire to compensate for her neglected education inspired her to undertake an extensive course of home study. When this did not satisfy her needs, she opened a correspondence with Catherine Beecher, Lyman Beecher's older daughter, who ran a girl's school in Hartford. Catherine paid her a visit in Philadelphia and invited her to Hartford to see the school for herself. Angelina was greatly taken with the place when she visited it in the summer of 1832, and also charmed with Catherine's sister Harriet, who had not yet moved to Cincinnati with her father. Here were enterprising young ladies after her own heart, full of notions and attainments, and very different from her sober Quaker companions. Angelina returned to Philadelphia filled with enthusiasm for her plan of going to Hartford to prepare herself as a teacher. She was promptly rebuffed, however, by the Friends. They sternly reproved this notion of "going among strangers" and "abandoning her charities." Yielding reluctantly, she settled back in the stultifying routine, more discontented and rebellious than ever.[99]

In spite of the singular and forbidding photograph taken somewhat later,[100] Angelina is described as an attractive woman in her youth, tall and graceful, with curly chestnut hair and sparkling blue eyes. Both she and Sarah had love affairs while they were living in Philadelphia, though Sarah's occurred some ten years earlier than Angelina's. Both affairs ended unhappily. Sarah's lover inspired in her "a state of tranquil & subdued feeling," and she took his loss with characteristic resignation and despair. Angelina's emotions seem to have been somewhat more tempestuous, though she described the young man as "the clear & placid sky against which every object in the checquered landscape of life is drawn," and her love as "not the result of excited feeling, but of the calm deliberate conviction that he is the friend designed by Almighty Goodness to be my earthly guide." If he shared this conviction, as she thought, he never confessed his feelings. Impatient of masculine reticence, Angelina complained of "the embarrassing situation in which his not speaking to me places me" since "every body is talking about us." He died after a brief illness on October 10, 1833, and Angelina, like her sister before her, was plunged into mourning and melancholia.[101]

One great source of comfort and consolation remained to the sisters in their distinguished brother, Thomas Smith Grimke. By all accounts he was a thoroughly admirable figure. Throughout the bitter nullification struggle in Charleston, he had courageously taken the Unionist side, and yet could claim "more strong and attached friends among the nullifiers, than all the Union Leaders put together."[102] His cousin Robert Barnwell Rhett, leader of nullificationists, believed that none of Grimke's political opponents "ever entertained a doubt of his simple integrity and disinterestedness in the opinions he professed."[103] And Thomas Grimke professed some notably unpopular opinions. Not only was he the leading pacifist in the South, nationally known as a leader of the peace movement, but he was an outstanding educational reformer and a champion of the temperance movement.

In the lives of Sarah and Angelina, their brother played the role of confessor and guiding inspiration. Sarah spoke of him as "my tutelary god, my idolized brother," and Angelina poured out her heart to him in long letters of an essay type on such subjects as religion, education, peace, and reform.[104] The intimate tie with their brother served also as the one link that held between the exiled sisters and their past—family, home, Charleston, and the South. Sarah had seen much of him when she visited Charleston in 1831, but Angelina had not seen him since she left home in 1829. In September, 1834, Thomas paid his sisters a visit in Philadelphia. A month later he was dead of the cholera.

Suffering an "agony intense" over the loss of her brother, Sarah turned back once more to her religion in search of consolation.[105] Angelina could expect no real comfort from her religion, for her alienation from the Friends was even further advanced than that of her sister. Bereft of lover and of brother within a year, an exile from home and family, and a stranger within her church, Angelina had to search further afield for a new meaning for her life and consolation for her losses. Her diary is silent for several months after her brother's death. It was during that period, however, that she became "deeply interested in the subject of Abolition." So powerfully did this interest develop in her that in May, 1835, she wrote: "Truly I often feel as if I were ready to go to prison & to death in this cause of justice, mercy & love." She even confessed a premonition that if she were called to return to Carolina, "it will not be long before I shall suffer persecution of some kind or other."[106]

Certainly there was no cause with which she could have identified herself that would have so completely justified in her own eyes her alienation and exile from her home and her growing estrangement with the Society of Friends. While there had long been a deep strain of anti-slavery feeling among the Quakers, sentiment divided the membership among gradualists, colonizationists, and immediatists. To avoid schism and embarrassment the Society frowned upon all discussion of the subject, and especially upon the agitation of the abolition movement. Nothing in the record indicates anything but conformity with the Quaker position on the part of the sisters up to this time. Both of them had expressed disapproval of slavery, but neither of them manifested any interest in the stirring events of the early abolitionist movement. "I had long regarded this cause as utterly hopeless," wrote Angelina.[107] But in the spring of 1835 she attended some lectures by the English abolitionist, George Thompson. In spite of Sarah's remonstrances she began to read abolitionist literature, "and for the first time saw that slavery, under all circumstances, was sinful."[108]

Among the abolitionist publications Angelina read was William Lloyd Garrison's *Liberator*, and it was an editorial of his that led her to make her first public commitment to the cause. As might be expected, there was nothing half-hearted about the commitment. Garrison had published an "Appeal" to the citizens of Boston against mob violence of the pro-slavery elements. "I confess I could not read it without tears," Angelina wrote Sarah, "so much did its spirit harmonize with my own feelings. This introduced my mind into deep sympathy with Wm. Lloyd Garrison.... It seemed to me I *must* write him."[109] And write him she did, after prayerful hesitation. Angelina's letter identified her completely, heart and soul, with Garrison and his aims and methods. She took no exception to the harshness of his creed nor the violence of his language. She wished that "thousands may adopt thy language, and be *prepared* to meet the Martyr's doom." She urged him never to retreat or compromise or give an inch. "The ground upon which you stand is holy ground: never—never surrender it," she implored. "If you surrender it, the hope of the slave is extinguished, and the chains of his servitude will be strengthened a hundred fold.... But remember you must be willing to suffer the loss of all things—willing to be the scorn and reproach of *professor* and profane." To convince the slaveholder of their earnestness abolitionists must be "willing to suffer the loss of character, property—yea, and life itself, in what we believe to be the cause of bleeding humanity." Martyrdom was to be deliberately courted. In fact, she wrote, "a hope gleams across my mind, that *our* blood will be spilt, instead of the slaveholders'; *our* lives will be taken, and theirs spared." Thus might slave insurrection and war be avoided. "If persecution is the means," she declared, "which God has ordained for the accomplishment of this great end, EMANCIPATION; then, in dependence upon Him for strength to bear it, I feel as if I could say, LET IT COME; for it is my deep, solemn, deliberate conviction, that *this is a cause worth dying for*. I say so, from what I have seen, and heard, and known, in a land of slavery, where rests the darkness of Egypt, and where is found the sin of Sodom. Yes! LET IT COME—let *us* suffer, rather than insurrections should arise."[110]

Of all the pronouncements of the new Southern recruits to abolitionism, Angelina Grimke's commitment was the most ardent and unqualified. Neither the testimonials and confessions of the Southern students in the Lane debates, nor James Thome's address to the Antislavery Society convention in New York, nor Birney's letter denouncing colonization quite so thoroughly captured the true believer's spirit of dedication and willing martyrdom as did

Angelina's letter to Garrison. The editor of the *Liberator* promptly published it in his columns without asking leave.[111]

It is evident that Angelina had not brought herself to face fully the consequences of her act when she wrote the letter. "I felt that it might involve me in some difficulties," she wrote in her diary, "& therefore it was written in fear & after it was written I hardly knew whether to send it or not.... I had some idea it would be published but did not feel liberty to say it must not be, for I had no idea of my name being attached to it if it was."[112] Her name *was* attached, of course, for it was her name and her Charleston background, as Garrison pointed out, that gave the letter its real significance. Not only did the editor use her name, but coupled that of her beloved brother Thomas with it in his praise of her act.

Angelina's first reactions to the publication of her letter were more those of the Charleston patrician than the dedicated abolitionist. "Blushing, and confusion of face were mine," she admitted in her diary, "and I thought the walls of a prison would have been preferable to such an exposure. Then, again, to have my name, not so much *my* name as the name of Grimke, associated with that of the despised Garrison, seemed like bringing disgrace upon my *family*, not myself alone. I felt as though the name had been tarnished in the eyes of thousands who had before loved and revered it. I cannot describe the anguish of my soul." The reproval of her sister Sarah, who thought Angelina had "listened to the voice of the tempter" and had been "given over to blindness of mind" was, she said, her "greatest trial." The stern opposition and remonstrance of her Quaker brethren and the disapproval of her closest friends seemed likely to crush her at first. "But I was truly miserable," she admitted, "believing my character was altogether gone among my dearest, most valued friends. I was indeed brought to the brink of despair, as the vilest of sinners." Pressure was brought upon her to write Garrison retracting some of her statements, or at least expressing disapproval of his publication of her letter. "Nevertheless," she wrote, "I could not blame the publication of the letter, nor would I have recalled it if I could." Angelina had taken her stand, and as was usual with her, there was no thought of turning back.[113]

It was nearly a year after Angelina pledged her faith in Garrisonian abolitionism that Sarah finally came around to the same position. In the meantime she had continued her unhappy religious strivings with no more reward or encouragement for her ambitions as a minister than before. Then one day at meeting while she was speaking the silent opposition that she had felt "for nine long years" suddenly became public. Jonathan Evans, presiding elder of the Yearly Meetings, sometimes called "Pope Jonathan" because of the authority he exercised, interrupted her remarks with the request that she be silent. It was an "entirely unprecedented & unsanctioned" act, said Sarah. "I of course instantly resumed my seat & never felt more peaceful & the conviction then arose that my bonds were broken." Following that rebuke she wrote a letter which she expected to result in her "disownment."[114] It was shortly after this experience of the "broken bonds," and apparently as one consequence of the liberation, that Sarah wrote Angelina withdrawing her opposition to her sister's abolitionism and joining her in the cause.

"O Sister," wrote Angelina gratefully in reply, "I feel as if I could not only give up friends but life itself for the slave if it is called for. I feel as if I could go any where to serve him, even down to the South if I am called there."[115] They were not "called" southward, as it turned out. But the two of them were at last free of their cramped frustrations and on the eve of a revolution in their lives. As Angelina put it, "The door of usefulness among *others* seem to have been thrown open in a most unexpected and wonderful manner, whilst the door of usefulness in our S[ociet]y seems as if it was barred and double locked."[116]

Notes

1. [note missing]
2. [note missing]
3. [note missing]
4. [note missing]
5. [note missing]
6. [note missing]
7. [note missing]
8. [note missing]
9. [note missing]
10. [note missing]
11. Charles Beecher (ed.), *Autobiography, Correspondence, etc., of Lyman Beecher, D.D.* (New York, 1874), II, 313.
12. William Birney, *James G. Birney*, 105–7.
13. Ibid., 107–10.
14. Thomas, *Weld*, 33; Fladeland, *Birney*, 52–53.
15. Weld to Birney, July 24 and September 27, 1832, in Dumond, *Birney Letters*, 13, 27.
16. "The Journal of Cyrus P. Bradley," *Ohio State Archaeological and Historical Quarterly*, XV, 218–22.
17. Robert S. Fletcher, *A History of Oberlin College* (Oberlin, 1943), I, 44–53.
18. Ibid., 52–53.

Chapter II: The Year of Decision   159

19. Henry B. Stanton to Theodore Weld, August 4, 1832, *Weld-Grimke Letters*, 85.
20. Fletcher, *History of Oberlin*, 54–55.
21. Beecher, *Autobiography of Lyman Beecher*, II, 321.
22. Fletcher, *History of Oberlin*, 56–57.
23. Weld quoted in Beecher, *Autobiography of Lyman Beecher*, 314–15.
24. Weld to Birney, September 27, 1832, in *Weld-Grimke Letters*, 27.
25. Thomas, *Theodore Weld*, 49; Beecher, *Autobiography of Lyman Beecher*, II, 314; H. B. Stanton, E. Weed., S. W. Streeter, and C. Waterbury to Weld, August 2, 1832, *Weld-Grimke Letters*, 78-90.
26. Beecher, *Autobiography of Lyman Beecher*, II, 289
27. Ibid., 321.
28. Weld to a Member of his Family, June, 1833, *Weld-Grimke Letters*, 109–12.
29. Weld to Birney, September 27, 1832, ibid., 27.
30. Thomas, *Theodore Weld*, 50–51.
31. [Ibid.]
32. Weld's "Commission" is found in Elizur Wright, Jr., to Weld, December 31, 1833, in *Weld-Grimke Letters*, 124–25.
33. Lyman Beecher to Arthur Tappan, April 23, 1833, in Beecher, *Autobiography of Lyman Beecher*, II, 323.
34. Weld to Arthur Tappan, Joshua Leavitt, and Elizur Wright, Jr., November 22, 1833, *Weld-Grimke Letters*, 124–25.
35. [Ibid.]
36. Weld to Louis Tappan, March 18, 1834, *Weld-Grimke Letters*, 132.
37. Ibid.
38. Angelina Grimke to Sarah Douglass, April 3, 1837, in Weld-Grimke Papers, Clements Library.
39. Quoted in Beecher, *Autobiography of Lyman Beecher*, II, 322.
40. Weld to Louis Tappan, March 18, 1834, *Weld-Grimke Letters*, 132.
41. Weld to James Hall, editor of *Western Monthly Magazine*, May 20, 1834, ibid., 138–39.
42. Henry B. Stanton in New York *Emancipator*, March 25, 1834.
43. Augustus Wattles in New York *Emancipator*, April 22, 1834.
44. Ibid.
45. Stanton in New York *Emancipator*, March 25, 1834.
46. Ibid.
47. Ibid.
48. Thome quoted in New York *Emancipator*, May 13, 1834.
49. Boston *Liberator*, April 15, 1834.
50. Stanton in New York *Emancipator*, March 25, 1834.
51. Weld to Louis Tappan, March 18, 1834; Weld to James Hall, editor of *Western Monthly Magazine*, about May 20, 1834, *Weld-Grimke Letters*, 132–35, 137–46; *A*

Statement of the Reasons Which Induced the Students of Lane Seminary to Dissolve Their Connection with That Institution (Cincinnati, 1834).
52. New York *Emancipator*, April 22, 1834.
53. Weld to James Hall, about May 20, 1834, *Weld-Grimke Letters*, 141.
54. New York *Emancipator*, May 13, 1834; *Debate at the Lane Seminary, Cincinnati. Speech of James A. Thome of Kentucky Delivered at the Annual Meeting of the American Anti-Slavery Society, May 6, 1834* (Boston, 1834).
55. Elizur Wright to Weld, June 10, 1834, in *Weld-Grimke Letters*, 149–50.
56. James G. Birney to Ralph R. Gurley, August 23, 1832, *Birney Letters*, 23.
57. Id. to id., July 12, 1833, ibid., 11.
58. Id. to id., April 13, 1833, ibid., 71.
59. Id. to id., October 13, 1833, ibid., 33.
60. Birney to Messrs. Phelan and Woodwon, August 14, 1833, in Huntsville (Ala.,) *Democrat*, August 15, 1833.
61. Birney, "The Colonization of Freed Colored People," No. 2, in ibid., May 23, 1833.
62. Birney to Gurly, December 27, 1832, *Birney Letters*, 50.
63. Birney, "The Colonization of Freed Colored People," Nos. 5, 10, and 12, in the Huntsville *Democrat*, June 13, July 11, 25, 1833.
64. Birney to Clement C. Clay [December 1832], rough draft without date or address, *Birney Letters*, 47.
65. Birney, "Colonization of the Freed Colored People," No. 3, Huntsville *Democrat*, May 30, 1833.
66. Birney, "Colonization of the Freed Colored People," No. 8, ibid., July 4, 1833.
67. Birney, "The Colonization of Freed Colored People," Nos. 5, 6, and 7, in ibid., June 13, 20, 27, 1833.
68. Birney, "The Colonization of Freed Colored People," No. 7, ibid., June 27, 1833.
69. Birney to Gurley, September 24, 1833, *Birney Letters*, 89.
70. Id. to id., April 8, 1833, ibid., 65–72.
71. Id. to id., March 18, 1833, December 27, 1832, ibid., 61, 49.
72. Id. to id., December 3, 1833, ibid., 97.
73. Id. to id., January 24, September 24, 1833, ibid., 50, 88, 90.
74. Fladeland, *James G. Birney*, 73–74.
75. Birney to Gerrit Smith, November 27, 1833, quoted in William Birney, *James G. Birney*, 131.
76. Birney to Ralph R. Gurley, December 3, 1833, *Birney Letters*, 97.
77. Ibid.
78. Birney to Gurley, December 11, 1833, ibid., 98; Fladeland, *James G. Birney*, 75–77.
79. Birney to Gurley, December 11, 1833, *Birney Letters*, 98–109.
80. William Birney, *James G. Birney*, 134–35.
81. Birney Diary, September 16, 1834, Library of Congress.
82. William G. Ballentine (ed.), *The Oberlin Jubilee, 1833–1883* (Oberlin, 1883), 63.
83. Fladeland, *James G. Birney*, 82–83.

Chapter II: The Year of Decision   161

84. Weld to Birney, May 28, June 17, 1843, *Birney Letters*, 112–18.
85. James G. Birney, *Letter on Colonization Addressed to Thorton J. Mills* (New York, 1834), passim.
86. Weld to Birney, June 19, July 8, July 14, August 25, October 6, 1834, *Birney Letters*, 119–37.
87. Fladeland, *James G. Birney*, 86–87.
88. Elizur Wright, Jr., to Weld, August 14, 1843, *Weld-Grimke Letters*, 166–67.
89. Weld to Birney, August 25, 1834, *Birney Letters*, 130–31.
90. Id. to id., August 25, September 4, 1834, ibid., 130–34; Birney to Weld, September 9, 1834, *Weld-Grimke Letters*, 167–68.
91. Angelina Grimke to Sarah Grimke, August 5, 1829, Weld-Grimke Papers, Clements Library.
92. Angelina Grimke, Journal, February 21, 1830, Clements Library.
93. Sarah Grimke, Journal, April 28, 1831, loc. cit.
94. Angelina Grimke, Journal, April 27, 1829, loc. cit.
95. Ibid., December 16, 1828; Birney, *Grimke Sisters*, 94–95.
96. Sarah Grimke, Journal, November 2, 30, December 2, 1834, November 22, 1835, loc. cit.
97. Angelina Grimke, Journal, December 12, 1831, loc. cit.
98. Quoted in Birney, *Grimke Sisters*, 98.
99. Ibid., 98, 108–9.
100. F. J. and W. P. Garrison, *William Lloyd Garrison, 1805–1879* (New York: 1885–1889), vol.
101. Sarah Grimke, Journal, January 26, 1823; Angelina Grimke, Journal, October 21, 1831, June 2 [?] an uncertain date, 1832, and another, 1833. Angelina Grimke to Theodore Weld, March 8, 1838, Weld-Grimke Papers, Clements Library.
102. Thomas S. Grimke to Anna Frost, February 9, 1833, Weld-Grimke Papers, Clements Library.
103. Quoted in John. B. O'Neall, *Biographical Sketches of the Bench and Bar of South Carolina* (Charleston, 1859), II, 384–87.
104. Sarah Grimke, Journal, June 3, 1827, quoted in Birney, *Grimke Sisters*, 19; Angelina Grimke to Thomas S. Grimke, January 16, 1832, and May 6, 1833, Clements Library.
105. Sarah Grimke to Theodore Weld, January 21, 1837, Weld-Grimke Papers, Clements Library.
106. Angelina Grimke, Journal, May 12, 1835, Weld-Grimke Papers, Clements Library.
107. Ibid.
108. Sarah and Angelina Grimke to Editor, Boston *Liberator*, October 13, 1837.
109. Angelina Grimke to Sarah Grimke, September 27, 1835, in Birney, *Grimke Sisters*, 127.
110. Angelina Grimke to William Lloyd Garrison, August 30, 1835, printed as broadside, *Slavery and the Boston Mob*, in Weld-Grimke Papers, Clements Papers.
111. Boston *Liberator*, September, 1835.

112. Angelina Grimke, Journal, September, no day, 1835, Weld-Grimke Papers, 1835, Clements Library.
113. Quoted in Birney, *Grimke Sisters*, 130–31.
114. Angelina Grimke to Theodore Weld, undated, 1837, in Weld-Grimke Papers, Clements Library.
115. Angelina Grimke to Sarah Grimke, August 5, 1836, Weld-Grimke Papers, Clements Library.
116. Id. to id., July 25, 1836, loc. cit.

THE MESSENGER LECTURES
Spring, 1964

C. VANN WOODWARD
Sterling Professor of History, Yale University

THE FIRST RECONSTRUCTION IN THE LIGHT OF THE SECOND

Thursday, April 23, 4:30 p.m.
RECONSTRUCTION IN MYTH AND POLEMIC

Friday, April 24, 4:30 p.m.
THE FEAR OF FREEDOM

Thursday, April 30, 4:30 p.m.
THE PARADOX OF LOYALTY

Friday, May 1, 4:30 p.m.
THE CONSERVATISM OF NORTHERN RADICALS

Thursday, May 7, 4:30 p.m.
RADICALISM FOR CONSERVATIVE SOUTHERNERS

Friday, May 8, 4:30 p.m.
DID THE NORTH REALLY MEAN IT?

ROOM 120, IVES HALL
Open to the Public

Photographic facsimile of the advertising flyer for "The Messenger Lectures, Spring 1964, C. Vann Woodward, Sterling Professor of History, Yale University" (MS 1436, box 64, folder 23), C. Vann Woodward Papers (MS 1436), Manuscripts and Archives, Yale University Library. Cornell University misprinted the title of Messenger Lecture V. Woodward titled this lecture "Radicalism for Southern Conservatives."

The Messenger Lectures
The First Reconstruction in the Light of the Second

In the Spring of 1964, C. Vann Woodward delivered the Messenger Lectures on the Evolution of Civilization at Cornell University. His six lectures, bearing the title "The First Reconstruction in Light of the Second," work as a chronological political history, centering on the motivations and concerns of the formerly enslaved, northern and southern radicals, and northern and southern conservatives during the era of Reconstruction from 1865 to 1872. The purpose of the series is to explain why Reconstruction failed. The problem involved, among others, the Republican Party's lack of a genuine commitment to racial equality, a crisis of loyalty among white southerners who were never able to reconcile allegiance to the union with region, white southern radicals' indiscriminate support for substantial structural change, and the abysmal conditions faced by the formerly enslaved such as disease, hunger, and violence. Woodward anticipated integrating these lectures into a larger book on Reconstruction, but, as the introduction makes clear, he never completed it. The lectures remained untouched—with the exception of a hybrid piece derived from portions of the second half of lecture four and the first half of lecture six that was recycled twice as a presentation and three times in print. The first lecture is missing. Thus the five extant lectures appear here for the first time as a set.

MESSENGER LECTURE II
The Fear of Freedom

AN EXPERIENCE AS momentous in the history of a race as liberation from centuries of bondage should have had all the poignancy and drama with which legend and song have endowed the liberation of the Negro slaves by the Civil War. The coming of freedom has been described as the fulfillment of long forbidden and secretly cherished hopes and dreams. Folk memory through generations turned the event into poetry and myth and embodied it in song and story. W. E. B. Du Bois called it "the Apocalypse," and described it in passages that are hauntingly lyrical:[1]

> This was the coming of the Lord. This was the fulfillment of prophecy and legend. It was the Golden Dawn, after chains of a thousand years. It was everything miraculous and perfect and promising.... There was joy in the South. It rose like perfume—like a prayer.... A great song arose, the loveliest thing born this side the seas.... It was a new song and its deep and plaintive beauty, its great cadences and wild appeal wailed, throbbed and thundered on the world's ears with a message seldom voiced by man. It swelled and blossomed like incense, improvised and born anew out of an age long past, and weaving into its texture the old and new melodies in word and in thought.

This vision, this great myth has sustained the hopes and aspirations of a whole people, and after a century it still inspires a mighty upsurge of effort toward final fulfillment. The ideal of freedom and the faith in democracy has been supported in the past by less substantial myths than this. To lay rude hands on the myth of liberation would be a wanton and heedless thing.

The historian is more properly concerned with the buried and forgotten realities out of which the myth was born. He would take into account the moment or days of wild delirium and ecstasy where they occurred (though many slaves did not share the experience in these ways), but he will search beneath and beyond these transitory outbursts for the substance and meaning of the experience of liberation. He will seek to discover how the terrible but familiar insecurities of the old order were exchanged for the strange and unfamiliar insecurities of the new order, how freedom was tested, its limits explored, its meanings and disappointments slowly and painfully learned, its potentialities dimly perceived.

It is rare that the Negro who went through the experience was articulate and literate enough to leave contemporaneous record of his feelings. Amos Beman, one of the few who did, wrote movingly of the newly emancipated: "They awake as from a troublesome and bitter dream; they find themselves invested with all the responsibilities of manhood and looking around..."[2]

For many the bitter dream did not end with the awakening. One difficulty with the apocalyptic conception of emancipation is that it was not accompanied by revelation. Nor did it come all at once. Perhaps as many as a third of all the slaves were involved in some form of degree of liberation before the surrender at Appomattox. It took the form of fugitives from the plantations swarming after the invading Union army. "They regarded the Union soldiers as deliverers from bondage," writes Bell I. Wiley, "... and in every locality where the 'Yankees' made their appearance the Negroes flocked to their camps in quest of freedom."[3] No arguments or commands could stop them. The process began in 1861 and continued throughout the war. John Eaton, General Grant's chaplain, witnessed the awesome spectacle in Tennessee in 1862: "The arrival among us of these hordes was like the oncoming of cities," he wrote. "There was no plan in this exodus, no Moses to lead it.... But their interests were identical, they felt, with the objects of our armies a blind terror stung them, an equally blind hope allured them, and to us they came. There were men, women, and children in every stage of disease or decrepitude, often nearly naked, with flesh torn by the terrible experiences of their escapes.... Such ignorance and perverted notions produced a veritable moral chaos. Cringing deceit, theft, licentiousness—all the vices which slavery inevitably fosters—were the hideous companions of nakedness, famine, and disease."[4] Three years later, near the end of the war, William Gannett described hundreds of freedmen arriving at Savannah sent back from Sherman's army by boat: "One half of the number had to be helped up the plank; they would drop half way from weakness. Four men only were strong enough to carry up those who could not lift a limb. Long, bony, and still, they lay along the decks, the flies swarming around them as if they lit upon the dead. The silence of four *was* that of death; and, before I had them all landed, the four were six. And yet their case has been that of thousands."[5]

For the slaves in the interior who remained beyond Federal lines or out of touch with the army at the end of the war liberation usually came with less dramatic suddenness and traumatic impact. Many were kept in ignorance or in doubt of their right to freedom for weeks or months after the return of peace. In the lower South the Freedmen's Bureau continued to issue circulars and publish notices assuring Negroes and warning planters of the reality of emancipation as late as August of 1865.[6] Even then for more than a year there were reports of remote plantations of the Southwest where slaves worked on apparently unaware of the news.

Whenever and however the news came, however, whether with the authority of the master himself or otherwise, the most common response was the immediate departure of all who were able to walk. This was what set in motion the black Volkerwanderung of 1865, the planless, uncontrollable marching of freemen back and forth across the South during the summer and much of the fall. Unlike the exodus of massed hordes that followed Grant and Sherman during the war years, the migrations of 1865 were in smaller groups and more diffuse in purpose. These people were not pursuing freedom, but testing it and for the first time using it in its most available and elemental form—that of uninhibited motion. The motion might have a well-defined objective—finding lost parents or children, or more vaguely seeking the forbidden pleasures of town and city, returning to the old home from which they had been sold or "refugeed" during the war. The second exodus was not always voluntary. Impoverished masters sometimes evicted them from their cabins. "I don't know as I 'spected nothing from freedom," testified one ex-slave, "but they turned us out like a bunch of stray dogs, no homes, no clothing, no nothing, not 'nough to last us one meal."[7]

The refugees who did not return to the plantation congregated by the thousands in filthy, disease-ridden, starvation camps that clustered near every town of any size. A North Carolinian described such a place at Beaufort, where a thousand arrived in two weeks. "Their condition is wretched indeed," he wrote. "They are nearly naked and half starved. They lie about on the ground in the sun and seem to have lost all of their energy." He told of one freedman broken out with small pox who lay by the side of the road for two days.[8] Near Atlanta a traveler saw the body of a Negro woman by the side of the road and asked two children who sat beside what was the matter with her. "She perish to def, sir," replied one, "but she free, dough."⁹ In Macon "ten were picked up dead in the streets" during one week of October.¹⁰ In the immediate vicinity of Vicksburg a thousand were reported to have died of cholera.¹¹ Exposure, malnutrition, and epidemics of cholera and small pox sometimes killed off the miserable population of the refugee camps faster than they could be buried. The sufferings of this second exodus recall at times the horrors of an earlier ordeal of the race, those of the Middle Passage.

The physical sufferings of the liberated who joined the exodus of 1865 were so striking and spectacular that they attracted wide attention. In the first place, no one had ever seen black people collected together in such great numbers before. Slave ships had arrived furtively and rarely in the living memory of men, but ever in the full tide of the trade in the eighteenth century their cargoes rarely ever exceeded 200. The coffles and barracoons of the domestic trade rarely assembled more at one place and one time. In the very nature of the plantation discipline slaves had been kept dispersed and largely immobilized. The appalling mortality rates in the towns and cities encouraged the growing belief that the race was doomed to early extinction, a delusion that became almost an article of faith among whites and was often repeated.

The psychic costs of liberation were more personal and obscure and the evidence was not easily perceived. The very rejoicing of the freedmen over deliverance from bondage seemed of itself to constitute denial of emotional distress. Yet testimony of the liberators as well as the liberated and old masters as well reveals that under the surface disturbance was not uncommon. On his own plantation in South Carolina Dr. St. Julien Ravenel noted in his diary that, "The negroes are completely bewildered at the change of their condition. Many are truly distressed. . . . All is in a chaotic state."¹² On one of the Sea Islands a Negro woman told a Northern missionary that her people "had all been so 'confuse,' they did not know what to do; did not know where they belonged or 'anything about we.' "¹³ Ben Simpson, born in Georgia and freed belatedly in Texas remembered that, "I was 'fraid of everybody. I just went wild and [took] to the woods. . . ."¹⁴

In the words of E. Franklin Frazier, the sociologist, "Emancipation was a crisis in the life of the Negro that tended to destroy all his traditional ways of thinking and acting."¹⁵ Those "traditional ways" were the ways of slavery, the discipline of generations that had isolated its victims from contact with freedom and in Frazier's opinion, erased the heritage of pre-slavery culture from their minds. "What authority was there," asks Frazier, "to take the place of the master's in regulating sex relations and maintaining the permanency of marital ties? Where could the Negro father look for a sanction of his authority in family relations which had scarcely existed in the past?... In the absence of family traditions and public opinion, what restraint was there upon individual impulse unleashed in those disordered times?"[16] Weak enough at best under slavery, parental authority and family integrity disintegrated rapidly with the collapse of the old order.

The atomizing effect of the weakened ties of family identity was aggravated by loss of personal identity as well. Virtually all the freedmen chose new surnames for themselves, and regularly did so without regard to kinship. "Our teachers," reported a Pennsylvania missionary in South Carolina, "have had to contend with difficulties growing out of a confusion of names. All the slaves of one master take his name. In one school will be a squad of Seabrooks, or Chisholmes, or Middletons, bearing no relation whatever to each other. Even a wife does not assume her husband's name if she belongs to another plantation."[17] Names offered little clue to identity and freedmen themselves complained of the loss. "They named theirselves big names," said a former slave from South Carolina, "then went roaming round like wild, hunting cities. They changed up so it was hard to tell who or where anybody was."[18] Not only that, but for these and other reasons it was often difficult for the freedman to retain with conviction a sense of his own identity.

It was easier for many freedmen to maintain identity by clinging or returning to the only life they knew, even to the old master, than to identify with some ill-defined and illusive freedom. "That they regarded themselves as more intimately connected with their former masters than with their liberators," write Simkins and Woody, "is indicated by the fact that in almost no instance did they assume such names as Lincoln, Sumner, Garrison and Phillips."[19]

One of the most cherished and often repeated legends of the white South was that of the faithful slave who refused to leave or returned to his old master. It has been embellished with sentiment and told in a thousand forms. One does not have to accept the traditional and self-serving interpretation of the legend to credit it with a basis of reality. Slaves did remain or return in large numbers. How many will never be known. Benjamin C. Truman estimated that as many as a third were back with their former masters by November, 1865.[20] While reunion between former slaves and former master varied greatly according to their former relationship, there are authentic accounts of reunions characterized by hysterical displays of affection on the part of the freedmen. Chief Justice Salmon P. Chase was witness to such a scene on St. Helena Island when "not less than a hundred" of Dr. Richard Fuller's former slaves, whose faces "fairly shown with joy and excitement" crowded around, "feeling the Doctor's hair, passing their hands over his shoulders, clustering lingeringly about him, and joining with deep-throated emphasis in the chant" of welcome.[21]

One possible explanation for such scenes is that the ex-slave was still playing the role he had been assiduously taught and aptly learned to play for generations. But neither role-playing nor the benevolent father image was sufficient to assure for many masters the repetition of such a performance. The extended hand was sometimes rejected and sullen looks were not concealed.

During the war years the conduct of those slaves who were in the path, or within range, of invading armies had already done much violence to the legend of "the faithful slave." Acts of devotion and loyalty, embellished by retelling down the years, undoubtedly did occur. But they were the deeds of a small minority of the slave population. That such acts were "exceptional" and that "insubordination seems to have been more common than submission" is the conclusion of close investigation by Bell I. Wiley. Such insubordination not only took the form of insolence, plundering, cooperation with invading forces, and refusal to submit to punishment and take orders, but in a few cases it reached the point of personal violence, rape, and attempts at insurrection.[22]

With the end of all Confederate resistance and the collapse of slave discipline, wild and vague fears of insurrection and massacre seized many whites. A citizen of Wilmington, North Carolina, wrote Governor W. W. Holden of "daily outrages" that "excited serious and well-grounded fears.... Our people of all classes are alarmed.... It will inevitably result in a *massacre*." Holden reported that "similar complaints" had come in from other communities.[23] No massacre or insurrection occurred, nor anything approaching one. But the record does not sustain the claim of Carl Schurz that, "The transition of the southern negro from slavery to freedom was untarnished by any deeds of blood..."[24] Such deeds were remarkably rare, but a few occurred during the war and a few after. The former slaves of James Clinton of Pickens City, Alabama, shot him from ambush and beat him to death with clubs.[25] A union officer wrote from Huntsville that, "The negro population is unsettled & restless. They suspect even their best friends. The white man is their hereditary enemy.... I have been surprised to find something of that feeling in my own regiment—the suspicion of all white men, northern or southern. A few days ago the negroes on a plantation near here burned their master's house.... It is certainly a very dangerous precedent, & Southern men so read it."[26]

One incident of this sort in slavery times was sufficient to panic whole states with rumors of insurrection. Emancipation heightened rather than diminished white susceptibility to panic of this kind—at least for a time. Before apprehension of the new insecurities of freedom began to subside, exaggerated reports of a massacre of whites in Jamaica in 1865 revived the historic nightmare of the Santo Domingo insurrection that tormented the sleep of two generations before the war. If thirty years of British emancipation and reconstruction could end in bloody deeds in Jamaica, what was the prospect for American emancipation in the South?[27]

As the old regime crumbled about their heads the masters and their families watched every gesture and expression of their servants. No one knew for sure what would happen. During the war years Mary Boykin Chesnut had speculated often about "these sphinxes" and what went on behind "their black masks." In May, after the surrender, she noted, "I do not see one particle of alteration. They are more circumspect, politer, quieter; but that's all." In June her friend Stephen Elliot from Beaufort told her, "They waited on me as before, gave me beautiful breakfasts and splendid dinners; but they firmly and respectfully informed me: 'We own this land now.'" And in July she heard stories of betrayal, defiance, and plundering. "Before this," she observed, "everyone had told me how kind and faithful and considerate the Negroes had been."[28]

On June 8 a master in Tuscaloosa wrote that "the servants that remain are even more docile & obedient than before," and that "Nothing has been said or done ... about ... changing their status in any respect. And things go on, as before."[29] But on June 15 a diarist of the same town watched in wonder while a Union officer lectured masters in the presence of their former slaves. "And they stand and ask questions of this yankee captain," he wrote, "as to their new relations toward their slaves!" To him it was fantastically unreal. "It seems a gigantic dream," he said. Only a few weeks before, the captain "would have been hung on the nearest tree, & left there."[30]

The meaning of liberation as loss of property was, for most masters, clear enough. What seemed incomprehensible was the loss of *authority*—authority over their former property and all the rights and sanctions, the instant deference and unquestioning obedience that went with it. Appealing for military assistance to put down "insubordination," a planter of southeastern Georgia explained that when his hands finished work, "they roam about just as they please, and when I tell them to go to their quarters they do not mind me."[31] The letter of an overseer to a planter of Baldwin County, Georgia, was eloquent with sheer bafflement: "som of them go when tha pleas and wher tha pleas an pay no attention to your orders nor mine ... "[32] Dr. St. Julien Ravenel observed the reactions of his class with the rare detachment of a scientist: "We are very apt to retain former feelings," he wrote, "& wish to exact more service than what would be implied in a fair contract with the white man. Especially is this the case when the former slaves are retained in service. *The former relation has to be unlearnt by both parties.*"³³ This great unlearning process proved painfully slow for both parties.

Among the freedmen the most hopeful signs appeared in some of the Negro troops. An army surgeon in New Orleans observed of those in uniform that "the slavish timidity and undue deference is rapidly disappearing and is being replaced by a more manly bearing."³⁴ Outside army ranks, however, the commonest observation was that of a missionary in North Carolina who "met thousands every day in the street" and found them "civil, respectful, almost servile in the presence of whites."³⁵ In despair a minister of abolitionist background reported that, "When addressing their masters, they take off their hats, and speak in a hesitating, trembling manner, as though they were in the presence of a Superior being."³⁶ The attitudes of both races recall the still unresolved American racial dilemma posed by Tocqueville: "To induce the whites to abandon the opinion they have conceived of the moral and intellectual inferiority of their former slaves the negroes must change, but as long as this opinion exists they cannot change."³⁷

The limits and boundaries of freedom could only be discovered by experiments of the bold who tested them. Where did freedom begin? How far down the big road? Was it to be found only in town, or on the plantation as well? If so, when did it start? Only after sundown? Or in work hours as well? The first thing a Georgia freedman remembered about emancipation was "someone saying—asking a question—'You got to say "Master?"' And somebody answered and said, 'Naw.' But they said it all the same. They said it for a long time."³⁸ Some learned to say "Yes" and "No" without adding "Massa" or Missus" in the army, but few tried it elsewhere. The steps from "Massa" to "Cap'n" and on to "Boss" were longer and more daring than many dared make for a long time.

For as long as she could remember, Mercia, a slave who belonged to Mr. Thompson of Chapel Hill, had made her master's fire every morning and brought him water three times a day. She continued to do so until one morning in November after the war when she asked for pay. Whereupon the old man took the pail and fetched his own water, passing through the kitchen filled with his former slaves. They watched silently. His wife Eliza reported further rebellion: "They say they won't sow the wheat unless Mr. Thompson will give them a living chance. Nobody knows what that is as they have stolen nearly all his sheep killed his calves taken as many chickens as they please ... they say they won't be bound in writing the Yanks told them they must draw a writing They say they have been niggers long enough They intend to be free."³⁹

For Andrew on the Manly plantation in Alabama, being free meant taking the wife his master had forbidden him to take at the cost of leaving the plantation. For his former wife Binkey it meant successful resistance to a whipping at the same cost. So it was for Annie and for twenty-one others on the Manly place who left rather than submit to discipline. Those who remained submitted to punishment or avoided it by strict observance of orders. The whip continued in use, as did other symbols and methods of the old regime.⁴⁰ In Texas Negroes were reported objecting "to anything that reminds them of the old system," and some of them were striking "against being summoned to and from the fields by the blowing of a horn or the ringing of a bell, because that was the old fashioned way."⁴¹

Among some freedmen [were signs of] the fear of freedom and its insecurities that was manifest in docility and compromises with the old master and the old discipline. One abolitionist believed that some "pined for the old allegiance with its careful providences."⁴² The Sambo role was for some not so much an act as an ingrained habit, and the skilled performer was still rewarded. The rewards combined with the temptations and coercions were too much for them.

To combat these temptations and coercions and dispel the fear of freedom, the freedmen enjoyed for a few months two underestimated resources of their own. One was the promise of land and the other was the presence of Negro troops. As late as July 15, 1865, there were still 123,156 Negro soldiers in the United States Army. They were organized in 139 regiments and the great majority of them were on garrison duty in the South, replacing rapidly demobilized white units. The Freedmen's Inquiry Commission had early noted that the freedman was already "to some extent a changed being," and that "No one circumstance has tended so much to these results as the display of manhood in negro soldiers."⁴³ The pride and confidence they inspired was clearly manifest in the conduct of the freedmen. For it was most frequently in the neighborhood of these garrisons that freedmen cast off docility and made their strongest demands for civil rights and fair treatment, and where whites complained most bitterly of insolence and insubordination.

The promise of land was less tangible, but it was real, and the demand for fulfillment was associated with the presence of the Negro troops. Between the spring and fall of 1865 there lay unresolved—suspended ominously in irresolution and tense conflict—what was potentially the most revolutionary feature of Reconstruction. This was the disposition of between 800,000 and 900,000 acres of abandoned and confiscated farm lands in the hands of the Freedmen's Bureau, together with 485,000 acres of Sea Island estates to which 40,000 Negroes held possessory titles under General Sherman's Special Field Order Number 15. On one side of this conflict were the former rebel owners and claimants of the land working with relentless pressure through President Johnson for restoration of ownership. On the other side were General Oliver O. Howard of the Freedmen's Bureau working with his associates with tactics of delay and evasion for the distribution of the land among freedmen.[44]

Far from passive spectators or uncomprehending dupes, the freedmen in their own way were active participants in this conflict. Their agitation and propaganda was popularly labeled a "delusion," the forty-acre-and-a-mule delusion, but it had folk shrewdness of purpose. Another widely used device contributing to the same purpose was their refusal to make contracts with planters on the ground of free land by Christmas. Those who held disputed title to land held on with great tenacity and some with show of force. In the neighborhood of Negro garrisons their agitation was boldest. From Wilmington, North Carolina, came report that, "The Negroes firmly believe that all the property is theirs of right and that every day of delay in the assertion of their rights is rendering their claims weaker.... If they read an official denial of such intentions on the part of the Government . . . they are utterly incredulous, and become impatient until their faith is bolstered by assurances from the negro soldiers or others of like ideas."[45]

By early fall President Johnson had resolved the conflict on all scores against the freedmen and in favor of their former masters. In response to demands from Southern whites the Negro garrisons were greatly reduced or replaced by white troops.[46] More important still, on September 4, Johnson directed Howard to restore to pardoned rebels all abandoned lands and all lands condemned but not yet sold. Within a month the Bureau had lost nearly all the lands once held for allotment to freedmen, together with the plea that pardoned rebels set aside a ten-acre homestead for Negro heads of families.[47] It then became the duty of General Howard to disabuse the freedmen of the "delusion" to which he had tried so hard to lend some substance of reality. In speeches, circulars, and bulletins scattered all over the South he labored to kill the hope that persisted. His most painful personal appearance was on Edisto Island before representatives of the 40,000 who held possessory title to lands which he told them had to be restored to their owners. "They did not hiss," he observed, "but their eyes flashed unpleasantly, and with one voice they cried, '*No, no!*'"[48] A few held on to their small acres, but only a few, and while

Lecture II: The Fear of Freedom

the great hope died more slowly than it did on the interior, it died along the tidewater too.

The "delusion," the hope, the propaganda—whatever one chooses to call the aspiration of landowning status for the freedmen—reached its climax among the Negroes in the Christmas holidays of 1865 and collapsed immediately thereafter. "I never witnessed in so short a time," wrote John T. Trowbridge, "so complete a revolution in public feeling."[49] He meant the feeling of the whites on the altered future of the freedmen—from that of an independent black yeomanry to what J. D. B. De Bow called "effective hirelings."[50] As General Howard put it in an address to Negroes in Jackson, Mississippi, they would in the future be "dependent on the white race, the property owners, for employment and support; their true interest was to cultivate harmony and good will . . ." He also suggested that "if they were polite and obedient as slaves, they must be more so as freedmen." The Mississippi editor who reported the speech pronounced it, "all that could be desired."[51] The General's emphasis on the black man's dependence upon the white man was echoed by a Confederate veteran of Georgia:

> Why, he can't even live without the consent of the white man! He has no land—he can make no crops except the white man gives him a chance. He hasn't any timber—he can't get a stick of wood without leave from a white man. We crowd him into the fewest possible employments. . . . Even in this city [Atlanta] he can't get a pail of water from a well without asking a white man for the privilege. He can hardly breathe, and he certainly can't live in a house, unless a white man gives his consent. What sort of freedom is that?[52]

The answer is that it was freedom of a very circumscribed sort. It meant making terms with a man who not only held to the old slavery doctrine that the Negro would work only under compulsion and must be made to stand in fear. It meant also dealing with a man convinced by the first year's experiment with freedom that the old slavery doctrine was essentially sound. For the employer the first year of freedom meant vagrancy, thievery, irresponsibility, a year of jubilee on government relief; it meant unplanted, unweeded, or unharvested crops and no profit to show for it. In making a contract for the future he based his valuation of the freedman's labor on the previous year's experience, and that valuation was correspondingly low—terribly low.

After six month's work with Georgia planters, a Freedmen's Bureau agent declared that "These men have no faith in the system. They prophesy failure when the contract is made, and afterward with a triumphant 'I told you so,' announce its uselessness."⁵³ An agent in South Carolina was of the same opinion. "I know it to be the wish of nine out of every ten Southern men," he declared, "to make emancipation a failure."⁵⁴

To make emancipation work was to make the freedman work, and General Howard was deluged by mail with a single theme: "*Compel him! Compel him!*" It came from the New England textile industry and from the army of Northern men who had leased or bought plantations, as well as from Southern planters. Sensitive to the charge of reenslavement, Howard publicly renounced compulsory labor. But in numerous ways, some subtle and some not at all subtle, the Bureau condoned and directly used coercion. One way was the reduction of rations or cutting off from relief. Another was the enforcement and extension of state vagrancy laws of the new and old black codes. In Alabama a man was a vagrant whose employer swore he had been needlessly absent from work for three days in a month. In Virginia he could be declared a vagrant if he refused a fair offer of employment, and in Georgia an agent could make a contract for a Negro who neglected to make one for himself.⁵⁵

In extra-legal or illegal ways and ways winked at by authorities, Bureau agents coerced, recruited, and supplied black labor to planters. Howard complained of "a sort of morbid sympathy [of many agents] obtained from constant contact" with planters,⁵⁶ of "immoralities, corruption, neglected duty and incapacity" among agents,⁵⁷ and of officers who "invested their own means jointly with citizens in the planting interest."⁵⁸ An investigator officially reported that, "The Bureau in Georgia is practically under rebel rule, and managed exclusively for the benefit of the black man's oppressors."⁵⁹ Quite outside the Bureau sprang up a large traffic in supplying Negro labor at $40 a head, described as "a regular business, carried on by a class... who, before the war, were known as 'negro brokers' in the purchase and sale of slaves."⁶⁰

The main reliance of the Bureau for the governing of planter-freedman relations was the labor contract. Hundreds of thousands of these contracts were drawn up with Bureau approval, many times the number that could be adequately supervised and enforced. Even with adequate supervision and strict enforcement, however, the contracts would hardly have established anything resembling a just and stable system of free labor. Although General Howard complained bitterly of "the proneness of many agents" to approve wages that were much too low, he firmly refused to fix wages or even to set a minimum wage and clung to a laissez-faire policy.⁶¹ On the other hand planters of three states entered wage-fixing agreements, and elsewhere by less formal means employers generally managed to depress wages to the subsistence level or below. Freedmen often got wages far below the rent their masters once collected for hiring them as slaves. Many contracts contained strict limitations on freedom of movement and heavy penalties for violation of rules and failure to show proper respect and obedience. As the Virginia commissioner of the Bureau observed, the former masters sought "to retain by contract much of the power, which the slave system formerly gave him."[62]

It is quite true that the freedmen rarely understood and frequently violated their obligations of contract. But it was a poor example that many of their employers set them in this respect. As low as were the wages, or as small as was the share of the crop promised, freedmen were often turned off without any pay or deprived of any share of the crop they had raised. The assistant commissioner for Mississippi estimated that two-thirds of the laborers of that state had been cheated of wages, and the similar officer for Texas believed that seven out of ten who paid wages there did so only under compulsion. The Texas officer could not blame Negroes for their suspicion of contracts. "They have received, thus far, for their work, as a class, blows, poor clothing, and poorer food."[63] There were exceptions, to be sure, and authentic record of fair treatment and good relations. But equally authentic and more common were records of forced labor with ample evidence of mistreatment, neglect, abuse, and whipping—a discipline that differed little from slavery and was occasionally harsher.

What was there to be said on behalf of people responsible for such abuses? Part of it was said by General Thomas J. Wood, in charge of the Freedmen's Bureau in Mississippi. "The white people of this State," he wrote, "have been educated, and their habits formed, under the influence of negro slavery. We shall not do them justice, unless we remember that, with very few exceptions, they were fully persuaded that slavery was right—and beneficial to the colored race, as well as profitable and pleasant to the ruling caste. We must also remember that these opinions and feelings pervaded the whole white population.... Therefore all felt injured in the tenderest point by emancipation; their profit and their pride were assailed and destroyed."[64] That was part, but not all that was to be said. For many of the same abuses were practiced by new employers of freedmen from the North, who had no education in slavery. What can be said of them as well as the Southern employers is that the freedmen were a weak and relatively defenseless people and to many an irresistible temptation.

In 1866 nature conspired with history to make the second year of the experiment with emancipation appear to the freedmen a fraud and to their employers a total failure. Prolonged droughts in the early summer were followed by continuous and heavy rains in August and September, and on top of them came the army worm. The combination all but completely destroyed the cotton crop and much of the corn in large parts of the lower South. The disaster reduced the total production of cotton to the low level of the post-war crop of 1865. "The success of free labor under the contract system," reported General Sheridan from New Orleans, "has been greatly discouraged by the disastrous events which have almost completely destroyed the season's crops. The confidence of employer and employee in each other has been impaired."[65] Mutual confidence in that quarter had already suffered heavy blows, but the experience of 1866 was shattering, amounting to something like a general breakdown. Thousands of hands turned off without pay faced the winter destitute and when relief failed they resorted to thievery to feed themselves and their families. The whites retaliated with violence and terror. Racial bitterness deepened as lawlessness bred more lawlessness. The dogma that the Negro would not work without compulsion deepened among the whites and so did their determination to confine him in bounds of a rigid peonage.

In all probability too much attention has been focused in the past on the infamous Black Codes, adopted by the Southern state legislatures for the most part in 1866. What they did was to advertise and proclaim in a most conspicuous way the South's determination to establish a system of caste and peonage for the Negro. The harsh vagrancy and apprenticeship provisions, the discriminatory punishments and fines, the restrictions on freedom of movement, residence, employment, assembly, and possession of arms—all helped to turn conservative Northerners against President Johnson's reconstruction policy. Their significance was largely political. The Black Codes were soon nullified or repealed. But the purpose they embodied remained unaltered. And as Carl Schurz pointed out, "There are a hundred ways . . . which will serve the purpose."[66] "Indeed," wrote General Q. A. Gillmore, "the ordinary vagrancy and apprenticeship laws now in force in some of the New England States" could be easily be so administered as to serve the same purpose as the Black Codes.[67]

It was not so much the kinds of laws that mattered as the administration of the laws—who administered them, how they were administered, and to what purpose. As Whitelaw Reid observed, "all the concomitants and outgrowths of slavery . . . and beliefs which reject the possibility of free labor . . . remained in full strength" in 1866. "They were imbedded in constitutions, they were walled about by the accretions of a century's laws, they were part and parcel of the accepted faith of the people."[68]

Notes

1. W. E. B. Du Bois, *Black Reconstruction in America, 1860–1880* (New York, 1935), 122.
2. Amos Beman to George Whipple, Feb. 25, 1867, in Beman Papers, James Weldon Johnson Collection, Yale University.
3. Bell I. Wiley, *Southern Negroes, 1861–1865* (New York, 1953), 181.
4. John Eaton, *Grant, Lincoln, and the Freedmen* (New York, 1907), 1–3.
5. *Freedmen's Record*, 1 (June, 1865), 111; *National Freedman*, I (Feb. 1, 1865), 18.
6. Vernon L. Wharton, *The Negro in Mississippi, 1865–1890* (Chapel Hill, 1947), 47–48.
7. B. W. Botkin, ed., *Lay My Burden Down: A Folk History of Slavery* (Chicago, 1961), 247.
8. John A. Hedrick to B. S. Hedrick, April 11, 1865, in B. S. Hedrick Papers, Duke University.
9. Jackson (Miss.), *Daily Mississippian*, July 27, 1865.
10. *The American Union Commission* (New York, 1865), 13.
11. Wharton, *The Negro in Mississippi*, 53.
12. A. R. Childs (ed.), *The Journal of St. Julien Ravenel* (), March 4, 1865, p. 215.
13. Sherwood (ed.), Journal of Susan Walker (), 35.
14. Botkin (ed.), *Lay My Burden Down*, 76.
15. E. Franklin Frazier, *The Negro Family in the United States* (Chicago, 1939), 89.
16. Ibid.
17. *Pennsylvania Freedmen's Bulletin* (Dec., 1866), 5–6.
18. Interview with Lee Guidon in Botkin, *Lay My Burden Down*, 66.
19. Simkins and Woody, *South Carolina During Reconstruction*, 359.
20. Quoted in New York *Times*, Nov. 23, 1865.
21. Whitelaw Reid, *After The War* (New York, 1866), 120–21.
22. Wiley, *The Southern Negroes*, 72–84.
23. A. M. Waddell, Wilmington, to W. E. Holden, June 18, 1865; Gov. Holden to Gen. I. D. Cox, June 22, 1865, in Holden Letterbook, 1865, North Carolina Archives, Raleigh, N.C.
24. Schurz Report in *Senate Executive Documents*, no. 2, 39 Cong., I Sess., p. 27.
25. J. C. H. Jones, Mobile, to Gen. Thomas Kilby Smith, June 23, 1865, in W. L. Sharkey State Papers, Mississippi Department of Archives and History, Jackson, Miss.
26. Joseph R. Putnam, Huntsville, to James A. Garfield, Nov. 10, 1865, Garfield Papers, Library of Congress.
27. Raleigh *Daily Standard*, Nov. 16, 1865; New York *Times*, Nov. 19, 1865, July 6, 1865. Fourteen whites were reported killed, but in reprisal more than 400 Negroes were killed and more than that number flogged.
28. Ben Ames Williams (ed.), Mary Boykin Chesnut, *Diary from Dixie* (Boston, 1861), 292, 433, 536, 544.
29. B. Manly, Tuscaloosa, to Sister Jane, Montgomery, June 8, 1865, in Manly Papers, Alabama Collection, Folder 173, University of Alabama.

30. Diary of Josiah Gorgas, June 15, 1865, Gorgas Papers, University of Alabama.
31. Quoted in Carl Schurz, "Letters from the South," No. 5, Savannah, Ga., August 8, 1865, Schurz Papers, Library of Congress.
32. J. D. Collins to John A. Cobb, July 31, 1865, in Ulrich B. Phillips (ed.), *Correspondence of Robert Toombs, Alexander H. Stephens, and Howell Cobb* (Washington, 1913), 665.
33. Childes (ed.), *Ravenel Journal*, 269.
34. F. E. Piquette to W. R. Harmount, Jan. 12, 1865, in *National Freedman*, I (1865), 79.
35. William T. Briggs to F. G. Shaw, Jan. 10, 1865, in *National Freedman*, ibid., 4.
36. Rev. John Savary in *National Antislavery Standard*, Nov. 3, 1866. [Woodward wrote above the endnote "Note from Cap't W. A. Poillon appended."]
37. Alexis de Tocqueville, *Democracy in America* (Cambridge, 1862), I, 459.
38. Botkins (ed.), *Lay My Burden Down*, 225.
39. Eliza J. Thompson to B. W. Hedrick, Nov. 6, 1865; Id. to Ellen Hedrick, Nov. 30, 1865, in Hedrick Papers, Duke University.
40. B. Manly Diary, Aug. 26, 29, Sept. 2, 1865, Alabama Collection, University of Alabama.
41. *Flake's Weekly Bulletin*, Galveston, Texas, Feb. 14, 1866.
42. H. B. Sargent to John A. Andrew, March 3, 1862, in Andrew Papers, quoted by Willie Lee Rose (last p. Chap. III MS draft).
43. *Senate Executive Documents*, No. 53, 38th Cong., 1st Sess., p. 99.
44. George R. Bentley, *A History of the Freedmen's Bureau* (Philadelphia, 1955), 89–102.
45. A. M. Waddell to Gov. W. W. Holden, June 18, 1865. Holden Letter Book, 1865, North Carolina Archives, Raleigh.
46. Gen. U. S. Grant to Sec. E. M. Stanton, Sept. 6, 1865, Stanton Papers, Library of Congress.
47. O. O. Howard to Rev. George Whipple, Nov. 27, 1865, Letters Sent, Freedmen's Bureau, National Archives.
48. O. O. Howard, *Autobiography of Oliver Otis Howard* (2 Vols., New York, 1907), II, 238–39; O. O. Howard to E. M. Stanton, Nov. 24, 1865; O. O. Howard to President Johnson, Feb. 22, 1866, Letters Sent, Freedmen's Bureau, National Archives.
49. John T. Trowbridge, *The South* (Hartford, 1866), 368.
50. *De Bow's Review*, New Series, I (1866), 73, 267, 678.
51. Jackson, *Daily Mississippian*, Nov. 12, 1865.
52. Chicago *Tribune* quoted in *The American Missionary*, X (Feb., 1866), 38.
53. Capt. A. P. Ketchum, Savannah, to Gen. Rufus Saxton, Sept. 1, 1865, Box 487, Record Group 105, Freedmen's Bureau Records, National Archives.
54. Lt. H. H. Alvord, Orangeburg, S.C., to Gen. Ely, Sept. 8, 1865, ibid.
55. Howard, *Autobiography*, 312; Bentley, *The Freedmen's Bureau*, 84–85.
56. O. O. Howard to James E. Yeatman, July 10, 1865, Freedmen's Bureau, Letters Sent, National Archives.
57. O. O. Howard to All Assistant Commissioners, Feb. 23, 1866, ibid.

58. Circular No. 4, May 24, 1866, signed by O. O. Howard, Circulars and Circular Letters Issued from May 15, 1865, to July 19, 1869, ibid.
59. Stuart Eldridge to Gen. David Tillson, Nov. 24, 1866, Letters Sent, 1866, ibid.
60. Synopsis of Reports, Oct. 26–Dec. 24, 1866, p. 123, ibid. Also White, "The Freedmen's Bureau in Louisiana," (Ph.D. dissertation, Tulane University, 19--), 259–60.
61. O. O. Howard to James E. Yeatman, July 10, 1865, Freedmen's Bureau, Letters Sent, National Archives.
62. Bentley, *Freedmen's Bureau*, 79–86.
63. Col. Samuel Thomas cited in Trowbridge, *The South*, 362–63; Gen. W. E. Strong in *Report of the Joint Committee on Reconstruction*, Part IV, p. 38.
64. Report of Gen. Thomas J. Wood, July 13, 1866, Freedmen's Bureau Synopsis of Reports, 1866, pp. 342–44, National Archives.
65. Report of Gen. P. H. Sheridan for the year ending Oct. 31, 1866, Freedmen's Bureau Synopsis of Reports, Oct. 26–Dec. 24, 1866, p. 95; Report of Gen. Springer on Arkansas for Nov. 1, 1865–Sept. 30, 1866, ibid., p. 22. Report of Gen. R. K. Scott on South Carolina for Sept., 1866, ibid., p. 33, National Archives.
66. *Senate Executive Documents*, No. 2, 39th Cong., 1 Sess., 35.
67. Q. A. Gillmore to Carl Schurz, July 27, 1865, ibid., 48–49.
68. Whitelaw Reid, *After the War* (New York, 1866), 409.

MESSENGER LECTURE III
The Paradox of Loyalty

IT BEGAN LONG before armed resistance was overcome, and continued after all Confederate forces had surrendered. It went on unabated for years, and it amounted in the end to the most extensive and extended loyalty investigation in our history. This was, in effect, a grand inquisition on the loyalty of the defeated South. It was carried on at all levels, official and unofficial, formal and informal. And it overlooked no part of the South and no class, save only the freedmen. It was thorough or superficial, stern or indulgent, according to the purposes and resources of the inquisitor.

Newspapermen swarmed over the South first and filled columns with reports of the defeated and their devastated land. There was a great curiosity in the North about all aspects of the fallen Confederacy, but if the proportion of space devoted to the subject is any indication, the loyalty of the defeated—or the lack of it—was the matter of greatest popular interest. Three gifted journalists raced to get books into print within the year after the war—Whitelaw Reid, Sidney Andrews, and John T. Trowbridge. All three published large books, and in all the loyalty inquiry was foremost. President Johnson commissioned at least three investigations of Southern loyalty, those of Benjamin C. Truman, Harvey M. Watterson, and Gen. U. S. Grant, and had a third wished upon him, that of General Carl Schurz. Congress through its Joint Committee on Reconstruction conducted its own investigation with hearings that filled 1200 pages. Private, unauthorized, and voluntary inquisitors packed the letter files of politicians and public figures with their findings and speculations.

In the immediate background of the early phases of the loyalty inquisition were four years of war propaganda that had stamped on the Northern mind the image of an implacable rebel foe capable of the most unspeakable atrocities. Back of that lay a generation of anti-slavery propaganda that fastened upon Southern whites responsibility for an institution that was "the sum of all villainies," wickedness surpassing all others. And in the immediate foreground was the blood of the martyred war President and the dark suspicion of Confederate conspiracy behind it that was hard to dispel and slow to recede. Before this tide of suspicion and propaganda had begun to ebb, a new wave of atrocity stories about the Confederate war prisons spread northward to bolster old suspicions, arouse new ones, and harden the Northern heart. And on top of this came authentic pictures of the appalling condition of liberated slaves fresh from their bonds, emaciated and dying by the thousands in refugee camps, abandoned plantations, and Southern cities.

The congressional investigation of Southerners later conducted by the Joint Committee on Reconstruction announced as its purpose: "to ascertain how far their pretended loyalty could be relied upon."[1] Variations of this formally expressed purpose were pursued by scores of less official and more informal investigators. The great question was how far these people could be trusted. Could they be trusted to rule themselves? Their former slaves? The Southern Unionists who lived among them and the Northerners who moved there? Or could they be trusted to participate in ruling the nation they had attempted to destroy? Had the war finally beaten out the fierce spirit of disloyalty that had sustained four years of resistance? How much of it was left? Or had the war failed of its purpose and the sacrifice been in vain? What had surrender really meant beyond the obvious military consequences?

The army of investigators differed greatly in their findings, as they did in the expectations, their sympathies, and in what they set out to find and to prove by their findings. But on two things there was remarkable agreement among them. One was upon the overwhelming completeness of the Northern conquest, and the other and more important still was the readiness in the spring and summer following the surrender with which Southerners everywhere acknowledged defeat and submission. The consensus embraced not only the radicals but moderates and conservatives, civilian as well as military opinion, Northern as well as Southern. Grant agreed with Sherman and Sheridan, Truman with Schurz, Reid, and Trowbridge. Even the incorrigible Tennessee Unionist, Parson William G. Brownlow for a time agreed with the old fire-eating secessionist J. D. B. De Bow.

Early in May Charles A. Dana pronounced the "thoroughness of the subjugation" in the South "wonderful" and declared that "no people were ever so entirely conquered."[2] Whitelaw Reid thought it "evident that they felt conquered, and stood in silent and submissive apprehension."[3] A radical Union man told John T. Trowbridge that "There never was a rebellious class more thoroughly subdued."[4] An investigator commissioned by Secretary of War Stanton in July was "surprised to find how docile and submissive they were."[5] The Joint Committee on Reconstruction concluded as a result of its hearings that, "The testimony is conclusive that after the collapse of the confederacy the feeling of the people of the rebellious States was that of abject submission."[6] There was far less agreement, however, on what this mood meant, how long it lasted, how deeply it penetrated, and the extent to which it constituted the basis or supplied a substitute for loyalty.

The mood of many Southerners could only be described as a state of shock, a dazed and bewildered condition in which the terms loyalty or disloyalty had little meaning. Writing from Richmond on April 10, Captain Charles Francis Adams, Jr., said "For the first time I see the spirit of the Virginians ... completely broken; the whole people are cowed."[7] And a month after the fighting, Colonel Josiah Gorgas on his way home to Alabama found defeat "so overwhelming that I am as yet unable to comprehend it. I am as one walking in a dream, & expecting to awake." To him it was incredible that "a people that a month ago had money, armies, and the attributes of a nation should today be no more, & that we live, breath, move, talk as before. Will it be so when the Soul leaves the body behind it?"[8] "Their faces have changed," remarked a Southerner who served in the Union army. "They have a dazed look, like owls in a sudden light. To any one who used to see them in the old days of their pride and spirit, this is very striking."[9]

Such a bankruptcy of spirit and collapse of morale could accurately be called docility, whatever else it meant. "Nothing is more remarkable than the readiness to submit" observed Major William T. Walthall in Alabama. "The chief anxiety seems to be to know what the enemy are going to do with us—whether the yoke is to be a light or a heavy one."[10] There was ample reason for anxiety. "The people are most painfully anxious," wrote a Mississippian, "to know what they are expected to do."[11] President Johnson was still thought to be vengeful and known to have promised repeatedly "to make treason odious." There was reason to fear heavy and bloody punishments. The government had already confiscated much land and confiscations were continuing.

The President's Amnesty Proclamation of May 29 allayed some, but by no means all anxieties. Most people of prominence and all with $20,000 of property or more fell into one of the fourteen excepted classes who had to receive pardon from the President. Without pardon one could not reclaim confiscated lands, convey or receive title to properties, or carry on business of many kinds. He was not only deprived of political rights but threatened with confiscation and conviction for treason. For the first four months after the proclamation pardons were slow in coming. Only in September were pardons speeded up and not until November did it become reasonably clear that pardoned men might recover confiscated property. For some six months after the surrender, therefore, Southerners had good reason for tractability and submissiveness, whether that could properly be called loyalty or not.

In the fateful summer and fall of 1865 there grew and hardened in the South a consensus on loyalty, its limits and definition, a conception of what honor permitted and necessity required. It was essentially a passive and negative conception. Its most common formulation was the often-repeated phrase: "We were whipped and we accept the situation." What "the situation" included might vary, but at the minimum it included abandonment of resistance, and of hopes for independence and slavery. As a Memphis editor phrased the formula in apparent good faith: "We are done with secession; it is exploded; done with slavery; done with the idea of a separate Confederacy. Is not this loyalty?"[12]

The answer to that question was "No." That was not an acceptable definition of loyalty—especially not on the part of a people demanding full representation and restitution of rights in a government they had recently tried to overthrow. And within less than a year the dominant party had won Northern support for the reply framed by the Joint Committee on Reconstruction: that loyalty was "something more than an unwilling submission to an unavoidable necessity—a feeling if not cheerful, certainly not offensive and defiant."[13]

Northern critics of Southern loyalty could marshal impressive evidence to support their criticism and to substantiate their charge that it was a loyalty that was grudging, unrepentant, half-hearted, and divided between the past and the future. Even a temperate critic such as General Sheridan had serious reservations. "I believe they accept the situation," he said, "and have an earnest desire for the restoration of a perfect union, but exhibit, at the same time, an unmistakable desire to glorify rebellion."[14] And even so cautious a Southerner as General Wade Hampton could betray attitudes that support the charge. "And, brother soldiers," he said in an address to veterans, "whilst we acquiesce in the result, let us not admit that the cause of it was unjustifiable or wrong. I accept the terms upon which we laid down our arms, in good faith ... but whilst I do this, I shall never say that we had not right on our side."[15]

Surrender was tendered with qualifications, and pardon was requested without repentance. Alexander Stephens was explicit on this point in his application to the President for amnesty. "I did not and do not wish to be considered or looked upon in any manner or form as a base supplicant for mercy," he wrote. "I have not the slightest sense of being a criminal..."[16] And in the privacy of his diary Colonel Gorgas recorded: "I have today taken the oath of amnesty before a federal officer... and forwarded my petition for *pardon*!—pardon for having done my duty in a cause I deemed the best on earth!"[17] Since the President's policy placed such great stress on oaths, the public was especially sensitive on this score. Whitelaw Reid took it as a commentary on "the average value of oaths of loyalty" when an actor in New Orleans ad-libbed a line: "'Let me go; *I'll take the oath!*'" and "The whole audience burst out into uproarious laughter...."[18]

The provisional governors appointed by Johnson and the state governments elected under the Presidential plan of restoration have had many apologists and defenders among historians—especially Southern historians. But the official record left by those governments and their officers speaks for itself. It is simply not a record calculated to inspire faith in the unequivocal loyalty of the vanquished or confidence that they grasped the implications of defeat. Even as an "experiment," an unauthorized dress rehearsal, the performance left much to be desired. The record is well known. It will be recalled that the state conventions often indulged in an inordinate amount of legalistic caviling and quibbling in debate over voiding of secession ordinances, abolishing slavery, and repudiating Confederate debts. One of them refused to ratify the Thirteenth Amendment, two declined to repudiate the Confederate debt, and several debated in a trance-like air of unreality whether to "repeal" or "nullify" ordinances of secession in order to preserve "the principle." None of them made the slightest concession to qualified Negro suffrage, and prominent leaders took occasion to reiterate the dogma that theirs was "a white man's government," and it was "intended for white men only."

Following the conventions the states elected legislatures and other state officials heavily recruited from Confederate figures. The legislatures of Mississippi, South Carolina, and Louisiana enacted black codes with provisions that could have returned great numbers of freedmen to virtual slavery, that seemed to make a mockery of emancipation and to cheat the victor cynically and flagrantly out of the fruits of his hard won victory. On top of this ten of the reconstructed states elected to Congress a delegation of senators and representatives that included the Vice President of the Confederacy, freshly released from prison, four Confederate generals, four Confederate colonels, and numerous civil officials of the Confederacy, including five congressmen and six cabinet officers.[19]

Lecture III: The Paradox of Loyalty

What explains the South's shift from the submissive docility of the postwar trauma to the aggressive defiance and willful arrogance of the period following? Contemporary critics and opponents of Johnson were inclined to place the entire blame upon the President's shoulders. A generation later Johnson attracted a remarkable number of defenders among historians and his reputation underwent a complete rehabilitation. Recent scholarship, however, particularly that of Eric McKitrick, has gravely impaired the case for the President. It is now virtually impossible to exonerate the Tennessean from the charge of misleading the South. He failed to convey fully and plainly to the vanquished the just and reasonable expectations and demands of the victor. He was too permissive, too lenient with his pardons, too ready to compromise. He was too doctrinaire about state rights and too blind to the sufferings of the freedmen. He should have been firm in insisting on the wise policies he merely suggested, such as the one for qualified Negro suffrage. There is no denying these faults and no excusing Johnson for his share of the blame.

But is this the whole story? Could the mistakes and shortcomings of any man, even a President, account for a tragedy of such dimensions? For the failure of reunion is second only to the breakdown of union in the tragic dimensions of our history. The roots of the tragedy lay beyond the reach of Presidential policy. Johnson could, and doubtless should, have disallowed unwise laws and constitutions and disqualified unsuitable elective officials. But the trouble lay deeper than that. It lay in the hearts of the people of the South. It lay in their inability to reconcile loyalty to the nation with basic loyalties to home, to church, to state, to region, to a way of life. It found expression in defiance of the law, in contempt for its officers of enforcement, in ostracism and persecution of Southern unionists, in mistreatment and hatred of Northern people, in open disrespect for the symbols of union.

It is not as if the trouble were rooted out by the downfall of Johnson and the overthrow of his policies. That came swiftly and thoroughly. And hard upon these events followed the new policy of Radical Reconstruction. But the attitudes of the South outlasted not only Johnson and restoration, but Radical Reconstruction and Grant as well, and endured stubbornly and ineradicably beyond that era into another. A viable solution was reached only by concessions from the North that have disturbed sectional relations down to the present. The basic trouble was a crisis in loyalty.

The confrontation between democracy and totalitarianism in our own era has revived scholarly interest in the nature of national loyalty and disloyalty and stimulated fresh and fruitful inquiry into the subject. It is the contention of Morton Grodzins, in *The Loyal and the Disloyal*, that loyalty in a democratic nation differs from loyalty in a totalitarian nation. In the latter, national loyalty is achieved by breaking down or destroying nonnational loyalties, attachments to community, locality, and face-to-face groups, and substituting a direct, all-embracing loyalty to the nation. On the other hand, Grodzins holds, in the democratic society, "populations are loyal to the nation as a by-product of satisfactions achieved within nonnational groups, because the nation is believed to symbolize and sustain these groups." Instead of being inimical or antithetical to national loyalty, "Their very strength," he contends, "is the strength of national loyalty. They promote and encourage patriotism." He goes so far, in fact, as to hold that nonnational loyalties constitute "the most important foundation of democratic national loyalty." It is persuasively argued that national loyalty in a democracy is not monolithic but multistranded and many-faceted and dependent for its strength upon the strength of local, nonnational allegiances and their identity with the nation.[20]

From this point of view the outlook for restoring national loyalty in the post-war South was gravely prejudiced from the start. To an appalling degree the normal objects of the Southerner's local ties and allegiances and nonnational loyalties were smeared with disloyalty and tainted with treason. His loyalties to region, to state, to party, to church, to community, to ethnic values and dogmas, to a whole way of life were in some manner or degree compromised. His region itself was hard to dissociate from the ill-fated Confederacy. The state, for many Southerners a loyalty symbol superior to both region and nation, was associated with doctrines of sovereignty and rights that led to secession. His church was not merely Methodist, Baptist, or Presbyterian: it was Southern Methodist, Southern Baptist, or Southern Presbyterian—representing a spiritual secession that well antedated and long outlasted the political schism. His party, if he were a Democrat, quickly healed its ante-bellum sectional schism, but on the local level it was the old party of secession, and the local leaders of rebellion, reinforced by Southern Whigs who had nowhere else to go, who were still in command. On the national level, of course, he was constantly reminded that his was the party of treason and rebellion. His racial loyalties, deeper for the mass of Southerners than any other, were based on dogmas that justified and glorified Negro slavery. His allegiance to his superiors and his obligations to his subordinates were dependent in a hundred subtle ways on the discredited dogmas of an outmoded way of life.

If the normal sources of national loyalty in a democracy are to be found in local allegiances and attachments, then the springs of national loyalty in the post-war South were poisoned. The crisis of national loyalty arose from the alienation of local loyalties in the South. The two could not be reconciled. To

Lecture III: The Paradox of Loyalty

be loyal to one was to be disloyal to the other. The Southerner could not think of the nation as symbolizing his most cherished loyalties. Instead of being mutually sustaining they were mutually subversive, their values inimical, their leaders at odds. According to a federal officer in 1866, "Good faith in the government, in the judgment of the people at large in Texas, meant bad faith to the community."[21] And a former Confederate officer in New Orleans noted in his diary that, "In the newspapers and other public utterances, 'loyalty' means treason to one's native land & devotion to the Yankee government, and 'rebellion' means obedience to one's own government."[22] If slavery made a paradox of ethics by the question, What is a "good" slave? Reconstruction made a paradox of loyalty by the question, What is a "loyal" Southerner?

Few institutions in mid-nineteenth century America were the focus and repository of more loyalties than the church. Yet for the great majority of Southern communicants, loyalty to one's church meant loyalty to an institution anathematized by its Northern clergy, journals, and official pronouncements as apostate, sinful, and disloyal. Of the great national protestant denominations, only the Episcopalians—who were relatively weak in the South—achieved reunion and reconciliation of the sectional branches soon after the war. Others not only remained separate and distinct in organization, but deeply antagonistic for many years.

The sectional struggle over the churches transcended verbal and spiritual clashes and raged in ugly and embittered fights over legal title and physical possession of pulpits and church property. Inspired by crusading zeal, Northern missionaries came in great numbers to storm Southern churches, lay siege to congregations, expose heresy, and stamp out apostasy. Southern Methodist Bishops warned their churchmen formally "of a systematic attempt, already inaugurated, to disturb, and if possible disintegrate and then absorb our membership individually. Their policy is evidently our division and ecclesiastical devastation." Quoting this, a Northern churchman said, "Amen! Never was a truer word more unwillingly spoken. The church of the North of every [denomination] will march, like Sherman's army, from many states through the South, devastating that apostate church of every name, and rebuilding the whole region.... These organizations, hostile to the state and the Gospel, must disappear, as has the Confederacy into which they flowered—a fitting body for their sinful soul."[23] The New York *Christian Advocate* denounced "the treason-tainted Methodism of the South," and called for "a policy of earnest and antagonist aggression." Another Northern organ of the church declared that "any fraternity between the Southern and Northern Methodists would be a humbug and a delusion."[24] A conference of Northern clergy resolved that

Southern Methodism "had been so completely leagued with detestable sin that its... apostate church should be exterminated."[25]

If it came to a choice between loyalty to church and loyalty to nation, few Southerners appeared to hesitate. The Northern crusade against Southern apostasy, determined and prolonged as it was, came to frustrating and ineffective results. In the Valley of Virginia, where many churches had retained their Northern allegiance through the war, the crusade actually had the opposite of the intended effect. It inspired a post-war ecclesiastical secession in which the churches belatedly severed their Northern connections and joined the Southern apostates.[26] Clerical militancy of the North provoked increasing clerical militancy in the South. "It was in the churches," as Paul Buck has said, "that one found the utmost intolerance, bitterness, and unforgiveness" in the South after Appomattox.[27] If the church is a fair example, the subversion of local loyalties is not a successful way of strengthening national loyalties. The theory it implied was that national loyalty could only be satisfactorily established by the repudiation of most of the normal components of loyalty in a democratic state.

To many Southerners the new standards of loyalty seemed to make impossible demands. "No Southern man is loyal," said a Virginia paper, "if he retains any local attachments; he must contract a disgust for his ancestors, and snap all the ties and associations of the past."[28] A double standard of loyalty seemed implied, requiring of the South what was not required of the North. "Loyalty requires," said one protest, "that any prejudice against... the negro must not be cherished at the South, but is unblameworthy in Connecticut."[29] Nor was the Northerner required to repudiate his region, his church, or his local attachment in order to establish his loyalty.

So repelled were some that they wept to the extreme of rejecting the whole concept of loyalty as un-American. A Kentuckian held in Congress that "the term loyalty was inapplicable in this country. It signified submission to a feudal superior, whereas here where all were equal, no such things as legal or obligatory loyalty... could be required of an American citizen.... The whole superstructure of both the state and Federal governments were built upon the declared right of the people to alter, abolish, overturn, and reconstruct their political institutions at pleasure."[30] He seemed to be suggesting that loyalty, like religion, was inherently a matter of private conviction and definition. The same idea seemed implicit in the statement of a Georgian of high standing that, "there is no such thing as '*loyalty*' to the republic, but only to the Emperor, King, or Prince, &c., and that being a *citizen* of the United States his rights are equal with those of any other citizen, and the matter of 'loyalty' has no business in the connection."[31] Still others relieved their torments of conscience and their aggression against their tormentors by turning the term "loyal" into a derisive epithet. A North Carolina editor invariably spelled it "trooly loil" and applied it contemptuously to all his political enemies. His enemies, incidentally, were the great body of Unionists and Loyalists of the state.

One of the most tragic failures in the federal statesmanship of loyalty was the alienation of the Southern Unionists by Reconstruction policy. A large if ill-defined minority in the South, a powerful group in several states, the Unionists were found among those who opposed secession in the first place as well as those disaffected with the Confederacy during the war. They included certainly the 200,000 Southerners who had served in the Union army and probably a larger number of deserters from the Confederate army. Their main stronghold was in the Appalachian South, but many old Whigs in the Lower South, including some of the wealthiest and most powerful families in pre-war days, called themselves Unionists. The unprecedented swing to candidates of Whig background in the Southern elections of 1865 has been interpreted by a recent scholar as disaffection with the party most closely associated with secession and the Confederacy.[32]

It was to this disaffection and unionism that Governor W. W. Holden of North Carolina was appealing in his proclamation of June 29, 1865, "Your experience, fellow citizens, during the rebellion," he said, "should attach you by the strongest ties to the government of the United States. You have just been delivered by the armies of the Union from one of the most corrupt and rigorous despotisms that ever existed in the world." He went on to remind them that many of them had been "hunted down like wild beasts in the forest and forced into the rebel armies as conscripts," and others had been "subjected to imprisonment and tortures" for their unionist sympathies.[33] John T. Trowbridge, to his "continual astonishment" heard Virginians express a bitterness against secession leaders and the Davis government with a "fierce furnace-heat of hatred" that made Northern feeling on the subject "mild as candlelight" by comparison.[34] Disaffection was even more fierce in Tennessee and flamed in all the ex-rebel states.

Frank Klingberg has shrewdly pointed out that "The Southern Unionists were in a key position to consolidate disaffection to the Confederacy with latent Unionism into an effective movement," and that "with intelligent support from Washington . . . they might have helped to reestablish state governments which combined national purpose with permanent improvement in the conditions of the entire Southern community." But instead of enlisting the

Southern Unionists, government policy alienated them. "Congress came in," said Benjamin H. Hill, "lumped the old Union democrats and whigs together with the secessionists, and said they would punish us all alike." Indicted with their section for guilt by association, many were denied their citizenship and vote. When they came forward with claims for payment for supplies and goods furnished the Union army during the war, claims they had every reason to expect would be honored, they were met by suspicion, indifference, and virtual repudiation. Many more Southern Unionists had valid claims than could afford the stiff costs of prosecuting them and risk the hostility of Southern neighbors involved. Yet 22,298 of them, distributed fairly evenly among the Confederate states, did file claims for a total of more than $60,000,000 and 701 of them made claims for $10,000 or more. The great majority came out of the ordeal with little to show for their pains save a deep sense of betrayal by the Union itself and an abiding resentment.[35]

The root of the trouble was the test of loyalty required of the Southern Unionist. As Klingberg puts it, this "demanded a life of treason to the Confederacy." It had to be "constructive treason," too, not mere nonparticipation. Even the payment of Confederate taxes would disqualify one. To pass the test the Unionists had to disavow local and personal attachments and make continued post-war life in a Southern community almost impossible. To be pro-Union, one had to be anti-Southern, not merely anti-Confederate. Professing devotion to the Union, an Alabamian nevertheless said, "If you want me to say, or expect me to say, that I hate the South because they were at war with the Union, I cannot say it." And a Georgian under cross-examination struggled hopelessly to distinguish human from political loyalty: "My sympathies personally were with my friends who were exposed to danger and their homes to desolation, but politically my sympathies were with the country." And a Tennessean insisted futilely that, "Whatever sympathies I had with relatives & friends on the Southern side were sentiments of a personal character & not sympathies with the cause in which they were engaged."[36]

All too often the iron-clad, monolithic conception of national loyalty prevailed, and the Southern Unionists were confronted with a cruel dilemma. Addressing them with a shrewd appreciation of their dilemma, a writer in *De Bow's Review* counseled them: "Better the friendship of your neighbor across the road or in the next county, than your neighbor in Boston or New Hampshire. You cannot successfully oppose an overwhelming public opinion. Insist upon it, and sooner or later you go down. Acknowledge the fact . . . and you will be received back into the family fold . . ."[37] Southerners with loyalty fierce enough to withstand Confederate persecutions and pressures for four years of war often faced a lifetime of ostracism or worse with less fortitude and confidence. Potentially the greatest resource of national loyalty in the South, the Unionists were frequently driven to join their enemies and were consequently lost to the cause they had served.

Disloyalty is rare we are told by a modern student of the phenomenon, because of the heavy penalties attached to it. "Job, family, friends, comfortable existence itself," writes Grodzins, "are in this sense all hostages insuring loyalty." The disloyal person, he says, "runs the risk of losing his place in all social life. Since men depend upon society for sustenance in no less certain a manner than they depend upon food, this risk is one that few are willing to take."[38]

Normally this is no doubt true. But in the post-war South something suggesting the very reverse of the normal situation appears to have prevailed. "The great trouble," observed a Northern minister in Virginia in February, 1866, "... is the extensively prevailing and operative sentiment that the cause of the Union and the supporters of the Union are not respectable. The mass, for fear of losing social caste, speak and act 'southern,' so far as they may safely."[39] That is, the social penalties tended to be leveled against national *loyalty* instead of against disloyalty—whatever the legal penalties prescribed. A Southern Unionist observed in New Orleans in January, 1866, that, "It has got to be so that if a man does not wear gray clothes he is not regarded as being anybody. It is taken for granted that a man is a Yankee if he does not wear gray clothes." Identification with the gray was clearly a negotiable asset. "Take up any of the New Orleans papers," said the Southern Unionist, "and you will see as a recommendation by those who advertise the statement that they have 'served in the confederate army.'"[40] When Union officers were insulted and their wives were not waited on at [the] table in the St. Charles Hotel, they "were told they were not desired there as it might affect the custom of the house."[41] Unionist merchants and businessmen complained of boycott tactics against them, and a correspondent of Thaddeus Stevens reported "that Loyal or Northern Merchants are failing all over the South," while the rebel merchant was "rewarded for his disloyalty" by increased patronage.[42]

As rewarders of disloyalty and punishers of loyalty no vigilante committee, no boycotters, no nightriders could rival the effectiveness of Southern women. Even the friendly Benjamin Truman admitted that, "Over Southern society ... women reign supreme, and they are more embittered against those whom they deem authors of all their calamities than are their brothers, sons and husbands."[43] This was the consensus of the sympathetic and the unsympathetic, Southerners and Northerners alike. All noted it and none resented it more than the young men in blue uniforms who sought a different reception. They often met instead with cold stares and scorn, and their superiors, even those of highest rank complained of calculated insult administered in public.

There has been too much evasiveness and too little plain talk about this crisis in Southern loyalty. It is one thing to dismiss alarmist reports that Southerners were engaged in treasonous plots with Emperor Maximillian of Mexico for foreign invasion. And it is true that partisan propaganda sometimes exaggerated Southern outrages for political purposes and represented as typical what was relatively rare and unrepresentative. But authentic, detailed, and responsible reports are not to be brushed aside.

In January, 1866, Colonel Samuel Thomas while on a tour of inspection of Mississippi was openly greeted while in uniform "with such remarks as 'that's a damned yankee,' 'what does he want here.'" In his experience lower class whites of the state were "not disposed to treat any person representing the Government, who is unsupported by a military force, with any respect, or even common decency."[44] In July, Lieutenant Colonel Orrin McFadden reported from Alexandria, Louisiana, that "Union men, whether of Northern or Southern birth, are living in extreme jeopardy of their lives."[45] The following January Captain George Everett, while marching 200 recruits from Indianola to Austin, Texas, saw his men "openly insulted without cause."[46] Such experiences illuminate Whitelaw Reid's earlier observation that, while "At the North we think little of loyalty; here loyal men, and especially those in the service of the Government, seem drawn toward each other, as are men who serve under the same flag in a foreign country."[47]

Freedmen were a more vulnerable target and a more natural scapegoat than federal officers and soldiers. Bureau officers heard and acted on more than 100,000 complaints in a single year.[48] In the summer of 1866 twenty-nine freedmen of Arkansas were murdered in two months, and ten were murdered around Newberry, South Carolina, in four weeks, and in no case was anyone brought to punishment.[49] So regularly did such crimes go unpunished that a Bureau superintendent in Virginia wrote his superior officer that he felt "ashamed of the office I occupy and of looking a freedman in the face."[50]

Southern Unionists, even in states where they made up a large proportion of the populations, came under increasing persecution in 1866. The leading Unionist paper of North Carolina reported that in that state "Unionists are dejected, cowed, proscribed, under the ban socially, pecuniarily, and politically."[51] And a former surgeon of the Union Army wrote from Asheville that as terrible as were the sufferings of North Carolina Unionists during the war,

"The union men never have suffered so much severe persecution since the war was first talked of as they have since its close."⁵² From Texas General Edgar M. Gregory reported to the Bureau that, "The Union men are trembling for their lives," and that "the more timid are preparing to leave the State."⁵³

By January, 1867, General Sherman was ready to admit that he and the officers of the army under his command were unable to "prevent the shooting of negroes & poor Union men" in Arkansas. "I have been more embarrassed," he wrote, "by well proven cases of murder, with Grand Juries ignoring indictments, & turning loose murderers... than by any other cause. We want the poeple [sic] of the South restored to all natural & civil rights, but our poeple insist on that feature of our Constitution that guarantees to every citizen a right to go where he pleases to make his home." To an old Southern friend he declared that under the circumstances, "it is idle for me or any man to attempt an apology or excuse, to ward off the pressures of the extreme Radicals. . . . idle for any friend of the South to approach a popular assemblage North." He sympathized with President Johnson, but was convinced that "these multiple instances of violence—proven by witnesses whom we cannot discredit—take from him all chance of explanation."⁵⁴

A full explanation of the breakdown and failure of Presidential Reconstruction would take into account numerous forces. Many of them were entirely of Northern origin, motivated by Northern ambitions and needs. These motives were complex and sometimes devious, and it may be doubted that they consisted of pure philanthropy or pure patriotism or a compound of the two. But it is not necessary to resort to elaborate economic interpretations or to rely upon complex political maneuvers and conspiratorial manipulations or to stress unduly the shortcomings and short-sightedness of any one man to discover adequate reasons for what happened. The fact was that the South under this dispensation engendered more defiance and disloyalty than any nation could indefinitely tolerate, especially one that had so recently emerged from a hard-won victory over the offenders.

Notes

1. *Report of the Joint Committee on Reconstruction*, Part I, o, x.
2. Charles A. Dana to James S. Pike, May 10, 1865, in Robert F. Durden, *James Shepherd Pike: Republicanism and the American Negro, 1850–1882* (1957), 160.
3. Whitelaw Reid, *After the War* (New York, 1866), 136.
4. John T. Trowbridge, *The South* (New York, 1866), 189.
5. John Covode in *Report of the Joint Committee on Reconstruction*, Part IV, 114.

6. Ibid., Part I, xviii.
7. W. C. Ford (ed.), *A Cycle of Adams Letters, 1861–1865* (Boston, 1920), II, 263.
8. Josiah Gorgas Diary, May 4, 1865, Gorgas Papers, University of Alabama.
9. Trowbridge, *The South*, 189.
10. William T. Walthall Diary, p. 115, Walthall Papers, Mississippi Department of Archives and History.
11. George T. Swaub to Gov. William L. Sharkey, Gov. Sharkey State Papers, ibid.
12. *Daily Memphis Avalanche*, March 8, 1866.
13. *Report of the Joint Committee on Reconstruction*, Part I, p. xvi.
14. Ibid., Part IV, p. 122.
15. Charleston *Daily Courier*, August 27, 1866.
16. Stephens to Johnson, June 29, 1865, quoted in Jonathan T. Dorris, *Pardon and Amnesty under Lincoln and Johnson* (Chapel Hill, 1953), 248.
17. Gorgas Diary, Aug. 22, 1865, Gorgas Papers, University of Alabama.
18. Reid, *After the War*, 449–50.
19. Edward McPherson, *A Political History . . . of Reconstruction* (Washington, 1875), 107–9; James G. Blaine, *Twenty Years*, II, 113.
20. Morton Grodzins, *The Loyal and the Disloyal* (Chicago, 156 [1956?]), 29–30, 68–69. See also Harold Guetzkow, *Multiple Loyalties* (Princeton, 1955), and Merle Curti, *The Roots of American Loyalty* (New York, 1948).
21. Testimony of T. J. Mackey, May 17, 1866, in *Report of the Joint Committee on Reconstruction*, Part IV, p. 151.
22. William T. Walthall Diary, June 24, 1865, in Walthall Papers, Mississippi Department of Archives and History.
23. *The Independent*, Sept. 21, 1865.
24. Quoted in Hunter D. Farish, *The Circuit Rider Dismounts* (), 44–45. [Get p. no. for last quote].
25. Quoted in Ralph E. Morrow, *Northern Methodism and Reconstruction* (Ann Arbor, 1956), 65–66.
26. Testimony of Rev. E. O. Dunning, Feb. 3, 1866, *Report of the Committee on Reconstruction*, part II, p. 45.
27. Buck, *The Road to Reunion*, 38.
28. Charlottesville *Chronicle* quoted in Vicksburg, Miss., *Weekly Herald*, Feb. 3, 1866.
29. Ibid.
30. Cited in B. B. Kendrick, *Journal of the Joint Committee on Reconstruction*, 373.
31. Quoted by Capt. A. P. Ketchum, Savannah, to Gen. Rufus Saxton, Sept. 1, 1865, Box 487, Freedmen's Bureau, Record Group No. 105, National Archives.
32. Thomas B. Alexander, "The Persistence of Whiggery."
33. Raleigh *Daily Standard*, June 29, 1865.
34. Trowbridge, *The South*, 157–58.
35. Frank L. Klingberg, *The Southern Claims Commission* (), 17–19, 101, 157, 207, 209.
36. Ibid., 17, 194–95.

37. Anon., "A Talk with Radicals," *DeBow's Review*, XXXIV (1866), 346.
38. Grodzins, *The Loyal and the Disloyal*, 34–35.
39. Rev. Dr. Robert McMurdy, testimony of Feb. 10, 1866, *Report of the Joint Committee on Reconstruction*, Part II, p. 89.
40. Testimony of Dr. James M. Turner, March 14, 1866, ibid., Part IV, p. 127.
41. Diary of Cyrus B. Comstock, Feb. 5, 1866, Library of Congress.
42. Augustus Watson, Fredericksburg, Va., to Thaddeus Stevens, Dec. 9, 1865, #53377, Stevens Papers, Library of Congress.
43. *Senate Executive Documents*, 39 Cong., 1 Sess., No. 43, p. 6.
44. Report of Jan. 31, 1866, Freedmen's Bureau, Synopsis of Reports, I (1866), pp. 65–66. National Archives.
45. Lt. Col. Orrin McFadden to Lt. Nathaniel Burbank, July 15, 1866, Sheridan Papers, Library of Congress.
46. Capt. George Everett to Gen. Sturgis, Jan. 3, 1867, Gov. J. W. Throckmorton Letters, Texas State Archives.
47. Reid, *After the War*, 56.
48. Howard, *Autobiography*, 370–71.
49. Petition from freed people of Newberry, S.C., to Gen. Sickles, Freedmen's Bureau Synopsis of Reports (1866), p. 379.
50. Report of Superintendent of 4th District of Virginia to Col. Orlando Brown, April 21, 1866, ibid., 161–62.
51. Raleigh *Tri-Weekly Standard*, May 12, 1866.
52. Marion Roberts to Thaddeus Stevens, May 15, 1866, #54092, Stevens Papers, Library of Congress.
53. Inspection Report of Gen. E. M. Gregory, June 18, 1866, Freedmen's Bureau Synopsis of Reports (1866), pp. 309–10. National Archives.
54. Gen. W. T. Sherman to D. F. Boyd, Jan. 25, 1867, D. F. Boyd Papers, Louisiana State University Library.

MESSENGER LECTURE IV

The Conservatism of Northern Radicals

THERE IS MUCH in the historiography of Reconstruction to encourage a cynical view of history and historians. The long shelves of books on the period are filled with special pleading, partisan bias, sectional animus, racial prejudice, and hereditary spite. The subject seems to have had a special attraction for those who like to stress the conspiratorial theme in history and delight in disclosing sinister plots and underhanded motives. It has also appealed to some who prefer simplistic explanations of complicated developments as well as those who are inclined to simplify human motivation.

Many of these unfortunate characteristics find illustration in the traditional treatment of the politicians responsible for Congressional Reconstruction—or Radical Reconstruction, as it is loosely called. A few prominent leaders of this party have borne the brunt of the historians' animus. At a low level this aversion has found expression in a tendency to dwell unduly on unfortunate physical or personality traits of the men involved. One recalls, of course, the club foot, the ill-fitted wig, and the ugly scowl of Thad Stevens, or the crossed eyes of Ben Butler, or the pomposity of Salmon P. Chase, or the pedantry and arrogance of Charles Sumner. This verbal aggression has enjoyed a tolerance that would never have been extended to efforts to discredit the New Deal by reference to Franklin Roosevelt's physical handicaps, which would be about on the same plane of taste and ethics.

At a somewhat higher level one notices a tendency to stress the psychological deviations of Radical leaders with the result that a movement is associated, *ad hominem* with the pathological and the neurotic. Still another derogatory association is suggested by stress on the domestic misfortunes or scandals of a few—the mulatto housekeeper of the elderly Stevens, the deplorable marriage of the elderly Sumner, the misadventures of Chase's daughter Kate, Roscoe Conkling's involvement with Kate Sprague, the ludicrous seduction trial of Henry Ward Beecher, the involvement of another prominent radical Theodore Tilton. Granting a rather high incidence of domestic infelicity in one political camp, this scarcely establishes anything conclusive about the sincerity or validity of their political principles and policies.

More damaging to the Radical reputation for sincerity, good faith, and elemental candor is the economic interpretation of their motives. This interpretation holds that Radical Reconstruction, whatever its appearances to the contrary, "was a successful attempt by northeastern business, acting through the Republican party, to control the national government for its own economic ends: notably, the protective tariff, the national banks, a 'sound' currency."[1] In other words much of the talk and excitement and legislation about Southern disloyalty and atrocities, freedmen's status and civil rights, was not an end in itself but a means to ulterior ends. These ulterior ends were not humanitarian like the ones advertised, but selfish and material. According to this view the humanitarian program and the moral indignation with which it was adopted were in large part a sort of mask, a disguise for less laudable motives. What appeared to be an idealistic movement to protect and advance equalitarian and democratic gains of the Civil War was in reality a movement to advance material interests of a sectional minority at the expense of other sections and classes.

This reading of Radical Reconstruction has beguiled American historians for generations, but recent scholarship has demolished the foundations of the economic interpretation. Independent studies by Robert P. Sharkey and Stanley Coben have shown conclusively that Republican congressmen were deeply divided on all the economic issues on which they were alleged to be united. On the tariff issue there were both protectionists and free traders, and on money questions there were both soft money and sound money men. Furthermore, there were protectionist soft-money men and free-trader sound money men as well as free-trader, soft-money men and protectionist hard-money men—all possible combinations. Moreover, the business community of the Northeast as well as the labor spokesmen were sharply divided. Industrialists combined high tariff with greenback inflationist demands and won labor support. Banker and merchant capitalists on the other hand were low-tariff and sound-money men and were usually found aligned with President Johnson and the Democrats. Important capitalist interests opposed the national bank and those most interested in investing capital in Southern resources and development were often those most opposed to Radical Reconstruction. Under this criticism the picture of Reconstruction as a quasi-conspiratorial movement of industrial capitalism falls apart and has to be discarded.

This is not to say that economic and material considerations had no bearing on Republican Reconstruction policy. To do so would be to forget the ante-bellum image of the South as a block to "Progress," progress as conceived of in western expansion and development, homestead law, internal improvements, transcontinental railway grants, a national program of economic expansion. These frustrated objectives had been realized in the South's absence, and a restored South—particularly one under solid Democratic control—represented a menace to all these incidental but important benefits from the war. But, as an English scholar has recently observed, "the impetus in Reconstruction came not from what Northerners wanted to do with the South but from their fear of what the South might do to them."[2] This was undoubtedly part of the threat that a restored and unreconstructed South represented to the Republicans. And it was a negative not a positive force: a vague fear of loss, not an astute scheme for gain. It was more instinctive and defensive than it was conscious and aggressive. It will not serve as a substitute for the economic conspiracy thesis of radical motivation, and it will not account for such unity as the Republicans achieved for the program of reconstruction.

Republican party solidarity during the period of congressional Reconstruction is a truly remarkable phenomenon. It is practically without precedent in American political history. And barring the early months of the New Deal, it is without a sequel. In the seven vetoes of significant Reconstruction acts the party failed to muster the required two-thirds vote of both houses for repassage in only one instance, the first one, and that by only one vote in the Senate. The party repeated this feat of securing two-thirds of the House and the Senate for the Fourteenth and Fifteenth Amendments. In the impeachment procedure against President Johnson conviction failed by only one vote.

Such impressive consistency of party solidarity in a time of domestic crisis over a period of years is not to be dismissed lightly. It is not to be passed over by contemptuous reference to "strict party votes." It is not to be accounted for by the tyranny of a party whip, by the vindictive bitterness of a few leaders, or by the neuroses of anybody. Much less is it attributable to the masterminded schemes of a unified capitalist oligarchy which did not exist. It would seem to be high time for historians to abandon the attempt to explain this striking political phenomenon in terms of petty spite, elaborate plots, or mental aberrations and seek more reasonable explanations.

A reasonable explanation would certainly take into account the peculiar power, prestige, and elan of the Republican party in the years immediately following the Civil War. It was no run-of-the-mill federation of mutually suspicious interest and patronage factions such as the old Whigs and Democrats. It was still a young party with the youthful rebellion and heroic resolves of its origins still green in the memory. Its bold revolt against the compromises and frustrations of the 1850's had been crowned with a magnificent vindication within a decade. It had won the war, freed the slaves, and saved the Union. Its triumph was sealed with sacrifice and the blood of heroes. It had reason to take pride in its victory and to expect gratitude for its services to the country. It could look its critics in the eye with an unwavering gaze.

The party did not consist of fanatics and business tycoons, It contained both of these elements, but it was broadly and loyally supported by small enterprisers and farmers, labor and upper class. It claimed the devotion of a remarkably large proportion of the intellectuals, writers, and more articulate members of Northern society. If the Radicals had a proper regard for non-Southern property, they also had moral ideals and convictions for which they had shed blood. As W. R. Brock, the English historian, has pointed out, these American Radicals did not "stand alone in the Western world, for the same blend of business acumen, practical politics, moral conviction, humanitarian feeling and hostility to privilege was found on both sides of the Atlantic; it was no accident that Sumner was a friend of John Bright or that a young French reporter called Georges Clemenceau admired Thaddeus Stevens."[3] To this historian "the crisis of Reconstruction was a part of the world-wide crisis of nineteenth-century liberal tradition."[4]

There were important differences, however, that set the Americans apart and endowed them with moral resources denied their contemporary Gladstonians across the Atlantic. This was the Treasury of Virtue accumulated in the anti-slavery crusade and four years of war. It was the apocalyptic mystique that permitted ordinary men to picture themselves as instruments of divine wrath, fulfilling God's will with a "terrible swift sword." It inspired them with a sense of destiny. They were the wave of the future, and they were determined to see that their "truth goes marching on." Surely not all Republicans were filled with this vision or keyed to this pitch. But many of them had been during the war, and in the crisis of Reconstruction these passions could be revived to burn as fiercely as ever.

Within a few months after the total victory over the enemy and the complete triumph of their principles, this party of war winners, Union savers, and slave freers was confronted in the full flush of its pride with an ill-concealed outburst of defiance and intransigence in the defeated South. If our analysis is correct there were understandable reasons for the recrudescence of Southern disloyalty, reasons for which Northern blunders and policies, quite apart from those of President Johnson, share the blame. But to explain the phenomenon is not to deny its existence nor to condone it. Defiance in the South, as we have seen, took some ugly forms including ostracism of Northern immigrants, insulting military personnel, resisting civil officers, defying judicial orders, boycotting Yankee merchants, and persecuting both Northern and Southern politicians of the Republican persuasion. It also took the form of electing ex-Confederate politicians and military heroes to high office, including the United States Congress, and of flaunting and advertising in numerous other ways an attachment and loyalty to the Lost Cause.

Simultaneously the victors were confronted with Southern laws, policies, and actions toward the Negro freedmen that they had every reason to interpret as a mockery of emancipation. Bowing to the inevitability of the abolition of slavery, the South was nevertheless determined upon the substitution of a system of forced labor and peonage for the Negroes and equally determined to deny them the elemental rights of citizenship and subordinate them to a permanently degraded caste of menials. Southern racial policy could very naturally be interpreted as a deliberate mockery of the proudest moral justification the Union offered for its conquest.

And now the Republicans were asked to support the administration of a President who justified and defended the South in these policies, who pardoned and amnested rebel offenders, who connived at their shameful treatment of Northern officers and civilians, who sanctioned their offensive racial policies, and who endorsed their election of ex-Confederate heroes. Not only did President Johnson demand that a Republican Congress admit the Southern states into the Union on a basis of full equality and their elected representatives to Congress, but that Republican congressmen refrain from taking any part in the reconstruction of those states. Here was a man elected to office by Republican votes, and yet it soon became clear that he was pursuing a course that would drive the Republicans from power and restore the rival party of Democrats to office and the vanquished South to influence greater than it had enjoyed before its defeat.

This was simply too much to expect of any party, much less a party that had just fought and won a war to decide who would rule the country, reconstruct the South, and free the slave. It is no mystery why the Republicans reacted the way they did to Johnson's policies and Southern intransigence. The mystery is how the historians ever made a mystery of it. How could the Republicans have done anything but reject and overthrow Presidential Reconstruction and turn against Johnson himself? Was there any other reasonable course for them to take? The great majority of Republicans was persuaded, after a year of Johnsonian government, that there was no other reasonable course, and they acted accordingly.

On two of the three great issues of Reconstruction the Republican party achieved unity and acted with firmness and consistency. These issues were, first, who should reconstruct the South; and second, who should govern the country. The answer to the first was that Congress and not the President should reconstruct the South—a Congress completely under Republican control. The answer to the second was that the North would govern the country without participation by the rebel states until those states were reconstructed according to Congressional plan. On these two issues there was fundamental agreement within the party and no important differences between Radicals and Moderates or between East and West. Not, at least until the defection of the Liberal Republicans in 1872.

The third of the great Reconstruction issues was the future of the Negro. Now that the economic interpretation of Radical Reconstruction has been discredited and in large part abandoned there would seem to be a general tendency to return to Negro rights as the central explanation of motives and the focus of interpretation. This tendency is no doubt strengthened by the prominence that the issue of racial equality has assumed in the Second Reconstruction of the last decade. The temptation is to recruit the leaders of the First Reconstruction as prophets and ideologists of the Second and to read into their words and deeds our own thoughts and motives. The temptation is strong, for the identification of the First with the Second Reconstruction might serve to spur on our lagging resolution to fulfill long overdue promises and to emphasize as nothing else how long those promises have been overdue. To be conscious of this temptation is—or should be—to be on guard against it.

The Republican leaders were quite aware in 1865 that the issue of Negro status and rights was closely connected with the two other great issues of Reconstruction—who should reconstruct the South and who should govern the country. But while they were agreed on the two latter issues, they were far from agreed on the third. They were increasingly conscious that in order to reconstruct the South along the lines they planned they would require the support and the votes of the freedmen. And it was apparent to some that once the reconstructed states were restored to the Union the Republicans would need the votes of the freedmen to retain control over the national government. While they could agree on this much, they were far from agreeing on the status, the rights, the equality, or the future of the Negro.

The fact was that the constituency on which the Republican party relied in the North lived in a race-conscious, thoroughly segregated society devoted to the doctrine of white supremacy and Negro inferiority. "In virtually every phase of existence," writes Leon Litwack with regard to the North in 1860, "Negroes found themselves systematically separated from white. They were either excluded from railway cars, omnibuses, stagecoaches, and steamboats or assigned to special 'Jim Crow' sections; they sat, when permitted, in secluded and remote corners of theaters and lecture halls; they could not enter most hotels, restaurants, and resorts, except as servants; they prayed in 'Negro pews' in the white churches.... Moreover, they were often educated in segregated schools, punished in segregated prisons, nursed in segregated hospitals, and buried in segregated cemeteries."[5] Ninety-four percent of the Northern Negroes in 1860 lived in states that denied them the ballot, and the six percent who lived in the five states that permitted them to vote were often disfranchised by ruse.[6] In many Northern states discriminatory laws excluded Negroes from interracial marriage, from militia service, from the jury box, and from the witness stand when whites were involved. Ohio denied them poor relief, and Indiana, Illinois, and Iowa had laws carrying severe penalties against Negroes settling in those states. Everywhere in the free states the Negro met with barriers to job opportunities and in most places he encountered severe limitations to the protection of his life, liberty, and property.[7]

One political consequence of these racial attitudes was that the major parties vied with each other in their professions of devotion to the dogma of white supremacy. Republicans were especially sensitive on the point because of their antislavery associations. Many of them, like Senator Lyman Trumbull of Illinois, the close friend of Lincoln, found no difficulty in reconciling antislavery with anti-Negro views. "We, the Republican party," said Senator Trumbull in 1858, are the white man's party. We are for free white men, and for making white labor respectable and honorable, which it can never be when negro slave labor is brought into competition with it." Horace Greeley the following year regretted that it was "the controlling idea" of some of his fellow Republicans "to prove themselves 'the white man's party,' or else all the mean, low, ignorant, drunken, brutish whites will go against them from horror of 'negro equality.'" Greeley called such people "the on-horse politicians," but he could hardly apply that name to Lyman Trumbull, nor for that matter to William H. Seward, who in 1860 described the American Negro as "a foreign and feeble element like the Indians, incapable of assimilation," nor to Senator Henry Wilson of Massachusetts, who firmly disavowed any belief "in the mental or the intellectual equality of the African race with this proud and domineering white race of ours."[8] Trumbull, Seward, and Wilson were the front rank of Republican leadership and they spoke the mind of the Middle West, the Middle Atlantic states, and New England. There is much evidence to sustain the estimate of W. E. B. Du Bois that, "At the beginning of the [Civil] war probably not one white American in a hundred believed that Negroes could become an integral part of American democracy."[9]

As the war for Union began to take on the character of a war for Freedom, Northern attitudes toward the Negro paradoxically began to harden rather than soften. This hardening process was especially prominent in the Northwestern or Middle Western states where the old fear of Negro invasion was intensified by apprehensions that once the millions of slaves below the Ohio River were freed they would push northward—this time by the thousands and tens of thousands, perhaps in mass exodus, instead of in driblets of one or two who came furtively as fugitive slaves. The prospect of Negro immigration, Negro neighbors, and Negro competition filled the whites with alarm and their spokesmen voiced their fears with great candor. "There is," Lyman Trumbull told the Senate, in April 1862, "a very great aversion in the West—I know it to be so in my state—against having free negroes come among us. Our people want nothing to do with the negro."[10] And about the same time John Sherman, who was to give his name to the Radical Reconstruction acts five years later, told Congress that in Ohio "we do not like negroes. We do not disguise our dislike. As my friend from Indiana [Congressman Joseph A. Wright] said yesterday, the whole people of the northwestern States are, for reasons whether correct or not, opposed to having many negroes among them and the principle or prejudice has been engrafted in the legislation of nearly all the northwestern States."[11]

So powerful was this anti-Negro feeling that it almost overwhelmed antislavery feeling and seriously imperiled the passage of various confiscation and emancipation laws designed to free the slave. To combat the opposition Republican leaders such as George W. Julian of Indiana, Albert G. Riddle, of Ohio, and Salmon P. Chase advanced the curious theory that emancipation would actually solve Northern race problems. Instead of starting a mass migration of freedmen Northward, they argued, the abolition of slavery would not only put a stop to the entry of fugitive slaves but would drain the Northern Negroes back to the South. Once slavery were ended, the Negro would flee Northern race prejudice and return to his natural environment and the congenial climate of the South.[12]

The official answer of the Republican party to the Northern fear of Negro invasion, however, was deportation of the freedmen and colonization abroad. The scheme ran into opposition from some Republicans, especially in New England, on the ground that it was inhumane as well as impractical. But with the powerful backing of President Lincoln and the support of Western Republicans Congress overcame the opposition. Lincoln was committed to colonization not only as a solution to the race problem but as a means of allaying Northern opposition to emancipation and fears of Negro exodus. To dramatize his solution the President took the unprecedented step of calling Negro leaders to the White House and addressing them on the subject. "There is an unwillingness on the part of our people," he told them on August 14, 1862, "harsh as it may be, for you free colored people to remain with us." He told them that "your race suffers very greatly, many of them by living among us, while ours suffer from your presence.... If this be admitted, it affords a reason at least why we should be separated."[13]

The fall elections following the Emancipation Proclamation were disastrous for the Republican party. And in his annual message in December the President returned to the theme of Northern fears and deportation. "But it is dreaded that the freed people will swarm forth and cover the whole land," he said. They would flee the South, he suggested only if they had something to flee from. "*Heretofore*," he pointed out, "colored people to some extent have fled North from bondage, and *now*, perhaps, from both bondage and destitution. But if gradual emancipation and deportation be adopted, they will have neither to flee from." They would cheerfully work for wages under their old masters "till new homes can be found for them in congenial climes and with people of their own blood and race." But even if this did not keep the Negroes out of the North, Lincoln asked, "in any event, can not the North decide for itself whether to receive them?"[14] Here the Great Emancipator was suggesting that the Northern states might resort to exclusion laws such as three of them used before the war to keep the Negroes out.

The party that emerged triumphant from the crusade to save the Union and free the slave was not in the best political and moral position to expand the rights and assure the equality of the freedman. I have not been able to discover or identify any dominant organization of so-called "Radical Republicans" who were dedicated to the establishment of Negro equality and agreed on a program to accomplish their end. Both Southern conservatives and Northern liberals have long insisted or assumed that such an organization of Radicals existed and determinedly pursued their purpose. But the evidence does not seem to me to support this assumption. There undoubtedly *did* emerge eventually an organization determined to overthrow Johnson's policies and take over the control of the South. But that was a different matter. On the issue of Negro equality the party remained divided, hesitant, and unsure of its purpose. The historic commitment to equality it eventually made was lacking in clarity, ambivalent in purpose, and capable of numerous interpretations. Needless to say, its meaning has been debated from that day to this.

The Northern electorate the Republicans faced in seeking support for their program of reconstruction had undergone no conversion in its wartime racial prejudices and dogmas. As George W. Julian told his Indiana constituents in 1865, "the real trouble is that *we hate the negro*. It is not his ignorance that offends us, but his color... Of this fact I entertain no doubt whatsoever." In the years immediately following the war every Northern state in which the electorate was given the opportunity to express its views on issues involving racial relations reaffirmed usually with overwhelming majorities its earlier and conservative stand. This included the states that reconsidered—and reaffirmed—their laws excluding Negroes from the polls, and others that voted on such questions as office holding, jury service, and school attendance.[15] Throughout these years the North remained fundamentally what it was before—a society organized upon assumptions of racial privilege and segregation. As Senator Henry Wilson of Massachusetts told his colleagues in 1867, "There is today not a square mile in the United States where the advocacy of the equal rights of those colored men has not been in the past and is not now unpopular."[16] Whether the Senator was entirely accurate in his estimate of white opinion or not, he faithfully reflects the political constraints and assumptions under which his party operated as they cautiously and hesitantly framed legislation for Negro civil and political rights—a program they knew had to be made acceptable to the electorate that Senator Wilson described.

This is not to suggest that there was not widespread and sincere concern in the North for the terrible condition of the freedmen in the South. There can be no doubt that many Northern people were deeply moved by the reports of atrocities, peonage, brutality, lynchings, riots, and injustices that filled the press. Indignation was especially strong over the Black Codes adopted by some of the Johnsonian state legislatures, for they blatantly advertised the intention of some Southerners to substitute a degrading peonage for slavery and make a mockery of the moral fruits of Northern victory. What is sometimes overlooked in analyzing Northern response to the Negro's plight is the continued apprehension over the threat of a massive Negro invasion of the North. The panicky fear that this might be precipitated by emancipation had been allayed in 1862 by the promises of President Lincoln and other Republican spokesmen that once slavery were abolished the freedmen would cheerfully settle down to remain in the South, that Northern Negroes would be drawn back to the South, and that deportation and colonization abroad would take care of any threat of Northern invasion that remained. But not only had experiments with deportation come to grief, but Southern white persecution and abuse combined with the ugly Black Codes had produced new and powerful incentives for a Negro exodus while removal of the shackles of slavery cleared the way for emigration.

The response of the Republican Congress to this situation was the Civil Rights Act of 1866, later incorporated into the Fourteenth Amendment. Undoubtedly part of the motivation for this legislation was a humanitarian concern for the protection of the Negro in the South, but another part of the motivation was less philanthropic and it was concerned not with the protection of the black man in the South but the white man in the North. Senator Roscoe Conkling of New York, a member of the Joint Committee of Fifteen who helped draft the Civil Rights provisions, was quite explicit on this point. "Four years ago," he said in the campaign of 1866, "mobs were raised, passions were roused, votes were given, upon the idea that emancipated negroes were to burst in hordes upon the North. We then said, give them liberty and rights at the South, and they will stay there and never come into a cold climate to die. We say so still, and we want them let alone, and that is one thing that this part of the amendment is for."[17]

Another prominent member of the Joint Committee who had a right to speak authoritatively of the meaning of its racial policy was George Boutwell of Massachusetts. Addressing his colleagues in 1866 Boutwell said: "I bid the people, the working people of the North, the men who are struggling for subsistence, to beware of the day when the southern freedmen shall swarm over the borders in quest of those rights which should be secured to them in their native states. A just policy on our part leaves the black man in the South where he will soon become prosperous and happy. An unjust policy [in the South] forces him from home and into those states where his rights will be protected, to the injury of the black man and the white man both of the North and the South. Justice and expediency are united in indissoluble bonds, and the men of the North cannot be unjust to the former slaves without themselves suffering the bitter penalty of transgression."[18] The "bitter penalty" to which Boutwell referred was not the pangs of a Puritan conscience. It was an invasion of Southern Negroes. "Justice and expediency" were, in the words of a more famous statesman of Massachusetts, "one and inseparable."

The author and sponsor of the Civil Rights Act of 1866 was Senator Lyman Trumbull, the same man who had in 1858 described the Republicans as "the white man's party," and in 1862 had declared that "Our people want nothing to do with the negro." Trumbull's bill was passed and after Johnson's veto was repassed by an overwhelming majority. Limited in application, the Civil Rights Act did not confer political rights or the franchise on the freedmen.

The Fourteenth Amendment, which followed, was even more equivocal and less forthright on racial questions and freedmen's rights. Rejecting Senator Sumner's plea for a guarantee of Negro suffrage, Congress left that decision up to the Southern states. It also left Northern states free to continue the disfranchisement of Negroes, but it exempted them from the penalties inflicted on the Southern states for the same decision. The real concern of the franchise provisions of the Fourteenth Amendment was not with justice to the Negro but with justice to the North. The rebel states stood to gain some twelve seats in the House if all Negroes were counted as a basis of representation and to have about eighteen fewer seats if none were counted. The Amendment fixed apportionment of representation according to enfranchisement.

There was a great deal of justice and sound wisdom in the Amendment, and not only in the first section conferring citizenship and protecting rights, but in the other three sections as well. No sensible person could contend that the rebel states should be rewarded and the loyal states penalized in apportionment of representation by the abolition of slavery and the counting of voteless freedmen. That simply made no sense. Nor were there many in the North at least who could object to the temporary disqualification for office and ballot of such Southern office holders of the old regime as were described in the third section. The fourth section asserting the validity of the national debt and voiding the Confederate debts were obviously necessary. As it turned out these were the best terms the South could expect—far better than they eventually got—and the South would have been wise to have accepted them.

The tragic failure in statesmanship of the Fourteenth Amendment lay not in its terms but in the equivocal and pusillanimous way it was presented. Had it been made a firm and clear condition for readmission of the rebel states a lot of anguish would have been spared that generation as well as later ones, including our own. Instead, in equivocal deference to states' rights, the South was requested to approve instead of being compelled to accept. In this

I think the Moderates were wrong and Thad Stevens was right. As W. R. Brock put it, "The onus of decision was passed to the Southern States at a moment when they were still able to defy Congress but hardly capable of taking a statesman-like view of the future."[19] It was also the fateful moment when President Johnson declared war on Congress and advised the South to reject the Amendment. Under the circumstances it was inevitable that the South should reject it, and it did with stunning unanimity. Only thirty-two votes were cast for ratification in all the Southern legislatures. This spelled the end of any hope for the Moderate position in the Republican leadership.

After two years of stalling and stumbling, of fumbling and backtracking, of endless committee work and compromise, the First Reconstruction Act was finally adopted in the eleventh hour of the expiring Thirty-ninth Congress. Only after this momentous bill was passed was it realized that it had been drastically changed at the last moment by amendments that had not been referred to or considered by committees and that had been adopted without debate in the House and virtually without debate in the Senate. In a panicky spirit of urgency men who were ordinarily clear headed yielded their better judgment to the demand for anything-better-than-nothing. Few of them liked what they got and fewer still understood the implications and the meaning of what they had done. Even John Sherman, who gave his name to the bill, was so badly confused and misled on its effect that he underestimated by some ninety percent the number who would be disqualified from office and disfranchised. And this was one of the key provisions of the bill. It was, on the whole a sorry performance and was far from doing justice to the intelligence and statesmanship and responsibility of the men who shaped and passed the measure.

One thing was at least clear, despite the charges of the Southern enemies and the Northern friends of the Act to the contrary. It was not primarily devised for the protection of Negro rights and the provision of Negro equality. Its primary purpose, however awkwardly and poorly implemented, was to put the southern states under the control of men loyal to the Union or men the Republicans thought they could trust to control those states for their purposes. So far as the Negro's future was concerned the votes of the Congress that adopted the Reconstruction Act speak for themselves. Those votes had turned down Stevens' proposal to assure an economic foundation for Negro equality and Sumner's resolutions to give the Negro equal opportunity in schools, in homesteads, and full civil rights. As for the Negro franchise their provisions, like those for civil rights were limited. The Negro franchise was devised for the passage of the Fourteenth Amendment and setting up the new Southern state constitutions. But disfranchisement by educational and property qualifications were left an open option, and escape from the whole scheme was left open by permitting the choice of military rule. No guarantee of proportional representation for the Negro population was contemplated and no assurance was provided for Negro office holding.

Notes

1. T. Harry Williams, "An Analysis of Some Reconstruction Attitudes," *Journal of Southern History*, XII (1936), 470. See also Howard K. Beale, *The Critical Year: A Study of Andrew Johnson and Reconstruction*.
2. W. R. Brock, *An American Crisis: Congress and Reconstruction, 1865–1867* (London, 1963), 243.
3. Ibid., 94.
4. Ibid., 9.
5. Leon Litwack, *North of Slavery: The Negro in the Free States, 1790–1860* (Chicago, 1961), 97.
6. Ibid., 91.
7. Ibid., 93–97.
8. Quoted in Ibid., 92, 269–72.
9. W. E. B. Du Bois, *Black Reconstruction*, 191.
10. Quoted in Jacque Voegeli, "The Northwest and the Race Issue, 1861–1862," *Mississippi Valley Historical Review*, L (1963), 240.
11. *Cong. Globe*, 37th Cong., 2nd Sess. (April 2, 1862), 1495, quoted in Selden Henry, "Radical Republican Policy toward the Negro," 32.
12. Voegeli, "The Northwest and the Race Issue," op. cit., 240–41.
13. Roy P. Bassler, (ed.), *The Collected Works of Abraham Lincoln* (9 vols., New Brunswick, 1953), V, 371–72.
14. James D. Richardson, *Messages and Papers of the Presidents*, VI, 14–141.
15. [note missing]
16. [note missing]
17. [note missing]
18. [note missing]
19. [note missing]

MESSENGER LECTURE V

Radicalism for Southern Conservatives

UP TO MARCH OF 1867 the South continued to live a fantasy sustained by the encouragements of President Johnson and the Democratic press of the North. According to this fantasy Northern opinion did not support the reconstruction policies of Congress, the elections of 1866 were a miscarriage or a farce, the President's defiant vetoes would prevail, and if not there was always the Supreme Court. In any case the Fourteenth Amendment was infamous and they rejected it resoundingly, all ten legislatures with scarcely a handful of dissenting votes. Rather than submit they would stay out of Congress indefinitely, pursue their policy of "masterly inactivity," and take their stand on states rights and injured dignity.

Congress broke the spell with shattering suddenness by passing its Military Reconstruction Act and overriding the President's veto on March 2. The thing was done. The South's response was a change of attitude as swift and complete as the shift from submission to defiance that occurred more than two years before in the summer of 1865. Now the shift was back to submission, compliance, acquiescence. Confederate heroes of the rank of Lee, Hampton, Longstreet, and Taylor urged this.[1] So did politicians such as former governors Joseph E. Brown of Georgia and A. G. Brown of Mississippi, and Governors R. M. Patton of Alabama and Orr of South Carolina. "It is a nauseating dose," admitted Brown, the Mississippian. "But I know the doctor; if I don't take this, *and do it promptly*, he will, on the next round, give me something worse, and very likely stand by and make me take it."[2]

Few of the admonitions of compliance were so bitter. Summing up the Southern press reaction, the New York *Times* stressed "a remarkable moderation of tone," and remarked that there was "no whining, no grumbling, no abuse."[3] Northern Democratic papers filled long columns with propitiatory editorials from Southern papers, urging restraint, forbearance, and willing submission. They said the Reconstruction bill was "the law of the land," that the South no longer had to decide upon its own humiliation, as in the vote on the Fourteenth Amendment, but only to submit. The South, they counseled, should at long last face up to its defeat, to stern necessities, and for its own good make the most of a bad situation.[4]

Conservative leaders warned, however, that passive submission was not enough and that the South must rally for action to avoid the worst. The strategy they proposed, now that Negro suffrage was inevitable, was an all-out drive to win Negro support. The strategy had many advocates but was most often associated with the name of Wade Hampton, the South Carolina aristocrat. "If we cannot direct the wave it will overwhelm us," he reasoned. "Now how shall we do this? Simply by making the Negro a Southern man, and if you will, a Democrat, anything but a Radical."[5] To a mass meeting of freedmen in Columbia on March 18 Hampton asked: "Why should we not be friends? Are you not Southern men, as we are? ... I want to make you feel that you are Southern men, with all your hopes, your feelings and your interests, identified with the South, for that is the true position for you to occupy.... A stronger prejudice has always existed at the North against your people than here, and it exists still."[6]

The Hampton Plan won enthusiastic adherents among conservative leaders all across the South in every state. A few such as Governor Orr of South Carolina, ex-Governor Brown of Georgia, and future Governor Alcorn of Mississippi combined their approach to the Negro with varied commitments to radicalism. More typical were the paternalistic and patronizing approaches in all varieties used by Governor Worth of North Carolina, Governor Patton of Alabama, Governor Throckmorton of Texas, and General John B. Gordon of Georgia. They appeared to be in dead earnest. The campaign of Mississippi conservatives for Negro votes was described as "strenuous," and "almost frantic" in its zeal.[7] The usual tactics were great mass meetings addressed by distinguished whites and assorted Negro speakers who stressed harmony, friendship, and trust. These were supplemented by public dinners and huge barbecues. Attendance was bi-racial, but the prevailing white attitude was the "old-master" benevolence and condescension. The leading conservative paper of North Carolina carefully "mistered" Negroes and violently deplored any suggestion of "a white man's party."[8] By May twenty-two newspapers in Mississippi were supporting the strategy. Negro collaborationists of some standing, such as Beverly Nash in South Carolina, could be found, and the age-old, ingrained deference to white authority fostered and flattered conservative hopes. A thoroughly conservative Memphis paper predicted that "nine-tenths of all the negro votes" could be secured.[9] Whatever the mass of whites thought, all the bruised pride and injured self esteem of the old planter elite was at stake in the experiment. Much more was at stake besides and optimism abounded.

The conservative strategists discovered too late that instead of advancing to a new realism they had retreated to another fantasy. They would have done well to listen to the counsel of the wealthy Mississippi planter James L. Alcorn when he told them that "all which our people claim for the influence of the 'old master' on the freedmen is neither more nor less than nonsense. The terrible necessities of our position demand blunt speaking.... The 'old master,' gentlemen, has passed from fact to poetry!"[10]

The fact was that in response to the new dispensation the freedmen had undergone striking changes. Independent reports from officers of the Freedmen's Bureau in many states commented on these changes during March, April, and May. From North Carolina General N. A. Miles wrote that, "The military steps toward giving the colored people their rights ... already give evidence of their influence in the development of their manhood. They evince appreciation of their position..."[11] From Florida Colonel J. F. Sprague reported, "The freedmen begin to understand their rights, and utterly refuse to work for those who have ill-treated or defrauded them."[12] The Bureau commissioner for Mississippi found that, "Those who treated freedmen unfairly last season cannot now obtain hands at any price."[13] Similar reports came in simultaneously from South Carolina, Tennessee, and Louisiana.

In the cities a new Negro was also in evidence. In New Orleans the people of color demonstrated so persistently against the Jim Crow "Star Cars" established in 1864 that General Sheridan ordered an end to racial discrimination on streetcars of the city in May, 1867.[14] Negroes of New Orleans also staged demonstrations for integrated schools, and they actually materialized in that one city. In Richmond a squad of Negro troops marched around the Capitol building while the Legislature was in session and "vociferously cheered for the Union and the Shallabarger [Reconstruction] bill."[15] Other demonstrators threatened to "force their way into white churches," and still others put up such a demonstration against exclusion from cars that General Schofield opened four of Richmond's six street cars to "all complexions" and reserved two for "ladies."[16] About the same time General Sickles abolished racial discrimination in the public conveyances of South Carolina.[17] Other racial barriers hastily erected by the Black Codes of 1865 in town, shop, market, and farm began to crumble under the protest of freedmen and the orders of the new military commanders.

Black faces began to appear in wildly improbable, wholly unprecedented places—jury boxes, for example, in Texas, in South Carolina, in North Carolina. It was incredible, but it was true. "It is amazing," wrote Kemp Battle of Raleigh, "how quietly our people take negro juries, or rather negroes on juries."[18] Not all could contain their amazement, especially when the racial mixing was voluntary. Randolph Shotwell, a bitter conservative of Rutherfordton, confessed his dismay at seeing "long processions of countrymen entering the village by the various roads, mounted and afoot, whites and blacks marching together, and in frequent instances arm-in-arm, a sight to disgust even a decent negro."[19] It was his first glimpse of the "Red Strings," the interracial radical club of Tarheels. Even native white radicals had grave misgivings, for example the one who wrote to the Raleigh *Standard* that "the two races now eat together at the same table, sit together in the same rooms, work together, visit and hold debating societies together," and wondered what it would all come to.[20] Even a seasoned Tarheel abolitionist like Daniel R. Goodloe reported rather self-consciously on attending a political-social affair in New Bern "composed of blacks and whites" that he "spent a very pleasant evening, and affiliated beautifully."[21]

Native whites of the radical persuasion were embarrassed from the start in their overtures to the Negro by constraints and ambivalences and traditional revulsions. Conservatives were cynically confident the radicals would never carry it off. "At heart three-fourths of the Southern Radicals believe the same thing," declared one conservative. "No class of men among us are more averse to negro equality than they are."[22] Radical strategists were as keenly aware of their handicaps as anyone. As one of them from northern Alabama, Joseph C. Bradley, remarked, "The negro is the bitter pill." As a concession to aversions in that section he hoped that segregated registration might be arranged—but tactfully. Yet he insisted even more strongly, "we must have men who will mix with the negroes & tell them of their rights. If we don't have such men, we will be defeated."[23] And such men were found, native whites, too, and they worked with a will. They knew the necessity. As recent study shows, native white radical voters were an absolute majority in hardly more than five per cent of the Southern counties, and Negro allies were essential.[24]

Whatever the ambivalence of the white radicals, the freedmen did not hesitate long between the sort of fellowship they extended and the condescending paternalism and segregated barbecue the old masters served up. "At first blush," admitted a Texas radical, "it seemed as if the 'lost cause' party would manage... to handle the newly enfranchised freedmen, but each day is clearing away the clouds..."

Again and again, a conservative rally for freedmen would wind up in a "thorough radical demonstration" on their part. Negroes were proving "radical to a man." There was indeed much to justify his description of Negro conversion to radicalism as "a sweeping fire in a piney woods."²⁵

The fire was not spontaneous combustion. The firebrands were collected, organized, and distributed. The Congressional Union Republican Committee, headed by Robert C. Schenck together with Zach Chandler, John A. Logan, William D. Kelley, and Oakes Ames, plunged into the work of organizing the Republican party in the South immediately after the passage of the First Reconstruction Act. In eight months they dispatched 178 speakers and organizers and distributed 854,700 pieces of propaganda throughout the South.²⁶ A similar committee called the Massachusetts Reconstruction Association worked independently to the same end.²⁷ But by far the most effective and important work was done by the secret Loyal Leagues, which also went under the name of Union Leagues and Liberty Leagues. They had come south with the Union army and with the triumph of Congressional radicalism took on new life and zeal. By late August of 1867 they was "recruiting in every village of the South," claimed "over four thousand Councils," and a membership of more than a half million, and by mid-November they were established in nearly every county of the region.²⁸

Participants in the organization drive in the South included Republicans of highest party rank, and numerous Northerners of all ranks. Teachers and officials of the freedmen's aid societies were swept up into the political crusade, and Freedmens Bureau officials from the North were involved in large numbers. One of them from Ohio wrote his mother from Mobile, Alabama that "It is simply impossible to keep out of the councils and caucuses of the union men and blacks who, as if by instinct, turn to the Bureau for council.... Almost any intelligent northern man is received warmly as an accession to their ranks, and can be placed at once in office by the colored vote. If Will [his brother] were here he could have a place worth several thousand."²⁹ Prominent Negroes, like Frederick Douglass and John Mercer Langston were in great demand and in constant use. Some ante-bellum leaders of the antislavery crusade enlisted wholeheartedly.

The old abolitionists were in an ecstasy of anticipation and fulfillment, and many of them went south to join the new crusade. Wendell Phillips, who did not, declared in May, "We seem to be on the very eve of the accomplishment of all that the friends of freedom have ever asked of the nation ... the absolute civil and political equality of the colored man under our institutions of government."[30] "How great these days!" exclaimed the abolitionist E. L. Pierce. It seemed to him "there had never been since Christian martyrdom or the Reformation, the opportunity for equal devotion." He was sure that the Negroes were "at last upon their feet provided with all the weapons of defense which any class or race can have."[31] To Theodore Tilton civilization seemed to be "coming brightly out of the darkness of the dead ages" and to be working "greater changes than genii or fairy ever dreamed of."

In the light of history those soaring hopes and confident predictions of Phillips, Pierce, and Tilton appear more fantastic than the dream of restored hegemony that beguiled the old masters. It was, as we now know, utterly unrealistic of them to assume that the newly freed slaves were assured "absolute civil and political equality" or that they had been endowed with "all the weapons of defense" they might need for the protection of such rights as they had on paper, or that they were at all prepared for the crucial test that history had in store for them. For never in the history of the republic, never before in fact—not in Athens, or Rome, or in Paris in its wildest days, had the democratic dogma been subjected to so severe and extreme a test as that to which it was put in eleven states of the South.

And yet there was much to justify optimism in the conduct and appearance of the freedmen at their first awakening into political life in the spring and summer of 1867. Federal officials, even friendly ones, had been gravely apprehensive over what might happen at this first stirring of the black mass. Yet their initial reports generally registered favorable surprise. The Freedmen's Bureau head in Florida told of mass meetings of thousands, one of five thousand, in Jacksonville, Gainesville, Lake City, and Tallahassee "at which trouble was apprehended," yet which invariably "passed off in a satisfactory manner."[32] The commissioner in Arkansas commented especially on the "calmness and dignity" with which the freedmen conducted themselves and said there were "no noisy demonstrations."[33] Even Southern white conservatives were impressed with the sudden sobriety and earnestness of the freedmen. Reporting a political meeting of Negroes in Raleigh, the *Sentinel* of that city said, "We have rarely seen in the city of Raleigh so quiet, orderly and attentive a crowd." And a meeting of over 3,000 Negroes in the village of Tarboro was described by a local journal as presenting a "uniform appearance of order and decorum," and "not a single instance of outrageous or indecent conduct."[34] Here and elsewhere, as Bureau agents reported, was evidence of a dawning respect for the freedmen in the white world. The most conservative editor in North Carolina wrote that "both white and colored seem to be adopting themselves quietly and peaceably to the new regime posed by Congress. The colored people... are bearing themselves, for the most part, modestly and becomingly.... We see no evidence of immoderate elation no excitement beyond what might be expected, and they manifest no spirit adverse to the proper claims of those whom they have hither to regarded as friends and superiors. Least of all do we find any hostility to those who were their former masters."[35] James S. Pike, who later in his book, *The Prostrate State*, did so much to denigrate and discredit Negro politicians received an entirely different impression of them in an earlier visit to Columbia. In his journal he noted "an air of mastery among the colored people," and was surprised at "how reticent the whites are in their dealings with the blacks, & how entirely self contained & self asserting the blacks appear to be." He suppressed these observations later.[36] Governor Worth of North Carolina wrote President Johnson in April that, "The negroes, so far, are apparently more conservative than the white men who claim to be their special friend."[37]

Many of the Negro leaders who suddenly appeared were recruited from teachers, lawyers, and preachers who had come in from the free states or Canada. [Remarkably few rose out of the ante-bellum free Negro population of the South, or] from the foremen, drivers, and specially favored ex-slaves of the old regime.* Native Negro leaders and politicians sprang typically from the urban slave population, former mechanics, clerks, or waiters, many with more than a smattering of education. "There is something fascinating," writes Wharton of the local Negro leaders in Mississippi, "about the suddenness with which, all over the state, they emerged from the anonymity of slavery to become directors and counselors of their race."[38] One reads in July 1866 of George Ruby, a Negro school teacher, being beaten and kicked in Jackson, Louisiana, and a year later finds him a chief figure in the Loyal League of Texas. Another place of evidence that James Pike suppressed in his *Prostrate State* book was the observation of a conservative white state senator of South Carolina that the Negro members learned legislative procedures and rules "like a flash."[39]

In the meantime the registration of the new Southern electorate went forward with painful slowness due to lack of qualified registrars who could take the "Iron Clad Oath" and legal complications. The processes of disfranchisement of disqualified whites and enfranchisement of newly

---

* Woodward crossed out the phrase in brackets thus leaving a fragment sentence.

qualified Negroes went on simultaneously. When it was complete more than 703,000 Negroes and some 627,000 whites were registered as qualified voters in the reconstructed states. While only two states had a colored majority of population, five states were given a colored majority of registered voters. The male population of voting age in Louisiana in 1860 was 94,711 whites and 92,502 Negroes, but only 45,218 whites were registered as against 84,436 Negroes. Alabama's voting age population in 1860 was 113,871 whites and 92,404 Negroes, but only 61,295 whites were registered against 104,518 Negroes. While some states with white majorities in population were given colored majorities in their electorate, others had their white majorities drastically reduced, and two states with a preponderance of Negroes in population had overwhelming majorities of Negro voters.

The newly minted electorate of freedmen was rushed immediately to the polls to vote on the calling of constitutional conventions. Their appearance there in mass for the first time in history was a dramatic occasion. They are described at their first balloting in Alabama, which occurred during a torrential rain, "the crowd of ragged colored men standing for hours in the pitiless storm, waiting to slip in their tickets, and so fearful of losing their turns that one who had deposited his vote found no avenue of egress save that paved with the heads of those behind." They stood silent, solemn, and appeared embarrassed, wearing old blue or grey uniform jackets, with not "one unpatched garment in fifty," shabby, forlorn, pathetically vulnerable.[40] Never in history had the franchise been conferred on a proletariat so utterly deprived. Their material impoverishment was too total to be adequately described by the word "propertyless;" their educational equipment too meager to be encompassed by the category of "illiterate." As for the less tangible but psychologically more important endowments of status, self assurance, and inner security, their deprivations were appalling, unprecedented among legally qualified electorates of record.

The record left by the revolutionary experiment in freedmen's franchise has been widely used to discredit both the experiment itself and the democratic faith in general. Yet a close reading of that record, far closer than we have time for here, would render an accounting that is not wholly without comfort for those of the democratic persuasion. To look for a moment beyond the limits of the present study, we can at least say that the ex-slave electorate proved remarkably restrained in their demands, unaggressive in their conduct, and deferential in their attitudes. In no state, not even in the five in which they held an electoral majority nor in the two of those where they constituted an absolute majority, did they hold place and power in anything approaching their numbers and voting strength. The freedmen of Mississippi almost never took advantage of their numbers to seize control of local government, for a Negro majority in a municipal government seems to have been unknown, and only one Negro mayor took office. To the first Congress in which they were eligible to serve only three Negroes were elected in the whole country, and there were never more than eight at one time out of a total of more than one hundred members from the Southern states. In view of all this and the consistently subordinate role the freedmen took in politics, it can not be said that any state in the South was brought under Negro rule or "domination" at any time.

And yet in varying numbers and different states Negroes did occupy from time to time all the varieties of public office in existence, up to but not including the governorship. And this included policemen and supreme court justices, recorders of deeds and lieutenant-governors, sheriffs and prosecuting attorneys, justices of the peace and state superintendents of public education, mayors and United States senators. Some were awkward and even grotesque in their roles, but not all the awkward and grotesque officials were black, nor were they all elected in the South in that period. Some moral and political pigsties developed in which corrupt Negro officials figured, but the blacks were far outnumbered by the whites in the pigsties—North as well as South. It may be said in general that the black neophytes of the 1870s do not compare unfavorably with the hordes of white neophytes that poured in from southern and eastern Europe in the 1880s, and 1890s so far as their respective record goes in their first encounters with democratic political life. On the whole one is more impressed with the success that a people of such meager resources and limited experience enjoyed in producing the number of sober, honest, and capable leaders and public servants they did, than with their undoubted failures.

One thing became unmistakably apparent about the black electorate once they began casting votes. That was that they voted overwhelmingly, consistently, and religiously for the Republican ticket. There were too few exceptions to give any comfort to the old-master strategy.

Republicans of the other color were less numerous and more difficult to identify. Wherever found and however identified, however, the native white Republican was easily the most reviled, censured, and despised participant in the radical experiment. Neither the Negro nor the carpetbagger has been the target of so much contempt and bitterness in the South as the native white radical. He was a "scalawag," traitor alike to region and to race. The scalawags have been the subject of a vast amount of opprobrium and vituperation.

Their numbers, their habitat, their motives, and their political antecedents have remained largely a mystery or a subject of vague speculation. Were they formerly Democrats or Whigs, wartime Unionists or Confederate turncoats, Delta planters or mountain farmers? They have been identified as all these things but without persuasive evidence to back up the identifications.

New light is shed on these questions in a recent study by Professor Allen W. Trelease.[41] By a close study of those counties in the South where the Republican vote significantly exceeded the Negro voting population he has been able to find out much about the native white Republican voter. Basing his figures on the 1872 election, he estimates that the native white Republicans cast about one tenth of the votes recorded in the South, about one fifth of all the white votes, and about the same proportion of all the Republican votes. In all they constituted "in the neighborhood of 150,000," and about half of those were accounted for by the two states of Tennessee and North Carolina. Most of the rest came from Arkansas, Texas, and Virginia, in that order of importance. As few as they were they constituted the margin of victory in many counties and to an important extent held the balance of power during the years of Radical Reconstruction in the South.

Significant information about the economic status of the native white Republicans is revealed by the association of low per capita income with their appearance in strength. According to Mr. Trelease, "The larger the proportion of white Republicans ... the lower was the per capita wealth." In those counties where they were in the majority, the per capita wealth was only $90 as compared with $145 in the South as a whole. In the 125 counties where the Republican percentage of the vote exceeded the percentage of Negro population by as much as 30 the per capita wealth was only $106. With few exceptions, the per capita wealth of counties with important white Republican strength was significantly less than that of the state at large. They were also, with some exceptions, chiefly in Texas, areas of low soil fertility where plantation and slavery had made little penetration. The disparity between per capita wealth of white Republicans and white Democrats is likely much greater than the figures suggest. There were few white Republicans in the black belt, where the wealth was concentrated in the hands of whites, a concentration not revealed by per capita figures. The clear indication is that the white Republicans were poor folk in terribly poor sections, appreciably poorer than the average whites and strikingly poorer than the conservative or Democratic whites.

In view of all this, what can be said about the pre-war political affiliations of the white Republicans in the South? Were they primarily Whig, as described by Professor David Donald and others, or were they Democratic?

The black Belt counties were mostly Whig in prewar days, and it is true that these counties were overwhelmingly Republican during Reconstruction. But this was due to the new Negro voters, for the ex-Whig white minority voted almost solidly Democratic. Of the ex-Whig counties that were predominantly white in population only 53 of the 117 voted Republican in 1872, and 50 of the 53 were in Tennessee and North Carolina with a few in Virginia. And again, of those counties in which white Republicans were a majority of all the voters, only about half or 27 were predominantly Whig before the war. And of the 27 counties 26 were in Tennessee and North Carolina. The case for identifying postwar Republicans with prewar Whigs, therefore, is limited to the three states of Tennessee, North Carolina, and Virginia. And even in those states a great number of old Whigs became postwar Democrats. Those who joined the Republicans were Appalachian highlanders, small farmers, not planter-aristocrats or businessmen of the black belt. Outside those three states most of the white Republicans appear to have been prewar Democrats.

The identification of white Republicanism with wartime "Unionism" is frequently made on the basis of the geographic coincidence of the two groups. It is clear that Unionism was heavily concentrated in the mountainous parts of Tennessee, North Carolina, Virginia, Alabama, Arkansas, and also parts of Texas. And it is equally clear that white Republicans were most numerous in those same areas. It was particularly in those parts that Confederate disloyalty, desertion, and peace societies flourished. But there was another contingent of Unionists quite outside these areas. These were the large planters and their business and professional friends of the black belt. Conservative in all things, they generally opposed secession, but their Unionism was conditional. They usually "went along with their states" and supported the Confederacy with more or less consistency. Once the war was over their conservatism reasserted itself and became a bulwark of resistance to Radical Republicanism. It is true that a few of them, often prominent ex-Whigs, experimented with joining the Radicals to tame them. But the experiment was shortlived and unsuccessful. This type of Unionist—the upper class, ex-planter and his friends—never furnished many votes for the Republicans. The great majority of them became conservative Democrats. The dominance of the spirit of Whiggery in the new Democratic party of the South was in fact largely their work.[42]

Before the advent of Republicanism the political parties of the South, true to the national tradition, had never been class parties. The characteristic rhetoric of one may have been thought more appealing to the common man or to the elite than the other. But if the Whigs were called the "broadcloth" party, the party of the aristocrat, they were also, as we have seen, the party of many very plain folk of the hill country. And if the Jacksonian Democracy was the party of the common man, it was also the party of slavery and nabob planters.

The advent of Republicanism marked the advent of class politics in the South. As anomalous as it may be in view of the subsequent history of the party in the North, Republicanism was preeminently the poor man's party in the Reconstruction South. By something like a four to one ratio its poor-man constituency was black. The black portion was truly dirt-poor, poorer by any measurement—material or otherwise—than the constituency of any party in our history, including the protest parties of Populism, Socialism, or Communism. But its ties to Republicanism, as we shall see, were ultimately based on characteristics and problems that were not essentially economic and that they did not share with the white minority constituency.

The native white Republicans brought along with them into their new party a highly developed and ready-made set of class resentments—their historic feud with the planter class and plantation slavery. Long submerged in Whig or Democratic allegiances, their bitter class resentments were released and exacerbated by secession and Civil War. Republicanism supplied a convenient and appropriate means of discharging accumulated aggressions. The old enemy was no longer in the same party but in the "other" party. The old constraints were down, and what was long muttered could now be shouted—and it was, from the housetops. Class animosities became the standard rallying cry of the new party.

In an address "To the White working Men of North Carolina," the leading Republican paper of that state said: "Heretofore you have been stigmatized as 'mean whites,' 'poor white trash,' and 'greasy mechanics.' You have been imposed upon socially, politically, and pecuniarily by Southern aristocrats and secession oligarchs." He said, "You were forced into the late war against your wills. . . . and your innocent families . . . were nearly starved and became shoeless and almost naked. . . . Humble working men you have been scorned by 'Southern Chivalry. . . . Behold! There is now a party in full life and vigor in North Carolina which honors the working man."[43] Parson Brownlow made "the slave-breeding, slave-driving, slaveholding classes of the South," as he described them, the very stereotype of the Democratic opposition for white Republicans of Tennessee. "The feelings, opinions and interests of what they termed the 'poor white trash' were never consulted," he declared. "In a word, the poor whites had no rights which the slave aristocracy ever did respect."[44]

Republicanism offered this class of Southern whites, especially the majority of them who lived in the mountain and hill country, more than a ready vehicle for rhetorical aggression. It offered them an economic and social program of reform that fit their needs and revived demands they had been making for decades. "I am charged with inconsistency," Parson Brownlow told a Radical Convention in Tennessee, "in that I am, as an OLD LINE WHIG, advocating the principles of the Republican party. A Republican Congress has inaugurated HENRY CLAY'S AMERICAN SYSTEM—a system that I have advocated for the last thirty years."[45] They were a land-locked people scratching a meager living out of subsistence agriculture but surrounded by fabulous mineral resources, unharnessed water power, and inexhaustible labor supplies—all lying idle and awaiting development. The Republican program of government subsidy for internal improvement, railroad development, and encouragement of capital investment seemed made to their order to fit their long felt needs.

"It has been very fashionable to denounce Yankees and ridicule Yankee notions," said Thomas Settle, North Carolina Republican. "I tell you Yankees and Yankee notions are just what we want in this country. We want their capital to build factories, and work shops, and railroads, and develop our magnificent water powers. . . . We want their intelligence, their energy and enterprise to operate these factories, and to teach us how to do it." This was why "we endorsed the measures adopted by congress for the reconstruction of the Southern States." It meant "starting afresh," he said. "Let the dead past bury the dead, our thoughts and hopes should be on the future." He added succinctly: "I take it that you and the Yankees are just alike about money."[46]

Over this issue of which way the South should face there was a head-on clash with North Carolina conservatives. "Yes, we *have* a *new* North Carolina," wrote Josiah Turner, their spokesman. But it was a cause of "humiliation and sorrow" instead of rejoicing to those of the true faith. "*We* cling, in our affections, to the North Carolina of old. We have no fancy for the meretricious trappings of the new. We have no toleration for a state of things, where the Almighty Dollar is so potent, so selfish, the great object of worship, to the neglect of the things that make for solid and valuable character."[47] Eventually the conservatives of the New South school evolved a marvelous mystique which reconciled the old order with the new, but that was in the future. For the present the conservatives were dead against the economic hopes of the native white Republicans.

As for the economic hopes of the native black Republicans, the new party had briefly entertained some radical proposals of land redistribution—the old 40-acre scheme—but abandoned them. Apart from a few token land grants in the sea islands, the empty gesture of the Southern Homestead Act, and such ineffectual efforts as the Freedmen's Bureau in supervising wages, contracts, and relief, Republicanism had nothing in the way of an economic program specifically geared to the needs of the Negroes. Certainly nothing comparable in relevance to the one geared to the needs of the Southern white constituency.

But of course the Negro had more than economic needs, needs in which Republicanism had something to offer of utmost importance. These were urgent needs for protection in vital areas—freedom and life itself, among others. And the others included citizenship, justice, the franchise, and the whole new endowment of political and civil rights into which the freedmen had so recently entered and upon which they had so tenuous and precarious a hold. So long as the Republicans could—or would—protect them in the enjoyment of these rights, there was good prospect for the success of the Radical Republican experiment.

After all, the new party enjoyed unprecedented advantages in initial voting strength. Of approximately 1,330,000 registered as qualified voters under the Reconstruction acts in 1867 and 1868, some 703,000 were Negroes and about 627,000 were whites. Adding an estimated 150,000 of white Republicans to the Negroes gives the Republicans a reasonable claim of 64 per cent of the total Southern electorate. This was a greater margin of voting strength than any party had enjoyed in the South for more than a generation. Whigs and Democrats divided the Southern vote very equally so long as they contested it.[47] So long as substantial numbers of whites were disfranchised for participation in the rebellion the Republican voting advantage was formidable in many Southern states.

It was this racial alliance of colors, roughly 80 per cent Negro to 20 per cent white that ushered in the new order, wrote the radical constitutions, the new law codes, elected the civil governments, filled the judiciary, and at the start administered the government.

In spite of these impressive achievements and the formidable combination of voters that supported the new order—and had very good reasons for supporting it—it is my contention that the experiment was doomed at a very early stage. In fact almost from the start. In my sixth and final lecture I shall attempt to explain why.

Notes

1. New York *Times*, March 26, 1867.
2. Jackson *Daily Clarion*, March 12, 27, 1867.
3. New York *Times*, March 6, 23, 1867.

4. For example in New York *World*, March 6, 15, 1867; Jackson *Daily Clarion*, March 17, 1867.
5. Wade Hampton to John Mullay (Private), March 31, 1867, in Cauthen (ed.), *Family Letters of Three Hamptons*, 142–43.
6. Quoted in Charleston *Daily Courier*, March 23, 1867, and Raleigh *Daily Sentinel*, March 28, 1867.
7. Wharton, *Negro in Mississippi*, 142–43.
8. Raleigh *Daily Sentinel*, March 27, June 29, 1867.
9. Memphis *Avalanche*, January 5, 1867.
10. J. L. Alcorn, *Views on the Political Situation in Mississippi*, 3–4, quoted in Wharton, *Negro in Mississippi*, 142.
11. Freedmen's Bureau Synopsis of Reports, January 1, 1867 to December 12, 1869, p. 117, National Archives.
12. Ibid., 100.
13. Ibid., p. 93.
14. P. H. Sheridan to U. S. Grant, May 10, 1867, in E. M. Stanton Papers, vol. 32, #56412, Library of Congress.
15. Richmond *Times*, March 13, 1867 in Raleigh *Sentinel*, March 14, 1867.
16. Richmond *Examiner*, May 2, 1867 in Raleigh *Sentinel*, May, 3, 1867; Galveston *Flakes Weekly Bulletin*, May 15, 1867.
17. Woody and Simkins, *South Carolina During Reconstruction*, 70.
18. Kemp Battle to B. S. Hedrick, June 12, 1867, in Hedrick Papers, Duke University Library.
19. Quoted in J. G. de R. Hamilton (ed.), *The Papers of Randolph Abbott Shotwell*, II, 295–96.
20. Quoted in Raleigh *Standard*, March 16, 1867, from Olsen, Chap. VIII.
21. Daniel R. Goodloe to B. S. Hedrick, April 24, 1867, Hedrick Papers, Duke University Library.
22. Raleigh *Daily Sentinel*, July 10, 1867.
23. Joseph C. Bradley, Huntsville, to Gen. Wager Swayne, April 6, 11, 12, 23, 1867; Bradley to J. C. Keffer, April 17, 1867; Bradley to Col. W. H. Smith, May 1, June 29, July 4, 1867, in Swayne Papers, State Dept. of Archives, Montgomery, Alabama.
24. Allen W. Trelease, "Who Were the Scalawags?", *Journal of Southern History*, XXIX (1963), 445–68.
25. San Antonio *Daily Express*, May 1, 1867.
26. Rochester *Express* quoted in New York *Times*, Nov. 16, 1867.
27. *De Bow's Review*, XXXVI (Sept., 1867), 245–46.
28. San Antonio *Daily Express*, August 26, 1867.
29. Quoted in *National Antislavery Standard*, May 18, 1867, in Jim McPherson.
30. E. L. Pierce to J. M. McKim, April 20, 1867, McKim Manuscripts, in Rose, last chapter.

31. James J. Jenkins, Mobile, to Mother, January 8, 1867, in J. J. Gillette Papers, Library of Congress.
32. Col. John T. Sprague, Jacksonville, June 5, 1867, reports on Florida for May, 1867, Freedmen's Bureau Synopsis of Reports, January 1, 1867 to December 3, 1869, p.143 National Archives.
33. Gen. C. H. Smith reports for Arkansas for May, 1867, in ibid., p. 153.
34. Raleigh *Sentinel* in Greensboro *Patriot*, April 26, 1867; Tarboro *Southerner* in ibid., May 31, 1867.
35. Raleigh *Sentinel*, April 2, 1867.
36. Robert Durden, *James S. Pike*, 212–13.
37. Jonathan Worth to Andrew Johnson, March 29, 1867, in Hamilton, (ed.), *Correspondence of Jonathan Worth*, II, 926.
38. Wharton, *Negro in Mississippi*, 164.
39. Durden, *James S. Pike*, 210.
40. Cincinnati *Commercial* quoted in The American Freedman, II (March, 1868), 372–73
41. Allen W. Trelease, "Why Were the Scalawags?", *Journal of Southern History*, 445–68.
42. Thomas Alexander, C. Vann Woodward, *Origins of the New South*.
43. Raleigh *Standard* quoted in Knoxville *Whig*, April 1, 1868.
44. Knoxville *Whig*, February 27, 1867.
45. Notes for a speech of Thomas Settle shortly after March 27, 1867, in Settle Papers, Southern Historical Collection, University of North Carolina.
46. Raleigh *Semi-Weekly Sentinel*, December 12, 1868.
47. Charles Sellers, "Who Were the Southern Whigs," American Historical Review.

MESSENGER LECTURE VI
Did The North Really Mean It?

A SUDDEN SHIFT from defiance to acquiescence took place in the South with the passage of the Reconstruction Act of March 2, 1867. How deep the change ran it would be hard to say. The evidence of it comes largely from public pronouncements of the press and conservative leaders, and on the negative side from the silence of the voices of defiance. The mood of submission and acquiescence was experimental, tentative, and precarious at best. It cannot be said to have predominated longer than seven months, from spring to autumn of 1867. That brief period was crucial for the future of the South and the Negro in the long agony of Reconstruction.

The period coincided on the one hand with the climax of the radical drive to register, indoctrinate, and organize the Negro voters as the mainstay of their Southern support. It also coincided with the counter drive of the conservatives to enlist the freedmen in their own cause. The Hampton Plan encountered skepticism from the start among Southern whites. But the apparent docility and moderation of the freedmen aroused hopes for the strategy and it was pressed with great vigor in many quarters. Only at the polls did it become apparent what an utter and abysmal failure the Hampton plan had proved. The first shock of overt and concerted opposition by the Negroes fell with stunning effect. In Tennessee, where they first appeared at the polls, the Memphis editor who had predicted nine tenths of them would vote conservative wrote, "We cannot express our surprise and mortification at the result of the election in this city and county. The Radical vote astonishes us by its magnitude."[1] In Nashville the Freedmen's Bureau commissioner reported that "the rage of the conservatives was without parallel," that they discharged some two hundred Negro employees in retaliation, and that the Negroes replied with a boycott.[2] In Richmond, Virginia, the number of freedmen on relief jumped 412 as a result of "the closing of most of the tobacco factories and discharge of employed for exercising the elective franchise in a manner contrary to the wishes of their employers."³ Critics poured derision on the Hampton Plan, and by the end of August General Hampton himself admitted that, "Recent events show that there is no longer a possibility of that entire harmony of action among our people for which you and we have heretofore hoped and striven."⁴

Smarting sharply under the rebuff administered by their new Negro electorate, Southerners watched intently the forthcoming state elections in the North in October. They were expected to reflect Northern reactions to Radical Reconstruction and especially to the issue of Negro suffrage. There was much earnest speculation in the South. "It may be," said the Charleston *Mercury*, "that Congress but represents the feelings of its constituents, that it is but the moderate mouth-piece of incensed Northern opinion. It may be that measures harsher than any ... that confiscation, incarceration, banishment may breed over us in turn! But all these things will not change our earnest belief—*that there will be a revulsion of popular feeling in the North*."⁵

Hopes were aroused first by the elections in Connecticut on April 1, less than a month after the passage of the Reconstruction Act. The Democrats won in almost all quarters. The Radical *Independent* taunted the North for hypocrisy. "Republicans in all the great states, North and West, are in a false position on this question," it said. "In Congress they are for impartial suffrage; at home they are against it." In only six states outside the South were Negroes permitted to vote, and in none with appreciable Negro population. The *Independent* thought that "it ought to bring a blush to every white cheek in the loyal North to reflect that the political equality of American citizens is likely to be sooner achieved in Mississippi than in Illinois—sooner on the plantation of Jefferson Davis than around the grave of Abraham Lincoln!"⁶ Election returns in October confirmed this. Republican majorities in the New England states and in Nebraska and Iowa were sharply reduced, and in New York, New Jersey, and Maryland the party of Reconstruction went down to defeat. Democrats scored striking victories in Pennsylvania and Ohio. In Ohio Republicans narrowly elected the Governor by 8,000 votes but overwhelmed a Negro suffrage amendment by 40,000. In every state where the voters expressed themselves on the Negro suffrage issue—in New York, New Jersey, Kansas, Wisconsin, and Minnesota, as well as Ohio—they turned it down.

Horace Greeley read the returns bluntly, saying that "the Negro question lies at the bottom of our reserves ... thousands have turned against us because we purpose to enfranchise the Blacks. ... We have lost votes in the Free States by daring to be just to the Negro."⁷ The *Independent* was quite as frank. "Negro suffrage, as a political issue," it admitted, "never before was put so squarely to certain portions of the Northern people as during the late campaigns. The result shows that the Negro is still an unpopular man."[8] Jay Cooke, the conservative financier wrote John Sherman that he "felt a sort of intuition of coming disaster—probably growing out of a consciousness that other people would feel just as I did—disgust and mortification at the vagaries into which extremists in the Republican ranks were leading the party," especially "the inconceivably stupid *blunder* in Ohio"—the blunder of Negro suffrage.[9]

To the South the Northern elections seemed a confirmation of their hopes and suspicions. The old voices of defiance and resistance, silent or subdued since March, were lifted again. They had been right all along, they said. Congress did not speak the true sentiment of the North on the Negro and Reconstruction. President Johnson had been the true prophet. The correct strategy was not to seek the Negro vote but to suppress it, not to comply with the Reconstruction Acts but to subvert them. The New York *Times* thought that "The Southern people seem to have become quite beside themselves in consequence of the *quasi* Democratic victories" in the North, and that there was "neither sense nor sanity in their exultations."[10] Moderates such as Governor James W. Throckmorton of Texas who declared he "had advocated publicly and privately a compliance with the Sherman [Reconstruction] Bill" was now "determined to defeat" compliance and to leave "no stone unturned" in his efforts.[11]

The South's defiance was encouraged not only by the Northern elections and the Negro vote in the Southern elections, but also by the terrible sufferings of crop failures, famine, and starvation during the grim winter of 1867–1868. The immediate and inevitable scapegoat was the Negro. No longer courted for his vote, the Negro had few defenders in the South and grave doubt had been cast on the sincerity of his Northern champions. Aggressions of all sorts were increasingly released upon freedmen. "Since the late elections," reported the Freedmen's Bureau of North Carolina, "the feeling of a large portion of the white race toward the blacks has become one of intense hatred. The evidences of revenge are to be seen every day."[12] In Virginia the press was advocating coercive measures by planters and employers with "the view of driving as many blacks as possible out of the State, and of punishing with starvation those that remain."[13] In Mobile two Negro churches were burned in two weeks.[14] At a state convention of Conservatives in Macon, Georgia, President Benjamin H. Hill struck the key note of defiance by urging absolutely no compliance with the new laws. General Wright echoed him by the cry that, "This is a white man's government. Rouse! Rally and fight on this issue."[15]

The standard Southern reply to Northern demands was the endlessly reiterated charge of hypocrisy. Northern radicals, as a Memphis conservative put it were "seeking to fasten what they themselves repudiate with loathing upon the unfortunate people of the South." And he pointed to the succession of Northern states that had voted on and defeated Negro suffrage.[16] A Raleigh editor ridiculed Republicans of the Pennsylvania Legislature who voted 29 to 13 against the franchise for Negroes. "This is a direct confession, by Northern Radicals," he added, "that they refuse to grant in Pennsylvania the '*justice*' they would enforce on the South.... And this is Radical meanness and hypocrisy—this their love for the negro."[17]

There was little in the Republican presidential campaign of 1868 to confute the Southern charge of hypocrisy and much to support it. The Chicago Platform of May on which General Grant was nominated contained as its second section this formulation of the double standard of racial morality: "The guaranty by Congress of equal suffrage to all loyal men at the South was demanded by every consideration of public safety, of gratitude, and of justice, and must be maintained; while the question of suffrage in all the loyal [i.e., Northern] States properly belongs to the people of those States." Thus Negro *dis*franchisement was assured in the North along with the enfranchisement in the South. No direct mention of the Negro was made in the entire platform, and no mention of schools or homesteads for freedmen. Neither Grant nor his running mate Schuyler Colfax was known for any personal commitment to Negro rights, and Republican campaign speeches in the North generally avoided the issue of Negro suffrage.

Congress acted to readmit seven of the reconstructed states to the Union in time for them to vote in the Presidential election and contribute to the Republican majority. In attaching conditions to readmission, however, Congress deliberately refrained from specifying state laws protecting Negroes against discrimination in jury duty, office holding, education, intermarriage, and a wide range of political and civil rights. By a vote of 30 to 5 the Senate defeated a bill attaching to the admission of Arkansas the condition that "no person on account of race or color shall be excluded from the benefits of education, or be deprived of an equal share of the moneys or other funds created or used by public authority to promote education..."[18]

Not until the election of 1868 was safely behind them did the Republicans dare come forward with proposals of national action on Negro suffrage that was to result in the Fifteenth Amendment. They were extremely sensitive to Northern opposition to enfranchisement. By 1869 only seven Northern states had voluntarily acted to permit the Negro to vote, and no state with a substantial Negro population outside the South had done so. Except for Minnesota and Iowa, which had only a handful of Negroes, every post-war referendum on the subject had gone down to defeat.

As a consequence moderates and conservatives among Republicans took over and dominated the framing of the Fifteenth Amendment and very strongly left their imprint on the measure. Even the incorrigibly radical Wendell Phillips yielded to their sway. Addressing other radicals he pled, "for the first time in our lives we beseech them to be a little more politicians and a little less reformers." The issue lay between the moderates who wanted a limited, negative amendment that would not confer suffrage on the freedmen, would not guarantee the franchise and take positive steps to protect it, but would merely prohibit its denial on the grounds of race and previous condition. Opposed to this narrow objective were the radicals who demanded positive and firm guarantees, federal protection, and national control of suffrage. They would take away state control, North as well as South. They fully anticipated and warned of all the elaborate devices that states might resort to—and eventually did resort to—in order to disfranchise the Negro without violating the proposed amendment. These included such methods—later made famous—as the literacy and property tests, the understanding clause, the poll tax, elaborate and difficult registration tricks and handicaps. But safeguards against them were all rejected by the moderates. Only four votes could be mustered for a bill to guarantee equal suffrage to all states, North as well as South.[19] "This amendment," said its moderate proponent Oliver P. Morton, "leaves the whole power in the State as it exists, now, except that colored men shall not be disfranchised for the three reasons of race, color, or previous condition of slavery." And he added significantly, "They may, perhaps, require property or educational tests."[20] Such tests were already in existence in Massachusetts and other Northern states, and the debate made it perfectly apparent what might be expected to happen later in the South.

It was little wonder that Southern Republicans, already faced with aggression against Negro voters and terribly apprehensive about the future were intensely disappointed and unhappy about the shape the debate was taking. One of their keenest disappointments was the rejection of a clause prohibiting denial or abridgement of the right of office-holding on the ground of race. It is also not surprising that Southern white conservatives, in view of these developments, were on the whole fairly relaxed about the proposed Fifteenth Amendment. The shrewder of them in fact began to realize that the whole thing was concerned mainly, not with the Reconstruction of the South, but with maneuvers of internal politics in the Northern states. After all, the Negroes were already fully enfranchised and voting regularly and solidly in all the Southern states, their suffrage built into state constitutions and a condition of readmission to the Union.

If the Fifteenth Amendment was not about the South and Reconstruction basically, what then was it about, anyway? A recent study has drawn attention to the significance of the closely divided vote in such states as Indiana, Ohio, Connecticut, New York, and Pennsylvania. The Negro population of these states was small, of course, but so closely was the white electorate in them divided between the two major parties that a small Negro vote could often make the difference between victory and defeat. It was assumed, of course, that this potential Negro vote would be reliably Republican. Enfranchisement by state action had been defeated in all those states, and federal action seemed the only way. There is no doubt that there was some idealistic support for Negro enfranchisement, especially among antislavery people in the North. But it was not the antislavery idealists who shaped the Fifteenth Amendment and guided it through Congress. The effective leaders of legislative action were moderates with practical political considerations in mind—particularly that thin margin of difference in partisan voting strength in certain Northern states. They had their way, and they relentlessly voted down all measures of the sort the idealists such as Senator Sumner were demanding.[21]

For successful adoption the amendment required ratification by twenty-eight states. But in spite of elimination of radical features, the negative character of the amendment, the careful respect for state rights, and the endorsement of moderates, it proved impossible to muster the required support in the North. In fact, ratification would have been impossible without support of the Southern states, and an essential part of that had to come by requiring ratification as a condition of readmission of Virginia, and perhaps of Mississippi and Georgia as well.[22]

The Fifteenth Amendment has often been read as evidence of renewed notice to the South of the North's firmness of purpose, as proof of its determination not to be cheated of its idealistic war aims, as a solemn rededication to those aims. Read more carefully, however, the Fifteenth Amendment reveals more deviousness than clarity of purpose, more partisan needs than idealistic aims, more timidity than boldness.

Signals of faltering purpose in the North such as Fifteenth Amendment and the state elections in 1867 were not lost on the South. They were assessed carefully and weighed for their implications for the strategy of resistance. The movement of counter reconstruction was already well under way by the time the amendment was ratified in March, 1870, and in that year it took on new life in several quarters. Fundamentally it was a terroristic campaign of underground organizations, the Ku Klux Klan and several similar ones, for the intimidation of Republican voters and officials, the overthrow of their power, and the destruction of their organization. They used violence of all kinds, including murder by night, by mob, by drowning, by torch; they whipped, they tortured, they maimed, they mutilated. They used economic weapons and threats of all kinds, so that witnesses were afraid to testify and juries to convict. The federal troops stationed in the South, whose numbers have been greatly exaggerated, were an ineffective handful in the face of such numbers. The state militias that were organized finally after Congress belatedly authorized them in 1869 were made up mainly of Negroes inadequately led and proved incapable of handling the opposition. New state laws against the secret societies and their activities simply could not be enforced. It became perfectly clear that federal intervention of a determined sort was the only means of suppressing the movement and protecting the freedmen in their civil and political rights.

To meet this situation Congress passed the Enforcement Act of May 30, 1870, and followed it with the Second Enforcement Act and the Ku Klux Klan Act of 1871. These acts on the face of it would seem to have provided full and adequate machinery for the enforcement of the Fifteenth Amendment and the protection of the Negro and white Republican voters. They authorized the President to call out the army and navy and suspend the writ of habeas corpus; they empowered federal troops to implement court orders; and they reserved to federal courts exclusive jurisdiction in all suffrage cases. The enforcement acts have gone down in history with the stereotypes "infamous" and "tyrannical" tagged to them. As a matter of fact they were consistent with tradition and with democratic principle. Surviving remnants of them were invoked to authorize federal intervention at Little Rock and at Oxford, Mississippi. They are echoed in the Civil Rights Acts of 1957 and 1960, and they are greatly surpassed in the powers conferred by the Civil Rights Act of 1964 and the proposed bill of 1965.

Surely this impressive display of federal power and determination backed by gleaming steel and judicial majesty might be assumed to have been enough to bring the South to its senses and dispel forever the fantasies of Southern intransigents. And in fact historians have in the main endorsed the assumption that the power of the Klan was broken by the impact of the so-called Force Bills.

The truth is that while the Klan was nominally dissolved the campaign of violence, terror, and intimidation went forward virtually unabated save temporarily in places where federal power was displayed and so long as it was sustained. For all the efforts of the Department of Justice the deterioration of the freedman's status and the curtailment and denial of his suffrage continued steadily and rapidly. Federal enforcement officials met with impediments of all sorts. A close study of their efforts reveals that "In virtually every Southern state . . . federal deputy marshals, supervisors of elections, or soldiers were arrested by local law enforcement officers on charges ranging from false arrest or assault and battery to murder."[23]

The obvious course for the avoidance of local passions was to remove cases to federal courts for trial, as provided under a section of the First Enforcement Act. But in practice this turned out to be "exceedingly difficult." And the effort to find juries that would convict proved often to be all but impossible, however carefully they were chosen, and in whatever admixture of color composed them. The most overwhelming evidence of guilt proved unavailing at times. Key witnesses under intimidation simply refused to testify, and those that did were known to meet with terrible reprisals. The law authorized the organization of the *posse comitatus* and the use of troops to protect juries and witnesses. But in practice the local recruits were reluctant or unreliable, and federal troops were few and remote and slow to come, and the request for them was wrapped in endless red tape and bureaucratic frustration.[24]

All these impediments to justice might have been overcome had sufficient money been made available by Congress. And right at this crucial point once again the Northern will and purpose flagged and failed the cause they professed to sustain. It is quite clear where the blame lies. Under the new laws the cost of maintaining courts in the most affected districts of the South soared tremendously, quadrupled in some. Yet Congress starved the courts from the start, providing only about a million dollars a year—far less than was required. The Attorney General had to cut corners, urge economy, and in 1873 instruct district attorneys to prosecute no case "unless the public interest imperatively demands it." An antiquated judicial structure proved wholly inadequate to handle the extra burden and clear their dockets. "If it takes a court over one month to try five offenders," asked the Attorney General concerning 420 indictments in South Carolina, "how long will it take to try four hundred, already indicted, and many hundreds more who deserve to be indicted?" He thought it "obvious that the attempt to bring to justice even a small portion of the guilty in that state must fail" under the circumstances. Quite apart from the inadequacy and inefficiency of the judicial structure, it is of significance that a majority of the Department of Justice officers in the South at this time, despite the carpetbagger infusion, were Southern born. A study by Everette Swinney concludes that "Some marshals and district attorneys were either sensitive to Southern public opinion or in substantial agreement with it." The same has been found true of numbers of federal troops and their officers on duty in the South.[25] Then in 1874 an emasculating opinion of the Supreme Court by Justice Joseph P. Bradley in *United States v. Cruikshank et al.* cast so much doubt on the constitutionality of the enforcement acts as to render successful prosecutions virtually impossible.

There is also sufficient evidence in existence to raise a question about how much the Enforcement Acts were intended for application in the policing of elections in the South all along, as against their possible application in other quarters of the Union. As it turned out, nearly half of the cost of policing was applied to elections of New York City, where Democratic bosses gave the opposition much trouble. Actually the bulk of federal expenditures under the Enforcement Acts was made in the North, which leads one student to conclude that their primary object from the start was not the distraught South under reconstruction, but the urban strongholds of the Democrats in the North.[26] Once again, as in the purposes behind the Fifteenth Amendment, one is left to wonder how much Radical Reconstruction was really concerned with the South and how much with the party needs of the Republicans in the North.

Disenchantment with radicalism and disillusionment and discouragement with reconstruction and its results began very early in the Republican ranks. It was already pronounced in influential circles in 1869 before the Fifteenth Amendment was adopted. The irony of timing in the onset of reaction was that it came at the peak of Republican power, when the party was not only in complete control of both houses of Congress and all branches of the federal government but in control of the Southern states as well. It came while many old radicals who had fought and finally triumphed over the conservativism of Lincoln and Johnson were still occupying their seats in Congress, and it infected their own ranks quite deeply.

On the extreme left of idealistic abolitionism the reaction took the form of pessimistic despair on confronting actual conditions in the South. Representative of this reaction was that of Parker Pillsbury, dedicated friend of the freedmen. On a tour of the South in the fall of 1869 he could scarcely believe what he saw of the Negroes' condition—their degrading poverty, ignorance, and gullibility, their laziness, promiscuity, drunkenness, and thievery. He thought nineteen out of twenty as bad if not worse off than they had been under slavery. To him it seemed their worst enemies and most cynical exploiters were their pretended friends the Northern Republican politicians and employers in the South. The freedmen's efforts at self-government in South Carolina he pronounced a "burlesque on the very name of government." He concluded that "it is time one thing was told, and believed, too, everywhere; and that is that reconstruction, so far, is a failure. It is a bad failure. From the sole of its foot to its head, if it have any head, there is no soundness in it, none whatever."[27]

For Pillsbury and the dedicated few the obvious answer was the redoubling of efforts, rededication to the cause, and withering scorn of all complacency, compromise, half-measures, and partisan rationalizations. But for those of lesser involvement and weaker commitment there were easier answers. To them, to the independent editor, the respectable intellectual, it appeared that it was time to call a halt. They felt that the Fifteenth Amendment had "solved the Negro question," that it had fulfilled their commitment to the freedman, that his future now depended on self-reliance, self-education, and the slow work of time. Such reputable journals as the *Nation* and *Harper's Weekly* were inclined to this view. Typical of their attitude was the thinking of the New York *Times* in reply to the laments of Wendell Phillips: "Must we, then, go on building forever our political platform exclusively from that traditional 'wood pile' in which 'the negro' has been concealed, and whence for years he has been heard to halloo.... Everybody knows that slavery is abolished, and that the joyful era of peace is here."[28]

Native white radicals of the South who had staked all on Northern support watched with dismay the rapid withdrawal of the promised support. A Tennessee Republican wrote home from Washington in January, 1870, that "Our friends in Congress are heartily sick of this reconstruction legislation and they are anxious to get through with it and then give their whole attention to legislation necessary to relieve the industrial & commercial interests of the country. The press of the North are clamoring for reduced taxation and vigorously protesting against any action which will open anew the question of reconstruction."[29] As for the new administration, U. S. Grant was the last man to rebuild fires of moral enthusiasm, and from that quarter the fires went totally unfueled.

Quite apart from practical politicians and respectable journalists, the mood of withdrawal spread slowly into the ranks of men of conscience once famous for fierce moral commitments to racial justice. None had been more fierce and famous in this respect than Thomas Wentworth Higginson. But as he watched Negro Senators and congressmen elected in the South turned away from hotels and restaurants in Northern cities conviction drained out of him. He wrote that Northerners were "willing that the negro should be a man at the South, to spite the white man, but not willing that he should be a man at the North, where it offends their sensibilities." And in February, 1870, he was advising defeated and bewildered Negroes in the South that what they needed was "not special legislation, but centuries of time."[30] Early in 1869 Theodore Tilton, editor of the uncompromisingly radical *Independent* exhorted Americans not to abandon the Negro, that justice for him had not been won, that it was the most vital moral question before the country, that the fight had only begun. But two years later, in 1871, he could write: "If we do not misread the signs of the times, the negro question is at rest forever. We cannot foresee a reasonable apprehension that it will ever need to be revived." He considered it "settled in perpetuity."[31]

In the meantime a wing of the Republican party with strong Whiggish identifications was exploring a new and more conservative approach to the Southern problem. As formulated by Horace Greeley of the *Tribune* this policy called for a bill of universal amnesty that would enfranchise all the disfranchised rebels. So long as they were proscribed they would be driven into the ranks of the Democrats. They made up "the solid, conservative class," the natural rulers of the South whose natural economic interest and sympathies were in line with the Republican party, for many of them were old Whigs. They could be depended on to protect the Negro's rights against the persecutions of the mean whites who made up the Ku Klux Klan. Why alienate such men by continued disfranchisement and rely instead on impoverished hillbillies with their poisonous prejudices and limited outlook? Universal amnesty was the way to peace for the South, the Nation, and the Negro—not to mention the Republican party.[32]

What Horace Greeley and his friends had in mind was the abandonment of radical reconstruction in the South and the abandonment of the Negro to the custody of his former masters as the price of a political alliance with the masters along the lines of antebellum Whiggery. It was essentially the compromise eventually framed six years later in 1877 minus certain concrete economic underpinnings. It was around this "New Departure" that the Liberal Republican party rallied and took shape in 1871. To it were attracted the cream of moral aristocracy in the Republican party, many of the party's founding fathers who had invested it in its origins with antislavery idealism, men who had fought heroically through the years of the war and the Johnson administration to preserve party dedication to high moral purpose. They included such men as Carl Schurz, George W. Julian, Lyman Trumbull, Salmon

P. Chase, Charles Francis Adams, and in a confused and contradictory way Charles Sumner. Outside remained a few like Wendell Phillips and William Lloyd Garrison. But insiders included men who in 1865 and 1866 would have appeared the least probable defectors, the last who could abandon the Negro and compromise principle.[33]

In his famous report on the South in 1865 to President Johnson Carl Schurz had used his German accent to voice and awaken the conscience of a nation. Six years later he was desperately attempting to explain away everything he had said. In September 1871 Schurz launched Liberal Republicanism as a national movement at a speech in Nashville. His appeal was addressed directly to Southern whites, conservative whites. He told them the great issues of the war were at last settled, for they were "firmly imbedded in the fundamental law." The time had come for peace and order and reconciliation. There should be an end alike to carpetbaggery and kukluxery. He was for home rule and states rights and the way to them lay through general amnesty and an alliance between sane conservative Southerners and Liberal Republicanism. The South's response was enthusiastic and gratifying.[34]

The platform of the new party embodied the pledge that "Local self-government, with impartial suffrage, will guard the rights of all citizens more securely than any centralized power," and promised "the immediate and absolute removal of all disabilities imposed on account of the Rebellion," and that "universal amnesty will result in complete pacification in all sections of the country." On these pledges the conservative South temporarily shelved its mental reservations, swallowed its pride, and went down the line for Horace Greeley and New Departure Republicanism.

Alone among the Liberal Republicans, Charles Sumner insisted that reconstruction was not complete and that slavery was not fully scotched so long as the freedmen were universally denied equal civil rights. The old color caste system of the North segregating the races in schools, public accommodations, and common carriers did not provide equality. It was instead a source of insult and humiliation and degradation to the Negro. He presented to the senate innumerable petitions from Negro protest meetings denouncing segregation and demanding a civil rights bill. He piled up stacks of evidence documenting the widespread and growing discriminations against Negroes in all parts of the country. To remedy these injustices Sumner brought forth a civil rights bill for integration of races in schools, public carriers, and all public accommodations. He attached this as a rider to the pending Amnesty Bill. Sumner was willing to go along with amnesty for the rebels, but only on condition of civil rights for freedmen. On this he told the Senate:

You are about to decree the removal of disabilities from those who have been in rebellion. Why will you not with better justice decree a similar removal of disabilities from those who have never injured you? Why will you not give to the colored race that same amnesty you now offer to former rebels? Sir, you cannot go before the country with this unequal measure under the ban of exclusion. Therefore, sir, did I insist that amnesty shall not become a law unless at the same time the equal rights of all are secured.[35]

Relentlessly, incorrigibly, mercilessly Charles Sumner pressed his party to the wall and made it face the moral crisis of its very being. There was no shaking him off or evading his issue. The Republicans had a clear command of the Senate and it was plainly within their power to advance the cause of Negro rights and equality if they wanted to. Their desks were piled with evidence for the need of such legislation. Their mails were full of the Negro's desire for it. Their memories and consciences were crowded with promises, commitments, and pledges of no remote date. The more radical of them squirmed and fumed and raged. Senator Lyman Trumbull relieved his feelings by outrageous tirades of invective against Sumner. Senator Schurz maintained that the Civil Rights rider would defeat the Amnesty Bill. The old timeworn evasions and doubletalk and self-deceptions were repeated and repeated again. The result was foreseeable. Civil Rights went down to a total defeat. The rebels received their amnesty with the passage of the bill on May 22, 1872, but the freedmen were denied their rights.

On that day radical reconstruction may be said to have ended and the abandonment of the Negro to have dated. It is true that the Liberal Republican went down to defeat. The Negroes, urged by Phillips, Garrison, and leaders of their own race voted for Grant. For their pains they found in his inaugural address the assurance that he would "not ask that anything be done to advance the social status of the colored man." Troops remained in the South for four more years, but the conscience of the country was in the keeping of U. S. Grant and the cause of Negro rights and equality lay crushed.

It is quite false to blame the stolid General for it all. His bitter opponents the Liberal Republicans, with their fine sensibilities and their disdain of Grantism, had already forfeited the principles of which they were the self-appointed guardians. But the shame was not a partisan or a regional monopoly. It was national, American, and quite general. It was fully endorsed by the judiciary, from the Supreme Court down through the police courts and the justices of the peace. It was defended and endorsed and rationalized in the most respectable press of the country, including journals primarily launched as champions of the cause, such as the *Nation* and the *Independent*. It found sanction in the colleges and public schools and churches and the bar all over the land.

To those who look to the First Reconstruction either for sources of inspiration or reasons for frustration of the Second it might be said that they will look in vain. For the First Reconstruction really never was tried. The conviction drained out of the enterprise before it was fairly under way. The North never really meant what it said, and the South sensed that from the start.

You may be quite sure that in the Second Reconstruction the same old counterwailing forces of regional suspicion and distrust are at work. The South is watching every move of the North, every signal of disingenuousness and evasion—the mounting strength of a Goldwater, the inroads of Gov. Wallace, the backlash of Northern reaction to the militancy of Civil Rights demonstrations, the resegregation of desegregated schools in Washington, the growing *defacto* school segregation entrenched in residential segregation, the intransigence of Northern labor unions, the bloody racial clashes in Northern slums, the secret organizations for terror and violence in Harlem. The stock Southern reply to Northern agitation for Civil Rights in the South is the century-old charge of hypocrisy—the charge that the North does not really practice what it preaches, that it really does not mean what it says. The success of the Second Reconstruction like that of the First hangs on the validity of that charge. For in order to succeed its Second Reconstruction cannot be confined to a region. It will have to be national, for the problem is national— more so than it was a century ago.

Notes

1. Memphis *Avalanche*, August 2, 1867.
2. General W. P. Carlin, report of August 13, 1867, in Freedmen's Bureau Synopsis of Reports, Jan. 1, 1867, to March 12, 1869, p. 168, National Archives.
3. General Orville Brown, reports on Virginia for November, 1867, in ibid., 249.
4. Quoted in Woody and Simkins, *South Carolina During Reconstruction*, 86.
5. Charleston *Mercury* quoted in *DeBow's Review*, XXXVI (Sept., 1867), 250.
6. The *Independent*, April 4, 18, 1867.
7. Quoted in ibid., Nov. 21, 1867, p. 4.
8. Ibid., Nov. 14, 1867.
9. Jay Cooke to John Sherman, Oct. 12, 1867, #28298, John Sherman Papers, Library of Congress.

10. New York *Times*, October 19, 1867.
11. J. W. Throckmorton to B. H. Epperson, Dec. 19, 1867, Epperson Papers, University of Texas Library Archives.
12. Quoted in Raleigh *Daily Sentinel*, Jan. 4, 1867, in Scroggs, "Carpetbagger Influence," MS Diss., 115.
13. New York *Times*, Oct. 29, 1867.
14. James J. Gillette, Mobile, to Father, A. D. Gillette, Oct. 28, 1867, Gillette Papers, Library of Congress.
15. New York *Times*, Dec. 10, 1867.
16. Memphis *Avalanche*, Nov. 10, 1867.
17. Raleigh *Daily Sentinel*, March 11, 1868.
18. McPherson, *History of Reconstruction*, 337–41.
19. *Congressional Globe*, 40th Cong., 3d Sess., 1004.
20. Ibid., 863 (Henry, 255).
21. Gillette, Wm., "The Power of the Ballot The Politics of Passage and Ratification of the Fifteenth Amendment" (Princeton, PHD), passim.
22. Ibid., 108.
23. Everette Swinney, "Enforcing the Fifteenth Amendment, 1870–1877," *Journal of Southern History*, XXVIII (May, 1962), 210.
24. Ibid., 210–11.
25. Ibid., 212–16.
26. Robert A. Horn, "National Control of Congressional Elections" (Ph.D. Dissertation, Princeton University, 1942), 143, 154–55, 183–87, 232–34. Cited by Gillette, 124n.
27. Quoted in *Independent*, Nov. 4, 1869. See also Revolution, Oct. 14, and Nov. 4, 11, 1869.
28. New York *Times*, Nov. 12, 1869.
29. A. J. Ricks to O. P. Temple, Jan. 15, 1870, Temple Papers, University of Tennessee.
30. Quoted in *Anti-Slavery Standard*, May 30, 1868, and Feb. 5, 1870.
31. *Independent*, March 25, 1869, and G. Age, July 15, 1871.
32. New York *Tribune*, June 9, July 16, Aug. 7, 1869.
33. Patrick W. Riddleberger, "The Radicals' Abandonment of the Negro During Reconstruction," *Journal of Negro History*, XLV (1960), 90–91.
34. Ibid., 92–93.
35. *Congressional Globe*, 42nd Cong. (May 21, 1872), 3737–38 [Woodward wrote the word "Check" in brackets].

STORRS LECTURES - YALE LAW SCHOOL 1969

SLAVERY TO FREEDOM: AN AMERICAN FAILURE
~~The Failure of Freedom~~

I

The Problem of Failure in American History

Some day a historian should explore the full implications of the recent Civil War Centennial. It would make a marvelous subject. Such a study would be rich with instructive ironies. One of the most curious aspects of this affair was that the descendents of the vanquished were the most enthusiastic participants in the celebration of their defeat, while the descendents of the victors were for the most part apathetic in celebrating their victory. Mississippi, the poorest state in the Union, made the largest appropriation, which was 200 times that of New York, the richest state, which appropriated a mere $10,000 for the promotion of the celebration as compared with Mississippi's $2,000,000.

Of all the participants, the least enthusiastic and the most apathetic were the descendents of the class usually considered the chief beneficiaries of the war, the liberated freedmen. Few of the grandchildren of the slaves would have anything whatever to do with the commemoration of the war to which they owed their freedom. Some went so far as not only to withhold approval but to denounce the Civil War Centennial as "a farce, a mockery, a distortion, a negation of all that is right."

Photographic facsimile of page 1 of "Lecture I, The Problem of Failure in American History," from "Slavery to Freedom," Storrs Lectures (MS 1436, box 66, folder 66), C. Vann Woodward Papers (MS 1436), Manuscripts and Archives, Yale University Library.

The Storrs Lectures

Slavery to Freedom: An American Failure

C. Vann Woodward delivered the Storrs Lectures at Yale University Law School on August 23, 24, and 25, 1969. The series, "Slavery to Freedom: An American Failure," reflects Woodward's interest in comparative emancipations and reconstructions. Lecture I, which is included here, stands out. The first two-thirds of the lecture have never been seen in print. Woodward draws comparisons between the Civil War semicentennial and centennial, outlines the cycles of Reconstruction historiography, and contemplates the psychological traumas in the North and South engendered by Reconstruction. The last third of this lecture includes a section of a paper Woodward gave at the Southern Historical Association in November 1967 titled "Reconstruction and Revision," pieces of which appeared in print and in presentations in various incarnations. The second and third lectures are more explicitly comparative and expand on the foreign comparative framework Woodward advised pursuing in the SHA discussion. They explore the similarities and differences between post-emancipation societies that had been formerly under the control of colonial powers in the western hemisphere. Later, Woodward combined the second and third lectures, presenting the reconstituted version twice and publishing it three times, as late as 1989.

STORRS LECTURE I
The Problem of Failure in American History

SOME DAY a historian should explore the full implications of the recent Civil War Centennial. It would make a marvelous subject. Such a study would be rich with instructive ironies. One of the most curious aspects of this affair was that the descendants of the vanquished were the most enthusiastic participants in the celebration of their defeat, while the descendants of the victors were for the most part apathetic in celebrating their victory. Mississippi, the poorest state in the Union, made the largest appropriation, which was 200 times that of New York, the richest state, which appropriated a mere $10,000 for the promotion of the celebration as compared with Mississippi's $2,000,000.

Of all the participants, the least enthusiastic and the most apathetic were the descendants of the class usually considered the chief beneficiaries of the war, the liberated freedmen. Few of the grandchildren of the slaves would have anything whatever to do with the commemoration of the war to which they owed their freedom. Some went so far as not only to withhold approval but to denounce the Civil War Centennial as "a farce, a mockery, a distortion, a negation of all that is right."

On closer inspection, however, the attitudes of the heirs to the two causes and the heirs of the chief beneficiaries of the Civil War shed their appearance of paradox and take on the color of logic. This is especially apparent in the attitudes of the Negro toward the Centennial. For of all the eligible celebrators, he had the most cause for discomfort and suspicion of what exactly was being celebrated, in what mood, and upon what underlying assumptions.

As a matter of fact, the only assumptions upon which it was feasible to conduct the historical celebration were of a character wholly unacceptable to the Negro. Tacitly but unmistakably these assumptions announced that the issues over which the Civil War was fought, and the issues it eventually precipitated were now wholly resolved and that for four years the nation could unite in celebrating the Great Consensus by reliving memories of our Homeric period. It was to be, in effect, a formal reaffirmation of the Compromise of 1877, which concluded an agreement among white men that some of the most celebrated aims of the Civil War and the Reconstruction were impracticable and were thenceforth and forever abandoned.

By some fateful chance of history, however, the opening guns of the commemoration happened to coincide with the opening guns of the radical phase of the Second Reconstruction. They were simultaneous signals for Americans to start marching in opposite directions, toward opposing social commitments. It was the Negro's sense of the historical incongruity of these events that spelled the failure of the Civil War Centennial.

It might be instructive to compare the response to the centennial anniversary of the Civil War with the response to the semi-centennial commemoration. The contrast is striking. Although the celebration of 1911 was half a century closer to the "Irrepressible Conflict," it was approached and commemorated in a spirit approximating mutual acceptance and general consensus among whites. The national synthesis was broad enough to reconcile North and South, tolerant enough to absolve both personal and sectional guilt, and indulgent enough to purge whatever shame remained on the conscience of the nation. Negro opinion was not consulted, not even considered.

By 1911, the Civil War had come to be regarded as the great catharsis of American experience. It was tragic, it was probably inevitable, and it was the result of deep-seated causes. But at the same time it was the great resolver of conflict, the solver of otherwise insoluble problems, and the purger of evils. The general tone was one of satisfaction with the results of the war in both North and South. It had abolished slavery and preserved the Union. It was the historical foundation of the New Nationalism in which all right-thinking Americans of 1911 rejoiced.

In that year three American historians published books on the Civil War which reflected the dominant mood of the time. Frederic L. Paxson of Wisconsin decided that "honesty and intelligence were about evenly divided in the contest," that both sides were "thoroughly American," that both were "devoted to the Union as they knew it," and that "each [was] endeavoring to work out the best American interest as it saw it." Charles Francis Adams,

Jr., who had led a Negro regiment into Richmond in April, 1865, declared in 1911 that "every man in the eleven states seceding from the Union had in 1861 ... to decide for himself whether to adhere to his State or to the Nation," and that "whichever way he decided ... if only he decided honestly ... he decided right." Adams wrote that "under similar conditions I would myself have done exactly what Lee did. In fact, I do not see how I, placed as he was placed, could have done otherwise." And in the same year, Emerson D. Fite, teaching then at Yale, called upon "the present generation of Northerners" to "shake off their inherited political passions and prejudices, and pronounce the verdict of justification for the South." Impressed by what he called "the infinite pathos" of the Civil War, Fite declared, "Both sides were right! Neither could have given in and remained true to itself. The North was right in opposing slavery, the South was right in seceding from the Union in its defense."

In salving the national conscience, appeasing Southern sensibilities, absolving guilt and blame, and balancing right and wrong between sections, these three historians were sustained by the findings of William A. Dunning, John W. Burgess, James Ford Rhodes, and a host of lesser historians of their generation.

Thomas J. Pressly, who has done most to clarify our thinking about this and other generations of Civil War historians, would seem to suggest that there is some inconsistency in the "nationalist tradition" between its consensus on the Civil War and the old consensus on Reconstruction: that having pronounced the one productive of "much more good than evil," it should have reached the conclusion that the other was wholly productive of evil. Similarly, Professor Kenneth M. Stampp is impressed by the "odd relationship to one another" manifest in popular attitudes toward Civil War and Reconstruction. While the Civil War was "admittedly a tragedy" it was celebrated as a "glorious time of ... high idealism." But Reconstruction, which sought to realize the high ideals, "represented the ultimate shame of the American people."

I suggest that this inconsistency is more apparent than real. In fact, I would go so far as to say that whether the Nationalists were right about the Civil War and Reconstruction or not—and I confess to serious misgivings about their position—they were *not* inconsistent in holding the views they took of both subjects. Had they, in fact, endorsed the purposes, approved the methods, and shared the hopes of Reconstruction, it would have been impossible for them to have sustained the view they took of the Civil War. No national consensus *favorable* to Reconstruction was possible in 1911—or for that matter at any time before or since that date. The positive consensus on the Civil War came at the price of a negative consensus on Reconstruction and was possible only on that condition. Like the cavalier myth, the negative consensus on Reconstruction was a product of Northern as well as Southern needs. As Gunnar Myrdal pointed out, the North needed it "in order to rationalize the national compromise of the 1870's and the condoning, since then, of the South's open break with the spirit of the Constitution." The South's needs were obvious.

Back of any general interpretation, assessment, or judgment of the Civil War will be found a set of assumptions and judgments about Reconstruction. They may not be so confidently asserted or consciously formulated as the accompanying assertions about the war, but they are nevertheless sure to be present. "Reconstruction was, in fact," as William B. Hesseltine pointed out, "the basic issue of the Civil War. The desire to remake the South, to reorganize its social system, to bring its divergent economy into the main stream of American life, to impose peculiar concepts of government and of constitutional interpretation upon the Southern states had been the reason for beginning the war and for prosecuting it with vigor, despite tremendous losses in human life and costs in national wealth." Some degree of agreement on these issues and the period in which they were resolved is therefore essential to a meeting of minds on the Civil War.

The three historians quoted to illustrate semicentennial attitudes toward the Civil War had no difficulty on this score. They were of one mind on Reconstruction. Paxson pronounced it an "unsavory story," and described the experience as "worse than war for the South." Adams described "the outrages, and humiliations worse than outrages, of the period of so-called reconstruction" as "actual servile domination." And Fite called it a "horrible regime."

Daniel Boorstin has complained that, "Not the least remarkable feature of the Civil War—apart from the fact that it occurred at all—is that it was so unproductive of political theory." In the literal sense of theory this is no doubt true, especially when one thinks comparatively of the vast body of theoretical works produced by the English Civil War or the French and Russian variations. But in the broader sense the Civil War and its aftermath of Reconstruction have been enormously productive of political and social theory. In view of Boorstin's insight that Americans have habitually sought in their history—or rather in ingenious and often tortured reinterpretations of their history—a viable substitute for theory and a guide to policy and action, his observation about the unproductive results of the Civil War is all the more curious. As he has pointed out, to find out where they go from here Americans characteristically look, not forward, but backward to see what they did in the past. This is one thing that gives American history its edge of priority and its keen sense of immediacy. Few periods have been as productive of this type of history as that of Civil War and Reconstruction. For evidence of this one has only to consult the records of American jurisprudence, legislation, sociology, political science, and anthropology.

Like the history of the Federal Constitution and its framers, the history of Reconstruction and its authors has been searched and researched, revised and reinterpreted, debated and tortured endlessly—and for much the same reasons. That is, to establish or rationalize fundamental law, historic commitments and decisions, the very meaning of the Constitution itself. For after all, the authors of Reconstruction were second only to the original framers of the Federal Constitution as makers of constitutional law. Their contributions, in fact, especially the Fourteenth Amendment, have been for three quarters of a century the most bitterly contested, most litigated, and most controversial parts of the whole Constitution. It is little wonder, therefore, that law makers of Reconstruction, like the Constitution framers and Founding Fathers, should have been cross-examined and scrutinized for their "real" motives and the purity or impurity thereof. Were they what they seemed, what they themselves said they were? Or were they masking less worthy, secret, and selfish motives?

In the opinions of the United States Supreme Court there is ample evidence that the so-called "lessons of Reconstruction" have not been lost on American jurisprudence. It is manifest, for example, in the opinion of Mr. Justice Brown upholding the constitutionality of segregation laws. "The argument" of Plessy, he said in *Plessy v. Ferguson*, "assumes that social prejudice may be overcome by legislation, and that equal rights cannot be secured to the negro except by an enforced commingling of the two races. We cannot accept this proposition.... Legislation is powerless to eradicate racial instincts or to abolish distinctions based upon physical differences.... If one race be inferior to the other socially, the Constitution of the United States cannot put them upon the same plane."

It goes without saying that influences other than historiography were at work at the same time upon the same men and with much the same effect. But these influences were often intertwined and themselves bore testimony to the impact of the Reconstruction trauma and the historians' reading of it. William Graham Sumner, foremost American exponent of Social Darwinism, was obviously influenced by his reading of that experience in shaping his doctrine of the sovereignty of folkways and their imperviousness to what he called "stateways." "The whites [of the South]," he wrote, "have never been converted from the old mores," and attempts "to control the new order by legislation" had been quite vain, and "The only result is the proof that legislation cannot make mores." My suspicion is that much of American thought attributed by intellectual historians to Sumner, Spencer, and Social Darwinism—at least in the field of civil rights and racial policy—could be more legitimately traced to the impact of Reconstruction and its historiography.

The nationalist picture of Civil War and Reconstruction and its "lessons" was the one with which the Progressive generation lived and with reference to which it thought about its problems and policies. The two foremost Presidents of the progressive period, Theodore Roosevelt and Woodrow Wilson, have left testimony of the impact that Reconstruction and its current interpretation left upon their minds. Writing to Henry Cabot Lodge, who had in 1890 sponsored a bill to restore federal protection to Negro voters, Roosevelt said in 1916, "I believe the great majority of the negroes in the south are wholly unfit for suffrage, and that if we were able to succeed in giving them an unbought, uncoerced and undefrauded suffrage we would reduce parts of the south to the level of Haiti." He thought the whole idea preposterous and denounced "the evil folly of Sumner and Stevens in pushing the Fifteenth Amendment." In his own writings, as well as in his own racial policies as President, Woodrow Wilson left evidence that regardless of other differences the New Freedom and the New Nationalism saw eye to eye on the "lessons of Reconstruction." These lessons left their imprint on the legislative and policy record of progressive statesmen in the fields of immigration restriction, civil rights protection, Negro disfranchisement, segregation, racial discrimination, and federal employment practices. In all these areas progressives fully heeded the "mistakes" of Reconstruction.

In American thought and policy with regard to imperialism it is often difficult to distinguish cause and effect in reference to Reconstruction historiography. But the interrelation of these two influences is clearly recognized in the statement of Professor John W. Burgess in January, 1902, that "now that the United States has embarked in imperial enterprises ... the North is learning every day by valuable experiences that there are vast differences in political capacity between the races, and that it is the white man's mission, his duty and his right, to hold the reins of political power in his own hands for the civilization of the world and the welfare of mankind."

The Dunning-Burgess-Rhodes synthesis dominated thought on the subject long after its authors passed from the scene, long past the progressive period in which they flourished. In the 1920's and 1930's the old interpretation was supplemented by a new one that stressed economic factors. The interpretation by Charles Beard and Howard Beale did not supplant the old synthesis, for it did not really disturb or seriously question the fundamental assumptions of the old point of view. It certainly did not render the Reconstruction heritage of racial equalitarianism any more palatable, nor the doctrine of federal protection of civil rights any more reputable. What it did was to remove the whole subject from the sphere of ethical controversy. It did this by setting aside questions of right and wrong, justice and injustice, as irrelevant. Whatever their intrinsic merits, they were not the "real" issues and motives were concealed. The "real" issues underlying them were economic, and the "real" motives were essentially selfish—the aggrandizements of individual, class, or section. The authors of Reconstruction were not conceded the benefit of long-ranged patriotism, or unconscious, Hamiltonian enhancement of national welfare by its identification with the fortunate few. For their economic program was pictured as productive of injustice and deprivation to certain classes and sections—including the hapless freedmen—for the benefit of other classes and sections.

The older synthesis which this supplemented had been content to condemn Reconstruction for its methods and its results while conceding a measure of benevolence to its motives and intentions—however naïve and misguided they might be. The supplementary reading by the economic interpreters not only condemned the methods and results, but discredited the motives and intentions of Reconstruction as well. In so doing, they further entrenched and strengthened the tradition of attributing a cynical or sinister coloration to any effort to extend Federal protection to civil rights, any agitation of "outsiders" in behalf of racial minorities, any use of force to implement Supreme Court decisions, any measures for the guarantee of the franchise under the Fifteenth Amendment, any organized support to the efforts of Negroes to recover or protect their rights, and any challenge whatever to what had come to be known as "established folkways," including legal and extra-legal arrangements—mainly elaborated in the twentieth century—for racial discrimination and segregation.

It was with this intellectual baggage that Americans entered the era of the Second Reconstruction. They suddenly found themselves overwhelmed with issues they had been taught to believe were "settled." Actually, they were the issues that had been pushed out of public consciousness and swept under the rug by forgotten compromises, sectional bargains, party evasions, ethnocentric consensus, and nineteenth-century Supreme Court decisions—all neatly and learnedly rationalized by historians and jurists in the national synthesis on Reconstruction. And now all those ancient "settled" issues came clamorously and insistently alive: the Fourteenth and Fifteenth Amendments, right out of the 1860's, along with a ghostly host of historical specters with forgotten banners and old slogans and epithets such as home rule, states' rights, force bill, Negro rights, military intervention, bayonet rule, carpetbagger, and scalawag.

In congressional debates on civil rights from that of 1957 to that of 1966, as well as the touchy, hair-trigger Presidential decisions to send in federal troops to deal with school desegregation upheavals, protest demonstrations, and riots, the old vocabulary of recrimination, the old charges of devious political motives, the old suspicions of sinister conspiratorial activity were all brought into full play. The parties to these disputes were after all locked in controversy over the interpretation and enforcement of Reconstruction amendments, enabling acts, and statutes originating a century ago and reviving all of the same issues and arguments.

Surveying the scene of battle, an American editor of foreign origin (Max Ascoli of the *Reporter*) remarked in dismay: "We almost lose heart when we realize to what an extent everything in this desperate conflict between two sections of America seems to re-echo the past. Everything is so old." So old, indeed. It is a minor irony to find a European observer exclaiming that "Everything [in America] is so old." And yet it is a truer insight than he knew, and of broader applicability to the American political tradition than he intended.

In the Senate debate over the Civil Rights Bill of 1957 it was disclosed that Title III of the proposed measure indirectly invoked Section 1989 of the Revised Statutes, which dated from 1870 and authorized Presidential use of military forces in executing judicial processes. That power was available under other statutes, but the link with 1870 brought a dozen Southern senators to their feet. Senator Ervin of North Carolina was "completely convinced of the fact that the Civil War is over. My only regret, however, is that I cannot say the same thing about Reconstruction." Senator Byrd of Virginia "strongly suspect[ed] that the modern Thaddeus Stevens, now cloaked in the robes of Chief Justice of the United States Supreme Court" was implicated. Senator Johnston of South Carolina asked his colleagues if they wanted "to be responsible for a second reconstruction era or a second pillaging of the South." And Senator Russell of Georgia, who well knew the power of the legend of "The Tragic Era" and its appeal beyond the limits of his own region, declared that, "there are millions of people in this country outside the South who would not approve of another Reconstruction at bayonet point of a peaceful and patriotic South."

Lecture I: The Problem of Failure in American History

Liberal Senators of the North were also aware of the potency of the historical medicine the Southerners were making and its appeal to their own people. Senator Hubert H. Humphrey hoped that "any indirect reference in the bill to that dismal period in American history, the so-called Reconstruction period, will come out of the measure. I have to say this, for it is on my heart. I do not like to have the American people reminded in however well-meaning a way, of the dark and sad days of Reconstruction. It is a bad chapter. . . . I do not like to remember those days either." Senator Smith of New Jersey thought we should "be moving in the direction of obliterating the unfortunate and regrettable events of the Reconstruction days, a period which, I believe, represents the darkest chapter in our history." And Senator Wayne Morse of Oregon wanted to be sure the measure was "devoid of carpetbagging and strong-armed tactics." Senator Humphrey joined in sponsoring an amendment to the bill repealing the vile Section 1989 of such bitter memory. The amendment was passed by a vote of 90 to 0. It was the first time in the course of a century that the United States Senate ever achieved unanimity in a vote on a Reconstruction statute. That vote in effect represented national unanimity on a legend.

I think the country suffers from a pathological complex on Reconstruction and has lived with it for a long time. It takes two quite different forms—one for the North and one for the South, both arising out of the same traumatic event, but experienced in very different ways. In the North it resulted in a guilt-and-shame complex, in the South a dirty-deal complex. These are, of course, short-hand labels for very complicated psychological patterns.

The North emerged from the Reconstruction experience with a repressed sense of frustration and failure, of lowered self-esteem and gnawing self-reproach. It had won a total victory after fighting a bloody war which it had justified before the world with widely proclaimed war aims of the noblest humanitarian and equalitarian ideals. But after winning a total victory over the South it had failed to implement its high aims and had abandoned its noble ideals. This was a transgression of its own professed principles and it involved guilt, self-reproach. If guilt stems from self-reproach and results from failure to live up to one's own image of one's self, shame we are told results from disapproval from outside and the criticism and scorn of others. If so, there was ample cause for shame as well as guilt in the North's reaction to Reconstruction. It was not merely criticism for abandonment of principle. More important still, it was the shame of being exposed in pretending to be nobler than in reality one was. It was the shame of exposure in temporarily forcing standards of ethics on the South that the North was not able to enforce in its own treatment of the Negro in its own society. And it was also the exposure in profiting from political and material gains under cover of lofty and disinterested motives.

The South emerged from Reconstruction repressing many inner conflicts of its own. Among them were fear and anxiety, wounded pride and damaged self-esteem, impulses of aggression and hatred that could not well be discharged against logical targets—either the self or the victorious enemy. It had dealt with its oppressive problems in devious ways of bribery and fraud, under cover of night and disguise, in many ways that did not square with its professed standards of sensitive personal honor and public probity. In particular it had betrayed its professed code of paternalistic protector of the Negro, so much at issue in the sectional struggle. Unable to face internal defects and shortcomings, unable or unwilling to shoulder the burden of blame and guilt, the South resorted to the "dirty-deal" complex to explain everything and shifted its burden of guilt to Reconstruction.

With a common problem of guilt-evasion, whites of North and South were looking for suitable targets for what the psychologists call "projection." They found them in the classic manner of guilt-evaders—in the victims of their aggression: the Negroes and the so-called Radicals. It was they who were to blame for it all. Since the opposing sides were able to agree on their targets for projection, the national consensus on Reconstruction was all the more readily attained. Thereafter the period has constituted a block to national and regional self-understanding and insight. It remains a largely undigested lump of historical experience in the national mind.

Reconstruction is unique for another reason as the one great experience of failure for Americans—Southerners excepted—in the national history. The rest of American history, with the exception of the current war, can be told broadly in terms of successes. Heretofore, Americans have won all their wars, or have been convinced that they did, and have encountered no frontiers or problems that did not yield eventually to persistent effort or a large amount of good luck. Many of the major historic episodes have had their full share of guilt and shame, of betrayal, treachery, injustice, rapine, mass outrage, and criminal blundering. But, by and large, they have turned out well from a national, or at least majority point of view. Americans dwell on their history, or their legends, fondly and without undue remorse or guilt or self-reproach. The winning of the trans-Mississippi West, for example, is crowded with stupendous gluttony and criminal stupidity, with broken promises, and betrayed minorities. Yet we have managed to convert it into something called the

Frontier Experience, which is said to have had all manner of therapeutic and improving effects on the national character.

Of course, had some of these great episodes—such as the American Revolution—turned out differently, we would probably be hearing more about treason and treachery and scalawags and carpetbaggers and shamefully treated minorities than we normally do in connection with that event on the Fourth of July. Eating all those fine and mouth-filling words in the Declaration of Independence would probably have been as much of an undertaking as eating all the comparable words in the Fourteenth and Fifteenth Amendments and the Civil Rights Act.

Reconstruction did "turn out differently," so to speak, and Americans, with a few exceptions, have never fully faced up to the consequences. One way of dealing with the problem is that proposed by Professor Burgess in 1902. "It is best for the North," he wrote, "best for the South, best for the whole country, best for the world that this terrible mistake of the North and this terrible degradation of the South should be dealt with briefly and impersonally..." In other words, deplored and forgotten. Another way would be to turn the old synthesis upside-down—to make the Radicals the inspired and blameless heroes, turn the carpetbaggers into agents of progress, the freedmen into faultless patriots, and the whole thing into a glorious if abortive experiment in democracy. Given our sympathies with the movement for Negro rights and our impatience for its fulfillment, this alternative has attractions that have proved irresistible to some.

The historian, however, would better take his cue from the therapist, who does not encourage the patient to bury the traumatic experience in forgetfulness or to transform it into a fond memory, but who insists on restoring it to full consciousness and facing all the implications and insights it provides.

The ruins of two great failures dominate the landscape of American history. They stand close together in the middle distance, back to back, but separate and distinct. One is the ruin of the Confederacy, the South's failure to gain independence. The other is the ruin of Reconstruction, the North's failure to solve the problem of the Negro's place in American life. The South's failure was the North's success and vice versa. Each can be and, of course, has been described by its opponents as simply the wreckage wrought in preventing acknowledged wrong. But from the standpoint of their supporters and champions, there can be no doubt that each of these ruins represents a great American failure.

They stand out all the more starkly and conspicuously on the historical landscape because of their unique character. Failures and defeats on the grand scale are notoriously exceptional and uncharacteristic of the American experience. And so far, at least, these two stand as the only instances of striking significance, save only one in the immediate foreground. They are surrounded by monuments of success, victory, and continuity, features far more familiar to the American eye. Some of these monuments—the Revolution, the Constitution, the two-party system, the parties themselves, the basic economic institutions, all still live and going concerns—are much older than the two historic ruins. This side of the ruins in the foreground are more recent monuments in the traditional success style of the American Way. But the middle distance is still dominated by the two great historic failures.

The obvious task of the historian is to explain these unique failures. But their very uniqueness, the strangeness and un-American character of failure, seems to have inhibited or warped the fulfillment of these tasks. One evasive strategy of historians of the Confederacy has been first to acknowledge more or less candidly that the movement was misguided and perhaps destined to failure from the start and even to admit tacitly that it was best for all concerned in the long run that it did fail. But then to dwell at length on the high moments, the ephemeral triumphs, the selfless devotion, the nobility of leadership, and the hardships and suffering of the participants. Essentially romantic, the lost-cause approach emphasized the glory and tragedy of failure without too much attention to its causes and consequences. Recently the historians of the Confederacy have been addressing themselves more and more to the causes of failure and less to the ephemeral triumphs. But for a long time the South's refusal to face up to and accept its own failure contributed to the North's failure in the sequel to Appomattox.

Historians of Reconstruction have played variations on these Confederate themes without exactly duplicating the order or the mood. For a long time they too started with the assumption that the movement was misconceived and doomed to failure from inception and that, all things considered, it was just as well that it did fail. Since failure was regarded as both inevitable and fortunate, the problem of explaining it did not appear very challenging. With these more or less common assumptions, historians of the old school divided mainly on how they distributed their sympathy and admiration among the victims—the humble freedman, the misguided idealists, the bumbling Presidents, or the long-suffering Southern whites—and on their distribution of blame among villains—Radical Republicans, Carpetbaggers, Scalawags, or Negroes. They were in substantial agreement, however, in their homage to the

Lecture I: The Problem of Failure in American History

tragic muse. Whether the spotlight was focused on the victims or the villains, the overriding preoccupation was with tragedy—incidental comic relief to the contrary notwithstanding. And whether as a cause for satisfaction or lament, there was little equivocation about the verdict of failure.

In the last few years a shift has occurred in the common assumptions and preoccupations of Reconstruction historians, especially with regard to the aspect of failure. Failure is no longer regarded as inevitable, the movement as misconceived, or the outcome as fortunate. On all these matters there has occurred a complete reversal of attitude. The treatment is still fundamentally tragic, but the reading of the tragedy has changed. The tragedy was not that a misconceived movement has caused so much unnecessary suffering, but that a noble experiment had come so near to fulfillment and failed. Furthermore, the impact of failure itself has been blunted and the historical problem of explanation shelved by a new emphasis on the positive accomplishments of Reconstruction.

Much of the attention of recent revisionists has been focused on these aspects of the Reconstruction record, on correcting the excessively negative picture painted by the old school historians and exposing the injustice and crudity of the old stereotypes. New studies have pictured the old abolitionists as realistic and persevering champions of the freedmen instead of irresponsible defectors in the struggle for equality. The collective portrait of the Radical Republican congressmen that emerges from recent biographies and monographs is one of high-minded idealists who rose above selfish political and economic interests. Studies of Northern teachers and preachers who went south on missionary enterprises stress their seriousness of purpose and the devotion and fearless dedication of their service. Carpetbaggers of heroic stature and courageous statesmanship have been sympathetically portrayed. Scalawags of the new historiography often appear to derive either from wealthy Southern aristocrats or from sturdy Jacksonian yeomen, depending on one's technique of quantification. Among Negro leaders and statesmen revisionists have discovered a gratifying amount of talent, ability and vision. Swindlers, grafters, and corruption have been discounted by comparison with contemporaneous fraud and graft in Northern states. The result of all this has been a wholesale decimation of stock figures in the demonology of Reconstruction.

At the same time revisionists have brought to light more and more praiseworthy achievements of Radical Reconstruction. These include not only the legislative and constitutional foundations for Negro citizenship, franchise, and civil rights, but the training and preparation of freedmen for political action. Radical state governments are also justly credited with framing laudable and often durable state constitutions and law codes, with providing relief and welfare for the distressed, with establishing public schools, and with inaugurating new public services. Careful scholars have pronounced the Negroes' economic progress during Reconstruction, given their low starting point, a tremendous success and enumerated with pride their gains in land and capital. Others have pointed out the general progress of the South in economic recuperation and growth. The emphasis here, as in so many other areas of revisionist history, is not on failures but on the successes of Reconstruction.

A great deal, in fact the larger part, of revisionist critical energy has been aimed not at the old school of the 1900's but the old school of the 1930's. Two targets in the latter area have drawn most of the revisionist fire—the economic interpretation and the defense of Andrew Johnson. The assignment of economic motivation, like the assignment of party motives for Radical Reconstruction, naturally left a slur upon the sincerity and idealism of the whole movement. Revisionists have responded with a devastating barrage of blockbusters that ran the risk of becoming an "overkill." It left scarcely a sign of life stirring in the whole target area. I live in daily expectation of proof that the Compromise of 1877 was accomplished without the slightest reference to vulgar material considerations. Closer inspection of the fire pattern in the more sophisticated attacks will reveal that it was more selective than that, that it left a good deal of economic motivation standing, and that it only upset some of the more naïve correlations of the economic interpretation. The general impression created, however, was that the pocket nerve of the Radical Republicans was uniquely anesthetized. As an English historian phrases the new view, "It was this idealism, not tariffs or homesteads or western railroads which made Republicanism the great driving force that it was..."

Similarly the slur of political expediency and partisan gain as explanatory variables in Republican motivation have been purged of credibility and the politicians of political guile. This goes alike for Negro enfranchisement and Confederate disfranchisement, for the Fourteenth as well as the Fifteenth Amendment, for Grant's nomination as well as for Johnson's impeachment. Instead of serving as instances of covert or incidental increment of partisan aggrandizement ennobled by humanitarian and idealistic purposes, they appear in the new light of revision to have been undertaken disinterestedly in the face of grave risk to party interests. Such is the insistence upon purity of motive and sincerity of purpose—those elusively unquantifiable variables—that at times one catches glimpses of a truly unique specimen in the annals of politics—a great and remarkably successful political party bereft of the normal political instincts.

As for old Andy Johnson, that rather seedy hero of the 1930's—the last Jacksonian and the first New Dealer, crypto-Populist and proto-Progressive, sworn enemy of the old planter aristocrats and terror of the new money-bag monopolists—poor old Andy has had it. Never in our history, perhaps, has a hero of one generation been reduced so completely to the fall guy of the next. For in the new light the former champion of the common man, hillbilly vindicator on the Lincolnian model, is seen as the apotheosis of the poor white, the complete outsider, history's prime example of the misfit.

For this and other services of the new revisionists one should be duly grateful. So successful have the revisionists of the 1960's been that they have virtually wiped the revisions of the 1930's off the map. The two great revisionist efforts have in effect canceled each other out, so that, as David Donald has remarked, on the score of economic motivation we have landed back in the vicinity of the Dunning encampment and on the evaluation of Andrew Johnson we are in speaking distance of James G. Blaine and James Ford Rhodes. This is progress, as progress is measured in historiography, but a little more of it and we will arrive back in that tragic spring when lilacs last in the dooryard bloomed. A belated reveler from the thirties might observe, like Dilcey, "I seed de beginnin, en now I sees de endin."

The achievements of the new school of revisionists are impressive. But as a contribution to explaining the failure of Reconstruction they are somewhat anomalous and tend rather to complicate than to solve the enigma. For if, as they have demonstrated, the statesmanship of the Radicals was all that inspired and their motivation all that pure, if the freedmen were so responsive and capably led, if the missionaries and schoolmarms were so dedicated, if government by the Scalawag-Carpetbagger-freedmen coalition was all that constructive, and if the opposition were indeed headed by a misfit and a bumbler out of touch with the electorate, then success would seem more indicated than failure. The paradox reminds me of the first historical problem a Southerner of the writer's generation confronted as a boy. It went something like this: If Marse Robert was all that noble and intrepid, if Stonewall was all that indomitable and fast on his feet, if Jeb Stuart was all that gallant and dashing, and if God was really on our side, then why the hell did we *lose* that war?

This is not to write off the accomplishments of the revisionists. I hope the record is clear that I have aided and abetted and egged them on, presumed to teach some of them, read many of their manuscripts and all their monographs, praised what I could and encouraged when I could. What they did in the main much needed doing and I rejoiced in their work even when it wounded the feelings of old friends and mentors and lacerated old loyalties, personal as well as regional. In characterizing isolated implications of the whole school, if indeed it can fairly be called a "school," one inevitably misrepresents individual historians. Many of them intended no such implications and were as fully aware of the paradoxes and ironies involved as anyone.*

This brings me back to the old problem of failure. As I have remarked earlier, and in other connections as well, Americans have rather a thing about failure—about confronting it, confessing it, and accepting it, as well as about explaining it. That was true of the past and it is tragically true of the present. It is noteworthy that the great bulk of work done by the new school has been on Andrew Johnson's administration, not on the two Grant administrations, that is, on the period where, paradoxically, the ephemeral successes and triumphs multiplied, not the period of twice that length when the failures piled up or became unavoidably conspicuous. This may be mere coincidence, but my guess is that it is more than coincidence.

Another tendency might be called the deferred-success approach, the justification of failure in the First Reconstruction on the ground that it prepared the way for success in the Second Reconstruction, or maybe in the light of later events, a Third. Thus Kenneth Stampp, for example, writes that the failures of the First Reconstruction "dwindle into insignificance" in view of "the ultimate promise of equal civil and political rights" for the patient Negroes of the present day. This is the application to history of a familiar middle-age solution to personal problems—a generational shift of the burden of responsibility—"let Junior do it." But it must be recognized as essentially another strategy of evasion. And besides, Junior, for all his abolitionist rhetoric, his Civil War beard, and his insurrectionary haircut, hasn't *done it*! Not yet, anyway.

---

* In the 1967 Southern Historical Association version, Woodward ends this paragraph with the line, "I hope they will forgive me." See C. Vann Woodward, "Reconstruction and Revision," Box 63, Folder 21, C. Vann Woodward Papers (MS 1436), Manuscripts and Archives, Yale University Library.

Acknowledgments

THE GENESIS OF this project lies in the organization of a roundtable titled "The Legacy of C. Vann Woodward's *Origins of the New South*" for the 2015 annual meeting of the Organization of American Historians. Held almost sixty-five years after publication of the book, the roundtable—which initially included Sarah E. Gardner, Tammy Ingram, Natalie J. Ring, and Jonathan Daniel Wells, with Michael O'Brien as moderator—sought to reassess the shelf life of *Origins* and explore some of the key themes that still animate the field of southern history. In the second preface to the 1971 reissue of the book, Woodward wrote, "Changes in the present have always provoked new questions about the past and stimulated the rewriting of history." The statement may seem clichéd, but the bulk of Woodward's work embodies this dictum. We may be familiar with the ways in which the modern civil rights movement shaped Woodward's understanding of the post-Reconstruction South, but it also influenced how he thought about the antebellum and Reconstruction eras. This volume turns to his unpublished writings on these earlier moments to underscore, yet again, how much the historical events Woodward lived through shaped the history he wrote.

We are indebted to many scholars for their assistance and support. The four outside readers of the book proposal offered extremely useful suggestions on the best way to assemble this collection. Tammy Ingram, who helped catalog the C. Vann Woodward Papers, fielded questions about the missing first Messenger Lecture and pointed us in the right direction for an answer. William Deverell offered to retrieve a copy of Woodward's 1967 Southern Historical Association paper "Reconstruction and Revision" from his attic before we discovered the original version in handwritten text on yellow-lined paper buried in a folder in Woodward's papers. James C. Cobb shared information about Woodward's identification as a "therapist of the public mind." During one of our trips to the archives in New Haven, Glenda Gilmore reminisced about Woodward and tried to help us understand why he might not have finished the book on Reconstruction. Her enthusiasm for the project kept us moving forward at an important time. Steven Hahn, Amy Louise Wood, and Daniel Wickberg read a draft of the introduction toward the end. Their feedback was indispensable. Thanks also go to Daniel Wickberg for assistance with compiling a bibliography on the intellectual climate of the consensus period of the 1950s and 1960s. We are delighted that Edward Ayers agreed to write the foreword to our collection. We couldn't have imagined a better choice for the task. Natalie would like to thank Jonathan Scott Holloway for lunches in New Haven, despite his busy schedule as an administrator, and his continued support since graduate school. His scholarship as an intellectual historian serves as an inspiration. Finally, we did not have the opportunity to share with Michael O'Brien our vision for this volume, but his edited collection of C. Vann Woodward's letters provided a model. Sarah would also like to acknowledge the out-sized influence O'Brien has had on her understanding of southern history.

This collection would not exist without the aid of archivists, staff, and assistants. We appreciate the help we received from the Manuscripts and Archives division at Yale University's Sterling Library. Jessica Dooling helped with forms and always responded promptly. Judith Schiff met with us early on and furnished crucial information on publication and rights. Rachel Kyes, a recent graduate of the University of Texas at Dallas, visited the William C. Carleton Papers at the University of Florida and delivered unduplicated correspondence between Woodward and Carleton. Diane Dix saved us time by keying in Woodward's typescripts to Microsoft Word and deciphering his handwriting and notations. She turned around one lecture within twenty-four hours, and for her heroic efforts we are eternally grateful. This collection arrived more quickly than expected because of her hard work. The Genice Rabe Fund from the University of Texas at Dallas financed a trip to conduct archival research in the Southern Historical Collection at the University of North Carolina at Chapel Hill. The Spencer B. King, Jr., Center for Southern Studies and the Office of the Provost at Mercer University helped offset costs associated with this project.

The editorial team at Oxford University Press has been a joy to work with. Susan Ferber's recognition of the project's significance and her genuine enthusiasm was evident from the moment we pitched the idea. Susan is a writer's editor, and her attention to detail certainly made this a better collection. Her generosity at the end of the project, with time and resources, is much appreciated. We were delighted to discover that OUP assigned Joellyn Ausanka, who worked with Woodward at the press, to be our production editor. Her cheerful and prompt replies made the process an easy one.

Jon Daniel and Todd Leopold were behind us from the very beginning when the volume was still a top-secret seed of an idea and simply referred to as "The Thing." They were good sports about our frequent trips to Yale and marathon phone conversations, as well as our obsession with documenting Woodward's fits and starts, false beginnings, and repurposed stuff which taken together document his enduring iconoclasm. We faced a bumpy path, at times, to reach this point, so the end is most welcome.

We thank Yale University Library for permission to publish these unpublished lectures and chapters from "Southern Exiles," Fleming Lectures (C. Vann Woodward Papers, hereafter MS 1436, box 66, folder 59); "The First Reconstruction in Light of the Second," Messenger Lectures at Cornell University, Spring 1964 (MS 1436, box 64, folder 23); and "Lecture I: The Problem of Failure in American History" from "Slavery to Freedom: An American Failure," Storrs Lectures at Yale Law School, 1969 (MS 1436, box 66, folder 66).

Index

abolitionism
  Allan conversion, 138
  Birney, James G., 7, 60, 64–65, 67–68, 72, 124, 132, 133, 144–50
  vs. colonization, 137, 146–50
  Conway, Moncure Daniel, 79, 99, 88–89, 96, 99
  Emancipator, The (newspaper), 137
  Garrison, William Lloyd, 57, 68, 93, 156–57
  Grimké, Angelina, 7, 64–65, 93, 155–57
  Grimké sisters, 66, 68, 70, 71–72, 93–94, 103, 155–56, 158
  Helper, Hinton Rowan, 85–87, 95, 100, 104
  John Brown's Raid, 88
  Kentucky Anti-Slavery Society, 67–68, 148–50
  Lane Theological Seminary, 7, 62–63, 137–42
  Liberator, The (newspaper), 57, 69
  National Era, The (newspaper), 83–84
  northern abolitionists, 57, 64, 70, 82, 88, 95, 100, 101, 142, 150
  religion and, 61, 82, 128–29, 137
  southern advocates, 6–7, 55, 60–61, 66, 69, 70–71, 94, 128, 140
  Tappan brothers, 130, 137
  Thome, James A, 7, 61, 63, 71, 75, 102, 140, 143, 144
  Weld and, 61–62, 66–67, 102, 131–32, 137–38
  See also antislavery movement; dissenters

Absalom, Absalom! (Faulkner), 8, 105
Adams, Charles Francis, Jr., 186, 241, 250–52
African Americans
  American Colonization Society, 145–46
  Black Codes, 180, 209–10
  Civil Rights Act of 1866, 210–12
  civil rights movement, 4, 18, 23, 24, 26–27, 35–37, 50n168, 205, 243, 250, 255–56, 264
  coerced labor, 28, 30, 178–79, 180, 204, 209
  elected officials, 221–22
  labor contracts, 28, 176, 178–79, 227
  Fifteenth Amendment, 233–35, 239, 255
  Fourteenth Amendment, 212–13
  free labor, 78, 101, 177–78, 180
  jurors, as, 209, 217, 233
  mobility, 23, 168–79, 207–8, 210, 170
  newly emancipated, 167–75
  Republican Party, and, 239–43
  refugee camps, 185, 170, 185
  segregation, and, 22, 206, 209–10, 241, 243, 253–55
  soldiers, as, 174–75, 216
  suffrage, 17, 22, 188–89, 211, 213, 215, 220, 231–37, 240–41, 254, 262
  terrorism, 180, 196, 236–37
  vagrancy laws, 28, 178, 180
  voting block, as, 220–222
  See also emancipation; Freedmen's Bureau; Reconstruction

alienation of dissenters, 64, 108–27, 155
Allan, William T., 138–39, 141, 151
Allan brothers, 61, 63, 66–67, 72, 93, 102, 111, 132–33, 135
American Anti-Slavery Society, 62, 64, 68, 71, 93, 97, 137, 142–44, 149, 151, 156
American Colonization Society, 64, 125, 133, 144–47, 149
American Counterpoint (Woodward), 5, 25, 30
American exceptionalism, 31–32
American Philosophical Society, 25
American Slavery As It Is (Weld and Grimkés), 70–72, 104–5
amnesty, 240–42
Amnesty Act, 21
Anti-Slavery Manual, An (Fee), 85
antislavery movement, 59, 67–68, 76, 79, 82, 83, 85, 128, 130, 131, 137, 148. *See also* abolitionism; American Anti-Slavery Society; Lane Theological Seminary
Appeal to Southern Women (Weld), 92

Bancroft Prize, 10
Beecher, Catherine, 69, 153–54
Beecher, Harriet, 72, 136
Beecher, Henry Ward, 88, 201
Beecher, Lyman, 62, 134–42
Berea College, 82
Birney, James G.
  abolitionists, 7, 64–65, 67–68, 144
  American Anti-Slavery Society, 64, 68, 97, 151
  American Colonization Society, 64, 125, 133, 144–47, 149
  Civil War and, 103
  colonization, 64, 101–2
  dissenters, 60
  family history, 108–9, 120–21
  financial difficulty, 96
  Kentucky relocation, 147–48
  Letter on Colonization (Birney), 150
  Liberty Party candidate, 75, 96–97, 100–101
  Philanthropist, The, 72, 83
  political career, 121–23
  religious conversion, 123–24
  southern exiles, 92–95
  Weld and, 61–62, 70, 132–33
Black Codes, 179–80, 188, 209–10, 217
black power movement, 26
Boorstin, Daniel, 41n42, 252
Bradley, James, 62–63, 135, 141
Breckinridge, Robert J., 143–44, 148
Britain, 91, 102, 104, 109, 136–37, 149, 173
Brock, William R., 32, 203, 212
Brockway, George P., 17–18, 20, 44n91
Brownlow, William G., 185, 225–26
Brown v. Board of Education, 4, 10–12, 23
Burden of Southern History, The (Woodward), 1, 5, 50n168
Burgess, John W., 251, 254, 259

Cable, George W., 14, 59
Carleton, William G., 5, 14–16, 20
Chase, Salmon P., 171–72, 200–201, 207, 240–41
Cherokees, 124
citizenship, 25
Civil Rights Act of 1866, 210–12
Civil Rights Act of 1964, 24, 25
civil rights movement
  Civil Rights Acts, 24–25, 210–11, 236
  Civil War Centennial, 250
  Congressional debates on, 256
  Constitutional Amendments, 255–56
  Fourteenth Amendment, 255–56
  Messenger Lectures, 24–26
  northern hypocrisy, 243
  Reconstruction, 18
  Second Reconstruction, as, 4, 18, 23, 24, 26–27, 35–37, 205, 243, 250, 255–56, 264
  southern dissenters and, 7
  "What Happened to the Civil Rights Movement?" 50n168, 50n171
  Woodward and, 4, 18, 26, 35
Civil War, 102–4, 249–52. *See also* Reconstruction
class conflict, 85
Clay, Henry, 109, 121, 124–25, 226
clergy, 191–92

colonization, 64, 125, 133, 136–38, 140, 144–47, 149–51, 208, 210
Commonwealth Fund Lectures, 37–38n6
Commonwealth (newspaper), 103
"Comparative Approach to Emancipation History, The" (Woodward), 30
"Comparative Approach to Reconstruction History, The" (Woodward), 30
Compendium (Helper), 87–88
Confederacy, 25, 184–86, 187, 188, 190–91, 193–94, 215, 224, 259, 260
Confederate soldiers, 176, 188, 204
Congressional Reconstruction. *See* Radical Reconstruction
Congressional Union Republican Committee, 218
Conkling, Roscoe, 201, 210–11
"Conservatism of Northern Radicals, The" (Woodward), 21, 200–213
Conway, Moncure Daniel, 7–8, 76–77, 79–80, 83–84, 88–89, 93–96, 99, 103–4
Cornell University, 2, 18–20, 23–25, 38n8, 164, 165

De Bow, J. D. B., 177, 185
Democratic Party, 190, 194, 201–2, 204, 223–24, 227, 231, 238, 240
desegregation, 16, 24, 243, 256
"Did the North Really Mean It?" (Woodward), 21, 230–44
dissenters, 2, 6–9, 11, 14, 36–37, 58–62, 108–27
Donald, David Herbert, 8, 12–15, 29
Du Bois, W. E. B., 3–4, 23, 45–46n112, 167, 207
Dunning, William A., 251, 263
Dunning School, 3–4, 27, 251, 254, 263

economic reform, 23, 85–86, 226–27, 254–55, 262–63
education, 24, 63, 80, 86, 130, 141, 206, 212, 216, 220–23, 233–34, 239, 241, 243, 262
elections, 193, 208, 214, 230, 223, 232–33, 235, 237–38
emancipation
  Amnesty Act, 21
  Black Codes, 179–80, 188, 217
  citizenship, 25
  coerced labor, following, 28, 30, 178–79, 180, 204, 209
  "Comparative Approach to Emancipation History, The" (Woodward), 30
  crisis of, 170–71
  Emancipation Proclamation, 208
  family relationships after, 171
  fear of insurrection, 172–73
  Freedmen's Bureau, 169
  freedpeople, 168–70
  Gradual Emancipation Society, 124–25
  impact of, 28, 34
  international, 28
  land redistribution, 177, 226–27
  Lincoln and, 208
  peonage, 180, 204, 209
  racism, 207–08
  white northerners, 179, 210
  See also Reconstruction
Emancipator, The (newspaper), 137, 142
Enforcement Acts, 236–38
Episcopalian Church, 191
evangelical revivals, 7
expatriates, 7, 82

"Fear of Freedom, The" (Woodward), 23, 45–46n112, 167–83
Fee, John Gregg, 76–79, 82–83, 85, 88, 93–94
Fifteenth Amendment, 34, 36, 202, 233–36, 238, 239, 254, 255, 259, 262
Finney, Charles Grandison, 61–63, 102, 128–29, 135
First Reconstruction, 21–24, 27, 243
"First Reconstruction in the Light of the Second, The" (Woodward), 2–4, 165
Fleming Lectures
  invitation to, 5
  LSU Press, 2, 5, 9–10, 13–14
  "Men of the Fifties, The" (Woodward), 7, 75–90
  "Men of the Thirties, The" (Woodward), 7, 57–74

preparation for, 5–7
"Process of Alienation, The" (Woodward), 108–27
"Southern Dissenters in Exile" (Woodward), 2, 7–9, 11, 55
Thinking Back: The Perils of Writing History (Woodward), 10, 40n24
"Way of the Exile, The" (Woodward), 7, 91–107
Woodward and, 2–3, 5–9, 11, 14, 55
"Year of Decision, The" (Woodward), 128–62
Foner, Eric, 32, 34–35
Fourteenth Amendment, 21, 29, 210–11, 212, 214, 215, 253, 255–56
Fourth Reconstruction, 36
Franklin, John Hope, 10, 12, 28
free labor, 78, 101, 177–80
Freedmen's Bureau, 22, 28–29, 169, 176–79, 216, 218–19, 226–27, 230, 232
Freedmen's Inquiry Commission, 175
"From the First Reconstruction to the Second" (Woodward), 25
fugitives, 79–80, 207–8
Future of the Past, The (Woodward), 5, 31

Garrison, William Lloyd, 8, 66, 68–70, 93, 131, 146, 156–57, 241
Genovese, Eugene D., 3, 30
Goodloe, Daniel Reaves, 76–78, 82–85, 93, 103, 217
Gorgas, Josiah, 186, 188
Grant, Ulysses S., 169, 184–85, 189, 233, 239, 242–43, 264
Great Reaction, 36, 50n171
Grantham, Dewey W., 12, 13
Great Revival, 61, 76, 128–29
Greeley, Horace, 87, 206–7, 231–32, 240–41
Griffith, Mattie, 76, 105
Grimké, Angelina (sister), 115–20, 151–52, 155–57. *See also* Grimké sisters; Grimké, Sarah; Weld, Angelina
Grimké, John Faucheraeu (father), 60–61
Grimké, Mary Smith (mother), 110, 112, 115, 118–20, 153

Grimké, Sarah (sister), 97, 112–18, 132, 152–55, 157–58. *See also* Grimké, Angelina (sister); Grimké sisters
Grimké, Thomas Smith (brother), 154–55
Grimké sisters, 7–9, 60–61, 64–66, 68–72, 88, 93–94, 101, 103, 109–12, 152–56, 157–58
Grodzins, Morton, 189–90, 195
Guggenheim Foundation, 17–18, 33
Gurley, Ralph, 144, 147

Hampton, Wade, 187, 215
Hampton Plan, 230–31
Harper's Magazine (Woodward), 25, 35, 50n168
Harvard University, 8, 78, 79, 80
Hedrick, Benjamin Sherwood, 76–78, 80–81, 83, 85, 93, 103
Helper, Hinton Rowan, 7, 76–78, 80–81, 83, 85–88, 93, 95, 98–99, 100, 103–4
Hill, Benjamin H., 194, 232
historiography, 3, 6, 12, 17, 20–21, 29–35, 200, 247, 253–54, 261, 263
Hodges, C. S., 63, 111, 139, 141
Hofstadter, Richard, 8, 16, 28, 33
Holden, W. W., 172, 193
Homestead Act of 1862, 29
Howard, Oliver O., 29, 176–79

Impending Crisis of the South: How to Meet It, The (Helper), 81, 83, 85–88, 98
Indian Bureau, 28
Inquiry into the Causes Which Have Retarded the Accumulation of Wealth and Increase of Population in the Southern States (Goodloe), 84
integration, 22, 28, 82, 216–17, 241–42
involuntary labor. *See* labor arrangements
"Irony of Southern History, The" (Woodward), 14, 28

Jackson, Andrew, 117, 122
Jamaica, 173
James W. Richards Lectures, 4, 11, 19. *See also* *Strange Career of Jim Crow*
Jim Crow, 1, 4, 7–8, 11, 22, 24, 37, 206, 216. *See also* segregation.

John Brown's Raid, 82, 87–89, 103–4
Johns Hopkins University, 18–19, 33
Johnson, Andrew, 176, 184, 186–89, 201–2, 204, 211–12, 214, 262–64. *See also* Reconstruction
Joint Commission on Reconstruction, 184–87
Julian, George W., 207, 209, 240–41
jury trials, 217, 237–38

Kentucky Anti-Slavery Society, 67–68, 148–50
Kentucky Colonization Society, 150
Kloosterboer, Wilhelmina, 30, 32
Ku Klux Klan, 29, 236–37, 240, 241

labor arrangements
  contracts, 28, 176, 178–79, 227
  coerced, 28, 30, 178–79, 204
  free, 78, 101, 178, 180
  peonage, 180, 204, 209
labor unions, 243
land redistribution, 22, 23, 29, 175–77, 226–27
Lane Theological Seminary, 7, 8, 62–63, 72, 78–79, 132, 134–42, 149, 151
Letter on Colonization (Birney), 150
liberalism, 2, 3, 7, 12–13, 57, 85
Liberal Republicans, 205, 240–43
Liberator, The (newspaper), 66, 156–57
Liberty Party, 75, 96–97, 100–101
Lilly Foundation, 18, 33
Lincoln, Abraham, 95, 103–4, 185, 208, 210
Little, Brown & Co., 16–18
Litwack, Leon F., 22, 206
Louisiana State University, 2, 5, 7, 10, 55
Louisiana State University Press. *See* LSU Press
loyalty investigation, 184–86, 189–91, 194–95, 204
LSU Press, 2, 5–6, 9–10, 13–14

Manual Labor Society, 130–31
martyrdom, 59, 67, 98–99, 132, 156–57, 219
Massachusetts Reconstruction Association, 218
McFeeley, William S., 3, 30
McPherson, James, 20

"Men of the Fifties, The" (Woodward), 7, 75–90
"Men of the Thirties, The" (Woodward), 7, 57–74
Messenger Lectures
  Carleton and, 15
  during civil rights movement, 24–26
  "Conservatism of Northern Radicals, The" (Woodward), 21–22, 34, 200–213
  Cornell University, 18–20, 23–25
  "Did the North Really Mean It?" (Woodward), 21–22, 34, 230–44
  "Fear of Freedom, The" (Woodward), 23, 167–83
  "First Reconstruction in the Light of the Second, The" (Woodward), 2–4, 165
  "Paradox of Loyalty, The" (Woodward), 22, 184–97
  "Radicalism for Southern Conservatives" (Woodward), 22–23, 214–27
  Reconstruction history, 33–34
  Republican Party, 34
  Rose and, 21
  Woodward and, 2–5, 18–25, 26, 29, 33, 165
Methodists, 191–92
Military Reconstruction Act, 212, 214, 218

Nashville Agrarians, 12
National Association for the Advancement of Colored People (NAACP), 10
National Era, The (newspaper), 83–84, 88
nationalism, 13
Native Americans, 28, 32
Nat Turner rebellion, 57, 125
New England, 137, 180, 208
New Nationalism, 250–52, 254
New South, 1
nonconformists, 1, 6. *See also* dissenters
northern abolitionists, 57, 64, 70, 82, 88, 95, 101, 142, 143, 150
northern states, 206, 208, 211, 231–32, 233–35
nullificationists, 154

Oberlin, 8, 63, 66, 67, 82, 102
O'Brien, Michael, 12–13, 26, 31–32, 33

Oneida Institute, 130, 135–36
Origins of the New South (Woodward), 1–3, 5–6, 10, 21, 38n6, 40n24

pacifism, 154–55
"Paradox of Loyalty, The" (Woodward), 22, 184–97
pardons, 176, 186–87, 189, 204
Paxson, Frederick L., 250, 252
peonage, 180, 204, 209
Philanthropist, The (newspaper), 72, 83
Phillips, Wendell, 80, 131, 218–19, 234, 239, 241
Plessy v. Ferguson, 253
polls, 4, 221, 230
posse comitatus, 237–38
post-emancipation societies, 28, 30, 247. See also emancipation.
post-war era. See Reconstruction
Potter, David M., 28, 33
Presbyterians, 134
presidential impeachment, 36, 202, 262
President's Amnesty Proclamation, 186–88
"Problem of Failure in American History, The" (Woodward), 30, 247–64
"Process of Alienation, The" (Woodward), 108–27
Progressive Era, 254
public transportation, 216–17

Quakers, 65–66, 79, 114–18, 152, 155, 157–58
"Question of Loyalty, The" (Woodward), 14, 50n171

racial equality, 19, 22, 24, 27, 36, 165, 208–9, 217–19, 233, 255
racism, 22–23, 206–8, 254
"Radicalism for Southern Conservatives" (Woodward), 22–23, 164, 214–39
Radical Reconstruction, 27, 189, 200–203, 207, 223, 230–31, 238, 242, 261–62
Radical Republicans, 20–22, 25, 27, 31–32, 208–9, 223–27, 258, 260, 262
Reconstruction
  amnesty and, 240
  backlash against, 36

civil rights movement and, 18
"Comparative Approach to Reconstruction History, The" (Woodward), 30
consequences of, 1, 20–21
Democratic Party, 204
Dunning School, 4, 27, 251, 254, 263,
economic reform, 254–55
elections, 193, 208, 214, 230, 223, 232–33, 235, 237–38
Enforcement Acts, 236–38
Fifteenth Amendment, 34, 36, 202, 233–36, 238, 239, 254, 255, 259, 262
Fourteenth Amendment, 21, 29, 210, 211–12, 214, 215, 253
free labor, 78, 101, 177–78, 180
Grant administration, 239, 264
Johnson administration, 4, 22, 176, 180, 184, 186, 188–89, 204–5
Joint Commission on Reconstruction, 184–87
Joint Committee of Fifteen, 210–11
land redistribution, 23, 29, 175–77, 226–27
polls, 4, 221, 230
"Reconstruction: A Counterfactual Playback" (Woodward), 31–32, 49n155
Reconstruction Acts, 202, 207, 212, 214, 218, 227, 230–32
"Reconstruction and Revision" (Woodward), 27, 29, 30–31, 33, 38–39n11, 47n138, 247
refugee camps, 23, 170, 185
Reunion and Reaction: The Compromise of 1877 and the End of Reconstruction (Woodward), 1, 6, 21
revisionist history, 4, 20, 21, 27, 32, 35, 261–64
"Search for Southern Identity, The" (Woodward), 13, 39n14
"Seeds of Failure in Radical Race Policy" (Woodward), 25
Southern Unionists, 193–97
suffrage, 17, 22, 188–89, 211, 213, 215, 220, 231–37, 240–41, 254, 262
West, the, 16, 28–29, 30, 32, 47n138, 102, 258
Woodward research, 2, 3, 8, 15–20, 32, 33

Reconstruction (cont.)
   See also emancipation; Freedmen's Bureau; labor arrangements; Radical Reconstruction; Republican Party
refugee camps, 23, 170, 185
Reid, Whitelaw, 180, 184–86, 188, 196
religion, 61, 69, 76, 83–84, 85, 95, 112, 128–29, 134, 190–92, 206. See also abolitionism; individual denominations
Republican Party
   African Americans, 239–243
   colonization, 208, 210
   Compendium (Helper), 87–88
   Fifteenth Amendment, 234–35, 238
   Fourteenth Amendment,
   Homestead Act of 1862, 29
   John Brown's Raid, 87–89
   presidential election of 1868, 233
   racial equality, 34, 165, 205–9, 212, 241–42
   Radical Reconstruction, 202–3, 238, 262
   southern radicals, 22–23, 165, 217
   white southerners, 29, 222–26
   white supremacy, 22, 28–29, 34, 206–7
   See also Fifteenth Amendment; Fourteenth Amendment; Radical Republicans
Reunion and Reaction: The Compromise of 1877 and the End of Reconstruction (Woodward), 1, 6, 21
revisionist history, 4, 20, 21, 27, 32, 35, 27, 261–64
Rhett, Robert Barnwell, 61, 154
Rhodes, James Ford, 251, 263
Richards Lectures. See James W. Richards Lectures
Robinson, Marius R., 63, 141
Rose, Willie Lee, 21, 48n152

Schurz, Carl, 172, 180, 184–85, 240–42
Sea Islands, 176, 226
"Search for Southern Identity, The" (Woodward), 13, 39n14
secession, 61, 188, 190–92, 225
Second Reconstruction, 4, 18, 23–24, 26–27, 35–37, 205, 243, 250, 255–56, 264

"Seeds of Failure in Radical Race Policy" (Woodward), 25
segregation, 1, 22, 206, 209–10, 241, 243, 253–56. See also Jim Crow
Sheridan, Philip, 185, 187, 216
Sherman, John, 207, 212, 232
Sherman, W. T., 168–69, 185, 197
slavery
   abolished in Britain, 136–37, 149, 173
   American Slavery As It Is (Weld and Grimkés), 70–72, 104–5
   Bible and, 85
   Birney and, 124
   Colonization and, 64, 125, 133, 136–37, 145
   economics of, 61, 101, 102
   horrors of, 62, 66, 72, 142
   Nat Turner rebellion, 57
   romanticization of, 6
   sectional controversy over, 76, 84
   slave trade, 30, 139
   Testimonies Concerning Slavery (Conway), 99
   See also antislavery movement
Smith, Gerrit, 70–71, 96, 103, 151
Social Darwinism, 253–54
Southerner as American (Sellers), 12–14
Southern Conservatives, 22, 165, 215–19, 209
southern exiles
   abolitionism, 58, 61–73, 128
   Civil War and, 103–4
   isolation of, 92–96
   Lane Theological Seminary, 135–36
   martyrdom of, 59, 67, 98–99, 132, 156
   men of the fifties, 7, 58, 76–84, 88
   men of the thirties, 7, 57–74, 75–76, 128
   religion and, 61, 83–84, 85, 95, 112
   "Southern Dissenters in Exile" (Woodward), 2, 7–9, 11, 55
   "Way of the Exile, The," 91–109
Southern Historical Association (SHA), 10, 14–15, 27–28, 30–33
Southern Homestead Act, 226
"Southern Manifesto," 11–12
Southern Radicals, 22–23, 165, 217
Southern Unionists, 185, 189, 193–97

Stanton, Henry B., 139–40, 142, 144
states' rights, 29, 189, 211–12, 214–15, 235, 241
Stevens, Thaddeus, 22, 29, 32, 195, 200–201, 203, 212, 254, 256
Storrs Lectures
  Genovese and, 3, 30
  invitation to, 29–30
  McFeeley and, 3, 30
  recycled material, 3, 30, 31, 34, 38n11, 247
  "Problem of Failure in American History, The," 3, 35–36 249–64
  Woodward and, 2–3, 29–30, 34, 48n150, 247
Stowe, Harriet Beecher, 83, 135
Strange Career of Jim Crow, The (Woodward), 1, 4, 11, 19, 22, 24, 29, 37
suffrage, 17, 22, 188–89, 211, 215–16, 220, 230–37, 240–41, 254, 262
Sumner, Charles, 21–22, 29, 103, 200–201, 203, 211–12, 235, 241–42
Supreme Court, 4, 10–12, 36, 238, 253

Tappan, Arthur (brother), 134, 137, 141–42
Tappan, Lewis (brother), 61, 70, 94, 97, 131, 137, 138, 151
Tappan brothers, 130–31, 132, 134, 136–37, 142
taxation, 84–85, 239
terrorism, 180, 236–37. *See also* Ku Klux Klan
Testimonies Concerning Slavery (Conway), 99
Thinking Back: The Perils of Writing History (Woodward), 10–11, 40n24
Third Reconstruction, 27–28, 35–36, 50n168
Thirteenth Amendment, 188
Thome, James A., 7, 61–63, 66–67, 71, 75, 93, 102, 110–11, 132, 135, 139–44, 156
Thompson, Henry P., 61, 111, 135, 139, 141
Thornhill, Arthur R., 16–21, 33–34, 44n91
Tilton, Theodore, 201, 219, 240
Tindall, George B., 12, 13–14
Tom Watson: Agrarian Rebel (Woodward), 1, 7
Transcendentalism, 79
Trowbridge, John T., 177, 184–86, 193
Truman, Benjamin C., 171, 184–85, 195–96
Trumbull, Lyman, 206–7, 211, 240–42

Uncle Tom's Cabin (Stowe), 72–73, 83
Underwood, John Curtis, 7, 76
Union army, 168, 174–76
Unionism, 193, 224
Union Leagues, 23, 218
Unitarianism, 83–84
United States v. Cruikshank et al., 238

vagrancy laws, 28, 178, 180
voter registration, 23, 217, 220, 234
voting rights. *See* African Americans; suffrage
Voting Rights Act of 1965, 36

Walter Lynwood Fleming Lectures in Southern History. *See* Fleming Lectures
"Way of the Exile, The" (Woodward), 7, 91–107
Weld, Angelina Grimké (wife), 62, 70, 75, 92, 97, 103–5, 132
Weld, Theodore Dwight
  abolitionism, 62, 66–68, 71, 83, 131–32, 138
  American Anti-Slavery Society, 62
  American Slavery As It Is, 70–73
  Birney and, 68, 149–50
  colonization, 136–37
  economics of slavery, 102
  Great Revival, 61, 128–29
  Grimké sisters, 66, 70
  illness, 75
  Lane Theological Seminary, 62–63, 132, 136
  Letter on Colonization (Birney), 151
  Manual Labor Society, 130–31
  marriage to Angelina, 70, 75, 97–98, 102–3
  Oneida Institute and, 130
Western states, 29, 32, 207
"What Happened to the Civil Rights Movement?" (Woodward), 50n168, 50n171
Whig Party, 78, 223–24, 240
white supremacy, 22, 28–29, 34, 206–7, 232
Whittier, John Greenleaf, 70, 142
Wiley, Bell Irvin, 6, 168, 172

William and Mary College, 14
Wilson, Henry, 207, 209
women's rights, 68–70, 97
Woodward, C. Vann
   American exceptionalism, 27, 31–32
   American Philosophical Society, 25
   analogy's usefulness, 4, 23–26, 32, 37, 205
   Brown v. Board of Education, 4, 10–12
   Burden of Southern History, The (Woodward), 1, 13
   Carleton and, 5, 14–16, 20
   civil rights movement, 4, 18, 26, 35
   Commager and, 8
   comparative history
   dissenter, as, 6, 14, 36–37
   Donald and, 8
   Dunning School, 3–4
   emancipation consequences, 1, 21, 28
   Fifteenth Amendment, 34
   Future of the Past (Woodward), 5, 31, 32
   Guggenheim Foundation fellowship, 17–18, 33
   Hofstadter and, 8, 16, 28, 33
   irony and, 1, 11, 21, 24, 27–28, 29, 30, 45–46n112, 238, 256
   Japan trip, 9, 10–11
   Johns Hopkins, 18–19, 33
   Lilly Foundation, 18, 33
   Little, Brown & Co., 16–18
   LSU Press, 2, 5–7, 9–10, 13–14
   mentorship role, 33, 47n137
   National Association for the Advancement of Colored People (NAACP), 10
   northern segregation, 22
   Origins of the New South (Woodward), 1, 2, 3, 5–6, 10, 16, 21, 30, 34
   publishing contracts, 44n91
   "Question of Loyalty, The" (Woodward), 14
   race relations, 1, 22
   racial equality, 22, 24, 27, 28, 36, 165
   "Reconstruction: A Counterfactual Playback" (Woodward), 31–32, 49n155
   Reconstruction, failure of, 34, 197, 227, 239, 257–61, 264
   research, 2, 3, 8–9, 15–20, 32, 33
   Reunion and Reaction: The Compromise of 1877 and the End of Reconstruction (Woodward), 1, 6, 21
   revisionist history, 4, 20, 21, 27, 35, 261–64
   "Search for Southern Identity, The" (Woodward), 13, 39n14
   segregation, 1, 10, 22
   Southern Historical Association (SHA), 10, 14, 45n155
   Strange Career of Jim Crow, The (Woodward), 1, 4, 11, 19, 22, 24, 29, 37
   students of, 18, 27, 20, 21, 33, 47n137
   Thinking Back: The Perils of Writing History (Woodward), 10–11, 40n24
   Third Reconstruction, 27, 35–36
   Tom Watson: Agrarian Rebel (Woodward), 1, 7
   unfinished projects, 2, 31
   University of Oxford visiting Harmsworth Professor, 11
   unpublished works, 1–2, 38n8
   Voice of America, 28
   white supremacy, 28–29, 34
   W.W. Norton & Co., 17
   Yale University, 2, 3, 19, 29, 33
   See also Fleming Lectures; Messenger Lectures; Storrs Lectures
Woodward, Peter (son), 33
Wright, Elizur Jr., 66, 96, 137, 142, 144, 151, 232
W.W. Norton & Co., 17

Yale University, 2, 3, 19, 29, 33
"Year of Decision, The" (Woodward), 128–62

www.ingramcontent.com/pod-product-compliance
Ingram Content Group UK Ltd.
Pitfield, Milton Keynes, MK11 3LW, UK
UKHW022153230426
12049UKWH00003BA/67